GUSTAV MAHLER

MEMORIES AND LETTERS

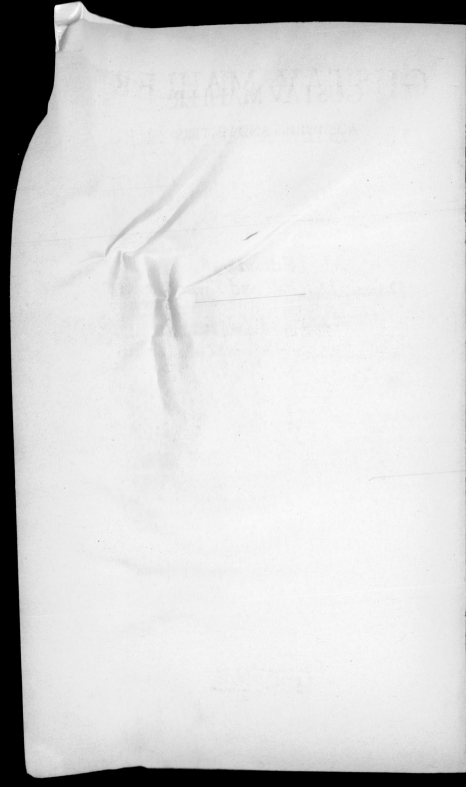

GUSTAV MAHLER

MEMORIES AND LETTERS

by Alma Mahler
(Translated by Basil Creighton)

Edited by
Donald Mitchell and Knud Martner

Fourth Edition (1990)
with additional Notes and Commentaries

CARDINAL

Contents

Introduction to the 1990 British Edition   ix
Introduction to the 1973 British Edition   xi
Introduction to the 1968 British Edition   xiii
Introduction to the 1969 American Edition   xxxi
Acknowledgements and a Note on the Text   xli
Preface to First Edition by Alma Mahler   xliii

PART ONE MEMORIES   1
First Meeting   3
January, 1902   27
Marriage and Life Together   33
Splendid Isolation, 1903   53
Splendid Isolation, 1904   62
Splendid Isolation, 1905   77
Splendid Isolation, 1906   96
Sorrow and Dread, 1907   106
Autumn, 1907   124
New World, 1907–1908   128
Summer, 1908   139
New World, 1909   148
Storms, 1910   164
Summer, 1910   172
Eighth Symphony, 12th September, 1910   180
Christmas, 1910   186
The End, 1911   188

PART TWO LETTERS 1901–1910   203
Biographical List   343
Notes and Commentaries by Donald Mitchell and
     Knud Martner   357
Index (by Roger Savage)   417

Illustrations

Gustav Mahler

Alma Maria Schindler (Alma Mahler), 1899

Alma Mahler and her daughter, Anna

Richard Strauss and his wife, Pauline, 1914. *Reproduced by kind permission of the Mansell Collection*

Gustav Mahler in Vienna with Max Reinhardt, Carl Moll and Hans Pfitzner, *c.* 1905

Gerhart Hauptmann (in foreground) with Alban Berg and his wife, Helene (left), and Countess Gravina (centre), and Margarete Hauptmann

A page of the libretto of *Rübezahl* in Mahler's manuscript *Reproduced by kind permission of Mr and Mrs Wolfgang Rosé*

Arnold Schoenberg

In Prague (1908), Bruno Walter talking to Gustav Mahler. On the right is Alma Mahler

'My God, I've forgotten the motor horn! Now I can write another symphony'

Gustav Mahler in New York, 1909

Gustav Mahler on board the *Kaiser Wilhelm II*, with his daughter Anna and Theodore Spiering. *Reproduced by kind permission of Miss Lenore Spiering*

Gustav Mahler as a conductor, silhouettes by Otto Boehler

A copy, in Mahler's hand, of one of his wife's songs, 'Erntelied'

Letter from Gustav Mahler to his wife, Prague, May, 1908

Chorus Mysticus from the Eighth Symphony in Mahler's manuscript

Page from the manuscript sketches for the Tenth Symphony

Introduction to the 1990 British Edition

Alma Mahler's reminiscences of Gustav Mahler, first published in Amsterdam in 1940, continue to rank as one of the principal sources of information about the composer and his music. The volume also includes one of the most important published collections of the composer's letters: his letters to his wife.

As time passes and perspectives both broaden and lengthen, we also come to recognize that Alma's memories of her husband, perhaps both knowingly and unknowingly, cohere to form a vivid portrait of her own personality, its fascinating merits and disconcerting – but no less fascinating – falsities and deceptions. About her overwhelming fascination, exercised on so many powerful creative figures in the twentieth century, and in so many areas of creative life, there can be no doubt, though we still await the serious, scholarly biography which will present something like the whole truth about this remarkable woman.

In the meantime *Memories and Letters* is rich in revelations and insights. The decades that have elapsed since the book's first publication have themselves been rich in tireless Mahler research and investigation: one thinks of Henry-Louis de La Grange in France, the pre-eminent biographer of Mahler, Kurt and Herta Blaukopf in Vienna, Edward R. Reilly in the U.S.A., Zoltan Roman in Canada and Paul Banks in the U.K., to name only a few of the many, many scholars all over the world who are engaged in Mahler studies. Their spirit of inquiry and pursuit of the truth about Mahler, along with our own research, allows us in this fourth and very substantially revised edition of *Memories and Letters* to add an entirely new section of *Notes and Commentaries* which we hope will bring to Alma's text fresh illumination and amplification, and – where needed – correction of wrong facts and faulty chronology. Not least, we have been able to establish a high proportion of accurate dates for the letters. The dates published in this edition are based on detailed investigation and it is only in relatively few cases that some uncertainty remains. When doubts still exist we have added an interrogation mark in editorial square brackets [?] after the date or month, as appropriate.

We are confident that this new edition will win many new readers for *Memories and Letters*, while for those already familiar with the book it will provide much fresh information about one of the most riveting marriages of modern times, an amalgam of glamour, love, tragedy, passion and deceit; and at the centre of it all was music and its evolution throughout the turbulent, innovative first decade of the new century.

D.M.

London,
March, 1990

Introduction to the 1973 British Edition

A new British edition of this book (the third) gives me the welcome opportunity to make two additions of substance to the revised and enlarged edition of 1968. Firstly I have included the Introduction which I wrote for the American printing of the 1968 edition, called there 'Editor's Note' (Viking Press, 1969). I think readers may be interested to have available in this form my commentary on *Waldmärchen*, the original Part I of *Das klagende Lied*, as well as a series of not insignificant corrections and amplifications (see pp. xxvii to xxxvii).

The second major addition takes the shape of an Appendix which includes an extensive Chronology as well as some new information, for the main body of which I am indebted to my friend Mr. Knud Martner, of Copenhagen, a formidable Mahler researcher, as his work here amply proves. I must confess that it was not until I was somewhat hectically in the midst of revising the letters for the 1968 edition that I came to realize how urgently they were in need of a fresh chronological disposition. (As Mr. Martner has pointed out to me, Alma Mahler (in *Mein Leben*, 1923–24, p. 137) was herself aware of the problem posed by the dates: 'It was hard', she wrote, 'to put the letters in order, because Gustav Mahler never wrote a date and I could only verify a date from the sense of the letter. Nobody but me could have done that!') At a rather late stage in the preparation of the revised 1968 text I did what I could to improve the chronological sequence, and I think made a fair start on re-ordering the correspondence, even though in so doing I risked the impatience of readers by burdening the letters with an elaborate network of anxious queries. Mr. Martner, with admirable method and a seemingly inexhaustible knowledge of Mahler's day-to-day affairs, has carried my initial investigations several stages further forward, as a result of which I am convinced that we have established here, for the first time, an authentic chronology for most of this important correspondence. More than that, Mr. Martner has generously provided all kinds of vivid and illuminating detail, not just dates, but information about Mahler's concerts, the programmes he performed, his travels, and many other aspects of his life. I think it will be worth any reader's time to read through the Appendix: he can only be better informed at the end of it. In order to simplify my patient publisher's task, I have written my own further corrections and amplifications (and some qualifying comments) into Mr. Martner's Appendix, but these are clearly distinguished by the use of square brackets and my initials.

A final word about the German edition of the 1968 English revision which was published by Propyläen Verlag, Frankfurt, in 1971. One must, of course, acknowledge the difficulty of reconciling the uncorrected German original with my English revision of 1968, and producing out of that coalition a revised German text in 1971. Nonetheless it must be said – if only in fairness to myself, whose name is on the title page of the German edition – that I was not editorially responsible for that edition, which unfortunately not only perpetuates a number of the former errors that I had corrected but also creates new confusions. It is to be hoped that an authentic German text, taking account of the revisions embodied in the successive English editions will soon be undertaken.

D. M.

Tangier/Barcombe,
January, 1973

Introduction to the 1968 British Edition

Alma Mahler's* reminiscences of her husband, Gustav Mahler, and of her remarkable marriage, are important on many counts. The very fact of the first publication of the book, and above all its appearance in English in 1946, was of peculiar significance. Up to that time, at least for English readers, the Mahler literature was scanty. Such scholarly or analytical commentary as existed was most of it in German and hard to come by, and hard to come by, of course, even in the German-speaking countries where Mahler's music and books about his music (with the exception of Nazi-inspired anti-Semitic tracts) were suppressed. For the rest, there were the odd comments in the press, given rise to by the most occasional performances of his music in England – at best some of the songs or the *Adagietto* from the Fifth Symphony – and these, more often than not, were excessively hostile in tone. (I shall always remember the late Eric Blom telling me authoritatively that 'We' – the English, that is – 'just don't want Mahler here', as if the great composer had been some kind of unwelcome musical immigrant, to be repelled if he dared to approach our shores.) Those of us with inquiring minds fared no better if we turned to works of reference, where Mahler was dismissed with a brevity that was none the less always ample enough to include the statutory reference to the extravagant length of his symphonies.

Far be it from me to rehearse the trials and tribulations of those who, in pre-war days and during the war, wanted to come to grips with a musical personality that nowadays forms a staple part of our concert life. Our opportunities were few, and we consumed the crumbs that fell to us most avidly. Perhaps there is something rather ironic about the fact that our enthusiasm for Mahler was based on as little practical experience of his music as the total condemnation purveyed by his opponents. But the little we heard was proof enough for us of the quality of the musical mind that we were so eager to explore. The little that his adverse critics

* Born in 1879, she died in New York in 1964.

heard, if indeed they had heard even a little, did not justify then, nor does it justify now, their wholesale, unrelenting hostility. There were, of course, honourable exceptions, Neville Cardus, Edward Sackville-West and Desmond Shawe-Taylor among them. But the roll-call on the other side was much more extensive and, one must suppose, influential; and for a picture of the dreadful parochiality that afflicted English musical life up to the war, we should not have to look much farther than the history of Mahler criticism. Our researches might prove narrow in subject (and undoubtedly tedious to read) but the taste, the flavour of those blinkered days would undoubtedly be there.

I only reminisce myself because the excitement of procuring Alma Mahler's memoirs cannot be sensed unless the context is evoked, at least in part. They were published at a moment when Mahler's music was on the brink – trembling on the brink – of its first break-through in this country, and it is absolutely certain that the book itself helped that break-through to happen. It was the first major document to fill out the details of Mahler, the man and the artist, and there were many passages, as I shall hope to show, which brought musical, as well as biographical, enlightenment. In more ways than one, indeed, the book was an instrument of our understanding Mahler. It was also, to state the matter crudely but plainly, useful propaganda. The publication of the book, plus the growing number of performances of his music – not to speak of the growing number of musicians and music lovers who wanted to hear more of his music – created an atmosphere which reversed and finally overthrew the hitherto sceptical majority posture.

Those who read Alma Mahler's memoirs then, and probably those who read them for the first time now, are more than likely to have been stimulated first by an interest in Mahler's music. Yet, even as a record of a remarkable love affair between a man of genius and a woman of clearly outstanding gifts, the book is surely compelling, perhaps unique. It might be that some people approach the book with a greater or lesser degree of sympathy for Mahler's art, but I should be surprised to find that even the least sympathetic reader was not profoundly stirred by the account of Mahler's last years, above all by the story of the last journey from New

York to Vienna, with hopes continually raised and as continually dashed. It is an epic tale, by any standards, and eloquently told.

It is true that part of the eloquence of these reminiscences resides in their frankness. Alma Mahler was frank about herself, about her husband – her portrait of him, devoted though it is, is far from idealized – and about their many friends. This rare ability to speak directly, and not to dissemble, lends her text its unmistakable ring of truth. At the same time one has to recognize that this very candour was one of the reasons why her memoirs, in certain circles at least, were coolly received. Biographies of great men, and especially of great artists, are all too often laboriously devotional in tone. Alma Mahler reverenced what mattered most, her husband's genius, but she had a sharp eye for human fallibility, and when Mahler faltered she did not fail to record the fact; nor, for that matter, was she sparing of herself. Her frankness, too, rested in her quite open manner of displaying her emotions. These are by no means emotions recollected in tranquillity but emotions re-lived and recorded with a substantial dash of their original force. Here again there were some who found this undisguised emotionalism not to their taste and out of place in a 'serious' biographical work. For others, the very fact that Alma Mahler was Mahler's *wife* seemed to constitute an insurmountable obstacle. These sceptics approached her book as if it were evidence presented in a court of law on her husband's behalf, and thus open to grave doubt. Of course, she *loved* Mahler – that is clear enough from her book. But it is a curious frame of mind that would exclude testimony – at any rate in artistic affairs – based on affection and sympathy, when it is just those qualities that provide the best chance of incomparable insights (qualities that play too minor a role in most criticism). What would we not give for the reminiscences of the wives of other great composers from the past? Alas, they did not have Alma Mahler's literary gifts.

I have dealt deliberately with some of the objections raised to her biography, not because I think a defensive position is necessary but because I wish to throw into relief my own conviction of the first importance of her book. No serious student of Mahler can afford to neglect it, for not only is it an unrivalled source of information about the composer's personality and mode of life but it also gives us concrete and illuminating facts about his methods of composing and about the compositions themselves. Take, for example, the Tenth Symphony, which has recently become known to us as an entity through the brilliant and devoted labours of Deryck Cooke. Alma Mahler recounts an event from 1907–8, when she was living with her husband at the Hotel Majestic, New York. She was visited by a friend, and hearing a noise, leaned out of the window, 'and saw a long procession in the broad street along the side of Central Park. It was the funeral cortège of a fireman, of whose heroic death we had read in the newspapers. The chief mourners were almost immediately beneath us when the procession halted, and the master of ceremonies stepped forward and gave a short address. From our eleventh-floor window we could only guess what he said. There was a brief pause and then a stroke on the muffled drum, followed by a dead silence. The procession then moved forward and all was over. The scene brought tears to our eyes and I looked anxiously at Mahler's window. But he too was leaning out and his face was streaming with tears. The brief drum-stroke impressed him so deeply that he used it in the Tenth Symphony'.

When I first read that passage I, like so many others, knew nothing of the Tenth Symphony but for the *Adagio* and the *Purgatorio* movement, which were the only movements available for many years in a performing edition. Mr. Cooke's reconstruction not only brought the whole work to life but also confirmed the essential accuracy of Alma Mahler's recollection. This was not just a vague recollection of a romantic incident but, on the contrary, proved to contain a kernel of valuable and enlightening musical information. For when we came to hear the whole work in Mr. Cooke's celebrated version, we also came to hear Alma Mahler's memory from the New York years translated into sound, indeed into a leading and unforgettable feature of Mahler's last symphony: there was the muffled drum-stroke, at the end of the second scherzo and in the wonderful introduction to the finale. Alma Mahler was right to make a note of the fireman's funeral procession in her diary. Its image, in the shape of a characteristic sonority, had bit deep into her husband's mind, into his supersensitive ear, and was turned to fascinating account in the Tenth.

Let me take another example of how later events, or later re-searches, proved to establish the authenticity of these recollections. Towards the end of his life, as Alma Mahler herself so movingly tells, Mahler became increasingly anxious about his relationship to his wife and decided to consult Sigmund Freud, the founder of psychoanalysis (the episode is described more fully on p. 175). I had always found this part of the text of peculiar interest, if only as evidence of a meeting between two legendary personalities. It was surely very much one of those encounters in history that one would much like to have attended as an eavesdropper. But there seemed little chance of discovering more about this particular matter, and I did not pursue it. In the 1950s, however, the late Dr. Ernest Jones published the first volume of his massive biography of Freud, and I was encouraged to write to Dr. Jones to ask him to let me know if any material on the Freud–Mahler meetings turned up during his investigations. He had not known of the reference to Freud in Alma Mahler's memoirs and doubted at first if anything would come to light. But something – and something very significant – did: a personal communication from Freud to Marie Bonaparte in 1925, which not only confirmed the fact of the meeting (at Leyden, in Holland) but also revealed a comment of Mahler's to Freud of no little musical importance. It has become familiar in recent years and, I fear, somewhat mis-used, but I think it still worth quoting here: 'In the course of the talk [with Freud] Mahler suddenly said that now he understood why his music had always been prevented from achieving the highest rank through the noblest passages, those inspired by the most profound emotions, being spoilt by the intrusion of some commonplace melody. His father, apparently a brutal person, treated his wife very badly, and when Mahler was a young boy there was a specially painful scene between them. It became quite unbearable to the boy, who rushed away from the house. At that moment, however, a hurdy-gurdy in the street was grinding out the popular Viennese air 'Ach, du lieber Augustin'. In Mahler's opinion the conjunction of high tragedy and light amusement was from then on inextricably fixed in his mind, and the one mood inevitably brought the other with it' (Jones, *Sigmund Freud: Life and Work*, Vol. II, p. 89, London, 1955).

If that story was known to Alma Mahler, and it would be my guess that it wasn't, she did not see fit to include it among her reminiscences. But we find that a hurdy-gurdy (or a barrel-organ, rather) does appear in her text, oddly enough, or appropriately enough perhaps, following on without a break from her account of the 'high tragedy' of the fireman's funeral procession which gave rise to the muffled drum-strokes in the Tenth Symphony. 'On another occasion,' she writes, 'when I was sitting in my room and Mahler in his, working, the silence was suddenly broken by a trickle of sound from far below. It was a tremulous and super-annuated Italian barrel-organ. I rang through to the office and begged them to move him on at once at my expense. The noise stopped at once. Then Mahler burst in: "Such a lovely barrel-organ – took me straight back to my childhood – and now it's stopped!"'

Now we know the Freud document, with what *retrospective* force that little incident strikes us, above all Mahler's remark, 'Took me straight back to my childhood.' Yes, indeed, we feel. He *would* have said that. More than that, with Freud's sober recollections to hand, we may think that he *did*. Thus it was that researches reaching into the 1950s threw light on Alma Mahler's memories of 1907 and 1908, a strong light that far from bleaching or negating the vivid colours of her book, only served to confirm their authenticity.

Of course, not all the events and incidents that are crowded into these memoirs can be independently tested. I have chosen to write about two examples which particularly interested me and in one of which I was personally involved. But I can testify that years of experience of the book, of laborious scrutiny of the text, have not shaken my confidence in its basic accuracy. I have no doubt that what Mahler told his wife, about his early years, for instance, is faithfully recorded in her memoirs; and for the early years, indeed, the only documentation that exists, exists here. We might all of us wish that there were greater detail, more facts, more dates. None the less, inevitable minor errors apart – some of which I hope to have corrected in this edition – these memoirs represent a major personal biography of Mahler and a major source of reference for musicologists, who still have to determine in its

final shape the by no means straightforward chronology of
Mahler's music.

It may strike the reader as curious that, although in a broad way
we 'know' at the present time all Mahler's major music, there is
still some music extant and unpublished that is not open to inspection and some, even some of the most familiar, that presents
intriguing chronological problems. Moreover, some steps forward
in our knowledge of Mahler are of very recent origin. The much-
played, popular First Symphony is a case in point. It was only in
1967, with the kind collaboration of the owner of the manuscript,
Mrs. James M. Osborn (New Haven, Connecticut, U.S.A.), that
the hitherto virtually unknown *Blumine* – the original second
movement in the first version of the symphony – was brought to
light. When the work was first performed, at Budapest in 1889,
it was in *five* movements, not four as it is today. The symphony
underwent considerable revision, not only of its instrumentation
– which was Mahler's normal practice (something we hear a good
deal about with regard to the Fifth, particularly, in these memoirs)
– but also of its total shape (a rare occurrence with Mahler). For
a few years he conducted the work himself in its five-movement
form, but before the first publication of the score in 1898 he
dropped the *Blumine* movement, which was thought to be destroyed or irretrievably lost. But no, in what must be the earliest
surviving MS. of the symphony, the original *Andante* is still
included, complete in almost every detail. Thus Mr. Benjamin
Britten, a long-standing admirer of Mahler's music, was able to
give the first performance of *Blumine* since the 1890s at the
Aldeburgh Festival, 1967, on 18th June.

Mention of his name in conjunction with Mahler's reminds me
of the vital work he did as a much younger man on Mahler's
behalf. These days we take performances of the massive Third
Symphony for granted, and would be horrified at the thought of
hearing anything less than the complete work. But it was not ever
so. In the past, and not the dim past at that, we often had to be
content with one movement, for example the charming Minuet
from the Third; and we might not have heard that, had it not
been for a skilful and persuasive reduction of the movement for
small orchestra by Mr. Britten, an economy version which

brilliantly maintained the essence of the original. It was in this way, at the start, that we managed to hear Mahler at all – in bits and pieces (another movement that cropped up now and again was the *Andante moderato* from the Second Symphony). The younger generation today, who sometimes wonder (to my amusement) if we are not subjected to *too much* Mahler, don't remember the time when isolated performances of isolated movements were rare and momentous events.

But let me return for a moment to *Blumine* and the First Symphony, because the circumstances surrounding them are not only of interest in themselves but also show how missing pieces, even at this late stage, turn up to help us fill out the jigsaw-puzzle-like picture of Mahler's total output: the main lines of the physiognomy are there but there remain some features still to be completed. In 1883, Mahler, in his early twenties, was appointed to a conducting post at the Cassel theatre. While there, he composed his only incidental music, presumably a suite or sequence of orchestral pieces, to accompany a dramatized version of Scheffel's once popular narrative poem, *Der Trompeter von Säkkingen*. Mahler scored a success with his incidental music, which received quite a number of performances – too many, eventually, for the composer's liking, who came to express his distaste for the whole undertaking. The music has never been recovered, and I have little doubt that the MS. score and parts, if indeed they survived that long, were destroyed in the Second World War. It seemed as if the *Trompeter* music would for ever remain an unknown quantity, and that we should have to remain content with a few bars of the opening melody (presumably the leading theme) quoted by Paul Stefan in his biography (*Gustav Mahler: eine Studie über Persönlichkeit und Werk*, revised edition, Munich, 1920, p. 36), where he was quoting not from his own memory but from the reminiscences of Max Steinitzer. The Stefan citation was as follows:

When I heard the *Blumine* movement, and above all, the expansive trumpet melody with which the movement opens, my memory of the Stefan quotation was aroused; and there can be no doubt that the *Blumine* melody presents us with the *Trompeter* theme complete.* More than that, I am certain myself that the movement itself is, in all essentials, one of the movements from the original suite of incidental music, perhaps the first movement and probably the movement that Mahler liked best – he must have liked it quite a lot, in fact, to have taken it into his First Symphony, though we must remember that the work was not so entitled at its première, when it was launched as an untitled 'Symphonic Poem' in two parts. Mahler, I think, was right to omit the movement which, charming and characteristic though it is, disrupts the integrity of the symphony as a whole; and to justify his musical instinct one could produce ample good musical reasons. What I think happened at the earliest stage of the work's life was something simple and human: Mahler had this movement to hand from the *Trompeter* suite, he liked it (whatever protestations he may have made to the contrary about the incidental music as a whole) and tried to make use of it, understandably enough, in his first big orchestral work, the structure of which may have been, originally, free in conception but in the event turned out to be anything but freely composed. Hence the intruder had to be dropped. None the less it is of some interest that already in this first, five-movement version of the First a principle was revealed that Mahler in fact followed up in his Second and Third Symphonies, in both of which relaxed character movements were followed up by Scherzos proper. The juxtaposition was there in the first version of the First.

With *Blumine* performed, and with the Tenth made known to us through Mr. Cooke's performing edition, there is little now that we may expect in the way of new Mahler discoveries. The only major manuscript source which still remains to be made

* In my book, *Gustav Mahler: The Early Years* (London, 1958), I was distinctly unenthusiastic about what I took to be the unpromising opening of the melody as disclosed by Stefan. The marvellous and original continuation and extension of the melody, as we hear it in *Blumine*, necessitates a radical revision of my earlier view. Indeed, the conception of it substantially anticipates the magic of the post-horn solo in the Scherzo of the Third. (One must also note that though the *Trompeter* music may have been in D, *Blumine*'s key is C major.)

accessible is the first part of the early cantata, ~~*Das klagende Lied*,~~ the ~~*Waldmärchen*~~ section, which was omitted when Mahler came to publish his revised version of the work in 1899/1900. It is doubtful whether this would prove to be a major musical revelation; on the other hand, it would be fascinating to have the opportunity of seeing, and possibly hearing, for ourselves how the youthful Mahler conceived his first large-scale composition.

Although new discoveries are improbable, there is still much detailed work to be done on established texts. For example, one of the best-known and most famous of Mahler's orchestral song-cycles, the *Lieder eines fahrenden Gesellen*, presents all kinds of chronological problems. This is not the place for a lengthy analysis of a peculiarly complicated history, but it would seem certain to me now – at least on the facts at present in my possession – that the songs did not achieve their orchestral guise until a much later date than has hitherto been supposed. Although it may be the case that Mahler thought of the songs as a cycle with orchestral accompaniment, it seems likely that the first version, which still exists in the composer's manuscript, was a piano score, for low voice, and entitled in those days (*c.* 1884), *Geschichte von einem fahrenden Gesellen*. But we should be mistaken in thinking that this MS. was the original of the piano score that is currently available today. There are not only significant musical variants, but the two middle songs in the early piano score are in different keys, respectively D flat and B minor (not D major and D minor as we have them today). So for a confusing start we have (a) an early piano reduction but no orchestral score and (b) a manuscript piano score and a published piano score that don't match up. As we continue our investigations, the problems and the queries grow in number. For instance we find on examination that the *published* piano score not only differs from the early MS. piano reduction but also from the *published* orchestral score – minor variants, maybe, but not unimportant ones.

A clear-cut answer to this tangle of questions seemed to be given by Natalie Bauer-Lechner, whose memories of Mahler were published in 1923. There she stated quite unambiguously that Mahler orchestrated the songs for a concert of his own music at Berlin on 16th March 1896, when he gave them their first performance. She was present at the concert and in Mahler's company during this period, so there is good reason to take her evidence seriously (indeed, like Alma Mahler's memoirs and Mahler's letters, Bauer-Lechner's reminiscences of her friendship with the composer represent a prime source of biographical information).

In the main, I have no doubt that Bauer-Lechner was correct, which means that the published full score we have today, and which is, of course, the work as we hear it performed, dates from 1896; and indeed the evidence of the music itself supports this date. It would have been strange if the chamber-musical perfection of the scoring had been within Mahler's grasp in 1884, when his First Symphony was not yet written, a work itself to be subjected to radical revision of its instrumental style. By 1896, however, Mahler had behind him the experience of his first two symphonies and was already at work on the Third. In these circumstances, the chiselled precision of the scoring of the *Gesellen* cycle makes excellent chronological sense.

At least, then, we can arrive at the conclusion that this first song-cycle of Mahler's, though composed in 1884, did not reach its final orchestral shape until 1896, in itself a fact of some interest. But can we as safely assume, on the basis of Bauer-Lechner's statement, that it was for the 1896 concert that the songs were *first* orchestrated? In the absence of Mahler's manuscript full score – i.e. the manuscript from which the full score was engraved (where is it?) – there seemed no reason not to accept the entry in Bauer-Lechner's diary. But in trying to seek out a reference to the whereabouts of this missing manuscript, I happened upon a reference to a manuscript orchestral score of the *Gesellen* songs, in Mahler's autograph, which forms part of the Willem Mengel-berg-Stiftung (Mengelberg Collection) in Amsterdam. The Curator of the Collection was kind enough to let me have a photocopy of the manuscript, which is indeed in Mahler's own hand and is just as certainly *not* the manuscript of the version we know today (there are substantial differences between the two versions, not differences in musical substance but radical differences in the orchestration). What, without doubt, the Amsterdam MS. gives us is an earlier orchestral version of the cycle, which means that we must qualify Bauer-Lechner's statement and now understand it to imply that Mahler was working in 1896 on his *final revision* of the orchestral version – this, Bauer-Lechner must have misunderstood as work on an orchestral version for the first time, which is something different. Unhelpfully, the Amsterdam MS. bears no date. On the other hand the score is inscribed, 'Older autograph score of the *Lieder eines fahrenden Gesellen* by Gustav Mahler, received as a present from the Composer at the end of 1895'. The inscription is signed 'Hermann Behn'.

How old is older? Not so old in this case, one may surmise, as what I have described as the first version of the songs, the piano reduction with the two middle songs in D flat and B minor; for in musical essence, orchestration apart, the Amsterdam MS. is identical with what we now know to be the final revision. Moreover, despite the absence of a date on the MS. from the composer, we can in fact allot the Amsterdam orchestration to a specific period: Mahler makes use of a manuscript paper, manufactured in Hamburg, of a brand that he also used for the Second Symphony, a clue which enables us to place the Amsterdam version not earlier than 1891 (when Mahler was appointed as first conductor of the Hamburg Opera) and not later than the end of 1895 (see the inscription).

Although the Amsterdam MS., dating from Mahler's Hamburg days, is indisputably the earliest orchestral MS. version of the *Gesellen* songs known to us, it is not impossible, of course, that there were earlier versions still that have been lost or were destroyed. But the balance of the evidence suggests to me the strong probability that there was a long gap in time before Mahler set about realizing his original intention to make the *Gesellen* cycle an orchestral set of songs (we must always remember that the first version, though a piano reduction, was inscribed 'für eine tiefe Stimme mit Begleitung des Orchesters' – 'for a low voice with orchestral accompaniment'). Speculation is always rash; but it is my guess that Mahler, having sketched out the songs for voice and piano, then became wholly immersed in the composition of his First Symphony, in which, of course, he borrowed freely from the *Gesellen* songs, and the cycle, in its orchestral guise at least, was stood on one side (which would mean, paradoxically, that the first orchestration of the songs occurred in the context of the symphony!); and it seems not illogical that Mahler returned to the orchestral conception of the songs during his Hamburg period, because it was just at this time in fact that he was composing the bulk of his *Wunderhorn* songs with orchestra. Until I am proved wrong, the following time-table seems to me convincing: 1884 – *Gesellen* songs composed (voice and piano): 1884 – First Symphony begun: after 1891 – first orchestral version of songs (Amsterdam MS.): 1896 – final revision and Berlin première of the orchestral version. Such is the complicated and still in part enigmatic history of one of Mahler's most popular works. (I will spare the reader an account of further complications, e.g. that the published vocal score not only fails to match up with the published full score, as I have mentioned, but also differs, in some particulars, from the Amsterdam MS.)

It is, however, this kind of searching after, and sorting out, of facts – if one is lucky enough to find any – that now constitutes the main task of Mahler students; and these memoirs of Alma Mahler have already greatly helped us in the process of detection and classification. They continue so to do, and here is a very fresh instance of how they can throw new light or bring confirmation of something one had previously conjectured. For some years I have been increasingly disinclined to believe in one of those established 'facts' that, alas, figure with stubborn monotony in almost every printed account of Mahler's life. The magic, seemingly ineradicable date is 1888, when Mahler is imagined for the first time to have discovered the famous collection of folk-poems, *Des Knaben Wunderhorn*, which was to serve him as a source of many of the texts of his songs. With the same regularity that the date is repeated, so too is the comment that Mahler had miraculously anticipated the *Wunderhorn* style in the texts that he himself had written some years earlier for the *Gesellen* cycle. Mahler was indeed an accomplished versifier and it is perfectly true that the *Gesellen* poems are very close in spirit and manner to the *Wunderhorn* anthology. But a fact that seems to be consistently overlooked, although it has been in circulation for a long time (Stefan, for instance, mentions it in the revised edition of his Mahler study), is Mahler's unacknowledged use of a *Wunderhorn* poem as the point of departure of his first *Gesellen* song. It may be of some interest to set Mahler's verses alongside the *Wunderhorn* original, when his debt to the latter (why he did not reveal it is not clear to me, but then he was just as cagey about the fairy-tale source of *Das klagende Lied*) is made very plain:

Des Knaben Wunderhorn	*Lieder eines fahrenden Gesellen*
Wann mein Schatz Hochzeit macht,	Wenn mein Schatz Hochzeit macht,
Hab ich einen traurigen Tag,	fröhliche Hochzeit macht,
Geh ich in mein Kämmerlein,	hab' ich meinen traurigen Tag!
Wein um meinen Schatz.	
	Geh' ich in mein Kämmerlein,
	dunkles Kämmerlein!
	Weine! Wein'! Um meinen Schatz,
	um meinen lieben Schatz!
Blümlein blau, verdorre nicht,	Blümlein blau! Blümlein blau!
Du stehst auf grüner Heide;	Verdorre nicht, verdorre nicht!
Des Abends, wenn ich schlafen geh,	Vöglein süß! Vöglein süß!
So denk ich an das Lieben.	Du singst auf grüner Heide!
	Ach! Wie ist die Welt so schön!
	Ziküth! Ziküth!
	Singet nicht! Blühet nicht!
	Lenz ist ja vorbei!
	Alles Singen ist nun aus!
	Des Abends wenn ich schlafen geh',
	denk' ich an mein Leid! an mein
	Leide!

If nothing else, this comparison shows that our surprise at Mahler's adroit *Wunderhorn* imitations in the *Gesellen* cycle should at least be qualified by the knowledge that, already in 1884, he was making use of an authentic *Wunderhorn* text; and more than that, I have ample evidence to hand which suggests that it would have been virtually impossible for him *not* to have been familiar with the *Wunderhorn* anthology long before 1888. This is not the occasion to bring all that evidence forward, but it is the moment to point to the confirmatory testimony that we find in these memoirs. The first English edition of the book was printed in conditions of stringent national economy, and some cuts were made, mostly in the Letters, but a few also in Alma Mahler's text. These – but for needless duplications – have been restored in this new edition, among them the excerpt from the diary of Frau Ida Dehmel, widow of the poet, Richard Dehmel. She records there a conversation with Mahler about the relationship between words and music, in which Mahler, she writes, referred to the *Wunderhorn* collection, interestingly enough, as 'poems ... not complete in themselves, but blocks of marble which anyone might make his own' – an exact description of his practice in the first song of the *Gesellen* cycle. But what, for my present purpose, is even more striking and apposite is the immediately preceding sentence: 'He himself had only appropriated some few bits from the *Wunderhorn* – *from earliest childhood* his relationship to the book had been particularly close.' (The italics are mine, and, I think, self-sufficing.)

I would excuse anyone who yawned with exasperation at this point, to ask: Does it really matter whether it's 1888 or earlier? I certainly have no wish to emulate Mr. Gradgrind, who pursued facts at the expense of life. But where a great composer is concerned, if the facts have a *musical* relevance, then it seems to me to be worth while getting them right; and for Mahler, the whole question of his association with the world of the *Wunderhorn* poems is of such fundamental importance, and is linked to such a wide stretch of his composing – not just the *Wunderhorn* songs themselves, but *Das klagende Lied* and the first four symphonies – that it is of some creative significance if it can be shown that, far from dropping into the *Wunderhorn* world at the age of twenty-eight, he was steeped in its atmosphere and climate throughout his youth. And perhaps most satisfying of all, it is a conclusion that the music itself justifies even more tellingly than any biographical documents, enlightening though these may be.

Somewhere a halt must be called, because there could be no end to the piling of postscripts on postscripts; and with almost every page of these reminiscences there comes a temptation to digress or to add some stop-press information. I cannot resist, however, including one last fact that has come to light since this book was first published. Alma Mahler writes a good deal about Mahler's youthful and turbulent friendship with Hugo Wolf. In particular, she mentions an idea both of them had, to compose a fairy-tale opera, *Rübezahl*. As the attentive reader will observe, the libretto, in Mahler's own hand, survived, and eventually became the subject of a dispute between him and his sister, Justine (see pp. 143–144 and 307). Although it appears that Mahler wanted to destroy the manuscript, or said he wanted to – his will, happily for us, was often weaker than his intention in this respect – the libretto outlived all those who were variously irritated by its existence, and by kind permission of its present owners we are able to include a photograph of one of the pages of the original manuscript (see illustration) and thus reproduce for the first time part of a very early project of the young Mahler which has hitherto only lived on as a title.

Mahler was not averse to a cyclic shaping of his musical materials, so let me round off this introduction by a return to the topics with which I began. It is a fact which even Mr. Gradgrind would accept that there has been a revolution in the general appreciation of Mahler, a revolution which has taken place between the publication of the first edition of Alma Mahler's memoirs and the present day. The reader coming to them for the first time now enjoys the inestimable advantage of reading them in the sure knowledge that, if he so wishes, there is scarcely a note of Mahler's music that he cannot hear, either live or on disc. Mahler performances indeed are so well established a part of the musical scene in the 1960s that the 1940s and earlier seem like some far-off dream.

Voices are heard, of course, in varying degrees of protest or scepticism. The older generation of critics, still not reconciled and perhaps irreconcilable, talk of a Mahler 'fashion', with the implication that his inflated reputation will eventually die a natural death. Fashion is a complicated subject, but one would be willing to discuss the proposition more seriously if the spectre of 'fashion' were not raised only when a composer is received with enthusiasm and rides high in public esteem. Where were the brave voices of protest when it was the fashion not to perform Mahler at all?

Or if it is not the bogy of fashion that is evoked, then it is some mysterious movement in public taste which has enthroned Mahler in the place of Tchaikovsky, the implication being that the gullible, tasteless public has exchanged one kind of high romantic, 'self-indulgent' music for another. A preposterous assertion this, and only worthy of note because it makes painfully clear that by one body of critical opinion at least, Tchaikovsky is no better understood than Mahler; and by 'understanding' I mean the bringing to bear of the kind of critical sensibility and sympathy which ought to attend works of genius.

One must be wary, however, of that most boring of all occupations, the rehearsal of ancient battles, especially if one has had the fortune to be, as it were, on the winning side. In the past a measure of pugnacity was obligatory: after all, one had to fight to secure Mahler a hearing. Now, in a very real sense, his music belongs to an immense and diverse public, spread throughout the world. It may well be that his reputation will fluctuate? What major composer's reputation doesn't, from time to time? But I do not foresee a period, given that our musical civilization persists, when the essence of Mahler – that is, his unique voice as a composer – will go unheeded. To someone like myself, whose life has been immeasurably enriched by his art, this would seem to be no more than the most sober of claims and least extravagant of predictions.

D.M.

Barcombe Mills,
Sussex,
August, 1967

Introduction to the 1969 American Edition

In my Introduction to this book, which I wrote in 1967, I said, '... there is little now that we may expect in the way of new Mahler discoveries. The only major manuscript source which still remains to be made accessible is the first part of the early cantata, *Das klagende Lied*, the *Waldmärchen* section, which was omitted when Mahler came to publish his revised version of the work in 1899/1900.'

By a stroke of unexpected fortune, I have now – in 1969 – been able to consult a MS. of *Waldmärchen* – Part I of what was originally a tripartite cantata – and thus am able to report on this last and hitherto missing link with Mahler's youth. (*Waldmärchen* was performed in 1934 and 1935 under the direction of Mr. Alfred Rosé, the son of Arnold Rosé and Mahler's sister Justine, but has never been published or made generally available.)*

This is not the place to embark on a full-scale examination of *Waldmärchen*, which space forbids. But it seems appropriate to give at least an indication of the character of the music and to speculate, one hopes profitably, about the probable reasons for Mahler's omission of the section at the stage when he was revising the work for its eventual publication. In fact, of course, these two considerations are inextricably bound together, and when one is discussed, the other is inevitably brought to the fore.

Perhaps then it may be concisely stated that in character the music of *Waldmärchen* differs little from the subsequent sections we know now as Parts I and II of the published version, i.e., *Der Spielmann* and *Hochzeitsstück*, and that it was probably for this very reason that Mahler at length decided to exclude the section from the revision. This bald statement, I think, is less uninformative than it may appear at first sight. For one thing, the fact of the section's omission, in the absence of the music itself, has naturally

* For further details, see my *Gustav Mahler: The Early Years* (London, 1958), pp. 153-157 and p. 118. There I had to rely in my account of *Waldmärchen* on reports generously contributed by Mr. Rosé and Dr. Hans Holländer. Clearly, these must now be revised in the light of the information I bring forward on this occasion.

suggested that it was the actual quality of invention that was found wanting by the composer when he came to make a mature assessment of the score as a whole. But on the contrary, at least in my view, the acknowledged freshness, exuberance and youthful originality of *Der Spielmann* and *Hochzeitsstück* are no less evident in *Waldmärchen*; and if we are seeking for the reason for Mahler's rejection of the first part of his work, it is not to be found in any lack of inspiration or scarcity of compelling ideas in the original Part I. (Having now seen the music for myself, I find Dr. Holländer's view that *Waldmärchen* represents 'a preliminary sketch' wholly untenable.)

It seems to me that there were two good reasons why Mahler applied the surgeon's knife. First, there is the question of overall shape. *Waldmärchen*, we find, begins with an impressive and elaborately worked out orchestral prelude of over 120 bars,* very close in length, style and manner to the prelude which opens the next section, *Der Spielmann*. (The prelude to *Hochzeitsstück*, on the other hand, is very much briefer, indeed only about one-third of the length of the other preludes, and in no way as elaborate in the meticulous, mosaic-like exposure and combination of leading themes and motives.) I have little doubt that it was, so to speak, an embarrassment of preludial riches which in part prompted Mahler to make his revision also an abbreviation: in a very real sense, the cantata in its original version gives the impression of beginning twice over.

Why then, one may well ask, did Mahler not confine his revisionary strategy to adjusting the proportions of the preludes to his original Parts I and II? The case, I think, is altogether less simple than that. On my reading of *Waldmärchen*, concede though one may its inspirations, one also has to admit that the section is very close indeed in its mingling of lyrical and dramatic incident to the style and matter of the immediately ensuing *Der Spielmann*; and also, of course, in its alternation of solo, choral and orchestral passages, though this is characteristic of the cantata as a whole. (One notes too that *Waldmärchen* introduces a bass soloist, who is not employed elsewhere in the work, an extravagance that might well have influenced Mahler to economize in his revision.) In

* *Waldmärchen* complete runs to over 600 bars.

short, though the inspirations of *Waldmärchen* may, as I suggest, be quite the equal of those in *Der Spielmann* or *Hochzeitsstück*, they may also be regarded as duplicate inspirations and thus expendable when scrutinized by a composer in his maturity.

More important, and here perhaps we approach the heart of the matter, it seems to me that Mahler's later dramatic sense must intuitively have told him that the excision of *Waldmärchen* greatly served to heighten and intensify the drama. Because, with all three sections *in situ*, we have in fact a needless duplication of the narrative, i.e., although the first section unfolds the actual murder of the young knight by his envious elder brother, the essentials of the tale are retold in retrospect during the succeeding second and third sections, through the medium of the bone-flute (the instrument that the wandering minstrel unknowingly fashions out of one of the murdered youth's bones). It is surely undeniable that the drama of the fairy-tale is immeasurably tightened by the omission of the expository first part, which, if anything, blunts the edge of the macabre narrative by making too much explicit at an early stage. Musically too, the gains are self-evident. For example, in his original version Mahler introduces the flute as a dramatic character in the preludes to both *Waldmärchen* and *Der Spielmann* in virtually identical musical terms, which is once too many. The retrospective narrative device is altogether more telling.

Though there may be good reasons why Mahler deleted the first part – and I think on the whole his judgment was completely sound – this is not to suggest that an occasional performance of the original version in its entirety would be anything but welcome.* The music of *Waldmärchen* is as fresh and enchanting as any music in the published version, and knowledge of the unfamiliar score enables us to see how the young Mahler envisaged the cantata as a whole. It is fascinating, for instance, to trace in this original first part the source of themes and motives which we have come to know so well in the bipartite final version of *Das klagende Lied*. The descending minor scale which winds – or unwinds, rather – *Hochzeitsstück* to its A minor close, and which also appears in *Der Spielmann*, is continuously used in *Waldmärchen*, as indeed is the octave motive ('Ach Leide!') which the scale fills out. Another

* As I write, I learn that a performance is planned in the U.S.A. for January, 1970.

link is the urgent, thrusting phrase to which the minstrel places the flute to his lips in *Der Spielmann*; again, in *Waldmärchen*, this particular idea is prominently used, appropriately enough in close association with the incident of the murder itself.

These are only two examples among many, of course; and they represent only what we should expect: evidence of Mahler's use of thematic and motivic connections between the parts to secure an overall unity and a cogently worked out scheme of themes, motives and keys with specific dramatic associations. It is a mode of operation which means, inevitably, that we have always known something of *Waldmärchen*, simply because its materials were necessarily deployed later in *Der Spielmann* and *Hochzeitsstück*; and in the published version of the cantata there are indeed quite extensive stretches of music, as distinct from themes or motives, which are, in substance, based on comparable passages from *Waldmärchen*. This duplication of musical incident was doubtless another reason why Mahler felt able to declare his original first section redundant: *Waldmärchen*, surviving its amputation, has lived on in *Der Spielmann* and *Hochzeitsstück*.

On the other hand, *Waldmärchen* certainly has its own distinctive inventions – the ingenious quasi-chorale treatment of some of the choral commentary is an example – and also clearly reveals an expository relationship to the succeeding sections. We find on occasion that what we know today as a prominent theme or motive in the revised version was much more extensively treated in the omitted first section. This is true, for instance, of the two quotations I happen to mention above, the descending scale and the phrase which carries the crucial text, 'Der Spielmann setzt die Flöte an', both of which are more insistently stated in *Waldmärchen* than in the ensuing sections. Thus part of the unique character of *Waldmärchen* – and one has to recognize the loss of it – was its function as a formal musical exposition. This impression is further strengthened by the discovery of the detailed extent to which, as it were, Mahler foreshadowed the development and end of the work in its beginning: the haunting 'Ach Weh' motive of *Der Spielmann* is already clearly articulated in bar 28 of the prelude to *Waldmärchen*, though it is not developed in *Waldmärchen* itself; and likewise in bar 70 we encounter the germinal motive of the festive 'castle' music which only attains its apotheosis in the celebrations of *Hochzeitsstück*. One may respect Mahler's judgment in making his revision, but there is no doubt that the original version of *Das klagende Lied* shows how the ambitious young composer – and we have to remind ourselves that Mahler was little more than twenty when he completed the work – was very much in control of the fine detail of his cantata, even though the sheer abundance of ideas and fertile expression of them may later have been a cause of concern to him.

One point of overall formal organization is certainly – and interestingly – established by the MS. of *Waldmärchen*: whereas the published version of *Das klagende Lied* opens in C minor (the prelude to *Der Spielmann*) and ends in A minor (the close of *Hochzeitsstück*), inspection of the original Part I (*Waldmärchen*) shows us that the first version of the cantata was less arbitrary in its tonal scheme; i.e., the prelude to *Waldmärchen* is launched with a tremolo on A which clearly looks forward to the clinching A minor of the work's final bars. (Also, F sharp minor, the key which eventually rounds off the unpublished first part, emerges early in *Waldmärchen*, in bar 5.) To have the whole work before us may indeed confirm the impression, which was perhaps Mahler's, that here was too much of a good thing. But one is also left inescapably admiring the thorough organization which underpins the total concept.

Possibly, though, the most fascinating aspect of *Waldmärchen* is the extent to which it demonstrates Mahler committed in musical style to the world of *Des Knaben Wunderhorn*, the world which embraces not only his *Gesellen* and *Wunderhorn* songs but the first four symphonies. In *Waldmärchen*, the use of fanfares (poetic and dramatic), the quasi-folk vocal melodies, the juxtaposition of major and minor, the march rhythms, the outbreaks of impassioned lyricism, the colourful key contrasts, the tramping basses founded on drum fourths – all these typical gestures fill out, most valuably, our knowledge and experience of Mahler's first period. Most striking of all, when the fated younger knight lies down to rest ('zur Ruhe') beneath the willow tree, the musical imagery is virtually identical with the famous passage in the *Lieder eines fahrenden Gesellen* (which Mahler later quoted in his First Symphony) where the travelling hero sinks to sleep and oblivion claims him. Only the tree is different: a lime, not a willow. For this remarkable anticipation of a masterpiece still to come, *Waldmärchen* must be reckoned an historic document of the first significance.*

The other new material I have to bring forward is of less substance but nonetheless demands notice. I much regret having inadvertently failed to include a paragraph which formed part of Alma Mahler's original German text but was omitted in the abbreviated English edition of 1946. I am sorry not to have repaired the omission in 1967 and take this opportunity now to supply the missing text, which should follow the paragraph ending 'The production was on a very high artistic level' (line 27) on p. 35. This is the passage in question, one of some interest because there is a reference in Letter 122, from 1907, which suggests that the encounter in Warsaw in 1902 left a marked impression on the Mahlers:

On our journey home to Vienna we had a curious experience in Warsaw. Although we were without any money, apart from a cheque for conducting fees, we very much wanted to do some sight-seeing. We boarded a hotel bus and rattled into town. It was still Advent and everything seemed sad and the shops were shut. When we arrived at the entrance of a hotel, which had its lights on, we considered our situation to be rather bleak with only five roubles in our pockets, so we told the porter that we would return later and strolled off into the dark streets. Not a soul about! We must have behaved in rather a suspicious way, for suddenly we realized that a shadowy individual was following at our heels. The man, wearing a Havelock, whispered to us softly, something about nightclubs and shady entertainment, but we hastened quickly along. The pursuing shadow kept up with us – we were hurrying into a dark side street; but we pulled ourselves together, jumped into a small cab, which came along empty, and drove off to the railway station which, with its lights, welcomed us as a place of refuge. We ate some eggs there, and felt secure. What remained of the five roubles I gave to a poor, old Jew who was selling matches there. Mahler was very happy about this small gesture of identification. From this poor, old Jew I learnt much, felt that I had to ask forgiveness of all Jewry and, in this one moment, comprehended the entire burden and sorrow of Israel. In the warm

* This passage discloses in fact the first appearance of a 'farewell' motive which was to remain a constant feature of Mahler's music.

sleeping compartment I found a gold piece, tucked away in a crease of my purse, which (had we found it in time) would have improved our stay in Warsaw.

I am grateful to Dr. Mosco Carner for pointing out this lapse in his review of this edition of the book in the *Musical Times*, London, January, 1969. Two further facts he lists are also worth noting. The critic who became one of Mahler's bitter enemies – in connection with the withdrawal of his version of Mozart's *Zaïde* from the Vienna repertory (see p. 49) – was Robert Hirschfeld of the *Wiener Zeitung*; and Dr. Carner further clarifies an incident described by Alma Mahler on p. 126; it was none other than Anton Webern who piped up with an answer to Mahler's question about Dostoyevsky, not a 'chorus of youthful voices.' (See also Willi Reich's *Alban Berg*, London, 1965, pp. 31–32.)

Dr. Carner also usefully, and sometimes correctively, comments on aspects of the translation. It is not possible to specify all his suggested improvements here, but I commend his review to the attention of interested readers. I shall certainly heed his emendations when the opportunity occurs to undertake a detailed revision. It must be emphasized, meanwhile, that my main editorial labour was concentrated on annotating the text and, above all, in establishing a more correct chronology for the letters.

I have to thank Mr. Peter Heyworth, the music critic of *The Observer* (London), for bringing to my notice the fact that Thomas Mann had Mahler in mind when writing his famous story, 'Death in Venice'. A letter of Mann's (from 1921) makes it clear that his portrait of the artist, Gustav von Aschenbach, was modelled on his vivid memories of Mahler. This information provides a fascinating footnote to Letter 174, the last letter in this book. Undoubtedly 'the impressions of 12th September' – the occasion of the première of the Eighth Symphony in 1910 – were deep indeed.

Mr. Heyworth has also queried the reference in Letter 26 to the 'electric railway'. Those with an expert knowledge of the history of Vienna's transport system assure me that this should read 'tramway'.

On p. 33, I myself raise a footnote query about the date of Mahler's marriage. This can now be settled. Alma Mahler was correct. The 9th March, 1902, is confirmed by the signed entry in the marriage register. I should also like to put straight what is, I think, a misleading reference on p. 96 to the 'great Quartet' from Mozart's *Seraglio*. I am sure now that what Alma Mahler actually had in mind was not the celebrated quartet from Act II of the opera, but the eminently singable *Vaudeville* which concludes Act III. Further, I regret the diminution, on p. 226, of the appropriate status of the Zend-Avesta, which should, of course, be preceded by the definite article.

In Letter 142, there is an unidentified reference to *Kaiser Karls Geisel*. This was a play by Gerhart Hauptmann. On p. 120, two philosophical works by the Italian Giordano Bruno rather quaintly appear with German titles. The Italian titles should read respectively, *Spaccio della Bestia Trionfante* and *Cena della Ceneri*; and on p. 351 of the Biographical List I was in error, under the Reger entry, to write of a 'volume of tributes to Mahler's memory'. This in fact appeared in 1910, when Mahler was still alive.

In my earlier Introduction, I tried to make clear how mistaken I thought this book's detractors were, who were so vociferous when it was first published. It seems now as if we may expect another bout of scepticism, concentrated once again on the vivid personality of Alma Mahler. Henry-Louis de La Grange, whose biography of Mahler has been long awaited, spent some time in the issue of *The Saturday Review* for 29th March, 1969, presenting what was described as a 'New Image' of Mahler. He suggests, if I understand him correctly, that this new image can only be achieved if, so to speak, we dent Alma Mahler's image; or, rather, amend the distorted portrait of her husband that her book promotes.

Perhaps we should wait until Baron de La Grange's book appears before assessing the weight of his strictures. But he seems to rely in the main on quotations from Alma Mahler's unpublished diary, *Ein Leben mit Mahler*, for his conviction that she indulged in 'the most serious distortions of the truth ... deliberately introduced and fostered in her two books *Mein Leben* [*And the Bridge is Love*, as it is known in English] and *Gustav Mahler* [the present volume].'

I think I have sufficiently shown that Alma Mahler's recollections of incidents and musical events – many of them of the greatest importance and first brought to our attention in this book – are exceptionally well founded and accurate, even though she may have erred in detail now and again. But then, to do Baron de La Grange justice, he does not dispute the facts so much as suggest that Alma Mahler falsified the account of her life with her husband and depicted him as someone and something he was not: 'Not only does Frau Alma describe him as sickly, but in page after page she refers to him as an ascetic and egotistic man, incapable of loving anyone wholeheartedly.' As for Alma Mahler, we must understand her to be – though not without considerable attainments – ambitious, calculating, domineering and preternaturally fickle.

All this strikes me as dangerous and treacherous ground for a biographer, who should avoid retrospective involvement in the emotional lives of those he studies, when all too often it is the biographer's emotions which begin to loom uncomfortably large. I am sure, of course, that Baron de La Grange is right in thinking that Alma Mahler's biography must be read, necessarily so, as a one-sided record; and clearly we must interpret what she writes against our knowledge of her complex personality. But the trivial evidence he produces from the unpublished diary seems to do little more than confirm what she makes abundantly clear herself in this book and even more emphatically in the disastrous reminiscences of *And the Bridge is Love*: that she was incurably – to use Baron de La Grange's own polite word – 'flirtatious'. The unpublished diary would appear to add nothing of significance to her own public tally of infidelities of thought and deed. Why assume, moreover, that a private diary embodies the whole truth and nothing but the truth? Private 'confessions' can be as fallible and variously motivated as those made for public consumption. The private fantasy, in fact, is as common a phenomenon as the public deceit.

There are three straightforward observations to be made on Baron de La Grange's 'New Image'. First, he does not always give the impression of having mastered the text on which he comments. For example, he rather grandly tells us that Mahler's previous biographers have acknowledged his 'Wagnerian fervour' but 'have not always insisted sufficiently on his equally strong love of Mozart'. I doubt if this is generally true; but in any event it is certainly not true of Alma Mahler, who writes unambiguously on p. 22 of this book, 'It was he [Mahler] who gave the signal to the whole world for the Mozart renaissance'; and there is more in the same vein. Secondly, it must surely be an eccentric person, who, after reading Alma Mahler's biography in its entirety, can seriously hold the view that, in substance and intent, it presents a hostile portrait of her husband. Thirdly, while it is true that we read the wife's account of her life with her husband with no counterpart document to hand from Mahler, there is, after all, the long sequence of his letters which rounds off this volume, from which an explicitly affectionate and admiring portrait of Alma Mahler emerges – a portrait based, one must add, on an acquaintance with the composer a good deal more intimate than Baron de La Grange's. Are we to believe that this was nothing other than a massive illusion? It is unrewarding enough to advise the living about their matrimonial affairs. One cannot but think that it is likely to prove even less profitable to set up as a kind of Marriage Guidance Counsellor to the dead.

D.M.

Aldeburgh,
Suffolk,
June, 1969

Acknowledgements
and a Note on the Text

I have a number of friends to thank, all of whom have helped me in various ways, by supplying illustrations, by answering queries or clarifying obscurities. First, however, I must thank the composer's daughter, Anna Mahler, for her patience in answering many tiresome questions, for her help with compiling the illustrations, and for her encouragement. Without the generous collaboration of Dr. William B. Ober and Mr. George Ozaki, certain materials located in New York could not have been reproduced in this book, and without the warm interest and enthusiasm of Mr. and Mrs. John Murray, the whole enterprise would never have been brought to fruition. I also wish to thank: Mr. Sergei Hackel; Mr. William Mann; Mrs. Margot Milner; Mr. Harold Rosenthal; Mr. Alfred Rosé; Mr. and Mrs. Wolfgang Rosé; Dr. Roger Savage; Miss Lenore Spiering; Miss Annie Steiner; Dr. Felix Steiner; and Frau Ida Wagner. I have been further helped by Mr. Martin Kingsbury and Mr. Charles Ford, while to my wife, Kathleen, who has shouldered much of the labour of checking, correcting and typing, I owe a special debt of gratitude. What errors remain are, of course, mine.

Perhaps it will not be out of place here to include a word about the text, and also an important word of thanks to the translator, Mr. Basil Creighton, who has not only provided translations of the passages and letters restored to this new edition but patiently acquiesced in the many suggestions and emendations I have put before him. Numerous corrections and (I hope) improvements have been made throughout the text. It would have been pedantic and superfluous to show most of them, but any matter appearing in square brackets, and there are a few instances, is of editorial origin. It is not the reminiscences that have raised most problems, but the letters, where I have often altered the chronology, or indicated transpositions, to make a better sequence. The sources of the facts that I have used to establish a fresh and, I hope, more convincing order are too numerous to list here, but I should like to pay tribute to a Czech edition of Mahler's letters, which includes the *Briefe* 1879–1911, published in Vienna in 1924, and also some of the letters from this volume. It appeared in Prague in 1962, edited by František Bartoš, and translated into Czech by Marie Bartoš and František Bartoš. This is the best available edition of Mahler's correspondence and is full of valuable incidental information, of which I have made liberal use and warmly acknowledge.

D.M. (1968)

A Note on the German and English Texts

The following letters are omitted from this edition. (Page references refer to the German edition.) Letter to Mahler from Mengelberg's father (p. 297); note from Pfitzner (p. 356); note from Dehmel (p. 370); letter from Burckhard (pp. 402–3); letter from Ignacio Zuloaga (pp. 403–4); two letters from Mengelberg (pp. 404–5 and 409–10); and a letter from Peter Rosegger (p. 473). Omitted letters from G.M. to A.M.: letter from Salzburg, 1906 (pp. 365–66); telegram from Salzburg (p. 367); excerpt of 10 lines after end of Letter 148 (pp. 438–39); letter from Toblach, 1909 (pp. 439–40); note of 9 lines, Toblach, July, 1909 (p. 442); a note of 9 lines, Graz-Tobelbad (p. 457); and a letter, Toblach nach Tobelbad (p. 458). My footnote on p. 332 of the English edition refers to the omission of some poems by Mahler and other lyrical texts: these are all to be found between pp. 459 and 464 in the German edition (and belong to the summer of 1910). For the rest, the only omissions are of needlessly duplicated or otherwise redundant examples of G.M.'s endearments, e.g., the last 6 lines of Letter 22 (p. 290 in the German edition), and A.M.'s transcription (p. 479) of G.M.'s anguished comments on the manuscript of the Tenth Symphony. It is better to consult these in the facsimile edition of the sketches.

D.M. (1973)

Preface to First Edition

I wrote this book many years ago, and my only reason for doing so was because no one knew Gustav Mahler so well as I and because I did not want the experiences we shared and the expressions of his thought to be crowded out of my own memory by the pressure and hurry of life.

It was not originally my intention to have the book published during my lifetime.

But now the whole of Europe has been rocked to its foundations and nothing stands where it did. Rodin's bust of Mahler, which I presented to the Vienna Opera and which was unveiled by the last President of Austria, has now been removed from its pedestal. The wide street in Vienna named after Gustav Mahler has been renamed Meistersinger Street.* The large sum of money subscribed throughout the world for a Gustav Mahler monument has been appropriated without ceremony to one of the usual welfare funds of annexed Austria. I therefore have no scruple in saying openly what I know from experience of persons who live their lives and play their parts in the Third Reich. The doors have been slammed. And not from one side only. All that I say of Richard Strauss is taken from the daily entries in my diary. It should not be forgotten that Richard Strauss, the greatest master of contemporary music in the first decade of this century, was Gustav Mahler's only rival.

Only those who were there at the time, and able to appreciate it, know what Mahler did for Vienna during the glorious years of his reign there. Today Germany is deprived of his music, and the memory of his life and compositions is carefully effaced. In other countries the great conductors, Willem Mengelberg, Bruno Walter and Otto Klemperer exert themselves on his behalf, and the best of the young conductors follow their example. They keep the torch alight and hand it on, until the day when the doors

* The Mahlerstrasse is back, and the bust was restored after 1945. (D.M.)

of his own country are thrown open again and his work is joyfully welcomed there once more.

I myself live a wholly different life today, and for me these
pages from past days are faded. But the work and personality of
Gustav Mahler have not faded. And so I give to the world these
recollections of years of pain and joy as a testimony to him.

ALMA MARIA WERFEL-MAHLER

Sanary sur mer,
Summer, 1939

Part One

MEMORIES

First Meeting

One afternoon in November, 1901, as I was walking along the Ring with some friends, I happened to meet the Zuckerkandls. Zuckerkandl, besides being an eminent anatomist, was an extremely intelligent person and full of humour.

'We've got Mahler coming in tonight – won't you come?'

I declined. I did not want to meet Mahler. In fact I had purposely and with considerable difficulty avoided meeting him that summer, because of all the stories people told about him. I knew him well by sight; he was a small, fidgety man with a fine head. I was acquainted also with the scandals about him and every young woman who aspired to sing in opera. I had been to the concert when he conducted his First Symphony [18th November 1900], a work I had thoroughly disliked and even angrily rejected. At the same time, he was of importance to me as a conductor and I was conscious of his mysterious and powerful fascination. But this I now belied.

My 'no' was scarcely uttered when Frau Zuckerkandl broke in: 'It wouldn't do in any case. I had to promise his sister, Justine, that there wouldn't be anyone else. He can't bear strangers.'

'Nonsense,' Zuckerkandl shouted. 'I insist.'

But I was resolute.

A week later Bertha Zuckerkandl wrote that Mahler had put them off after all, but proposed himself for the following Sunday, which was always their day. She had asked Gustav Klimt and Max Burckhard and several more, and urged me to come, as she did not now feel bound by her promise to Justine. Klimt, the well-known painter, and Max Burckhard, the idol of my youth, director of the Burgtheater and poet, most liberal-minded of Austrians and my fatherly counsellor – I should be among friends, and I accepted. I went there feeling rather intimidated. Mahler had been in Paris, giving concerts with the Philharmonic orchestra,* and there, at the Austrian Embassy, he had met Madame Sophie

* 18th–22nd June 1900. (D.M.)

Clemenceau, sister-in-law of Georges Clemenceau and a sister of Berta Zuckerkandl. She was extremely cultivated, and they had agreed to meet at the Zuckerkandls' when she was next in Vienna.

From the very first moment Mahler observed me closely, not simply because of my face, which might have been called beautiful in those days, but also because of my piquant air. He studied me long and searchingly through his spectacles. The last guest arrived and we went in to dinner. I was between Klimt and Burckhard, and we three made a merry trio and laughed a lot. Mahler, at the other end of the table, looked on and listened, covertly at first and then without disguise. At last he called out enviously: 'Mayn't we be allowed to share the joke?' His unfortunate neighbour was ignored that evening.

Then a belated guest turned up. He came straight from a recital of Kubelík's and was so enthusiastic about his playing that it was impossible to keep silent. When he asked me whether I had heard Kubelík, I said that soloists' recitals didn't interest me. Mahler chimed in approvingly. 'Nor me,' he said loudly from the other end of the table.

After dinner the party broke up into groups and there was a discussion about the relativity of beauty. 'Beauty!' Mahler said. 'The head of Socrates is beautiful.' I agreed and added that in my eyes Alexander von Zemlinsky, the musician, was a beauty. He was almost the ugliest man I had ever seen – and yet the force of his intellect was felt in every glance of his eyes and in every one of his abrupt movements. Zemlinsky was a disciple of Brahms and almost all the musicians of his day and of the next generation too were recruited from among his pupils. Mahler shrugged his shoulders. That was going a bit too far, he thought.

I fired up and made a point of bringing the talk round to Zemlinsky. 'Now that we are talking of him – why don't you do his Hofmannsthal ballet, *Das goldene Herz*? You promised him you would.'

'Because I can't understand it,' Mahler rapped out.

I had been instructed in the somewhat confused symbolism of the poem by Zemlinsky himself. 'I'll tell you the whole story and explain what it means.'

Mahler smiled: 'I'm all eagerness.'

'But first,' I said, 'you will have to explain for my benefit the full meaning of the *Bride of Korea*.'* (This ballet was a standing item in the Vienna repertory and incredibly confused and stupid.) Mahler laughed loudly, showing all his flashing white teeth. He went on to ask me about my musical studies and I told him I studied composition with Zemlinsky. He begged me to bring some of my work to the Opera for him to see.

We had long ago drawn apart from the rest, or else they had left us alone. There was that magic circle round us which quickly encloses those who have found each other. I promised him to come one day, when I had something good to show him. He smiled ironically, as though to say that he would have a long time to wait, and then invited me to the dress-rehearsal next morning of the *Tales of Hoffmann*. Madame Clemenceau and Frau Zuckerkandl came up at that moment and he invited them also. I hesitated at first: my composition for Zemlinsky was not done yet. Then my feelings carried me away and I accepted. There was just time before we parted for a quick question:

'Where do you live?'

'Hohe Warte —'

'I'll take you —'

But I did not want to go on foot. It was late and I was tired.

'Well, you'll be at the Opera? For certain?'

'Yes indeed, as long as I can get my work done.'

'Then that's a promise?'

It was over. I was not pleased with myself. I had the distinct feeling of having put myself in a false light. Owing to my wretched, inborn shyness I could never be my real self in company and when I met people for the first time. Either my obstinate silence was broken only by distracted replies, or else, as tonight, I was as bold as brass and kept nothing back.

My stepfather, Carl Moll, talked to me at length about this new friendship, which did not altogether please either of us. Mahler by that time had got into the way of talking as though he addressed an assembled crowd. 'Yes, but I tell you —' That was how he

* By Josef Bayer (1852–1913), composer and director of ballet music at the Vienna Opera. (D.M.)

talked. He had wielded power so long, encountering only abject submission on every hand, that his isolation had become loneliness. I thought no more of my impressions, but I was certainly flattered by the exclusive attention he paid me.

But it is time to say something of Mahler's family and upbringing.

His father was a man of strong and exuberant vitality, completely uninhibited. He married a girl of a good Jewish family named Frank; being lame from birth, she had no pretensions to a good match. The man she loved did not give her a thought and so she married Bernhard Mahler without love and with utter resignation. The marriage was an unhappy one from the first day. There were children in plenty, twelve in all. Her martyrdom was complicated by a weak heart, which grew rapidly worse owing to the strain of child-bearing and housework.

They began their married life in a small way at Kalischt, a village in Bohemia. He had a distillery* there, which his family called in joke the manufactory. Immediately the Jews were granted the freedom to move from place to place, Bernhard Mahler migrated to Iglau, the nearest town of any size, and there set up in his business again. His pride and reserve cut him off from other people and he was left to himself. He had what might almost be called a library, and was goaded on by the ambition to better himself, but he was uncertain how this craving was to be satisfied. So he decided that his children should achieve what was denied to himself.

His mother, Gustav Mahler's grandmother, was a woman of masculine energy. She was a hawker and even at the age of eighty went from house to house with a large basket on her back. In her old age she had the misfortune to transgress some law regulating hawkers and was given a heavy sentence. She did not for a moment think of putting up with it. She set off on the spot for Vienna and sought an audience of the Emperor, Franz Joseph, who was so much impressed by her vigour and her eighty years that he granted her a pardon.

---

* In fact, the family business was a good deal more humble than 'distillery' suggests. It was more like a shop or small pub. (D.M.)

Mahler certainly inherited his inflexibility in the pursuit of his aims from his grandmother.

His talent for music was shown at an early age. Once on a visit to the parents of his mother, who because of her superior refinement was jokingly called the 'duchess', Gustav could not be found. After a long search he was at last discovered in the attic, strumming on an old piano. From that day on his father was convinced that he was destined to be a musician. He was then four years old.

Five of his brothers and sisters died at an early age of diphtheria. The sixth, a boy, died at twelve of hydrocardia after a long illness. This was the first harrowing experience of Gustav Mahler's childhood. He loved his brother Ernst and suffered with him all through his illness up to the end. For months he scarcely left his bedside and never tired of telling him stories. To all else he was blind. Indoors and out he lived in a dream; he dreamed his way through family life and childhood. He saw nothing of the unending tortures his mother had to endure from the brutality of his father, who ran after every servant, domineered over his delicate wife and flogged the children.

Every day his father exploded over the untidiness of Gustav's drawer – the one and only place where tidiness was demanded of him; and yet every day Gustav forgot all about it until the next explosion burst about his ears. It was quite beyond him to bear this one trifling command in mind. These scenes did not stop at words, but nothing could break in on his day-dreams until the day when his father sent him to Prague to be placed with the celebrated music firm of Grünfeld to study music. Here he came into touch with the ugliness of life for the first time. His clothes and shoes were taken from him and worn by others and he had to go barefoot, and hungry also. All this he scarcely noticed. When he told me about it he added: 'I took it as a matter of course.' His worst experience was being the involuntary witness, when he was sitting in a dark room, of a brutal love-scene between the servant and the son of the house, and he never forgot the shock of disgust it caused him. He jumped up to go to the girl's help, but she did not thank him for his pains. He was soundly abused by both of them and sworn to secrecy.

This episode left a deep mark. Just as one can be angry all day long with people who have annoyed one in a dream, so Gustav never forgave the young pianist who had given him this shock.

At last his father heard by a side-wind in what a state of neglect he was living. He found the boy in a pitiful condition and took him straight off to the inn he was staying at to eat his fill for once, and then returned to this odd specimen of a pension to collect what was left of his son's wardrobe. Gustav meanwhile sat in the inn and never stirred until his father returned in a fury and took him to the station for the train to Iglau. Mahler's passivity as a child, his power of obstinate endurance, is illustrated by another episode which I have given elsewhere.* His daughter in her child-hood had the same faculty: she could sit and wait for hour after hour as though in a physical trance.

His mother patiently bore her lot and, as the years passed, her joy in Gustav's expanding life was her greatest and at last her only happiness. His father gave way to his temper whenever the mood took him. I have never heard Mahler say an affectionate word of his father, but his love for his mother had the intensity of a fixation, then and always. Often and often he has told me with bitter remorse how when playing the piano as a child he used sud-denly to feel there was somebody there, and it was always his mother listening at the door, in the covered gallery. Then he used to stop playing and show his annoyance. His harshness to her in those days haunted him in later years.

In due course he arrived at the Vienna conservatoire to study with Julius Epstein and Robert Fuchs. He must have been an odd pupil. Fuchs himself told me: 'Mahler always played truant and yet there was nothing he couldn't do.' His fellow-students regarded him as a marvel and spoke of him as 'another Schubert'. He won the first prize for composition. His fellow-student and friend, Hans Rott, an extraordinarily talented musician, was unsuccessful. Mahler went home and told them proudly of the prize he had won. His mother wept tears of indignation and said: 'All the same, Rott's work was better than yours.' It was just like his mother.

(Rott went out of his mind while he was quite a young man.

* Alma Mahler refers to her edition of Mahler's correspondence (1924). (D.M.)

He composed continually in the asylum. He used the sheets of music-paper he had written on for a very different purpose and said with a grin of delight: 'That's all the works of man are worth.')

Mahler's eldest sister, Leopoldine, was yoked to an unloved husband and died in early life of a tumour on the brain. In after years Mahler reproached himself, as though he were partly to blame for her unhappiness, because he was too young and ignorant of life to know what went on in his home.

Justine, his second sister, had an unusually vivid imagination. The practice of lying was systematically inculcated in her by her father's short-sighted harshness. It was long before she awoke from a nightmare of whippings. This little story – a legend, as it were, of her life – is thoroughly characteristic of her. While still a child, she stuck candles all round the edge of her cot. Then she lay down and lit the candles and firmly believed that she was dead.

And now for Gustav's brothers. Otto, the elder, a very talented musician, but lacking in seriousness and perseverance, was by far and away his favourite. Mahler employed a tutor and got him through his school-work by hook or by crook. In later years he found him jobs as répétiteur in small German towns, but all to no purpose. Otto grumbled and complained. He thought himself as good as his brother and envied him his greater success. Again and again he threw up the livelihood provided for him. Finally he shot himself. He left a note saying that life no longer pleased him, so he handed back his ticket. He was a fanatical disciple of Dostoyevsky's and philosophized about his approaching death, in the manner of the great Russian, with an old friend of Mahler's, a woman, who, however, did nothing to prevent it. People of his kind, who know too much, often cut a very sorry figure in life.

The second, Alois, sickly from birth – all the children, Gustav included, were handicapped by their mother's heart-disease – was rather a fool than a freak. He was crammed full of senseless absurdities. One day he hired an old horse and had riding-breeches made with one leg blue, the other red. He rode up and down the streets of Iglau as a German mercenary, to the joy of all beholders but to the bitter shame of his family. 'You wait,' he said. 'I'll ride past the castle in Vienna like this, and the Crown Prince will ask: "Who's that fine young fellow on horseback?" He'll summon me to his presence and I'll get some wonderful post.' Once he accompanied Justine to Bolzano, where Gustav sent her for a cure. During the *table d'hôte*, which in those days was served at long tables, she suddenly heard him loudly boasting of the year he had served as a volunteer in a smart cavalry regiment. A man at the table, an officer on the active list who was in civilian dress, asked him about some of his fellow-officers, of whom of course Alois knew nothing whatever, but about whom he lied volubly. The officer was astonished and Justine beside herself. In another moment her brother would be held up to public disgrace. There was a reprieve in the nick of time, when the company rose from the table. She left Bolzano then and there.

Alois later called himself Hans, because it sounded less Jewish, ran into debt, forged notes and finally had to flee to America. When he wanted to look smart, he wore a top-hat, a flowered waistcoat and white spats.

These anecdotes – Justine's death fantasy; the half-wit ambition of Alois, who talked of going to Vienna in medieval garb to win broad acres; the sinister suicide of Otto, the Wandering Jew – all betray features which one may call Gustav Mahlerish. They are the sheet-lightning, which portends the real thing, the chaotic elements which precede creation.

Mahler passed in rapid strides from Hall, Laibach, Cassel and Leipzig to Budapest, where he directed the Opera. His parents, to his great satisfaction, lived to see all this. Then his father died suddenly, and in the same year, after a lingering illness, his mother followed. Justine nursed her until her death and Mahler loved her as his beloved mother's dying bequest. He sent for her to join him at Budapest and, although quite inexperienced, she kept house for him there. He was so much concerned by her weakness after the fatigue of nursing their mother that he carried her in his arms every day up the four flights to his flat.

His engagement at the Royal Opera came to an abrupt end. There was a quarrel with the Intendant, the one-armed piano-virtuoso, Count Zichy, and next morning Mahler found his office door at the Opera bolted and barred against him. He lodged a formal protest; nevertheless his engagement was terminated, but with the payment of an exceptionally large sum as indemnity. Meanwhile he had accepted an offer from Pollini to go to Hamburg.

There were now five of his brothers and sisters depending on him for their education and financial support. The business had been sold, badly of course, since none of them understood anything about it. The meagre inheritance was shared out. Mahler gave up his share to his sisters and demanded the same sacrifice of his brothers. They obeyed, but Otto was indignant and Alois furious. Mahler now had difficult times to face – drudgery and worries without end.

He took a large flat for the family in Vienna, and Justine, the eldest, was put in charge. It was too much for a scatter-brained girl of twenty. She could be of little help. Her task was to run the household while the rest were to set to work learning something. They learnt nothing. Mahler had to keep on sending money and very often, as he once wrote in a letter, could not afford to have his shoes soled. Letters flew to and fro, bearing demands for money from the one side and exhortations to economy from the other. Then Otto came to his tragic end. It was a terrible blow to Mahler. He broke up the household in Vienna and took his two sisters to live with him in Hamburg. Alois, meanwhile, had got a job somewhere.

Mahler fell in love in Hamburg with a singer, M. [Anna von Mildenburg.] He confided in Justine, who clung to him jealously, and therefore did all she could to inject his feelings with suspicion. He suddenly felt the throttling coils and decided to break loose.

It was a wholly self-seeking love on the part of the singer. She insisted on his coaching her for hour after hour, when he came back worn out from rehearsals. At first he enjoyed it. She was a talented singer and he was in love with her. But soon there were rifts; the enforced rehearsals became a torture to him, and his feeling for her died down just as hers for him reached its zenith. Often she lay in wait for him at night after the performance at the Opera and wept and fell on her knees and behaved like a mad woman. He found these scenes so unpleasant that the last spark of affection for her was extinguished.

He decided to leave Hamburg and to get a foothold in Vienna. He went there for an interview and found out on his arrival that M. had gone behind his back and, helped by the intrigues of her teacher, Rosa Papier, signed a contract to sing in Vienna herself. He asked her to come and see him and mercilessly told her to her face that all was over between them; that it was solely because of her he had left Hamburg before he meant; that it was never again to be 'Du' between them, and that he forbade her ever to cross his threshold again.

Once during the winter she succeeded in enticing him back to her on the plea that she was ill. Without warning him she asked a Benedictine monk called Father Ottmar to be present, and begged him, before Mahler arrived, to marry her then and there to her lover, who, she said, would be willing. The Father replied that he could do nothing of the sort in the circumstances and she stormed at him up to the very moment of Mahler's arrival. She hoped by staging this operatic scene to induce him to take the plunge, in spite of his shyness of the marriage tie. Father Ottmar told me all this many years later.

And so he bade farewell to Hamburg and, in spite of all the intrigues set on foot against him, particularly by Cosima Wagner, who could not tolerate a Jew as Director of the Opera in Vienna, he secured his engagement, first as conductor of the orchestra and heir-presumptive of Wilhelm Jahn and, before many weeks had gone by, as Director. He was thirty-six. The sufferings of his earlier years as a conductor are an ever-recurring theme in his letters to his parents.

He often said to me: 'You are lucky. You were born with a silver spoon in your mouth. You can go your flowery way – no grim past, no family round your neck – but I have had to stagger on all my life with clods of earth weighing down my feet.'

Justine got to know the distinguished violinist, Rosé, leader of the orchestra at the Royal Opera, immediately she arrived in Vienna. They fell in love and embarked on a love affair which they kept a secret from fear of Mahler's strict morals. Many of the dissensions which dogged Mahler to the end as Director of the

Opera were due to this intimacy of his sister with the leader of the orchestra.

Justine was in a terrible dilemma. She loved the violinist, but she loved her brother quite as much, and to be parted from him seemed to her impossible. A friend of hers, who although she was old and ugly was in love with Mahler and hoped for the return of her passion, bargained to keep her secret if Justine would put her in the way of being much alone with him. If this service were refused her, she threatened a betrayal. And so, all through the summer which preceded the inevitable catastrophe, whenever Mahler was ready for the usual walk with his sister, Frau B. [Natalie Bauer-Lechner] confronted him, in the full hope of the reversion of his love. When he asked impatiently what had happened to Justine, he was put off with one excuse after another for her absence and got more and more annoyed with her. So it went on until, as had to happen, they all betrayed each other.

Mahler was extremely puritanical. Up to now he had been in a sense married to Justine. He regarded himself as bound to her by vows of fidelity and deliberately eluded all temptations. And there were many; not only at the Opera; everywhere he went he caused a flutter. He was not in the ordinary sense good-looking, but he had a great fascination. He exacted without mercy the same self-denial of Justine, who was much too temperamental and too young to tread the stony path.

Often and often in these years he had inklings of Justine's intimacies with Rosé, but whenever he taxed her with them he was given delusive answers: it was friendship, comradeship and all those other things which since the beginning of the world have been called into play to veil love affairs from profane eyes. The fear he inspired was such that there was no possibility of confiding in him honestly.

When he discovered that his trust had met only with deceit he was so disconcerted that he refused to speak to Justine for weeks; and when at last it came to painful scenes and explanations he insisted that she should either break with Rosé or marry him. At the same time he told her that he now regarded himself as entirely free. So far he had rejected the thought of any other tie for her sake, but now if he met a woman he liked he would not keep out of her way but take his share of happiness like another. His love of her, great as it had been, was now done with for ever. He trusted people blindly, but once his eyes had been opened his distrust knew no bounds.

In the early spring of 1901 Mahler had a severe haemorrhage which was only stopped by an immediate operation the same night. Two more very painful operations followed and then he was sent off to Abbazia, where he slowly recovered. For months afterwards he walked with two sticks. I saw him conduct twice on the very day of this disaster. I did not know him then. In the afternoon, the Philharmonic concert; in the evening, a performance of the *Meistersinger*. He looked like Lucifer: a face as white as chalk, eyes like burning coals. I felt sorry for him and said to the people I was with: 'It's more than he can stand.' That night he had the haemorrhage.

It was impossible to work two such miracles on the same day without perishing, considering the intensity of his interpretation.

The moment they heard of his illness the Philharmonic Orchestra, relentless enemies of Mahler's, chose Joseph Hellmesberger, a young conductor of mediocre gifts, to take his place without even first making sure of his resignation.

His domineering manner, the way he stamped his feet at rehearsals when his patience gave out, the stabs of his baton aimed at some miscreant who did not play or blow quite cleanly, or came in a moment late – all this embittered the orchestra, whose hearts were in any case hardened against him by the growing antisemitism of those days. When one violinist remarked to another: 'I don't understand why you find Mahler so infuriating – Hans Richter pitches into us far worse,' the reply was: 'Yes, he's one of ourselves. We can take it from him.'

This attitude of the Philharmonic was one of the many causes of his being later driven from Vienna.

All this took place before my acquaintance with Mahler began. On 10th November, the day after meeting him for the first time at the Zuckerkandls', I called for Madame Clemenceau and Frau Zuckerkandl first thing in the morning. Mahler was

impatiently awaiting us at the Opera. He helped me out of my
coat and impolitely omitted to do the same by the other two.
Keeping my coat over his arm he ushered us with an embarrassed
air into his office. My two companions began a conversation,
apparently unaware of the tensely emotional atmosphere of the
room. I went to the piano and turned the pages of the music I
found there. I was not in a state to join in the commonplaces of
conversation. Mahler stole glances at me, but I was in a malicious
mood and would not help him out. I was in all the glory of
untrammelled youth and not to be imposed upon by fame or
position. The one thing that might have humbled me, his inner
significance, was at that time almost hidden from me. And yet I
was puzzled by a sense of awe in face of his outstanding genius
and it threatened to cloud my untroubled serenity. 'Fräulein
Schindler,' he called out to me, 'how did you sleep?'

'Perfectly. Why not?'

'I didn't sleep a wink the whole night.'

I made some silly reply, which, thank God, I have forgotten.

This dress-rehearsal of the *Tales of Hoffmann** was the first at
which I was present in close proximity with him. I have never
known a greater producer. The rehearsal went without a hitch.
The orchestra was intoxicating. The small audience was keyed
up and scarcely seemed to breathe. The performance was only
broken off once and this was when Gutheil-Schoder came on
as Julietta. Mahler ordered her off in a fury. Her dress was slit
up each side to the waist and had to be stitched up instantly on
account of the gross indecency. As soon as the poor lady had
vanished he continued to rail for some time over the heads of the
orchestra at Schoder's shamelessness in coming on to the stage
in such a state of undress. If he had dreamed that ten years later
whole rows of more or less naked women would crowd the stages
of the 'straightest' theatres (to mention only *Franziska*, or *The
Legend of Joseph†* at the Opera) he would have lost his faith in
the drama. To him, it was sacred. Too sacred almost. Prince
Liechtenstein, an official at Court, remarked once at a rehearsal:
'You needn't shift the scenes yourself.' It was not only a metaphor.

---

* At Vienna under Mahler for the first time on 11th November 1901. (D.M.)
† By Richard Strauss. *Franziska* was a play by Wedekind. (D.M.)

I was still without a suspicion and never imagined I had made so deep an impression. I was overawed, and yet my work for Zemlinsky still came first.

By the next morning's post I received some verses of great beauty:

> Das kam so über Nacht.
> Hätt' ich's doch nicht gedacht,
> Daß Contrapunkt und Formenlehre
> Mir noch einmal das Herz beschwere.
>
> So über eine Nacht
> Gewann es Übermacht.
> Und alle Stimmen führen nur
> Mehr homophon zu einer Spur.
>
> Das kam so über Nacht
> – Ich habe sie durchwacht –
> Daß ich, wenn's klopft, im Augenblick
> Die Augen nach der Türe schick'.
>
> Ich hör's: ein Mann – ein Wort!
> Es tönt mir immerfort –
> Ein Canon jeder Art:
> Ich blick' zur Tür – und wart'.

My mother gave a sharp look at my anonymous letter. She took it out of my hand and asked whom it could be from. I said it could only be from Mahler. She replied that I need not imagine that a man like Mahler would write verses to a raw girl and laughed at me. Somebody, she said, must have been playing a joke on me.

But my instinct told me the poem could only be from him. I walked along the streets in a dream, loving him not yet, but unable to think of anything else. I did not answer him. A fortnight later my mother and I went to the Opera. It was Gluck's *Orpheus and Eurydice*. Almost at once I discovered Mahler in the Director's box. There was nothing wonderful in that. Every opera-fan knew Mahler's box. What was a wonder, however, was that he had discovered me at once too. After that a full-dress flirtation began – a thing nobody would have believed possible of a man like him, who, if anything, carried seriousness too far.

In the interval we went into the foyer and there stood Mahler as though conjured up from the floor. He hurriedly requested to be introduced to my mother, who was not present on the evening of our first meeting. Soon we were surrounded by inquisitive onlookers, and so Mahler proposed our retreating to his private room, where, since the occasion of the dress-rehearsal, I felt myself at home. I sat down as before at the piano and left my mother and Mahler to themselves. A mutual sympathy drew them together immediately and for ever.

'You live on the Hohe Warte? That is my favourite walk.'

'Then you must come and see us one day —'

'I certainly shall. But when? Soon?'

'That is for you to say.'

He got up to consult his large engagement book and suggested the following Saturday. I was asked whether I was at liberty that day. I had a lesson in counterpoint with Robert Gound, but I promised to put it off.

As we left I said I should like to be engaged as a conductor at the Opera and he promised in all seriousness to let me try my hand: it would give him at least great pleasure. I replied that that was not enough: his verdict would not, I thought, be impartial. To which he replied: 'No verdict is ever impartial.'

We parted in high spirits, feeling that something great and beautiful had come into our lives.

My mother and I had a rendezvous with Moll and Max Burckhard in a restaurant after the performance. My mother told them guilelessly of our encounter with Mahler, but it would have been better to have said nothing. Moll was furious.

'You mean to tell me you took an innocent girl, your own daughter, into the private room of a *roué* like him?'

Mahler, ascetic though he was, had a lurid reputation. In fact, he was a child and women were his dread. It was only because I was a stupid, inexperienced girl that I took him off his guard.

Max Burckhard knew life too well to be taken in. He saw the whole truth more clearly than even Mahler or I.

'He was head over ears in love – the other night.'

'I didn't notice it,' I replied.

'Now, what are you going to do about it if he proposes?'

'Accept,' I said calmly.

I did not know then that Mahler and Burckhard had left the Zuckerkandls' together and that on their way home Mahler had tried to put Burckhard through a regular catechism about me. Mahler told me all about it years later. Burckhard had declined to give any information about me whatever. What he actually said was: 'Those who are acquainted with Fräulein Schindler know what she is. Those who are not, have no right to ask.'

But now, as we sat there after *Orpheus*, his concern for me was for the first time seriously aroused. He bent all his mind and knowledge of life to the task of curing me of what he clearly saw to be a rising fever.

'It would be a positive sin,' he said in his ironical way. 'A fine girl like you – and such a pedigree too. Don't spoil it all by marrying an elderly degenerate. Think of your children – it'd be a sin! Besides, fire and water, that's all right. But fire and fire, that's all wrong. It would be for you to give way, not him. And you're too good for that.'

He practically forbade the match. But whether he forbade it or not, I longed for Saturday and for Mahler to come. Later on, I confess, I often recalled what he had said, waking, as I did, from years of silence, searching in vain for any prospect of my own, finding to my horror that my life was forfeit.

On Thursday afternoon, just as I was working out figured basses under Robert Gound's eye (I had changed his day to Thursday), the servant burst into the room. 'Gustav Mahler is here!'

He was a celebrity even in the servants' hall.

And that was the end of counterpoint for ever and a day.

We had just moved into a new house and my books were still waiting to be installed. Some lay flat, some stood on end, some were on the shelves, some in heaps all round the room. Mahler walked to and fro, inspecting them. My taste appeared to please him, except for a complete edition of Nietzsche, at which his eyebrows went up in horror. He demanded abruptly that it should be cast then and there into the fire. I refused and said that if his abhorrence had any justification it would be easy enough to convince me; and it would be more to his glory if Nietzsche stayed where he was and I refrained from reading him than if I consigned him to the flames and yet yearned for him ever after. He was put out, but not for long. He proposed that we should go for a walk. We met my mother in the hall, and in that unruffled way which was her peculiar charm she invited him to stay to dinner.

'There's *Paprikahendl* and – Burckhard. Do stay —'

'I'm not very fond of either. But I'll stay all the same.'

And then we walked over the crunching snow, side by side – so near and yet apart – down to Döbling, and there he wanted to telephone to his flat to say that he would be out that evening. Every other minute his shoe-laces came undone and he selected the highest point of vantage to put his foot upon and tie them up. His childlike helplessness went to my heart. In Döbling we went to the post office, but he did not know his own number; and so he had to ring up the Opera. His message gave no explanation of his absence, a thing unexampled in all the nine years Justine and he had lived together. Then we climbed the hill again in silence.

Suddenly he burst out: 'It's not so simple to marry a person like me. I am free and must be free. I cannot be bound, or tied to one spot. My job at the Opera is simply from one day to the next.'

A feeling of suffocation came over me. He laid down the law without thinking of consulting my feelings. After a moment's silence I said:

'Of course. Don't forget that I am the child of artists and have always lived among artists and, also, I'm one myself. What you say seems to me obvious.'

I can still see the sparkle on the snow as we passed each lamp-post. I can recall how we both without a word drew attention to its fairy-tale beauty. We did not speak another word all the way home. He seemed cheerful and reassured. We went by tacit agreement straight up to my room. There he kissed me and went on to talk of a speedy marriage, as though it went without saying.

Those few words on the way up seemed to him to have settled everything. Then why wait?

And I – I was silent – silent. He had simply made up his own mind about it. We went down to join the rest, both of us in a strange sort of enchantment. Burckhard and M., an architect [probably Kolo Moser], an old admirer of mine, were already there. The elemental undercurrent of that evening drove poor M. from our house for ever. Mahler, in the company of the others, now revealed all his charm, all the resources of his mind. We argued about Schiller, whom he loved and I at that time did not. He knew him almost by heart and there was such a fascination in the way he rose up in his defence that I, after letting him kiss me without really wishing it, and speed on the wedding before I had even thought of it myself, knew now that in both he was right and that I could no longer live without him. I felt that he alone could give my life meaning and that he was far and away above any man I had ever known.

One of our early discussions was about Jesus Christ. Although I was brought up as a Catholic, the influence of Schopenhauer and Nietzsche had made a free-thinker of me. Mahler contested my point of view with fervour. It was paradoxical that a Jew should hotly defend Christ against a Christian.

Many years later I experienced the very same thing a second time. Mahler was a disciple of Dostoyevsky's and was always saying: 'How can one be happy while a single being on earth still suffers?' I have noticed that it is egocentrics mostly who talk like this, and even downright egoists. Exalted pity for the 'insulted and injured' is often expressed, but seldom leads in given cases to any tangible result.

Mahler did not always live up to his convictions, but that he always wished to is certain.

It was at about this time I met Ludwig Karpath, the music critic, at a party. He and Adalbert von Goldschmidt (a somewhat dissipated person of great originality) were my neighbours at table. We talked of Mahler. Goldschmidt said: 'He – that little hop o' my thumb. He's not a man. And his music is not music.'

I was soon to learn why he was so enraged against Mahler. He had submitted his opera *Gaea* and it had been refused.

Karpath became very earnest in Mahler's defence, more especially as a composer. 'Surely I ought to know. I made him in Vienna,' he said.

Neither of the two knew that I was even acquainted with Mahler, let alone secretly engaged to him. Next day I told him about this occasion. He wanted to know all about it and all we had talked about, and I innocently repeated what Karpath had said. I knew little of him at that time except that he was the nephew of the celebrated composer, Carl Goldmark. Mahler was obviously annoyed and I felt I had said too much.

A day or two later Karpath happened to be seeing Mahler at the Opera. Mahler leaned back in his chair at his writing-table and his manner was very much *de haut en bas*. Their talk proceeded very haltingly and at last Karpath prepared to take his leave. Mahler left his chair and went close up to him.

'Before you go I really must thank you for having made me in Vienna.'

Karpath was utterly taken aback.

'Did Fräulein Schindler tell you that?'

Mahler replied that he did not know me. But a few days later our engagement was in the newspapers. Mahler had no sense of humour in such matters and after this experience and some others of the kind I learned to hold my tongue. He was very touchy.

Ludwig Karpath was not far off the truth. He had great influence as a journalist and a critic, and had in fact exerted it to the utmost to get Mahler's works performed in Vienna. Perhaps Mahler was all the more angry just because there was some truth in it. After this occurrence Karpath was for years an unpleasant enemy of Mahler's.

Early on in our secret engagement Mahler once conducted the *Magic Flute* for me alone. He sent me his official pass. His sister did not know what to think when the pass, which was always at her disposal, was not to be had that day. But Mahler said nothing and she dared not ask. At the end of each act he stood for a long while at the conductor's desk, chatting casually to Rosé, the first violin, so that we could see one another better. I gave him my impressions in a letter, as he had asked me to do.

Productions of Mozart's operas, not only in Vienna, were very drab and down-at-heel before Mahler's day. Mahler went so far as to emend the libretto of *Figaro*, to clarify the action of the comedy. He used motifs of Mozart's for the recitatives he had to compose. He did all this to make the work more living. It was he who gave the signal to the whole world for the Mozart renaissance.

The younger generation grew up to take Mozart as a matter of course. To me he was unfamiliar, and also I was too young in those days to appreciate his genius. Mahler had first to teach singers to sing in the Mozart style, hitherto beyond their power. Later Roller came to his help as stage-designer.

Shortly after this Mahler went to Berlin and Dresden. He wrote a lot to me and put us both on the rack. Then he sent for Justine to join him at Dresden and put her on the rack as well by firing off questions such as: 'Should a middle-aged man marry a young girl?' 'Has he the right to do so?' 'Can autumn chain spring to its side?'

Justine, feeling herself narrowly observed, was filled with foreboding and could only reply: 'Oh, yes – oh, no.'

In one of these letters he said I might speak to my mother on his behalf, because he wanted to be accepted by her as a son immediately he got back. However, just before his return to Vienna our first serious quarrel occurred. I happened to say that I could not write any more that day as I had some work to finish, meaning composition, which up to now had taken the first place in my life. The idea that anything in the world could be of more importance than writing to him filled him with indignation, and he wrote me a long letter, ending up by forbidding me ever to compose any more. It was a terrible blow. I spent the night in tears. Early in the morning I went sobbing to my mother, and she was so horrified by his unreasonable demand that, deeply as she loved him, she urged me to break with him. Her unqualified support brought me to my senses. I recovered my calm and confidence and finally wrote him a letter, promising what he wished – and I kept my promise.

His man was to come for my answer before he would see me

again; for, as he had told me in his letter, he would not know where he was until he had had it. In my agitation I went out to meet his messenger. I gave him my letter, but he had brought one for me, and in it Mahler, clearly uneasy about the effect of his earlier letter, was less exacting in his demands. He came that afternoon, happy and confident, and so charming that for the moment there was not a cloud in the sky.

But there was. I buried my dream and perhaps it was for the best. It has been my privilege to give my creative gifts another life in minds greater than my own. And yet the iron had entered my soul and the wound has never healed.

It was at about this time that my stepfather, Moll, guileless man, came to me and said: 'Alma, my dear, I've a sort of idea Mahler takes an interest in you, you know. I think we ought to have a talk about it.'

I was sitting on the piano-stool and I whipped round and stared him in the face. Could it be possible he had observed no more than this? But he went on, unperturbed.

'It isn't exactly what I should have wished for you. He's not young. To my certain knowledge, he's in debt. He's not strong. And then, it's all up with his job at the Opera.' (This was common talk in Vienna for ten years before he went; by the time he did go these rumours had all died down.) 'He's certainly no beauty. Composes, too, and they say it's no go.'

At that I burst out laughing and he went out shaking his head, no wiser than when he came in.

Mahler now came to see me every day and stayed until late at night. He often had to walk the whole way from the Hohe Warte to the Rennweg, as the buses had stopped running. But that did not worry him. He sang and whistled on his way.

Mahler kept our secret from Justine out of fear of her jealousy. One day they went for a walk after lunch. When they reached the Ringstrasse, he greeted a man whom she recognized as the painter, Moll; they had both got to know him on the same occasion not long before. 'What a charming man he is,' she said. 'Yes,' he replied without thinking, 'but you ought to know her mother —!'

The murder was out. Justine's riddle was solved. She had felt sure that only a woman could account for his being out night after night, but, closely as she watched him, she had failed to discover who it was. After this she was initiated by degrees and soon he brought her up to the Hohe Warte to see us. Before this I had paid her a visit at his wish. It was not a great success.

By degrees Mahler got to know all our friends and he particularly took to the painter, Kolo Moser, and Theobald Pollak. As he and Pollak were walking home together after spending the evening with us, he remarked that the first time he met me he had felt as if he had been suddenly taken out of a stuffy room into the fresh air. Kolo Moser, too, said to me once: 'As soon as Mahler came into the room you suddenly went as still as the sea when oil is poured on it.'

He brought me his Fourth Symphony one day. I did not, at that time, care for it. He played some of it to me and asked me how I liked it. I said frankly: 'I feel Haydn has done that better.' He laughed and said I would live to think differently about it. The same day we played it as a duet. I missed a semiquaver. He laughed and said: 'I make you a present of that semiquaver. So I would if it had been a quaver, or a crotchet. Yes, or the whole lot! – myself!' When we joined my mother, he said to her: 'Mamma, after playing the piano with her, I ask you once again for your daughter's hand.'

After our engagement was made public a delegation from the Vienna Philharmonic Orchestra waited on me with the request that I would set Mahler free from the dangerous influence of their leader. I was then twenty and incapable of carrying out such a mission. Rosé was on friendly terms with the members of the orchestra and with Mahler too; and there is no doubt that. sometimes purposely, sometimes unconsciously, he did influence Mahler's decisions, which were not always just, and that the members of the orchestra always knew the source of them; but there is no doubt, either, that Mahler not only listened to him but pumped him very often too. In after years I was able to avert many an injustice, but it was too late: Mahler's relations with the Philharmonic and theirs with him were ruined by then.

Christmas came, the first we had spent together. Sacred to me from my childhood, it meant nothing to him, and he took my suspense and excitement as an affectation. His 'friends' were already making mischief. He was full of suspicion and scented danger on every hand; and so a period of martyrdom set in for me. Everything in me which had so far charmed him became of a sudden suspect. My style of hairdressing, my clothes, my frank way of speaking, everything, in fact, was interpreted as being directed against him; I was altogether too worldly for him. Wrought upon by envious tongues and by his so-called friends, he lived a life of torment and inflicted torments a thousand times worse on me.

Our lovely beginning had turned to gloom and misery. His friends could not ever be friends of mine. Since his early youth he had had them clamped to his feet like irons, and I could never regard them with anything but dislike. There was an old barrister, dull and obtrusive; and there was Siegfried Lipiner and his set. Brahms said of him once: 'That lying hound of a Pole interests me.' The description could not be bettered; but while Brahms might find his society an amusing distraction, I was quite incapable in those days of putting up with cads of his sort. These friends formed a group round the 'celebrity' and the Director of the Opera, whose box they treated as their own; and they had no intention of budging an inch for any claims of mine.

Lipiner was introduced to me at Mahler's flat. He patronized me, called me 'my dear girl', and put me through my paces; he expected me to agree with him that Guido Reni, who meant nothing to me, was a great painter, and I refused to. I was reprimanded for reading the *Symposium* – it was far above my head. I had never before encountered such aridity in any human being – if he was a human being.

Then came the full-dress review. There were present Lipiner, whom our first meeting had made my avowed enemy; his first wife; his second wife; his current mistress (Mahler's one-time friend, M.); his first wife's husband (Lipiner's bosom friend); Rosé, Justine's friend; my mother; Moll and Kolo Moser. I shall never forget the grandiose and festive air which so completely belied the hollowness of that occasion. No one spoke, but angry hostile eyes followed every movement I made. Then M. said: 'What is your opinion of Gustav's music?' I replied in a temper: 'I know very little of it, but what I do know I don't like.'

Mahler laughed out loud. The others let their heads hang lower than before. My mother blushed for my bad manners. The atmosphere became unendurable. Then Mahler took me by the arm and we went into Justine's little room. 'It was frightful in there,' he said. 'We'll do better on our own for a bit.' So there we were – together again, happy and free of care. But in the next room my downfall was decreed.

Siegfried Lipiner was undoubtedly a very clever man – an all-round scholar without a single idea of his own. Even in conversation he always brought quotations to his aid in order to make anything clear; he never had anything of his own to say. He may have had originality in his youth; if so, that spring had prematurely dried up. Nietzsche had hopes of him; Wagner too. But his surviving work is eclectic in matter and turgid in manner. He was an ill-natured, harsh-tempered brute – his eyes much too close together and surmounted by an enormous bald skull. He had a stammer; he was a bogus Goethe in his writing and a haggling Jew in his talk. Mahler was always overcome by his stupendous knowledge.

The only thing of his which might survive is his translation of Mickiewicz's *Dziady* [*Forefathers' Eve*].*

* The famous Polish patriotic play. (D.M.)

January

1902

From that evening onwards his friends launched a regular campaign against me, which ended only with Mahler's retirement from the Opera in Vienna, although during the latter years their smouldering hatred emitted only an occasional spark. Mahler, however, was from the first so firmly attached to me that all their plots miscarried. All they achieved was his final severance from themselves. In those days he conducted a great deal. One morning, owing to the indiscretion of someone we had taken into our confidence, the newspapers all came out with headlines proclaiming our 'betrothal'. We went to the Opera the same evening. Mahler was conducting. I was in such a state of agitation and agony of mind that I heard nothing and saw nothing. I don't know why it was, but I was ashamed in those days to be seen in the street. I felt that everybody stared at me. As soon as Mahler appeared there was such a prolonged outburst of clapping that he had to bow his acknowledgements again and again. It was the congratulation of the public on his engagement.

At the end of January there was the première of Richard Strauss's *Feuersnot*,* and Pauline Strauss shared our box for the occasion, raging the whole time. Nobody, she said, could possibly like that shoddy work. We were simply lying if we pretended to, we knew as well as she did that there wasn't an original note in it, all stolen from Wagner and many others, yes, even from Schillings (Maxi, as she called him) whom she liked a great deal better than she did her husband. In short, she raved. We could only put on our silliest faces, taking good care not to speak, let alone agree with her, because she would be quite capable of turning round and exclaiming with equal vehemence against what she had just said herself.

After the performance, which Mahler had not conducted

* The Vienna première took place on 29th January 1902. (D.M.)

because he had a horror of the work, we were all to adjourn to the Restaurant Hartmann. But this plan suffered a delay. Strauss, after taking endless curtains, joined us in our box in obvious elation.

'Well, Pauksl, what do you say to that for a success?'

But he had come to the wrong address. She sprang at him like a wild cat:

'You thief, how dare you show yourself in my presence? I'm not coming with you – you make me sick.'

Mahler had had enough and bundled the two of them into his large office, and we all awaited the end of the debate in the next room. Wild outcries were heard, and Mahler, who had had more than enough, knocked at the door and called out that we could not wait any longer and were going on ahead to the restaurant. At that the door flew open and Strauss reeled in followed by Pauline.

'You can go now,' she shouted. 'I am going to the hotel and I shall spend the evening alone.'

'Can't I take you there?' he begged.

'Ten paces behind me – not otherwise.' She went off, Strauss following at a respectful distance.

We went on to the restaurant in silence. Soon Strauss joined us in a state of exhaustion, sat down beside me and said in these very words: 'My wife's a bit rough sometimes, but that's what I need, you know.'

Strauss himself even in my eyes came out in his true colours that night. Throughout supper his mind ran on nothing but money. He tormented Mahler without ceasing with calculations of the exact royalty on successes great or middling, with a pencil in his hand the whole time which he now and then put behind his ear, half by way of joke, and behaved in fact just like a commercial traveller. Franz Schalk, the conductor, whispered to me, 'And the sad part of it is that he is not putting it on. It's deadly earnest.' He had become an unashamed materialist, weighing his own advantage at every turn, a gambler on the stock exchange and an exploiter of the Opera. I saw Pfitzner and Schoenberg standing as stylites on either side of him and he as the worldling in between.

Meanwhile preparations for our wedding were going forward, and for that of Rosé and Justine as well. Mahler went to

Semmering for a few days after the première of *Feuersnot*. He
always went up there once or twice during the winter for the sake
of the high air.

When he was in Dresden just before our secret engagement, a
panic seized him while he lay sleepless in bed. 'Suppose I am too
old,' he thought. After that, this thought never left him and he
was an altered man when he returned to Vienna. He was nerve-
ridden and ill.

He had lived the life of an ascetic and was completely at a loss.
The strain of apprehension and self-torture was terrible; sometimes he longed for death, sometimes for life at its fiercest.

We were sad and had no one to guide us.

'Oh,' he said, 'if only you had had a love affair or were a
widow, it would be all right.'

These outbursts were painful to me. Up to now my virginity
had always seemed a glory. It never occurred to me that all good,
even this too, is relative and that he was only blurting out what
many think who secretly wish for 'an experienced woman'. That
I certainly was not; and so we tormented ourselves not from love
so much as fear of love. At last the only natural solution occurred.
The consequences soon followed and I suffered bitterly. In every
convention there is a core of truth, as we soon had to recognize.

The rehearsals for the first performance in Vienna of the Fourth
Symphony and *Das klagende Lied* came on. It was the first time I
had ever heard any work – let alone a work of his – rehearsed day
by day from the first reading-rehearsal onwards. A work which
was new and strange to me, very strange at the outset, became
by degrees so familiar that I soon knew its every beauty and how
each instrument came in. After that I shared the experience with
him of hearing each of his works from the sounding of the first
note up to the last time he conducted it. They were the most
unforgettable and exalted hours of my life.

Mahler was in a state of nervous exasperation just at this time
and so prejudiced, into the bargain, against the Philharmonic
Orchestra owing to the persistent agitating on the part of some of
its members, that these rehearsals threw me into paroxisms of
fright. He raged, he stamped; he picked on victims for special

castigation and shouted at the orchestra as a whole until they played unwillingly, and some even made a show of leaving in the middle of the rehearsal. It took us all our time to calm him down in the brief pauses, and even so these rehearsals were a martyrdom for players and audience. A young musician asked my leave to look over my score. I was very glad to share it with a musician; and I could sympathize with his enjoyment of the passages which came through best. It was Gustav Brecher, the since celebrated conductor.

The performance took place on 12th January 1902.* It was in the afternoon and I was not feeling well. I was stared at as Mahler's fiancée and I found it hard to bear. I was more conscious of the blood singing in my ears than I was of the music.

The Fourth came to an end; I looked round the hall and caught sight of an old friend, the President of the Society of the Friends of Music, in the Director's box. He smiled and bowed to me and I was glad to see a face I knew. The friends of Mahler, however, had their eyes glued to me and before the interval was over they reported me to him for flirting outrageously throughout the whole performance.

Das klagende Lied began and ended without giving me any real pleasure. I was too much ruffled by all I saw and felt. M. was lying on the sofa in the artists' room simulating a fainting attack. I was ignored by the 'friends' and Mahler treated me as a criminal. I was beside myself. I knew nothing of the clouds which had gathered about my head in my absence. His friends had been dinning it into him that whereas M. sacrificed herself for him (she had sung the chief part in the *Klagende Lied*) and gave her last breath for him, I sat and flirted all through the concert. Mahler was in consternation over this. He begged M. to spare herself and thanked her again and again. To me he was exceedingly chilly. The plot had worked.

* The chronology needs tidying up here: (1) *Das klagende Lied* was given its first performance in Vienna on 17th February 1901; (2) Mahler's Fourth Symphony was given its first performance in Munich on 25th November 1901; (3) the first performance of the Fourth Symphony in Vienna took place on 12th January 1902; (4) what Alma Mahler seems to refer to here is a special concert which took place on 20th January 1902, when both the Fourth Symphony and *Das klagende Lied* were given in the same programme – the *second* Vienna performance of the cantata and a *repeat* performance of the symphony. (D.M.)

This was their last assault. We walked back by ourselves, the baying of the hounds died away, and we had it out as we walked. By the time we reached his flat we were blissfully happy. Justine saw that we could never now be separated.

After the sensational disclosure of Mahler's engagement in the press, M. invaded his private room at the Opera and made a scene, at the end of which she once again had a fainting-fit. But he had taken the measure of her theatrical faintings. He asked her to come out with him and in the street she could not avoid controlling herself.

This scene showed that up to the last moment M. had not given up hope. She had recovered her composure in the street and begged him to restore the 'Du' of earlier days. He said he could not make up his mind without consulting me, and so she put her request in another way by begging for friendly relations with an apparent desire to include me. He was caught out and promised to bring me to see her in a day or two.

I refused at first; for even though Mahler, by his own confession, had never been on intimate terms with her, they had at least been on affectionate ones, and her sudden interest in me could not be genuine. We arrived at Hietzing, where she was living in a dreary hotel. Disregarding the common politeness due to a visitor, she sat me down in a corner with the barest of apologies and gave me a book to look at. She then took Mahler into the next room, whence I soon heard raised voices. I glanced occasionally at the piano score of *Tristan and Isolde*, with Stassen's horrible illustrations.

We were in a very bad humour on the way home and started on an argument about these illustrations, which Mahler liked and I did not. As it had nothing really to do with Stratz, but everything to do with those deep influences to which Lipiner looked in his efforts to set Mahler against me – in this case it chanced to turn on M. and Stratz – I fought like a lion; and being the daughter and stepdaughter of painters I knew something of pictorial art, although at the moment it was the last thing on earth I cared about.

These people in their blindness had badly miscalculated. They thought my unpractised youth was an instrument ready to their

hand. Their plan was to degrade me in his eyes, to show me up
in my raw immaturity; and so to wound his pride. But they had
not reckoned with my fierce spirit of independence or my sensitive pride. In any case, as Mahler hated nothing more than argument and thrashing things out, he simply kept more and more out
of the way of his trusty old friends. They achieved exactly the
opposite of their designs.

Marriage and Life Together

We were married on 9th March 1902, and on the 10th, the day after we had left for our honeymoon, Justine and Arnold Rosé followed suit.

Mahler went to the church on foot in galoshes, as it was raining hard; my mother, Justine and I drove. There was no one in the Karlskirche except ourselves and the witnesses, Moll and Rosé. It was early in the day. When it came to kneeling down, Mahler misjudged the hassock and found himself on the stone flags; he was so small that he had to stand up again and make a fresh start. We all smiled, including the priest. There were six of us at the wedding-breakfast, a rather silent occasion, and our guests took their departure immediately afterwards, leaving us alone to pack and drive to the station. As the wedding had been publicly announced to take place in the evening, a crowd of inquisitive people must have come to the church in vain.

Once in the train for St. Petersburg we breathed again. His clouded spirits cleared as though by magic; and I too, alone at last, was no longer oppressed by the need to conceal my condition. He had been invited to conduct three concerts in St. Petersburg and so we had decided to make this trip our honeymoon. Unfortunately, Mahler caught a severe feverish chill on the journey, induced in this case by the overheated compartment of a Russian train. He suffered all his life from these infections and his fatal illness was partly due to one of them. I was aghast as I saw him rushing up and down the corridor – his face as white as a sheet, incapable of uttering a syllable. He jumped out at every station and walked about the platform, in thirty degrees of frost without hat, coat or gloves. The Russians, who kept out the cold with huge fur caps and gloves, were greatly amused.

I sat in our compartment, waiting anxiously for his martyrdom to end, as I was often to do during these onsets of his.

He arrived in St. Petersburg with a temperature and a cough, so hoarse that he could hardly speak, and afflicted further by chilblains; and I soon caught his cold. But in spite of all, those three weeks were unforgettably beautiful. He could only whisper at the rehearsals, but he was so perfectly understood that the result in every case was a magnificent performance. In this strange, faraway world, I heard the *Liebestod*. As I was still unwell and might be unable to sit it out, I was allowed to stand behind the orchestra, and so could see his face, which had a divinely beautiful expression. His exaltation when he was conducting was always intense and the sight of his face on these occasions, uplifted and openmouthed, was so inexpressibly moving that I felt a thrill of utter conviction: I knew once and for all that it was my mission in life to move every stone from his path and to live for him alone.

He conducted works of Haydn and Schubert, the *Funeral March* from *Götterdämmerung* (it was encored) and the *Eroica*. At the end of the *Eroica* – I was this time sitting among the audience in the hall – I heard two people say in French: 'Mahler's tempi are not at all what we are accustomed to, but it's beautiful, and new, like that.' The other replied: 'Of course, and why not?' Imagine such a criticism among us in Vienna, where everyone has a leasehold on his own Beethoven and his own tempi.

Mahler had a cousin there, called Frank, who was high up in the public service. He showed us all the wonderful sights and street scenes of Petersburg; the Hermitage, the palaces – all of it so strangely foreign and impressive. The Neva was frozen over and tram-lines were laid down across it. Towards evening it was a lively, crowded scene: elegance and fashion turned out to skate with an ease and gaiety which were fascinating to watch.

There was another side to the picture: now and then a member of the orchestra was missing and when Mahler asked the reason he was told it was not impossible he had been sent to Siberia.

The devoutness of the people, which an effort has since been made to stamp out, was very touching. We were always driven about in a small, low sledge, with three horses harnessed abreast, not knowing at first that no Russians ever drove in an open troika at this time of the year. When we did know it, we persisted all the same because we enjoyed it so much. One evening, as we were passing the Kazan Cathedral in a bitter wind and driving snow, the coachman got down from the box and threw himself on his knees in the snow to pray. He did not give us a thought. When we were frozen to the very marrow and he had turned into a snowman, he quietly got up and drove on again without a word.

We saw a good deal of high society, as it is called. I often asked Mahler to go alone if I did not feel well enough; but in the concert-hall I could not avoid these introductions, and I found the arch-dukes I spoke to easier and more amiable in manner than our nobility at home. Conversation was in French. But as for what was actually said, we felt there was no difference: it meant just as little to us.

Among them there was a beautiful old lady of hysterical tendencies, who years later when Mahler was in Russia by him-self summoned him and told him that she felt her death to be near, and would he enlighten her about the other world, since he had said so much about it in his Second Symphony. He was not quite so well informed as she supposed and he was made to feel very distinctly when he took his leave that she was displeased with him. He gave me a description of this scene in a letter.

What surprised us more than anything was that scarcely any-one was acquainted with Dostoyevsky; people only sniffed when Mahler mentioned his name.

We saw nothing of the theatre except a good production of *Eugene Onegin*. It was Advent and all the theatres were closed. This was a charity performance and permitted for that reason. The production was on a very high artistic level.

Our charming flat awaited us in Vienna, and the life we lived for six eventful and yet – up to the final shock – happy years began. The flat now consisted of three larger rooms and three smaller rooms. It was smaller before our marriage.

Mahler had suffered from a great infliction there; an officer occupied the small room next his bedroom and had such a hatred of him that he gave orders to his servant always to turn on the gramophone during his working hours. Having unearthed this plot, we bribed the man and after this he put on a record only when his master came in sight.

I had to take over the domestic finances in a state of virtual bankruptcy. There were debts upon debts; for although Mahler had been paid a big indemnity in Budapest and earned large salaries ever since, his brothers and sisters, with Justine at their head, squandered his money to such a tune that in Hamburg he was borrowing from his friends even at the beginning of nearly every month, because he was completely cleaned out. Justine showed me a letter of his in which he wrote: 'Do, for heaven's sake, be more careful. I have been waiting for months to get a pair of shoes soled and never have the money.' And this was the principal conductor of the Hamburg State Theatre. He said to me when we married: 'Justine, unfortunately, did not understand housekeeping. I resigned myself long ago to being perpetually in debt. But now, see what you can do.'

I found that, reckoned in Austrian gold crowns, he owed 50,000. Besides this, he had the building of his house at Maiernigg to pay for; and first of all I had to pay his two sisters their share of the patrimony. I had been brought up in such a modest way that the strict economies of our early married life were no hardship. On the contrary, I took a pride in getting him out of debt. But to him these five long years of parsimony were very trying. Once when I took Justine to task for her wild extravagance, she replied: 'Well, if the worst had come to the worst, *I would have gone begging with him from door to door.*'

In May, 1902, the *Sezession** got up a private festival in honour of Max Klinger. The *Sezession* painters self-sacrificingly painted frescoes, all of which were lost except those of Gustav Klimt; and these were peeled from the walls at extravagant cost. The subjects of all of them were allegories referring to Beethoven, and Max Klinger's monument to Beethoven was to be exhibited for the first time in the centre of the gallery.

Next, Moll approached Mahler with the request that he would conduct at the opening and he kindly agreed. He arranged part of the chorus from the Ninth Symphony for wind and brass instruments only, and rehearsed it with the wind and brass from the Opera orchestra.

* See note, p. 62. (D.M.)

Ihr stürzt nieder, Millionen?
Ahnest Du den Schöpfer, Welt?
Such' ihn über'm Sternenzelt.
Über Sternen muß er wohnen.

He conducted the chorus on the day and with the new instrumentation it rang out as starkly as granite. Klinger, who was a very shy man, came in just as the first note clanged out above his head. He was so moved that tears ran slowly down his cheeks.

We saw a lot of him at that time. His personality was not impressive and it seems likely that he was overestimated in those days. He was entirely dominated by Assenjeff, a red-headed Russian woman, who had him completely under her thumb. She was hysterical, and on one occasion suddenly burst into tears at table, because she had once had a jaguar she loved and it died. Klinger tried to control her by glances of despair, but it was no use. Some scene or other broke out at every moment, and we felt sorry for him.

He never said anything very much to the point, and so his company was no particular joy to us and we dispensed with it by degrees. He was a great drinker and his days and nights were invariably spent over the bottle, for which we had neither time nor inclination. He was the owner of a champagne factory and it cannot have done him much good.

The next première* – *Butterfly* – was not one of Mahler's productions. Puccini attended the final rehearsals, but took no part in them. Mahler and he had not a particle in common. During the dress-rehearsal the maestro never took his eyes off the Royal Box, in which, as he took pains to find out, were two archduchesses. He requested Mahler to have him presented to them; and Mahler reluctantly did so. He was no courtier, although on given occasions very strict in his observance of form. Puccini, in spite of his genius, was utterly enamoured of the outward show.

Mahler's attitude to the aristocracy was peculiar. He resisted the Emperor's orders but stood to attention if an archduke or the

---

* Alma Mahler's chronology seems to have gone astray at this point. The opera itself was not first produced until 1904 and the Vienna première did not take place until 31st October 1907. It is more than likely that she had in mind *Bohème*, the Vienna Opera first performance of which was given on 25th November 1903. (D.M.)

superintendent passed by. Once we fled across the Michaelerplatz
to escape Princess Pauline Metternich, celebrated as a ghost of
the Second Empire, who had caught sight of him from her carriage
and was in pursuit. She overtook us at the bottom of the Kohl-
markt. I retreated into the entrance of a house and Mahler went
up to the carriage door, where she kept him talking for some
time. She was always trying to enlist his influence on somebody's
behalf or to get hints of future operatic events from the fountain-
head. When at last he joined me, he spat on all sides. 'Horrible
woman – those scarlet lips.' The worst he could think of in the
intervals of spitting was not bad enough. When he lost his temper
over bad taste of this sort he never refrained from relieving his
feelings on the spot. It was his nature to react with violence against
any annoyance.

The first complete performance of the Third Symphony took
place at Crefeld on 9th June 1902.* I was in the middle of my
pregnancy and we travelled to Cologne in a heat-wave. Mahler
did his utmost to make the time pass by playing jokes on me. I
was always asking impatiently when we should arrive and he
kept me in such a state of suspense by inventing one answer after
another that when at last we arrived I utterly refused to believe it.

First drafts of the programme of the Third Symphony:

I. THE HAPPY LIFE
A SUMMER NIGHT'S DREAM
(*Not* after Shakespeare. Critics and Shakespeare scholars please note.)

1. *What the forest tells me*
2. *What the twilight tells me*

* Many drafts exist for the titles and sequence of the movements of the Third
Symphony. The second quoted by Alma Mahler is of some interest for its instrumental indications: the Introduction to the first movement as we know it today bears
out Mahler's thoughts as noted in this draft. He eventually dropped the titles, but it
may perhaps be useful to set down the order of the movements in their final form,
together with their original titles: (1) Introduction: *Pan erwacht*: followed by *Der
Sommer marschiert ein*; (2) *Was mir die Blumen auf der Wiese erzählen* (Minuet); (3) *Was
mir der Kuckuck erzählt* (Scherzo) – this movement was also known as *Was mir die Tiere
im Walde erzählen*; (4) *Was mir der Mensch erzählt*; (5) *Was mir die Engel erzählen*; (6) *Was
mir die Liebe erzählt*. At one stage Mahler contemplated a seventh movement: *Was mir
das Kind erzählt*. This was his setting of a *Wunderhorn* poem, *Das himmlische Leben*, for
soprano and orchestra, which existed as an independent song and eventually became
the finale of the Fourth Symphony. Indeed, it was *into* this song that the Fourth was,
so to say, composed. (D.M.)

3. *What love tells me*
4. *(What the twilight tells me)*
5. *What the cuckoo tells me*
6. *What the child tells me*

II. A SUMMER NIGHT'S DREAM

1. *Summer marches in*
   (Fanfare and lively March) (Introduction)
   (Wind only with solo double-basses)
2. *What the forest tells me* (1st movement)
3. *What love tells me* (Adagio)
4. *What the twilight tells me* (Scherzo) (Strings only)
5. *What the flowers in the meadow tell me* (Minuet)
6. *What the cuckoo tells me* (Scherzo)
7. *What the child tells me*

The rehearsals at the Gürzenich were unique. Mahler came to me at the end of each movement and we discussed it in every detail. After the first movement, which had never been played before, he came up to me laughing, calling out from a distance: 'And he saw that it was good!'

I made notes in my score of the passages which did not seem to me to come through. A small boy, sitting behind me, looked with lively interest over my shoulder; so I held my score up for him to see. A short time ago the pianist, Edwin Fischer, thanked me for my kindness on that occasion to a child whom I did not know.

We stayed at the Dom hotel. We always drank Moselle or Rhine wine at dinner there (a thing we seldom did, as Mahler drank little). After lunch, for which owing to the long rehearsals we were always late, we went for a drive through the flat country. We became completely one during those wonderful days together. For hour after hour as we were driven along we discussed the first hearing of this stupendous work – the entry of the oboe, for example, in this passage, or the dynamic effect of the strings in that. Often he fell asleep with his head on my shoulder.

When the rehearsals were over we moved on to Crefeld to stay with some wealthy silk manufacturers, who were undisguisedly put out by our arrival. We were assigned a bridal chamber, where we scarcely dared move for fear of toppling some ghastly knick-knack from its ghastly stand. Ancient myrtle-wreaths mouldered beneath domes of glass.

They regarded Mahler as the great Director of the Opera, who to please himself had composed a monstrous symphony and now to pain everybody else was having it performed. Any donkey felt himself entitled to pass judgement on him. All the beauty of the days of the rehearsals was blotted out. A mob of musicians and critics surged about us wherever we went: there was no escape. We felt that the liberty to come and go as we pleased was taken from us and cursed the place for having no hotels; we were obliged to accept hospitality which was not spontaneously offered but extorted from our hosts by a committee. It was the first time and the last we ever accepted an invitation of this kind.

There was one cheerful little episode. The house was tall and narrow and we were on the second floor. We emerged from our room, ready to go out. Mahler stopped a moment at the top of the stairs to polish his spectacles and then, stepping out in his impulsive way without looking where he was going, he kicked against a large pail of water which was on the edge of the top step. It went bouncing in a cascade to the bottom, where, as we had every right not to expect, our hostess happened to be standing. She held up her hands in consternation. 'Well, Herr Mahler, the Graces assuredly did not preside at your cradle!'

And now for an example of the retentiveness of the human memory: at the Mahler festival at Amsterdam in 1920 a lady came up to me with a message from Frau X. of Crefeld, who wished me to know that she treasured in her memory the 'unforgettable' days Mahler had once spent in her house. *Così fan tutte.* They all 'remember' today; but at the time these people were for the most part extremely discouraging and quick to take offence.

On top of all the rest, our unconventional appearance caused an unwelcome sensation. I was wearing a so-called reform dress (designed by Kolo Moser) and was well advanced in my pregnancy. Mahler always went about bare-headed, with his hat in his hand and his head poked forward; his gait too was peculiar, unrhythmical, urgent and stumbling. Whatever his suits cost he always looked badly dressed. In short, the schoolchildren followed us about, at first in two's and three's and then in a crowd. On one occasion, one of them advanced and shouted amid the tumult: 'You've lost your hat, sir!' A roar greeted the announcement. It was quite true. He had left his hat in a tea-shop. It was the last straw. Back we had to go to recover it. We were hunted through the streets again as we made for the refuge of a wretched little hotel. The Rosés were expecting us upstairs, and helped us to pour water on the heads of our persecutors and put them to flight.

The performance was awaited with breathless suspense, for the rehearsals had done something to reveal the greatness and significance of the work. A tremendous ovation broke out at the end of the first movement. Richard Strauss came right up to the podium, applauding emphatically as though to set his seal on its success. The enthusiasm rose higher with each movement and at the end the whole audience got up from their seats in a frenzy and surged to the front in a body. Strauss had become more and more subdued and at the end was not to be seen.

I was sitting among the audience by myself, as I did not wish to be with my relations. I was in an indescribable state of excitement; I cried and laughed softly to myself and suddenly felt the stirrings of my first child. The hearing of this work finally convinced me of Mahler's greatness, and that night I dedicated to him my love and devotion with tears of joy. I saw what hitherto I had only surmised.

Strauss gave a further and final proof of his coolness before the night was over. We had supper after the concert at a small inn. Strauss, as he passed our table, gave us all his hand in a lordly way and went on, without noticing Mahler's extreme agitation or addressing a single word to him. Mahler took this very much to heart. For some time he could not speak. His spirits sank and the public acclamation now seemed of no account.

I owe my lasting friendship with Hans Pfitzner to those days at Crefeld.

Mahler and I were in our large bedroom, where in an alcove, curtained off with black curtains, there was an enormous double bed. A visitor was announced and Mahler, after a glance at the card, asked me to retire for a few minutes within the matrimonial recess, as he wished to speak to the man alone.

Next I heard a thin, high voice interceding urgently with Mahler; and what I heard affected me deeply. It was painful and degrading – an artist, and that he was one I could hear in his very first words, pleading for the production of his work: *Die Rose vom Liebesgarten*.* And Mahler refused, coldly, calmly, tersely.

He must have forgotten his own youth.

'No singers – libretto too bad – whole symbolism incomprehensible, too long, far too long.'

And at intervals the pleading voice broke in. One trial – last hope – Mahler, the only musician who could understand him—otherwise, despair. The two voices rose higher as the door was reached. I could not hold myself in any longer. I jumped up, pulled the curtains apart, ran to Pfitzner and squeezed his hand to show how deeply I sympathized. I shall never forget the look he gave me. Then he went out. Mahler was not angry. To my astonishment, he was not angry!

We went straight from there to Maiernigg, where we lived a life of utter peace and concentration. Mahler wore his oldest clothes there and was almost unrecognizable. He got angry if anyone spoke to him on his long walks. He had the sketches for his Fifth Symphony with him, two movements completed and the rest in their earliest stages. I tried playing the piano very softly, but when I asked whether he had heard me he said he had, although his studio was far away in the wood. And so I changed my occupation; I copied all he had ready of the Fifth straight away, so that my manuscript was ready only a few days behind him. He got more and more into the way of not writing out the instrumental parts in the score – only the first bars; and I learnt at this time to read his score and to hear it as I wrote and was more and more of real help to him.

In the intervals of work we walked a lot. Too much. He counted too much and too proudly on my youth, and as we were both as thoughtless as children my stock of health was squandered in the common cause. I had to climb over fences and creep through hedges. My mother paid us a visit at this time. She was horrified when he dragged us up a hill which was almost perpendicular.

* See also pp. 60 and 81–84. (D.M.)

The house at Maiernigg had been built for Mahler, in a some-what philistine style, by a Wörthersee neighbour. Its position was as enchanting as its interior was frightful. Mahler once caught me standing on a chair tearing down the fretwork ornamentation from the tops of the cupboards. He understood and gave his approval. There were two large verandas, one open and one shut in. The open one gave access to the sitting-room and my bedroom, the closed one to the dining-room and spare bedroom.

High above, the balcony of Mahler's bedroom had a magnificent view over the lake. He had a large studio-bedroom with an enormous writing-table, and next door a small dressing-room. There was a very large spare bedroom next the sitting-room, very close therefore to my bedroom, but this by the second year had been turned into a nursery.

During the early years of our married life I felt very uncertain of myself in my relations with him. After I had conquered him by my audacity before I knew what I was about, all my self-assurance was undermined by the psychological effects of becoming pregnant before being married. From the moment of his spiritual triumph, too, he looked down on me and did not recover his love of me until I had broken his tyranny. Sometimes he played the part of a schoolmaster, relentlessly strict and unjust. He soured my enjoyment of life and made it an abomination. That is, he tried to. Money – rubbish! Clothes – rubbish! Beauty – rubbish! Travelling – rubbish! Only the spirit was to count. I know today that he was afraid of my youth and beauty. He wanted to make them safe for himself by simply taking from me any atom of life in which he himself played no part. I was a young thing he had desired and whose education he now took in hand.

Frau M. [Anna von Mildenburg], envious as ever, settled down promptly in our immediate neighbourhood. In the evenings she paid us visits uninvited, accompanied by a mangy dog she had bought from a loafer out of pure kindness of heart, as she carefully pointed out, and from other no less elevated motives. Nevertheless, Mahler had a horror of the beast. His love of animals was theoretical only. He escorted her home for the first few times, and this was the object of her manœuvres, but finally her manœuvring annoyed him. He sent the servant home with her and at once her regular visits ceased.

She came one day punctually at the outbreak of a terrific thunderstorm and dragged Mahler out on to the terrace for closer contact with the fury of the elements. I was afraid, in the condition I was in, of being hit by the branches of trees which came hurtling through the air. But I had never been afraid of thunder. On the contrary, I loved its grandiose effects. The great Wagnerian soprano let her hair fall about her face and played Valkyrie and Ortrud in the same breath. She called to me to come and when I made a sign of refusal she turned in scorn to Mahler: 'She's a coward.'

On another of her descents I was alone in the house and she began to play Ortrud in good earnest for my benefit. She was vulgar as well as voluble about Mahler and about his sister, giving intimate details, which, if I had not known his whole life from his own lips, would have suffocated me. But I knew more than she. I knew that he had really loved her for a time in Hamburg and that she during that time had been a torment to him; that she had later done her utmost to keep him at any cost, but he was finished with her and 'disgusted' (his own word) and wanted to be left in peace. I knew from his own lips why he had fled from Hamburg.

He had been baptized before he left Hamburg.* He was afraid lest otherwise he might find it difficult as a Jew to get his engagement in Vienna. His account of his recalcitrance and doubts during his instruction in the Catholic faith, of the embarrassing questions he put to his catechist and the sudden surging up of Old Testament pride was delightful. Then he arrived in Vienna, where the fullest powers were guaranteed and where he hoped to carry out at last all his far-reaching plans for stage and orchestra.

And now, on that afternoon at Maiernigg, M. poured out all her fury and tried to enlist me, of all people, in her war against him. This showed me that she could never have been a great tactician; or she would not have confided in me, her natural enemy, who could only be waiting for her to show her hand. I did not hesitate to report our conversation to him the same evening. He wanted

* On 23rd February 1897, at the Kleine Michaelskirche. (D.M.)

to forbid her the house at once and for ever; but I deprecated a scandal and suggested making a musical occasion of it when next she came. This we did. We played and sang the whole of the last act of *Siegfried* together. Her voice that afternoon was truer and her singing more beautiful than they had ever been on the operatic stage; and as our concert carried right down to the lake, there was a crowd of boats in front of our house by the time we had done, and an outburst of enthusiastic applause. This was the last of our meetings.

Mahler's daily programme during the next six summers at Maiernigg never varied. He got up at six or half past and rang for the cook to prepare his breakfast instantly and take it up the steep and slippery path to his hut, which was in a wood nearly two hundred feet higher up than the villa. The cook was not allowed to take the usual path, because he could not bear the sight of her, or indeed of anyone whatever, before setting to work; and so, to the peril of the crockery, she had to scramble up by a slippery, steeper one. His breakfast consisted of coffee (freshly roasted and ground), bread and butter and a different jam every day. She put the milk on a spirit-stove, matches beside it, and then beat a hasty retreat by the way she had come in case she might meet Mahler climbing up. He was not long about it; he was very quick in all he did. First he lit his spirit-stove, and nearly always burned his fingers, not so much from clumsiness as from a dreamy absence of mind. Then he settled down comfort-ably at the table and bench in front of the hut. It was simply a large stone building with three windows and a door. I was always afraid it was unhealthy for him, because it was surrounded by trees and had no damp-course; but he was so fond of this retreat that I could do nothing about it.

He had a piano there and a complete Goethe and Kant on his shelves; for music, only Bach. At midday he came noiselessly down to the villa and went up to his room to dress. Up in the wood he delighted in wearing the oldest rags. After that he went down to the boat-house, where we had two beautiful boats. On each side of it there was a bathing-hut with a platform of planks in front. The first thing he did was to swim far out and give a whistle, and this was the signal for me to come down and join him. Once I had both little children with me in the bathing-hut. Mahler went off with one under each arm and then forgot all about them. I was just in time to catch one of them as she was falling into the water.

I usually sat down on the boat-house steps. When he came out of the water we talked and he lay sun-bathing, until he was baked brown; then he jumped into the water again. As I watched this procedure I always felt a terrible anxiety about his heart. I was ignorant in those days, but I knew at least that it could not be good for him. But nothing I could say could induce him to give it up, and he persisted in heating himself up and cooling himself down, often four or five times running. After this he felt invigorated and we went home for lunch, making a tour of the garden on the way. He loved the garden and knew every tree and plant in it. The soup had to be on the table the moment we got in, and the food had to be simple, even frugal, but perfectly cooked, and without a trace of fat or seasoning. Its purpose was to satisfy without tempting the appetite or causing any sensation of heaviness. In fact he lived all his life on an invalid's diet. Burckhard's opinion was that it was enough to ruin a man's stomach for good and all.

We sat and talked for half an hour afterwards. Then up and out, however hot or however wet it might be. Sometimes our walk was on our side of the lake; sometimes we crossed to the other side by the steamer and then set off on our walk – or run, rather. I see now that his restless energy after meals was his way of escape from the pressure of a full stomach on an overworked heart. It was purely instinctive. He could not bear lying down after meals, but he never knew the real reason.

Our expeditions were fairly long. We walked for three or four hours, or else we rowed over the dazzling water, which smote back the glare of the sun. Sometimes I was too exhausted to go on. We invented a hypnotic cure for my collapse: he used to put his arm round me and say, 'I love you'. Instantly I was filled with fresh energy and on we tore.

Often and often he stood still, the sun beat down on his bare head, he took out a small notebook, ruled for music, and wrote and reflected and wrote again, sometimes beating time in the air. This lasted very often for an hour or longer, while I sat on the grass or a tree-trunk without venturing to look at him. If his inspiration pleased him he smiled back at me. He knew that nothing in the world was a greater joy to me. Then we went on or else turned for home if, as often happened, he was eager to get back to his studio with all speed.

His remarkable egocentricity was often betrayed in amusing little incidents. Sometimes he liked to break off work for a day or two in order to go back to it with his mind refreshed. On one such occasion we went to Misurina. My mother was with us and we had three rooms next door to each other. My mother was in my room and we were whispering cautiously, as our habit was, for Mahler's ears detected the slightest sound and the slightest sound disturbed him. Suddenly my door flew open and was banged shut and there stood Mahler in a fury. 'Do you hear that? Someone banging a door again along the passage. I shall make a complaint.' For a moment we looked duly horrified and then burst out laughing.

'But, Gustav, you've just done the same thing yourself.'

He saw the absurdity of it.

One of his favourite quotations was from Schopenhauer's *The World as Will and Imagination*: 'How often have the inspirations of genius been brought to naught by the crack of a whip!'

His life during the summer months was stripped of all dross, almost inhuman in its purity. No thoughts of fame or worldly glory entered his head. We lived on peacefully from day to day undisturbed in mind, except for the occasional letter from the Opera, which was sure to bring trouble.

In the autumn he played me the completed Fifth Symphony. It was the first time he had ever played a new work to me and we climbed arm in arm up to his hut with all solemnity for the occasion. When he had done, I told him of all that won my instant love in this magnificent work, but also that I was not sure about the chorale at the end. I said it was hymnal and boring. He disagreed.

'Yes, but Bruckner —' he protested.

'He, yes; but not you,' I said, and on the way down through

the wood I tried to make clear to him the radical difference between his nature and Bruckner's. I could not feel he was at his best in working up a church chorale.

I was touching here on a rift in his being which often went so deep as to bring him into serious conflict with himself. He was attracted by Catholic mysticism, an attraction which was encouraged by those friends of his youth who changed their names and were baptized. His love of Catholic mysticism was, however, entirely his own.

Soon after this our holidays came to an end and we returned to Vienna. The Fifth was completed and he worked at the fair copy all through the winter, in this too following an invariable practice, for his winter programme was as strict as his summer one. Up at seven, breakfast, work. At nine, to the Opera. Punctually at one, lunch. His servant telephoned from the Opera as soon as he left, and as soon as Mahler rang the bell on the ground floor, the soup had to be on the table on the fourth. The door had to be open to avoid the slightest delay. He stormed through all the rooms, bursting open unwanted doors like a gale of wind, washed his hands, and then we sat down to lunch. Afterwards, a brief pause just as at Maiernigg; and then either a race four times round the Belvedere or the complete circuit of the Ringstrasse. Punctually at five, tea. After this he went every day to the Opera and stayed there during part of the performance. I picked him up there nearly every day and we hastened home to dinner. If he was still busy in his office, I sometimes looked in at whatever opera was on, but never stayed on after he was free. That is why there are many operas I have seen a part of but never seen to the end. Now and then he told me the end, adding every time that I hadn't missed anything, in which, in the case of many operas, he was perfectly right. They were often more interesting as torsos. After dinner we sat together on a sofa and talked, or else I read aloud.

This first winter, of course, I had the birth of my first child to think of. It took place on 3rd November. Owing, as the doctor said, to the fatigues I had undergone during my pregnancy, the child had got misplaced. Mahler was not told of this, for fear of agitating him; but he read it in the faces of the doctor, the nurse and my mother, and raced through the streets as though frantic. When a friend of his, Guido Adler, asked how I was, he shouted at him: 'Idiot, I forbid you to ask me.' I could hear him raging up and down in the next room, waiting in a frenzy of anxiety for the end of this frightful delivery. When at last it was over, he cried out: 'How can people take the responsibility of such suffering and keep on begetting children!' He was crying hard when he came to my bedside. When I told him subsequently that it had been a breech birth he laughed uncontrollably. 'That's my child. Showing the world straight off the part it deserves.' He loved this child beyond measure from the first day. It was christened Maria after his mother, but the happiness of keeping her was denied him and us, and although I recovered, my recovery was very slow. We saw her in all her beauty only to lose her; within a few months she fell ill and lay for long unconscious, between life and death. She was given hot and cold frictions. Mahler carried her about in his arms and was convinced that his voice alone recalled her to life.

In October he had studied and rehearsed an entrancing little opera of Mozart's, *Zaïde*. It was not given often and then vanished altogether from the repertory. He had to pay dearly for dropping it. It had been adapted by a critic, who drew the royalty; and when it vanished so quickly from the repertory, he protested and said that Mahler ought to go on giving it, which the box-office receipts made it impossible to do. The man was Mahler's bitter enemy ever afterwards and harried him in the press at every opportunity.

The critics in general were inexcusably unjust to him. At first they all turned to him in the hope that he would listen to their advice, but as soon as they saw that he had an unbending will of his own, they first of all withdrew in silence and later became more and more aggressive. During his last years in Vienna he was surrounded by a mob of enemies. We opened the evening paper with dread. 'Another incident at the Royal Opera' – in large type, and all because some young lady had a complaint and some reporter lent a willing ear. Or else it was that Mahler made a short journey to conduct one of his symphonies. At once he was accused in the press of neglecting his duties at the Opera. It was intolerable.

In December, 1902, Mahler prepared for performance Tchaikovsky's *Queen of Spades*. We enjoyed this enormously. He took me to many of the rehearsals and was always playing bits of it to me. For weeks we lived with no other music in our ears. Our life was very quiet. The only people we ever saw were my parents, the Rosés, the Zuckerkandls, the art-historian Strzygowsky, Burckhard, Gustav Klimt, and Pollak, who idolized Mahler.

Strauss too came to Vienna at about this time with his wife and gave some concerts. He was still the much debated, eccentric composer and she an ambitious wife. She sent word to me at once, asking me to come and see her. I went and found her in bed. There was a concert that evening, at which she was to sing, but she did not rise from her bed. Then the door burst open and Strauss came in with a little case in his hand. 'I've got your ring and now you'll get up, Pauksl, won't you?' And Pauksl got up at once and the concert came off, an expensive one for Strauss; for it was a large diamond ring. She asked me at the end of this little scene to bring her some books to read: 'Something light, you know, thrillers.' On this occasion Strauss conducted to a completely empty hall. We sat in the front row and while he conducted he kept up a conversation in a loud voice with Mahler about the idiotic public, which deserved only trash, and so forth. He rejoiced in his own audacity and we found him charming.

Next, they came to see us when several friends of ours were there. As his wife was put out by any kind of serious conversation Strauss got up and said: 'Come along, Mahler – let's go into your room for a bit.' From this moment she began to rage. 'Yes, you can laugh – but it's no joke bein' the wife of a misunderstood genius. I tell you, it's frightful! We never have a penny and I never see him to speak to. Soon as he's done workin', out he goes to play skat and I'm always alone.' She burst into tears and laid her head on the table. We felt most uncomfortable. To soothe her was not easy. I got up quietly, and brought Mahler and Strauss back into the room. Her face cleared at once. Strauss asked her what was the matter. 'Nothing,' she replied. 'Good,' he said, turning to Mahler. 'Then we can continue our conversation.' They stayed in the room with us after that and began discussing Mommsen's *History of Rome*. Mahler loved it. Strauss thought it unsound. They argued the question at length. Pauline sat in a corner and beckoned me to her. 'I say, which is the best hairdresser in Vienna?' I could hardly reply.

Next they discussed Beethoven. Strauss preferred early Beethoven to late, to which Mahler replied that a genius such as he could only get better as he grew older. Strauss maintained the contrary: inspiration often failed him in his later years. The spontaneity of youth was worth all the rest. Mozart, for example —

'And blouses – where do you go for them?'

I got up and left her to herself. I was not going to miss another word of that evening's talk. Mahler and Strauss enjoyed talking to each other, perhaps because they were never of one mind.

'The mistake you make, for example, in your production of opera is in preferring the player who can't sing to the singer who can't play. You have a fellow like Demuth, a woman like Kurz – and enthuse about Mildenburg, or Schoder.' And Strauss shuddered over these foes of *bel canto*, these barbarians of the voice, and called them 'singing players'.

He said too: 'I travel about conducting until I've collected enough money and when I've collected enough I settle myself down in peace to compose.'

Mahler observed to me afterwards: 'But by that time he's gone near to losing his soul.'

We all took Mahler's side about operatic singing, because we had been educated by him, and he by Wagner, to appreciate the German school of singing. In those days we scorned *bel canto*. And yet, during his last years, Mahler fell more and more under the charm of Italian voices in New York, whereas Strauss was seduced into composing title-roles for German singers – Mildenburg as Clytaemnestra, Schoder as Elektra, and so on. His taste had come round to what Mahler's turned from in his last years.

Here are some observations of Mahler's on conducting:

The tempo is right if it allows every note its value.

If a phrase can no longer be grasped because the notes run into one another, the tempo is too fast.

The extreme limit of distinctness is the right tempo for a presto. Beyond that, it has no effect.

He said that if an adagio seemed to be lost on the audience, he slowed the tempo down instead of quickening it, as was commonly done.

The following anecdote is amusing and also sheds light on his attitude to Wagner. One day on his way to the Opera he met Goldmark.

'Well, Master, won't you come along to the Opera?'

'No, I never listen to Wagner. I'm afraid of getting too like him.'

'But,' said Mahler, 'you eat beef without becoming an ox.'

Splendid Isolation

1903

I give this title to the following years because it was a favourite phrase of Mahler's to describe our completely solitary way of life.

There was a landing-stage at Unterach on the Attersee, and there, before the arrival of every steamer, all the good people of Unterach gathered, to see – and to be seen, which was quite as important – and to be well up in whatever was going on.

'We don't go and stand on the landing-stage, and that's unforgivable,' Mahler used to love saying.

We were always a centre of interest and therefore always enveloped in a cloud of gossip, of which, thank heaven, we were mostly unaware. We lived as though under a cloche.

After the première of *Euryanthe* – it was given on 19th January 1903 – we all, my parents, the Rosés, Roller and a young musician, went out to supper as our custom was on such occasions – to let off steam, as Mahler called it. 'I must let off steam after a production, hear what people think and talk about it until I calm down.'

It happened that Mahler went ahead with the others and I followed on with Roller and the young musician. We spoke with indignation as we walked along about the wretched libretto, and the musician said that it was entirely the fault of the libretto if that divine music refused to come to life. We all arrived at the same moment at the Restaurant Hartmann. Mahler turned round in the doorway and called out to us: 'Don't you agree that the libretto of *Euryanthe* is really not at all bad? When you think of it, all the characters in *Lohengrin* are foreshadowed – Elsa is Euryanthe, Lohengrin is Adolar, Ortrud is Eglantine, etc. In spite of all her feminine nonsense, Wilhelmina von Chezy was a talented playwright.'

The musician replied without a moment's hesitation: 'Exactly what I was just saying.'

Mahler's power of suggestion was irresistible.

In the course of studying *Euryanthe* afresh, Mahler had revised the whole libretto, making great alterations both in the wording and the sense. He was always very much amused by the childishness of the librettists of these early operas. When, for example, an ensemble was called for, all the characters were brought together by chance in a wild ravine. 'Our jolly rustics all united once again,' he said with a chuckle. So, with *Euryanthe*, he endeavoured to steer clear of its absurdities, but he did not altogether succeed. In any case, the opera could not hold its own in its renovated dress.* The young man was right.

His defence of the libretto was due to his passionate engrossment in his work. All through the rehearsals he was determined to find excuses for it. He identified himself so completely with any work he studied that even though it impressed him only moderately before and after, he loved it without reserve and fought its battles with fury at the time.

We paid my mother fairly frequent visits up at the Hohe Warte, where painting was the chief interest. Mahler got to know there the friends of my childhood, and among others Alfred Roller. They fell at once into a discussion of the technique of the stage and Roller remarked that he had never missed a performance of *Tristan*. But he could only listen to the music – never look at the stage, because the stage-setting as it was managed up to now destroyed the whole illusion. Mahler asked him what he would do about it himself and Roller replied by unfolding schemes of such magnificence that Mahler gave him an appointment at the Opera next day. 'That's the man for me – I'll engage him,' he said to me on our way home.

Sure enough, Roller was commissioned the very next day to design new scenery for *Tristan*, and shortly afterwards he was appointed permanent stage-designer.† It was taking a colossal risk, as Roller had never in his life before been behind the scenes; and there were indeed the most absurd ructions during rehearsal. M., who was accustomed to her old time-honoured properties,

---

* According to Specht, it was not until 19th January 1904 that the production with Mahler's revised text took place. (D.M.)

† The première of the new production of *Tristan* was given on 21st February 1903. (D.M.)

burst into tears. 'I don't care if I have to tear up the footlights,' she screamed, 'I won't stand it.'

Mahler sent Roller to pacify her and in a very brief space all went smoothly; for M. had fallen in love with him. Mahler and I were now to learn that the tales he told of her were no exaggeration. We were all three about to have supper together in Mahler's large studio during one of the evening performances. A servant came to the door in ill-concealed mirth with a message from M. Would Herr Roller please go to her immediately, as only he could put on her bracelets. Mahler was extremely angry. He sent back word that Roller was not able to come just then, as he was engaged in an important discussion with the Director. After a few minutes the man came back, this time grinning broadly, with the message that she would not sing again, unless Herr Roller came immediately. We thought better of it, and he went.

The production was wonderful. The great yellow awnings made an illusion of such sunlight as is seen only in the desert or on the sea. But Mahler was tired. The haemorrhage, a year before he got to know me, had sapped his vitality. After the second act he lay on the sofa; his face was white, he could hardly pull himself together to conduct the third act. 'If only someone would take it off my hands,' he said.

It was then Justine lost all that was left of my love for her. As we stood looking down on Mahler lying there half asleep, she said under her breath: 'One thing delights me – I had his youth, you have him now he's old.' A sister's jealousy seems to be more dangerous than a mistress's or a wife's because it is without hope. Justine was wounded in her very soul. She had hoped that Mahler would miss her and her advice now and then and would turn to her, and she could not understand it when all he wanted was to be alone with me. Night after night. He wrote to her from Petersburg that he was utterly happy and asked nothing more of this world than what he had. The letter was handed to her at the Opera and she fainted when she read it at the stage-door. Yet Mahler, great psychologist and babe-in-arms, thought he was giving her pleasure.

At the conclusion of a scene between them at the Opera when I was not present, she exclaimed, wringing her hands: 'But,

Gustav, after all, I am flesh of your flesh.' To which he replied: 'Dirt of your dirt, you mean.' He repeated this to me with great delight when he came home. He believed only in the predestination of the spirit, not in the influence of heredity. He had no wish to be reminded of origins, family, race, those emblems of the weight of earth.

I could forgive her enraged and jealous persecution of me on one ground: all Mahler's friends were envious, but they had not the justification of having shared his life for nine years, as she had, only to be ruthlessly cast aside. Yet all of them, one after another, made themselves so impossible by their intrigues that they could not expect friendship to survive.

The lengths to which these old friends of his carried pedantry, tedium and priggishness passes description. They were nothing but M-counters.* Nothing but life-cripples. Proffering advice when none was needed or desired. Their initial attempts to fit me into their Procrustean bed of friendship came to grief. I utterly refused to see any more of people who purposely misunderstood me. Mahler with my approval tried it, but came back full of resentment, and after that we were left in peace.

One day in January he told me he had had a very remarkable opera sent him. 'It doesn't inspire great confidence in the piano score, but the full score is brilliant and dramatic. Couldn't be otherwise. It was the hit of this year's opera season in Paris.'

It was Charpentier's _Louise_.

Rehearsals began at once. A double cast, as there always was with any production of Mahler's. Schrödter, Foerster-Lauterer,† Slezak, Schoder. Charpentier preferred Foerster's simple, homely appeal. He said of Madame Schoder: '_Oh non, ce n'est pas ma Louise!_' From the first she was too sophisticated for him. Demuth was the father in both casts.

One morning during rehearsals Mahler and I were walking along the Ring to the Opera House. There was a man in front of

---

* Dr. Joseph Fränkel, a common friend of ours, of whom more will be said later, called these cranky Jews M-counters, by which he meant that they made it their life's business to count the M's in the Talmud, without making any real study of it, let alone understanding it. (A.M.)

† The wife of the Czech composer, J. B. Foerster, a close friend of Mahler's during his Hamburg years. (D.M.)

us in a flapping black cape, which made him look like a gigantic bird. It was Charpentier. Mahler pointed him out to me and we had a good look at him as we followed on behind. He looked like a perambulating windmill and was an odd sight altogether.

He had come to Vienna for the première at Mahler's invitation and was present at the final rehearsals.* He thought the scenery quite impossible. In a sense, he was the first of the Surrealists and his observations on the production were as incomprehensible to the producer as to Mahler. All Mahler could do was to postpone the première and leave the field to Charpentier. The whole setting was too 'grand' for him. The seducer now had to wear a red electric bulb beneath his dress-coat, so that when he opened it his heart was revealed. The ballerina, when she danced on Montmartre, had to come on in a short ballet-skirt, followed all the time by a pink spotlight. All realism was very properly eliminated as being out of date. Mahler learnt a great deal from these rehearsals; above all, lightness and a sense of humour, as he himself afterwards confessed. But he too was wonderful. He was not touchy about it. 'I was wrong,' he said from the first. 'After all, the composer must know best.'

We saw a lot of Charpentier. Indeed, he paid court to me, but was so clumsy over it that both Mahler and I found it merely comic. Besides, it was not courting in the accepted sense. *Louise* was his only love. We put our box at his disposal, as we did for all musicians from abroad. He made use of it daily and took with him a girl he had picked up. Rosé warned me against making a public appearance in such company. I should not have died of it.

But I had better let my diary tell of those days.

28 March, 1903.
Exciting days for us. The première of *Louise* is over.
A work of genius.
Charpentier a complete bohemian.
Have made great friends with him.
His manners are not all they might be. Spits under the table, bites his nails, draws your attention by a pressure of his knee or

* The Vienna première took place on 24th March 1903. (D.M.)

a nudge of his elbow. Trod on my foot last night in our box to call attention to the beauty of *Tristan*. But as it comes of his associating mostly with people of quite another sort I don't take it amiss. He's wonderful.

He called Mahler and me his two children. It did him so much good to talk to people who honestly said what they meant.

His method of composition is original. First of all he sees a picture, then he hears the music and finally writes the dialogue. You can feel it. After the first rehearsal I said to Mahler: 'Charpentier is a painter, as much a painter as a musician.' He's intoxicated by his success. He talks of his music as of a mistress. He sang some of *Louise* to us as he first wrote it – with great dramatic talent.

To me: 'You are very fortunate to have so great a man for a husband.'

To Mahler about me: 'You have there *un gamin, la clarté, la gaîté, le printemps* – we artists need that.'

My room is a flower-garden. A bouquet, beautifully beribboned, and inscribed: '*A Madame Mahler, gracieuse muse de Vienne, la muse de Montmartre reconnaissante.*'

His account of his life: member of an orchestra, great poverty. Began composing *Louise*, and got into such a fever of work that he couldn't go out to eat or earn money. Wrote on because he couldn't be parted from his composition. Nobody would give him tick, he hadn't a sou, he had lost his job in the orchestra by this time – only an old milkman brought him his daily litre of milk. Then he submitted his score by the hand of the milkman – and became a celebrity overnight. The première caused a sensation in Paris. He sat in the author's box, the milkman in smock and blue apron by his side. He's a socialist and wants to convert me. Has founded a workers' school of music. It's called 'Mimi Pinson'. The students of this conservatoire sent him a long telegram after the première here.

He told us he had composed a whole new opera. It was very lovely, but when he played it through again he woke up to find it was by Wagner. So he destroyed it. He bears the mark of genius on his forehead. He who has eyes may see it.

Paris: November, 1926. I have tried to see Charpentier again. I discovered his address with great difficulty. Everybody said: 'Oh, he's dead long ago.' But the Austrian Embassy found out for me where he lived. I drove there. It was in the outskirts. I climbed steep stairs. A girl came running down. 'Does M. Charpentier live here?' I asked. She said yes. 'Is he at home?' – 'Oh, *non*, Madame —' So I went downstairs again. I would have liked to see him once again. Although he is said to be worse than dead. I was told terrible stories. Probably only because he lives as he chooses, in a manner incomprehensible to conventional persons. Who knows?*

In the middle of June Mahler conducted his Second Symphony in the Cathedral at Basel. He went ahead of me, as always, because I could not be parted so long from my child. This time he came from Amsterdam where he had conducted the Third. Our contralto, Kittel, sang the contralto solo there, and now in Basel she sang *Urlicht*. Mahler made a life-long friend there, Willem Mengelberg, and so arrived at Basel beaming with joy.

No one who was there will ever forget the rehearsals, the dress-rehearsal or the performance in the Cathedral. The building, the galaxy of lighted candles, the lofty roof, and the music all combined to make an unforgettable impression. Oskar Nedbal knelt down outside and kissed Mahler's hand, and no one found it surprising. (Nedbal was a brilliant musician and has written some delightful music.)

We met Hans Pfitzner also, and Mahler immediately asked him to a meal with us. The friendship between him and me grew apace. He asked me if he might send me his string quartet. Our friendship, and my respect for him, have gone on growing ever since.

Summer had come, and with it we resumed our life at Maiernigg and its unvarying and peaceful routine. Mahler soon began

* Now – 1939 – I have seen Charpentier again. He is just the same. All he told me was full of courage and high spirits. He has kept as young as his own *Louise*, which is as lovely as on its natal day. (A.M.) Charpentier died in Paris in 1956. (D.M.)

working. This time it was the first sketches for the Sixth Symphony. He played a lot with our child, carrying her about and holding her up to dance and sing. So young and unencumbered he was in those days.

The hot walks through woods and scrub came round again, and utter tranquillity.

One day a letter announced the arrival of Hans Pfitzner's string quartet in manuscript,* and the manuscript followed. He asked me in his letter, with a touching nonchalance, to take good care of it, as it was the original and he had no copy. When the manuscript came, I took it up to Mahler in his hut. He came down two hours later.

'It is the work of a master,' he said with emphasis, delighted to give his approval.

In the autumn Mahler as usual went back to Vienna before I did, and being left to myself I took out the piano score of *Die Rose vom Liebesgarten*. I grew more and more enthusiastic and told Mahler so in every letter I wrote; and when I got back to Vienna soon afterwards the opera was always on my music rest. And since the piano in any room of ours was always open and Mahler automatically played whatever he found there, he came to share my enthusiasm for *Die Rose vom Liebesgarten* so fully that he decided to produce it, in spite of all his previous objections. It was the one and only time during all the six years I lived with him while he was Director of the Vienna Opera that I purposely and openly influenced him; and I certainly had no cause to regret it.

Two movements of the Sixth were finished in the summer and the scheme of the others had taken final shape in his head.

I used to play a lot of Wagner, and this gave Mahler the idea of a charming surprise. He had composed for me the only love-song he ever wrote – *Liebst du um Schönheit*† – and he slipped it in between the title-page and the first page of the *Valkyrie*. Then he waited day after day for me to find it; but I never happened to open the volume, and his patience gave out. 'I think I'll take a

---

* This would have been the first (1903) of Pfitzner's three string quartets. (D.M.)
† The second of Mahler's five settings of poems by Rückert, for voice and orchestra. (D.M.)

look at the *Valkyrie* today,' he said abruptly. He opened it and the song fell out. I was overwhelmed with joy and we played it that day twenty times at least.

He and I were jealous of each other, at first I of him more than he of me. I was jealous of his past, which in my innocence I used to think very objectionable. He was jealous of my future, and that I can now understand.

Splendid Isolation

1904

At the beginning of this year the *Secession** held an exhibition of the work of Hodler and Amiet.

Ferdinand Hodler was like a tree, uncouth and gigantic. There was not a woman he did not deem his prey, without prelude or postscript. He even laid his hands on B.Z. [Frau Bertha Zucker-kandl], who gave him a resounding box on the ear. He came to a performance of *Tristan* – it was the first time he had ever heard this work – and sat in my box, showing every sign of discomfort. In the middle of the third act he got up to go. 'That kissing-match in the second act was all very well, but they can get on with their dying without me – I'm off.'

Once when he came to see us, he asked to see my child and I brought her in my arms. 'Hold it – don't move,' he shouted. 'I shall have to paint you like that!' More acclamations followed. But Mahler did not like it when I excited admiration of this kind. It put him in a bad humour and he did his utmost to see that it did not happen.

The first performance of Hugo Wolf's *Corregidor* took place on 18th February. Mahler rehearsed and conducted it himself, and Roller was responsible for the setting. Wolf had recently died after spending years in an asylum; the production was a debt of honour owed to his memory by the Opera and by Mahler. This was the keynote of the occasion, an evening at half-mast. It was not a great success, for a series of songs, however beautiful, does not make an opera. The box of the librettist, Rosa Mayreder, Hugo Wolf's friend for many years, was wreathed in flowers. Mahler went and spoke to her after the first act. But it all came too late.

* A body of artists who broke with academic tradition and institutions and devoted themselves to furthering the aims of modern movements in painting. Mahler's relationship to *Art Nouveau* is of no little interest or significance and worth more consideration than has yet been given to it. (D.M.)

Mahler himself told me the story of his friendship with Wolf and how it ended.*

Their friendship went back to their early life, when, with another man called Krzyzanowski, they shared a room for a few months. They were very poor and, as all three were musicians, extremely sensitive to noise; so when any one of the three had any work on hand, the other two had to tramp the streets. Once Mahler composed a movement of a quartet for a competition while the other two spent the night on a bench in the Ringstrasse.

Mahler gave lessons; Wolf did not, or only very few. When their money ran out, one of them gave a pupil notice. The plan was to ring the bell, say he was suddenly obliged to go away and request payment for the lessons already given. The ready money provided meals for all three for a day or two. On the other hand, a pupil was lost for ever.

Mahler did not come from a poor home, merely from one of soul-destroying narrowness; and while he was a student at the conservatoire, where his friendship with Wolf began, his parents often sent him parcels of food, which the others very quickly disposed of. In one of these parcels there was once a green overcoat as a Christmas present; but, as his father had sent it him to grow into, it trailed at his heels and caused such a sensation in the street that he became aware at last that something must be wrong. As soon as his two friends explained what was the matter, nothing would induce him to wear the coat again, and the long and lank Krzyzanowski became the fortunate possessor.

When he was twenty Mahler got an engagement at Bad Hall. Wolf would not accept any job and said arrogantly that he was going to wait until he was made 'God of the Southern Hemisphere'; and he went hungry until his death.

The three friends made their first acquaintance with *Götterdämmerung* together, and in their passionate excitement they bawled the Gunther–Brünhilde–Hagen trio to such effect that their landlady came up in a fury and gave them notice on the spot. She would not leave the room until they had packed up their

---

* Readers, however, should consult Frank Walker's authoritative biography of Hugo Wolf (London, 1951), who questions some of the details of these reminiscences. (D.M.)

scanty belongings, and then she locked the door angrily behind them.

One day, as they were talking, Wolf got the idea of writing a fairy-tale opera. This was long before Humperdinck and undoubtedly an original inspiration. They considered many themes and finally hit on *Rübezahl*.* Mahler was young and impulsive and he began on the libretto that very night and finished it next day. In all innocence he took it to Wolf for him to see. But Wolf also had made a start and was so put out by Mahler's having stolen a march on him that he threw up the whole idea and never forgave him. Outwardly they remained on friendly terms for some time longer, but they avoided each other's society. Many years later they met on the way to the Festspielhaus at Bayreuth and passed by with a curt 'Hallo'.

Soon after Mahler had been made Director of the Vienna Opera, Wolf was announced; and there he stood, lean as a skeleton, with burning eyes, and imperiously demanded the instant production of *Corregidor*. Mahler, knowing the work and its defects, made the usual evasions: no singers suited to it, etc. Wolf grew obstreperous and Mahler did not like the look of him. He had a special bell within reach for such occasions. He pressed it and his man came in with the prearranged message: 'The Intendant wishes to see you at once, sir.'

Wolf found himself alone. He rushed downstairs and along the Ring. His mind gave way; he thought he was the Director and on his way home. When he arrived at Mahler's flat, Auenbruggergasse 2, he rang the bell; and when the servant opened the door, he shouted at her to let him pass – he was the Director. She slammed the door in his face in terror. Shortly afterwards he was shut up in a lunatic asylum.

I saw Wolf myself in my father's house when I was a child. He came into the room and stared at the ceiling. 'Oh – so you've just moved in, have you?' The unadorned ceiling must have annoyed him. My father had stripped off all the mouldings, because he hated that sort of ornamentation. Wolf then sat down at the small upright piano and began to improvise wildly. When Papa shyly asked what it was he was playing, Wolf without stopping shouted:

* See Introduction, pp. xxv-xxvi (D.M.)

'*Aïda – Aïda*,' and hammered away madly. I was standing behind
the piano, sliding one finger to and fro over the surface. 'What's
she doing there? Is she a lightning-conductor, or what?' I was
sent out of the room. I have never forgotten that weird apparition.

Mahler was dissatisfied with the reception of *Corregidor*, and on
10th March he gave it a second time in its original version. It was
a labour of love, and had only a very short run in Vienna.

I was expecting my second child in June and this caused a
disturbance in our habits, one of which was to race every day after
lunch three times round the Belvedere or the Ring. But now I
often had to stay at home, and Mahler came back from his 'runs',
as he called them, in a surprisingly short time.

Verdi's *Falstaff* was given in German for the first time on 3rd
May; but I could not be at his side during the rehearsals as he
liked me to be.

On the other hand, our life was now much more sociable. Max
Burckhard tried to bring us into touch with his friends. It was not
easy. Mahler seldom felt happy when he went out anywhere and,
his gloom being infectious, everyone felt as if 'there was a corpse
under the table'. I am sure there was always a sigh of relief when
we left. But one day Burckhard invited us to meet Gerhart
Hauptmann, his friend, Margarethe Marschalk, whom he married
soon after, and Josef Kainz. Mahler reluctantly consented to go.
That evening was unforgettable.

It was the first of many talks Hauptmann and Mahler had together and I remember it very clearly. There was a great argument between Hauptmann and Kainz during dinner about the
end of the *Versunkene Glocke*, which Hauptmann had altered. In
the first version Rautendelein went back into the well as cheerfully
as she had emerged from it. Now he made her go back sadly,
which certainly is not in keeping with her elfish nature. Kainz
called it a concession to the public. Hauptmann had given him a
copy of the earlier version, and Kainz said with a laugh that if he
outlived him he would have it printed at his own expense.
Hauptmann said he did not mind what liberties were taken in the
future, as long as the edition already printed survived. Kainz has
since died, and what has become of the version he spoke of?

It was late when we left, and the long walk home from Frank-gasse, where Burckhard lived, to Auenbruggergasse near the Rennweg, where we lived, was made longer still because Mahler and Hauptmann were so engrossed that they stopped and talked at every lamp-post for a quarter of an hour at a time. Margarethe Marschalk, a lovely creature in those days, and I sat down on a seat and waited patiently until we could get a word in edgeways to remind them of our existence. At four in the morning I could walk no farther and we took a cab from the Michaelerplatz.

Next day we paid the Hauptmanns a visit at the Hotel Sacher. Margarethe was wearing a shirt and black satin trousers, and her short black curls hung down to her shoulders; I could tell at once that she and Rautendelein were one and the same. She and I were to go out together and Mahler to stay with Hauptmann. Hauptmann took me aside as we were starting. 'Do keep an eye on Gretchen,' he said. 'Don't let her enter a shop. She hasn't a notion of the value of money, and simply spends all she's got. Once, in Berlin, I gave her a thousand-mark note to keep for me until we got to Italy, but when I asked her for it she hadn't the faintest recollection I'd ever given it to her. It put me in a great difficulty because I'd been absolutely counting on it. So I made a search. And do you know where I found it? At the bottom of her trunk, screwed up in a ball. What do you say to that?'

I gave my promise, but it was not easy to keep it. She wanted everything she set eyes on in a manner entirely elfish. She pitched into me, too, for living in such poor style: I ought to see that I had an easier life of it. She had eight servants, she told me, and never did a thing for herself. Hard words have been said since of her extravagance, but my impression was that Hauptmann liked her for it. He encouraged in her the qualities he had given to Rautendelein and which, like another Pygmalion, he wished to bring to life and enjoy in her.

Their stay in Vienna this time was short, but there was a longer one to come, which was to mean even more to us.

In the spring, just before the birth of my second child, I went to Abbazia with my little Maria and a scatter-brained maid, who literally expected me to wait upon her, which in my condition was absurd. I have often experienced the same thing with servants.

Mahler soon followed me. He took a sleeper, as he always did, whereas I travelled in an ordinary compartment. I went to meet him at Mattuglie. He told me he had been persecuted the whole morning by two small boys, who spied on him through the curtains of his sleeper. Later on there was a coming and going along the corridor and he recognized them as the sons of the Archduke Otto. I was standing close to Mahler as they got out. The Archduchess Maria Josepha took the children up to him and told them not to forget having seen him. After greeting him very graciously she rejoined her attendants, who were looking on in surprise. She was very fond of Mahler, because he pensioned off the dancer, Schleinzer, Archduke Otto's extremely tactless mistress. When Schleinzer asked him why, he replied: 'I can't do with an archduchess in my company.' One of these two boys was later the Emperor Karl.

Mahler brought his work with him even to Abbazia. I never knew him to have a real holiday. We were given the privilege of having our meals served in our own rooms, which as they were in an annexe called Tusculum at the far end of the garden must have been somewhat troublesome.

I enjoyed the 'splendid isolation' as much as he did. Once or twice, to please our landlady, we joined the company in the dining-room, where as usual Mahler's presence caused an embarrassed silence, broken on this occasion only by the comedian, Treumann, who was unabashed and asked Mahler some foolish questions. He did not take them amiss; on the contrary, he was glad to have the solemn ban lifted.

We returned to Vienna a day sooner than we had intended. Mahler could never stay long anywhere. There was no rest for him. He was driven on without respite, either by his own work or his duties at the Opera.

On 14th June 1904, we went for a drive in the Prater, as we had every afternoon for the last few weeks. On our return we found the Rosés in the hall, on the point of going to the Burgtheater. They had come in the hope of persuading us to join them. It was *Der arme Heinrich*. Mahler was all the more glad to go when he saw how eager I was, and so we all four drove straight on to the theatre.

It was like wine to me. Kainz played Heinrich. I was shattered, which was not surprising in my condition. When I got home, Hauptmann's musical verse was still in my ears and I took the play to bed with me and read it through. The verse sounded on through my dreams and I suddenly woke, as though God had touched me with a finger. My hour had come – and still I heard Hauptmann. I did not want to wake anyone. I opened the window. It was 15th June; all nature bloomed; leaves rustled, birds sang. I had no fear. It was five o'clock by now, and the pangs were severe. I went to Mahler. He put on his clothes and hurried out in alarm to fetch the midwife, and then did all he could think of to mitigate my pain. But the best he could think of was reading Kant aloud. I sat at his writing-table and writhed in agony. The monotonous drone of his voice drove me crazy; I could not understand a word he read, and at last I could bear it no longer. But I know now he was right: mental concentration is the one means of overcoming pain. Only – the book, in the circumstances, was a bad choice; it was too difficult to understand.

The birth, at midday, in the middle of the week (Wednesday), in the middle of the month, in the middle of the year, might have been an allegory. From the first moment the child was a great joy to us and was nicknamed Guckerl, from her wide-open, blue eyes.

I was fast asleep later in the day and awoke with a violent start. An enormous stag-beetle hovered in the air an inch or two from my face. Mahler was holding it by a single leg, beaming with delight, in spite of his horror of beasts of all kinds. 'You're so fond of animals,' he exclaimed exultingly. 'I caught this fellow for you.' Once I had a sudden longing for a little piece of cheese. Such a thing never crossed our threshold, so Mahler ran out at once to the largest dealer in cheeses he knew of and bought an enormous wedge of strong Schwarzenberg cheese. I never knew till then that so large a piece could be seen at one time. As he would never carry anything in his hand he hung it on a button of his overcoat and promptly forgot all about it. He hurried along and the dangling cheese spread a pungent aroma abroad. They were repairing a gas-main in the Walfischgasse and, as there seemed to him to be a suffocating smell of gas, he turned aside into the Ring; but still there was the noxious smell of gas, and the faster he went the stronger it grew. At last he burst into my room. Even there the smell pursued him. We burst out laughing, and he was annoyed at first when we tried to persuade him that he himself was the origin of it all. Then he laughed too.

Mahler was extremely susceptible to suggestion. If I had a pain anywhere, he immediately had it too. He was also as credulous as a child in such matters and never had the slightest idea what did him good. He believed in any cure, whoever recommended it, and no medicine came amiss to him. When we moved from Auen-bruggergasse, our large dining-table at its full extent could scarcely accommodate all the medicaments he had collected, and our friends were able to lay in a stock to last them for years.

His sister once recommended unleavened bread, and it was sent to him every three or four days to the Tyrol. I, of course, had to eat it too and it lay like lead on my stomach. I endured in silence. But one day I had spasms and could think of no cause but this bread. Mahler was overjoyed. He jumped up and cried out: 'You can't bear it either? Thank God for that! It's given me hell for the last week. We won't eat any more of it.' We stopped it at once.

It was often like that.

There was an entertaining episode at a dentist's: Mahler had toothache, but was not sure which tooth ached. I had found it for him, and I was sitting in the waiting-room, which was full of people. Suddenly the door flew open and Mahler called out: 'Alma dear, which tooth is it actually that's aching?' He was astonished when everyone laughed.

We saw more of him at home now than ever before. He could scarcely bear to be parted from the children, and for each he had a special form of entertainment – stories jokes or funny faces. He loved telling the elder one Brentano's fairy tale – 'Gockel, Hinkel and Gackeleia.'

Zemlinsky paid us a visit in the summer (I had been playing with him a little in the winter; he revered Mahler as a god and Mahler got to like him more and more) and Roller also, of whom he had always been very fond; and so we were quite lively.

Mahler became more human and expansive. He finished the
Sixth Symphony and added three more to the two *Kindertotenlieder* already composed.* I found this incomprehensible. I can
understand setting such frightful words to music if one had no
children, or had lost those one had. Moreover, Friedrich Rückert
did not write these harrowing elegies solely out of his imagination:
they were dictated by the cruellest loss of his whole life. What I
cannot understand is bewailing the deaths of children, who were
in the best of health and spirits, hardly an hour after having kissed
and fondled them. I exclaimed at the time: 'For heaven's sake,
don't tempt Providence!'

The summer was beautiful, serene and happy. Before the
holidays came to an end he played me the completed Sixth
Symphony. I had first to get everything done in the house, so as
to have all my time free. Once more we walked arm-in-arm up
to his hut in the wood, where nothing could disturb us. These
occasions were always very solemn ones.

After he had drafted the first movement he came down from the
wood to tell me he had tried to express me in a theme. 'Whether
I've succeeded, I don't know; but you'll have to put up with it.'

This is the great soaring theme of the first movement of the
Sixth Symphony.† In the third movement he represented the
arhythmic games of the two little children, tottering in zigzags
over the sand. Ominously, the childish voices became more and
more tragic, and at the end died out in a whimper. In the last
movement he described himself and his downfall or, as he later
said, that of his hero: 'It is the hero, on whom fall three blows
of fate, the last of which fells him as a tree is felled.' Those were
his words.

Not one of his works came so directly from his inmost heart as
this. We both wept that day. The music and what it foretold
touched us so deeply. The Sixth is the most completely personal
of his works, and a prophetic one also. In the *Kindertotenlieder*,
as also in the Sixth, he anticipated his own life in music. On him
too fell three blows of fate, and the last felled him. But at the

* This is an example of the useful dates that can be deduced from these memoirs.
On the facts given here we can attribute completion of the *Kindertotenlieder* to the
summer of 1904. (D.M.)
† Alma Mahler refers to the movement's expansive second subject. (D.M.)

time he was serene; he was conscious of the greatness of his work. He was a tree in full leaf and flower.

One more word about his playing the work through to me: he always said he would never play an unfinished work, and he never did. It would, he said, be an immodesty. An artist could no more show unfinished work than a mother her child in the womb.

I remarked to him once during a walk: 'All I love in a man is his achievement. The greater his achievement the more I have to love him.'

'That's a real danger. You mean if anyone came along who could do more than I —'

'I'd have to love him,' I said.

He smiled: 'Well, I won't worry for the time being. I don't know anybody who can do more than I can.'

All the same, each of us was jealous of the other, though we belied it. He often used to say: 'If you were suddenly disfigured by some illness, small-pox, for example, then at last, when you were pleasing in the sight of nobody else – then at last I could show how I loved you.'

The load of debt I had taken over was heavy. Before we married, Mahler had entrusted its speedy liquidation to me with the words: 'In the name of God and my *Euryanthe*, I pray you may soon be done with it.' The apportionment of his income for this and all other purposes was my undivided responsibility. Mahler had all his clothes from the best tailor, his shoes in large numbers from the best English shoemaker, whereas I wore the same dress for five or six years on end. I was unable to accept an invitation to lunch with Baron Albert Rothschild, because I had not a hat to put on. It did not occur to either of us that I might buy one. Mahler went alone.

And so it was that the rigid economy, the cares of the household, which had to be run in exact conformity with his wishes, the children and the daily round all combined to wear down our love for each other; and yet his love, which in these mid-years of marriage seemed not only at its last gasp but already buried, awaited its resurrection.

Roller was now commissioned to design a new stage-setting for *Fidelio*.

Besides his wonderful scenery, there was an entirely new conception of the opera and a new grouping of the singers on the stage. The great *Leonore* overture (No. 3) now introduced the last scene; and the effect was indescribably beautiful. The music led the way from the sombre prison, through darkness to light; the curtain rose and the Bastille towered up in a flood of brilliant sunshine. It was a stroke of dramatic genius on Mahler's part,* and it has caught on. Toscanini plays the overture there to this day.

For the quartet '*Mir ist so wunderbar*' Mahler made the four players, who up to this moment had been in vigorous movement, suddenly form a tableau, and a ray of sunshine fell on the group through the window. The orchestra, the singers and every detail were studied and rehearsed to a pitch he had never reached in the production of any other opera. This was first given on 7th October 1904 and its influence still lives on.

Although I was nursing my youngest child, I did not want to miss the final rehearsals; and so I sat unobserved in a box and ran out to the telephone every half-hour to make sure the children were well. I was continually harassed by anxious forebodings, not without good cause, as the future was to show – to my bitter sorrow. I was to learn that anxious care and all else are of no avail, if God has so decided. At the end of September Mahler asked me to wean the little one as soon as I could. I did it, but with a heavy heart, and only for the sake of the first hearing of the Fifth Symphony at Cologne, which I was unwilling to miss at any cost.

We were to travel together to Cologne for the rehearsals; but nature will not be trifled with. I fell ill through the sudden drying up of my milk, and our hope that I might be able to follow later was disappointed. And so I lay in bed with a temperature while the Fifth was given its first hearing, the Fifth, which had been my first full participation in his life and work, the whole score of which I had copied, and – more than that – whole lines of which he had left out, because he knew that he could trust blindly to me.

* It has been argued that it was the difficulties of scene-changing that gave rise to Mahler's use of the overture. If today's mechanical facilities had been available, would this 'tradition' have ever begun? (D.M.)

Early in the year there had been a reading-rehearsal with the
Philharmonic, to which I listened unseen from the gallery. I had
heard each theme in my head while copying the score, but now I
could not hear them at all. Mahler had overscored the percussion
instruments and side drum so madly and persistently that little
beyond the rhythm was recognizable. I hurried home sobbing
aloud. He followed. For a long time I refused to speak. At last
I said between my sobs: 'You've written it for percussion and
nothing else.' He laughed, and then produced the score. He crossed
out the side drum in red chalk and half the percussion instruments too. He had felt the same thing himself, but my passionate
protest turned the scale. The completely altered score is still in
my possession.

Mahler, then, set off alone for the first performance in public
of a work I knew and loved so well. It took place on 18th October
at the Gürzenich, Cologne, and appears to have been very well
performed and a great success.* Mahler wrote me a detailed
account. He had to go on to Amsterdam, where he stayed with
Mengelberg and felt, as he always did there, more at home. He
conducted the Second and the Fourth. It was the first performance of the Fourth in Amsterdam and Mengelberg put it twice in
the same programme: Fourth Symphony. Interval. Fourth
Symphony.† Mahler conducted the first time, Mengelberg the
second, with Mahler sitting comfortably in the stalls to hear his
own work played to him. Mengelberg, he said, when he came
home, had so perfectly grasped his meaning that it was just as if
he had been conducting himself.

He arrived in Vienna from Amsterdam first thing in the morning, and his bath was ready for him. As usual, I was waiting to
look after him; and he told me all his experiences. Then he had
breakfast and went to the Opera. At that time he was conducting
there about twice a week. He made his own study for almost
every production, or took an active part if the rehearsals were
under another conductor. His industry was unflagging. He was
thoroughly familiar from frequent rehearsals with every opera in
the repertory, and worked indefatigably at fresh interpretations of

* See Letters 45–48. The Gürzenich (Diet House) was used as a concert hall. (D.M.)
† See Letter 53. (D.M.)

known works as well as for the first production of new ones. His early mornings only were given up to writing the fair copy of his scores.

In December his Third Symphony was given a great reception in Vienna* and the concert was repeated. Afterwards he entertained the orchestra at the Golden Birne in Mariahilf – a sacred rite which he never failed to perform – and spent an hour with them. He loved these occasions and the people he worked with, each of whom he valued and esteemed. If only his orchestra had known it, how happily they might have worked together.

Christmas came and the New Year. There were parties and also a dinner-party at a wealthy friend's. Mahler arrived in the middle, took an apple from the centre of the table, while the other guests stared so hard they forgot to eat; after smelling it exhaustively he laid it down beside his plate and hurriedly swallowed what was put before him. Then he jumped up before the last course and vanished into the smoking-room, with his host and his host's daughter at his heels. In vain he protested that he wished to be alone: they kept him company by turns until the dinner was at an end and the whole company noisily trooped in.

All stood in awe of him and all found him intriguing. But he did not help to make such evenings as this a success. There was a singer present who had persuaded his host that such a chance of singing before Mahler was not to be missed. But the moment the first notes of the accompaniment were heard and the singer had taken his stance, Mahler abruptly got up and left the room; after waiting, for decency's sake, until the song was over, he brusquely took leave of the company and hurried me off.

This dinner-party and one other at the house of some moderately cultivated persons of noble birth were the only so-called social occasions we took part in during the whole of our married life in Vienna. We reckoned afterwards that the cost of clothes and cab-hire would have paid for a holiday. When we talked it over and discovered that each of us was making a sacrifice to the supposed pleasure of the other, we naturally decided to forgo all such parties in the future.

Mahler lived the life of a Stoic – a small flat, no luxuries of any

* On 14th and 22nd December 1904. (D.M.)

sort. His one aim was to be unconscious of the body, so as to concentrate entirely on his work. Besides this, I myself had come to a strange pass. I was shy when I was a girl, but in Mahler's company the affliction got to such a pitch that I could scarcely make a rational reply when spoken to; I felt I was nothing but his shadow. His celebrity was such that the moment we were seen in the street people stood stock-still and loudly exclaimed: 'Look – there's Mahler with his wife.' They laughed, nudged each other and turned round to stare and made me feel so uncomfortable that I could hardly walk on. But Mahler saw nothing. His utter unconcern was sometimes ludicrous.

Once, for example, we were waiting for a tram in the Prater. Mahler's presence was a sensation. Every eye was on him. Just as the tram came in sight, it suddenly occurred to him to retire. An abashed smile passed from face to face and every eye was now fixed on me, who at such moments longed for the earth to open and swallow me up.

In a restaurant, too, it was his invariable habit to draw the waiter's attention to the dish somebody else was enjoying. If necessary, he stood up to point out the man whose luck he envied and desired to share, asking the waiter in a loud voice: 'Waiter, what's that gentleman eating over there?'

Another episode has its appropriate place here, although I was not myself present. Mahler told me the story, which belongs to the days when he directed the Opera in Budapest. He and Justine went for a walk and arrived at a fashionable café, where the tables were disposed on two terraces one above the other. Mahler felt a sudden urge to wash his hands. Characteristically, he got up and marched up to the balustrade with the water-bottle from the table and without a thought emptied it over his hands. An outcry arose from below, chairs were pushed back, dresses shaken out and then, after a look upwards, there was the exclamation: 'Oh – it's only Mahler!' Calm was restored after he had politely begged pardon; and he and Justine resumed their talk. Soon he felt the need to wash his hands once more. He took another water-bottle and carefully going to the other end of the terrace again poured water over his hands. To his great surprise the very same feminine outcry arose and looking down he saw the very same company as before, whom he had be-sprinkled for the second time. Fearing lest this might occur, they had removed themselves to the farthest possible distance.

I found this extraordinary ingenuousness and total unconcern ever more of an embarrassment. The upshot, in any case, was that I suffered more and more from a torturing sense of inferiority. Often I had to affect a cheerful air with tears ready to burst from my eyes. And I must not let him see. I could have found in my music a complete cure for this state of things, but he had forbidden it when we were engaged – and now I dragged my hundred songs with me wherever I went – like a coffin into which I dared not even look.

One day he came home unexpectedly and found me in tears. He asked me the reason. Then he put his hand on my head: 'Dreams that never flowered.' I could not restrain myself any longer but broke into heart-breaking sobs.

We came to an agreement while we lived in Vienna that, if I had heard any unpleasant news in the morning, I was to talk cheerfully during lunch, for fear of upsetting his digestion, and say nothing of my ill-tidings until he had been refreshed and invigorated by his brief siesta. How well I understand him today. Time has brought me the afflictions he suffered from years ago, and I have had no one to ward them off. I thank God I did as he wished in those days out of mere obedience to his will.

Another understanding between us, which I understood as little, was that what he said one day was not to hold good the next. It was therefore out of the question for me to say: 'But, Gustav, you said the very opposite yesterday' (as he very often did), because he reserved for himself the privilege of inconsequence. This characteristic of his was often a great shock to me. I could never be sure of what he thought and felt.

Splendid Isolation

1905

In the winter a new production of *Rheingold* was rehearsed. There was one row after another between Roller and the Rhine maidens, who rebelled at singing in baskets on long poles. Roller took disciplinary action, but his strictness, his harshness, indeed, made bad blood in the company. His settings were beautiful but awkward even for the other singers. And Mahler was defenceless against him; he began to domineer and Mahler's power dwindled.

DIARY: January 26. Concert yesterday: Zemlinsky–Schoenberg.* My surmise was correct. Zemlinsky, in spite of his many thoughts and charming inspirations, in spite too of his imposing knowledge, has not the strength of Schoenberg, who for all his wrong-headedness is a very original fellow. The audience kept leaving in droves and slamming the doors behind them while the music was being played. There were whistles and cat-calls as well. But for us two his talent was beyond question.

When I was twenty Zemlinsky taught me in composition, and through him I got to know his pupil, Schoenberg. He used to say when I confessed my lack of sympathy with Schoenberg: 'You wait. The world will talk of him before long.' In those days I could not work up any belief in him. But Zemlinsky, who was at first Schoenberg's teacher, later became his pupil. Nobody who entered the charmed circle of Schoenberg's spirit could resist his intellectual pre-eminence or the force of his logic.

In those days we used to go to Frau Conrat's, a friend of Brahms, every Sunday evening. After Mahler's First Symphony we all arrived late, because we had been arguing passionately all the way about the music we had just heard. It had filled us with anger.

* The first performance of Schoenberg's *Pelléas and Mélisande*. (D.M.)

I met Schoenberg again later. I was acquainted with Mahler by then, although nobody knew it. I asked Schoenberg whether he was going to hear the performance of the Fourth Symphony. He answered me by one of those paradoxes he was so fond of: 'How can Mahler do anything with the Fourth when he has already failed to do anything with the First?' This was true 'Schoenberg'. Yet he was to be Mahler's greatest and most convinced follower. Zemlinsky brought him to see us later on, and a strange sort of friendship evolved between the three of them. Zemlinsky, from an exaggeration of pride, was dry in manner with Mahler. 'I know,' he said. 'Everybody wants something from him and flatters him for that reason. He shall never say that of me.'

I told Mahler this and he sent word by me that he was not to be so disingenuous but take heart and be friendly.

Schoenberg, on the other hand, was inspired by a youthful rebelliousness against his elder, whom at the same time he revered. They used to come in in the evening. After one of our devastatingly simple meals, all three went to the piano and talked shop – at first in all amity. Then Schoenberg let fall a word in youthful arrogance and Mahler corrected him with a shade of condescension – and the room was in an uproar. Schoenberg delighted in paradox of the most violent description. At least we thought so then; today I should listen with different ears. Mahler replied professorially. Schoenberg leapt to his feet and vanished with a curt good night. Zemlinsky followed, shaking his head.

As soon as the door had shut behind them, Mahler said: 'Take good care you never invite that conceited puppy to the house again.' On the stairs Schoenberg spluttered: 'I shall never again cross that threshold.' But after a week or two Mahler said: 'By the way, what's become of those two?' I did not, of course, say: 'But you told me not to ask them again,' but lost no time in sending them an invitation; and they, who had only been waiting for it, lost no time in coming. Nevertheless, it was a long time before there was much solace to be had from their intercourse together.

Mahler once said when he came home: 'I've been stealing for

you today.' He took a sheet of paper folded in four from his pocket-book. It was the inner title-page of *Tannhäuser*. At the bottom in the right-hand corner were the words: 'I conducted from this score on the —. Richard Wagner.' Mahler had been conducting *Tannhäuser* that evening, and it had pained him, as it often had before, to think of this sacred page being turned over and thumbed by any conductor who happened to come along; and so it occurred to him to abstract it. I was wild with joy. Mahler said he had rescued it, for the various conductors paid so little heed to it that their thumb-marks had almost obliterated the words. We smoothed it out and had it framed; and I hung it up in our music-room in perfect innocence. Not long after, Rosé saw it there: 'What, *you've* got it? The whole opera's been looking everywhere for it. No, my children, that won't do.' He took it away, frame and all. And that was the last we ever saw or heard of it.

I should very much like to know where it is now.

All foreigners of distinction had free use of our box, and there were often so many that there was scarcely room for me. Mahler came home from the Opera one day and said: 'Richard Dehmel's in Vienna. I don't care for him, but I know he interests you. Shall I bring him along?' And so he came with his wife to see us. We had a good many people, the same company as usual. There were Roller, Klimt, Moser, my mother and Moll. Soon a fierce argument broke out about Wagner. Mahler and all of us took up the cudgels for Wagner. Mahler loved him unreservedly. Dehmel was hard-set in his up-to-date, jejune antipathy, and the argument was threatening to take an unpleasant turn, when Dehmel said abruptly: '. . . and, anyway, Wagner reminds me of a poppy, and I can't stand poppies.'

Silence fell, and the party broke up in gloom. And the odd thing is that such painful incidents live on, unforgotten and unforgiven, in the memories of all their victims.

There was another strange evening. Theodore Streicher, the composer, a neighbour of ours on the other side of the lake at Maiernigg, paid us a visit in the summer, which we returned. He did not appear to have any ulterior motive and little else passed between us. But he turned up again in the winter and out of his mouth came the words: 'I should like very much to play you some compositions of mine.'

'To what words?' Mahler asked.

'*Des Knaben Wunderhorn*,' he replied.

Mahler grunted.

The evening came. There were Streicher, his wife in an old-fashioned silk court dress, Schoenberg, Zemlinsky and Klaus Pringsheim (Thomas Mann's brother-in-law). At dinner we talked of anything but Streicher's compositions. But afterwards I made a sign to Mahler to ask him to play, but he only laughed and shrugged his shoulders. Conversation limped on. Streicher exchanged surprised glances with his spouse. Again I gave Mahler a reminder and at last when it was nearly midnight I succeeded in decoying him into the hall; and there, projecting far from the pocket of Streicher's overcoat we saw the menacing roll of paper. Mahler went back into the room with a smile, and Streicher, released at last from his suspense, fell first on him and then on the piano.

He played a song, then a second, and a third. Mahler said not a word, but he bit the inside of his cheek, a sure sign that he was bored. Schoenberg and Zemlinsky, finding the situation more and more painful, got up and stood like heraldic birds in support of Streicher, whose nervousness increased. In the kindness of their hearts they set about discovering little beauties. Streicher, who was so ill-advised as to read the words of each song aloud and then to expound them, was now encouraged to draw attention to happy inspirations and 'remarkable' modulations; he panted and perspired and committed the one unforgivable sin a man can commit in such predicaments: he played on. Mahler took not the slightest notice; he lay prostrate on the sofa. Pringsheim leant on the end of the piano. I stood behind the performer. We did not dare look at one another in case we burst into uncontrollable laughter. Frau Streicher fixed her eyes on each of us in turn. It was a painful ordeal. At last the Streichers took their leave with marked coolness, and we could give rein to our merriment. That was Mahler all over: he never could say even one solitary word he did not mean.

DIARY: January 28. Final rehearsal for the concert of Mahler's songs.* Keen interest on the part of the public. It was the first time people accepted Mahler's songs. Before, there was much hostility and criticism in the press, and among the audiences.

After much debating, for and against, the rehearsals of Hans Pfitzner's *Rose vom Liebesgarten* began at the end of March. Meanwhile Pfitzner had paid me the great compliment of dedicating his string quartet to me. Many letters had passed between us and we had become friends in spite of the distance which separated us. Now he came to Vienna for the first rehearsals. He was frightfully nervous; kept a stern eye on the slightest unpunctuality on the part of any member of the company and was so self-centred that no one could hope for indulgence. I was the only person who could always calm him down.

DIARY: March 21. Yesterday Pfitzner asked me to play some old songs of mine. He said they were good and that he was very glad to find I had a real talent for composition and a sound feeling for melody. 'I wish we could work together for a time. It's such a pity about you.' What a melancholy joy coursed through my veins! A moment's bliss.

March 22. Happy times with Hauptmann. He and Gustav together – it's a joy to listen to them. Last night was rather spoilt by Pfitzner's being there. He's somehow limited. He said that the deepest and truest thing in Wagner was his Germanness. Hauptmann and Gustav both replied that the greater an artist was, the further he left nationality behind. Pfitzner writhed like a worm and left in mortification soon after. Since then he has altered. This was after a performance of *Fidelio*. Pfitzner and I had stayed at home and spent the time playing first his songs and then mine. We were to meet Mahler and Hauptmann in Meissl and Schadn's beer-cellar. In the ardour of playing we forgot the time and were late, but no one took it amiss. Pfitzner played each of his songs about ten times, or as often as I needed in order to enjoy it more thoroughly.

* On 29th January 1905, repeated on 3rd February. The programme included the first performance of the *Kindertotenlieder*, with Weidemann as soloist. (D.M.)

Today there was another argument between Mahler and Pfitzner about '*das ewig Weibliche zieht uns hinan.*'* Anything less fruitful than this discussion it would be hard to imagine. Each purposely misunderstood the other and at the end each felt insulted. Besides, Mahler is jealous.

To get the better of his jealousy he constantly asked Pfitzner in and then left us alone. We spent hours making music together and talking, but Mahler was always there for me whether he was in the room or not. However, it was uncomfortable when the three of us were together, as he and Pfitzner were not made of the same clay; I was the only link between them and their brief moments of mutual understanding soon gave out. And so, in any case, it was a more peaceable and satisfactory arrangement.

DIARY: Lovely spring day. Rehearsals at the Opera – Pfitzner's *Rose*. Mahler had a brief rehearsal of his songs for orchestra (with Weidemann) coming on afterwards, and he asked Pfitzner, who naturally was present at the rehearsal of the *Rose*, to stay for this Weidemann rehearsal; but Pfitzner, once his own rehearsal was over, was in no mood to stay any longer to please Mahler; so he said something about urgent business and hurried off. Hurried off to me. On the way he stopped only to buy me a red rose, which without a word he laid upon the piano. This did not prevent him being in a very bad temper. It was the first of May and he had met a procession of working-men in the Ring. Furious at the sight of proletarian faces, he darted down a side street and scarcely felt safe from pursuit in my room.

Mahler soon followed. He was both amused and vexed when he saw Pfitzner's flight in its true colours. But he was too happy to care: he too had met the procession in the Ring and had even accompanied it for some distance. They had all looked at him in so brotherly a way – they *were* his brothers – and they were the future!

That was enough to start the battle. It raged for hours, with ill-nature on both sides and me in the middle.

* The last line from the last scene of Goethe's *Faust*. It was a text that Mahler was to use for the final chorus of his Eighth Symphony. (D.M.)

Pfitzner often complained to me that he could not make any contact whatever with Mahler's music. He didn't think it *was* music. Mahler was aware of his opinion, but all the same he worked himself nearly to death over the rehearsals of *Die Rose vom Liebesgarten*, conducted it magnificently and was so taken with it that he exclaimed at the end of the first act on the night of the première: 'Since the *Valkyrie*, Act One, there has been nothing written to touch it!'

He was delighted by the musicianship and success of the other man.*

Hauptmann, who had been in Vienna that winter for the first night of his *Rose Bernd* at the Burgtheater, had a tender affection for Mahler which was not altogether returned. But I had an instinctive feeling that his society was, or would be, a blessing to Mahler, and so I telephoned every morning to arrange a meeting that day. Every day Mahler was confronted by the *fait accompli* and every day was better than the last. There were always only the four of us. On one occasion they talked about Christ. Hauptmann wrote *Emanuel Quint* very soon afterwards. Mahler talked in a fine exaltation and Hauptmann listened in silence. When Mahler went out of the room (we were dining at the Hotel Erzherzog Karl), Hauptmann said: 'Your husband expresses clearly what I confusedly feel. I have never got so much from anyone as I have from him.' Mahler grew more and more fond of Hauptmann; yet he was easily made impatient by his slowness of mind and laboured expression.

I was right: these two geniuses of darkness and light were bound to harmonize and give out a beautiful note.

There was a very painful incident that winter. We were in Hauptmann's box for the first night of *Rose Bernd*. At the end of the first act the door opened and a friend of ours came in: 'It's a boring play, don't you think, and pretty bad.' He got kicks and pinches in plenty, but nothing could make him see that Hauptmann was there. Mahler jumped up and pushed him through the door. We never knew whether Hauptmann heard or not. We loved the play and the playwright.

.   .   .   .   .

* The Vienna première took place on 6th April 1905. (D.M.)

We celebrated the première of *Die Rose vom Liebesgarten* in April by giving a party after the performance. Max Reinhardt, a Berlin banker (a friend of Pfitzner's), Cossmann from Munich, Roller, the Zuckerkandls, my family, the Rosés and Pfitzner were there. Mahler, to whom Pfitzner's circle was somewhat unsympathetic, began to feel bored. He got up during supper (as he often did) and went into the music-room to read a book. Nobody took offence at this except the fat banker, who was so much upset that he said he would never enter the house again. Mahler hated long sittings at table. Whoever might be present, he frequently got up and went into the next room to smoke or read, and came back again after a time. All the same, he was eager to know what we were talking about and always shouted through the wall to ask. All our friends knew of this habit of his, and did not mind it in the least.

We lived simply, but very expensively. Everything was of the best quality even if there was no luxury. This must have seemed to many very odd, but we preferred it.

One evening Zemlinsky and Schoenberg came to dinner again. As usual there was only a dark beer (Spatenbräu, of which Mahler was very fond). At first, all went merrily, but then Schoenberg's brow clouded and a discussion on musical matters, which did not seem likely to arouse violent antagonism, ended in a regular orgy of paradox on his part. At last Mahler lost patience with him. 'Oh, do turn the tap off. That's enough of your beery fantasies.' To which Schoenberg replied: 'Well, really, it is not my fault if we don't get wine to drink.'

We saw more and more of these two. At their suggestion, Mahler was elected honorary president of a composers' club which had recently been started. On 29th January, he let them have the *Wunderhorn* songs and the *Humoresques** and, at a later concert of theirs, he conducted Strauss's *Sinfonia Domestica*. These were their best attended concerts, but the club faded out, as all such enterprises do in Vienna, and probably everywhere else, unless they have the backing of 'Society'.†

I meant to go to Maiernigg in May, but Mahler asked me to

---

* At one stage, Mahler entitled some of his *Wunderhorn* songs with orchestra, *Humoresques*. (D.M.)

† Schoenberg later founded his famous Society for Private Concerts (1918), 'the aim being to accustom the public to the sound of modern music' (Erwin Stein). (D.M.)

go to Strasbourg with him. I left the children with a heavy heart.
His two concerts were on 21st and 22nd May. Mahler conducted
only his Fifth in the first programme. Richard Strauss was there too.

21 May 1905.   Strasbourg.   Alsatian Musical Festival.
       Fifth Symphony ..   ..   .. Mahler
       (Conductor, Mahler)
       Rhapsody ..   .. Brahms
       (Frau Kraus-Osborne)
       Violin Concerto in G major   .. Mozart
       (Henri Marteau)
       Sinfonia Domestica ..   ..   .. Strauss
       (Conductor, Strauss)
22 May (Mahler conducting the whole concert)
       Coriolan ..   .. Beethoven
       Piano Concerto in G Major   .. Beethoven
       (Busoni)
       An die ferne Geliebte   ..   .. Beethoven
       Ninth Symphony ..   ..   .. Beethoven

The end of the *Rhapsody* in the first concert had to be given
again in response to persistent 'encores', and Strauss, who had
only appeared in time for the final rehearsal, began to feel anxious
about the performance of his own work. He foamed at the mouth
and became violently angry. The *Domestica* was wretchedly performed: nobody played when he should.

We arrived eight days before Strauss. Mahler as usual had many
rehearsals and his performances were magnificent. After the Fifth
he and I were sitting on a balcony to enjoy the evening air. It was
outside the round artists' room and we were hidden from view.
Suddenly we heard Strauss come into the room in a fury. 'What a
circus – she ought to be singing at the Venezia in Vienna, the
cow, not at a serious concert.' 'Repeat the end – repeat the end,'
he shouted over and over again. 'Tiring out my oboes until they
can't blow another note. But of course – an old pundit like Brahms!
If I had no more shame than to end on a common chord in C
major, I should have the same success!' He raged on like this
while we sat there not knowing what to do. At last the interval
brought Kraus, Frau Osborne's husband, on the scene; he had
been told of Strauss's insulting remarks and said that, failing an

apology to his wife in writing, for which purpose he drew up a document to be signed by us as witnesses, he would call him out. It all threatened to become very unpleasant. Mahler tried in vain to pacify Kraus. He merely shouted out: 'My wife does not sing at Wanamaker's.'* The interval ended and events took their course. Strauss went fuming downstairs and ascended the podium. Mahler and I had to leave our refuge and listen to the infernal racket. Just before it ended we slunk out of the hall in a daze and back to the balcony, where as the end came we heard a scraping of chairs as the audience got up to go. And yet Strauss's vogue was such in those days that even for this chaotic performance he got something like applause, mingled with hisses; but these were to be heard too after the faultless performance of Mahler's Fifth.

Strauss joined us – fuming, followed by one or two members of the committee, who after expressing regrets, although it was not their fault that Strauss had had too few rehearsals, stood there in dismay while Strauss raved up and down like a tiger, cursing all music-festivals and all committees. In spite of this, an attempt was made to invite Strauss, Mahler and me to the banquet, an invitation he cut short by a curt refusal on behalf of all three of us. The gentlemen of the committee retired trembling, and Mahler dragged Strauss into the open air. We walked back to our hotel together and his temper made a rapid recovery. Mahler took the opportunity of telling him that it was all his own fault for conducting his work without having rehearsed it. We went on to describe his exhibition of temper, to which he replied: 'I must write and tell my wife that. She doesn't believe I've got a temper at all. But you must tell her too – give her a good fright.' He agreed now to attend the banquet with Mahler so as to remove the bad impression he had made by his loss of temper. I stayed in the hotel; I always kept out of the way of these functions. After half an hour Mahler came back laughing. They had been received, he said, first with great astonishment and then with great cordiality. Strauss thereupon treated the committee to a tremendous oration. Mahler was forgotten and was able to make his escape unobserved.

* Strauss conducted at Wanamaker's in New York during shopping hours. I was long before he was forgiven for this in America. (A.M.)

This was not the only reason why we were much alone. The Association of German Composers made a point of avoiding Mahler. Schillings gave him only a timid greeting, Rösch looked the other way. Anti-Semitism was in the ascendant and Mahler was made to feel it. There was no mistaking it; we saw how they made up parties at neighbouring tables and left us out. We did not begrudge them; we were very glad of our enforced quarantine. We went for walks in the country and over the old entrenchments. They were all overgrown and green, and breathed the spirit of peace, not war.

Friends of ours arrived from Paris – General Picquart; Painlevé, the great mathematician, afterwards French premier; Paul and Sophie Clemenceau and Baron L'Allemand – the so-called quartet of the Dreyfus affair. They arrived at noon. Picquart went straight to the concert-hall before even going to his hotel, and there he sat with his hand over his eyes, patiently waiting for the time to pass. The reason was that he had been retired owing to the Dreyfus affair, but as he might at any moment be put back on the active list, he did not like to risk crossing the German frontier without official leave; so to avoid tedious formalities he had come incognito.

Picquart impressed everybody at the first glance as a man of fine character and nobility of feeling. His intervention in the Dreyfus affair was a great deal more courageous than Zola's, who challenged the world, heroically enough, with his *J'accuse!* But Picquart knew as a soldier that he lost all by standing firm in his indictment – his honour, his profession, his livelihood and perhaps his life.

The performance of Beethoven's Ninth Symphony on this occasion was the most perfect I have ever heard. The audience was wrought up to such a pitch that it looked from my seat in the gallery as though Mahler was in danger of his life; he seemed to vanish, as a wedge-shaped mass of frenzied men and women surged towards him. Picquart, Clemenceau and I ran down into the street and round the building in pursuit of him. We could see him running, his hat in his hand, at the tip of a monstrous tidal wave. He groaned with relief as soon as he saw us. Clemenceau hailed a comfortable old landau and, before the Bacchic maniacs could reach us and take the horses out of the shafts, we had got clear away. We had a meal in an obscure little pot-house, where nobody recognized us.

Picquart, the Clemenceaus and Painlevé drove out next morning to Sesenheim, and followed up every trace left by Goethe there. They formed probably the most cultivated circle in Europe. Picquart was scarcely a human being. He was a seraphic being with eyes like a mountain spring – they were so blue and clear. He spoke little and wisely. No one could meet him without feeling his strength of character and his genius. As soon as I looked into his eyes the first time, I knew that Dreyfus had been condemned unjustly, although until that moment the disgusting outcry in the press in his favour had made me think the very opposite. Picquart spoke fluent German, knew the whole of literature, knew Mahler's music – from playing it four-handed with L'Allemand. He was a man in whom one saw the fullest development of the human spirit and not only the very pattern of a soldier.

Strauss, in spite of all, was cheerful and communicative. He had finished *Salome*, and asked Mahler whether he might play it through to him from the manuscript score. There is a story behind this. When he told Mahler he was going to make an opera of Wilde's *Salomé*, Mahler was violently opposed. He had a thousand reasons; there was first of all the moral objection, but also, neither last nor least, that the production might be barred in Catholic countries. Strauss was unconvinced, but somewhat irritated all the same, though not for long. I told Mahler afterwards I was surprised he should have tried to dissuade him. It was if he had advised a man against marrying the woman he loved.

And now the composition of the opera was finished, and there was a note of triumph in his proposal. He had discovered a piano-shop and the three of us made our way to the showroom, where there were pianos by the dozen. It had huge plate-glass windows on every side and passers-by loitered and stood still to peer in at what was going on.

Strauss played and sang to perfection. Mahler was charmed.

We came to the dance – it was missing.* 'Haven't got it done yet,' Strauss said and played on to the end, leaving this yawning gap. 'Isn't it rather risky,' Mahler remarked, 'simply leaving out the dance, and then writing it in later when you're not in the same mood?' Strauss laughed his light-hearted laugh: 'I'll fix that all right.' But he did not. The dance is the one weak spot in the score – just botched-up commonplace. Mahler was won over. A man may dare all if he has the genius to make the incredible credible.

The new production and setting of *Don Giovanni*† was an event which the musical world awaited with eager suspense. Roller's new setting, with the flanking towers, which remained throughout the whole performance but made a succession of different scenes owing to the effective use of lighting, broke new ground in its day, though it has been put in the shade since. It was the first time this method of staging by suggestion was employed, or perhaps rediscovered. Roller at that time went a good way in it without having much insight into its future developments. For the finale of *Don Giovanni* he had black velvet rolled out over the whole stage, to give the impression of the Don being devoured by darkness. It was a good idea, but it did not come off. The old theatrical fire and brimstone was more effective.

In the summer of 1905 Mahler wrote the Seventh Symphony in one burst. The 'architect's drawings', as he called them, belong to mid-summer of 1904. As he wrote the serenade‡ he was beset by Eichendorff-ish visions – murmuring springs and German romanticism. Apart from this, the symphony has no context.

In between came the songs for orchestra.§

From the Diary of Frau Ida Dehmel (widow of the poet, Richard Dehmel):
22nd March 1905: *Mahler*. I heard his name for the first time from

---

* Alma Mahler refers to the famous *Dance of the Seven Veils*. (D.M.)
† 21st December 1905. (D.M.)
‡ The symphony's fourth movement, with its evocative and innovatory use of guitar and mandolin. (D.M.)
§ Mahler would have been preparing all his late songs for their publication in 1905. (D.M.)

Nodnagel in the year '95. Then, in the same year perhaps, I went
to a concert devoted to his compositions. All paper – scarcely
twenty tickets sold, a complete flop, twenty at most of those
present (including Lechter, Wolfskehl and me) recognized that
a new star had risen. Next I heard Weingartner conduct a movement of a symphony, it even had a title in those days, 'What the
flowers in the meadow tell me' – that was all.* Mahler attended
the Dehmel night at the Ansorge-Society and afterwards we paid
him a visit at the Opera. Even if I had never heard anything
whatever about him, I should have felt at once that he was a
genius, a man of *Gefühlswucht*† (the expression is Lublinsky's, I
believe), all nerve, all energy, with a forehead, a look, a voice, all
saying: Here the world finds a sounding-board. He was not as yet
thought worthy of being compared to Strauss, a comparison
which was soon to be run to death – as it was with Liliencron-
Dehmel. Strauss then is like Liliencron, Mahler like Dehmel. By
that I don't mean to equalize the two powers. Strauss dazzles
and sparkles, tells stories and keeps close to the earth. Mahler
both glows and illumines, points upwards and carries us with
him far beyond the individual destiny. So much I could read from
his personality that time in Vienna: I know it now from his
Fifth Symphony. You too were strongly drawn to him that time,
and we gladly accepted his invitation to hear the Berlioz *Requiem*
with him next day (conducted well enough by Schuch) and then
to a meal with him and his closest friends. That was a wonderful
afternoon. Besides us there were Carl Moll and his wife, Roller
and Klimt. It was one of those occasions when every sense is
gratified, leaving in the memory a feeling of complete satisfaction.
There was the sight of his radiantly beautiful wife, who made no
secret of her pregnancy; the bright, comfortable, even luxurious
flat, good food and good wine; and a company each member of
which could stand up and say, I am I. Among all the refinements
of Vienna, this was the strong note.

Then, in Weimar, in October 1904, another wonderful day,
bound up for me with Mahler. We were invited to breakfast at
the Ludwig von Hofmanns. There were Frau Förster-Nietzsche,

* The Minuet from the Third Symphony. (D.M.
† 'charged with feeling'. (D.M.)

Ansorge, Van de Velde and his wife and his pupil Fräulein von Scheel, Dora Hitz, Herr and Frau von Münchhausen (not Boerries), and Gerhart Hauptmann. It would have been even better with a few omissions. These charming art-lovers bring everything down to the same level of pleasant conversation. As for Frau Förster-Nietzsche, she only shows her metal as the roused lioness, and Grete Hauptmann and Baroness Munchhausen, piquant and charming as they are, haven't a trace of the proud dignity, the radiance or the resources of Frau Mahler and her mother. Hauptmann took me in and we talked of Mahler. The enthusiasm he expressed for his personality might be put down to hypnosis. For him Mahler is genius personified, even though he knows nothing as yet of his music and judges of him solely from his personality and as a conductor. His idea of perfect bliss is *Tristan* conducted by Mahler and produced by Roller. Whenever he sees that Mahler is conducting works of his own anywhere, he can hardly restrain himself from rushing off there.

So there we were, and Mahler with us. We were with him for two hours before the final rehearsal, said all we wanted to say after it, on Monday I heard his concert, and early on Tuesday while you were in Halle I travelled with him to Berlin. And now I may well allow myself to have an opinion both as a human and a musical being, and it is that if at first Mahler the man made me believe in Mahler the musician, I now believe so firmly in Mahler the musician that I am ready to forgive whatever symptoms of the all-too-human he may show. Sparing as I am in my use of the word, I now accord him the title of genius. This Fifth Symphony of his carried me through every world of feeling. I heard in it the relation of adult man to everything that lives, heard him cry to mankind out of his loneliness, cry to man, to home, to God, saw him lying prostrate, heard him laugh his defiance and felt his calm triumph. For the first time in my life a work of art made me weep, a strange sense of contrition came over me which almost brought me to my knees. The *Adagietto* may for me have lacked something, and in the last movement I noticed some check to the logical development. Nevertheless, this symphony is a master-piece of the first rank, and at a second hearing it was precisely the last movement which engaged my passionate attention: I positively drank in every note. Mahler had warned me in advance that the Scherzo might seem obscure – no critic so far had known what to make of it. It was the Scherzo that made the strongest impression on you, as by the way it did on Brecher too, who told us it came first in order of composition.

I was extremely interested, to come to human matters, by what you had to tell us of the Meier–Graefe questionnaire about a national slogan. There was a directness and lucidity in Mahler's reply which pleased me very much. He said he would never have anything to do with such queries because he thought them utterly superfluous and boring, and that he did not either feel the least need to set himself against them, and if he were to take any part in your questionnaire with its national reference, people would only ask what a Jew had to do with it. Besides, music was his means of expression, not the pen, of which he was a horribly clumsy and reluctant manipulator. 'Perhaps if I were better at it I might employ it more. But I doubt it. There's Wagner as a shocking example. What is the use of all those volumes he wrote? You have to forget them before you can begin to love the genius of Wagner as it deserves to be loved.'

He was delighted by the reception his symphony had had in Hamburg. The warmth of the applause after the rehearsal alone was a great satisfaction to him, and on the way to Berlin he told me more of what he felt about it. Travelling and particularly stopping in hotels was a martyrdom. 'But you travel all the same – for the sake of your children, no doubt,' I put in.

'Do you mean my real children or my musical children?'

I had meant only his musical ones.

'I have to think of both. Actually, I should like best to live only for my compositions, and, to tell the truth, I am beginning to neglect my operatic duties, but if I gave up my salary as Director of the Opera I should have to make it good in some other way, as a guest conductor perhaps. I doubt whether I shall ever make a penny from performances of my own works. So that's one reason for my travels. The other is this: my Fifth Symphony was performed the other day in Prague and Berlin, each time to little effect. So I thought to myself: Is it the fault of the symphony or the conductor? Now Hamburg has given the answer. We musicians are worse off than writers in that respect. Anyone can read a book, but a musical score is a book with seven seals. Even the conductors who can decipher it, present it to the public soaked in their own interpretations. For that reason there must be a tradition, and no one can create it but I.'

He asked my opinion of the settings of Dehmel's poems,* and was obviously delighted when I said we found Fried promising. That was his own opinion. We agreed too about Pfitzner. Only the way composers search for librettos seems to him ludicrous (in Pfitzner's case too). Music, he said, was superfluous for a completed drama; no professional playwright would leave his work uncompleted, so that a composer could bring out what he himself had passed over; and no music, however inspired, could make a great work of a bad play. No one, therefore, who had not both gifts, as Wagner had, should attempt it. It even seemed to him a profanity when composers ventured to set perfect poems to music; it was as if a sculptor chiselled a statue from marble and a painter came along and coloured it. He himself had only appropriated some few bits from the *Wunderhorn* – from earliest childhood his relationship to the book had been particularly close. The poems were not complete in themselves, but blocks of marble which anyone might make his own.

If you ask me when he seemed to me human, all-too-human, my answer is when he spoke of Strauss and the Strauss and Hauptmann marriages. He only spoke of Strauss's music very cursorily, but stressed Strauss's way of making a business of it. Strauss was the businessman first and foremost and an artist only in the second place: when the two came into collision it was the businessman who won. In this I detected a little envy of Strauss's success, in terms of money, that is. Of Strauss's marriage he spoke with contempt, even with disgust. He thought it verged on masochism. My own observations, I confessed, led me to the same conclusion. I was only once in Frau Strauss de Ahna's company, at 25 Parkstrasse, Pankow. She and her husband paid a call when Kessler and Hofmannsthal were there too. The exhibition she gave in that short space of time and in the presence

* Dehmel's texts attracted many composers, among them Richard Strauss, Pfitzner, Schoenberg and Max Reger. (D.M.)

of perfect strangers exceeded in tactlessness and vulgarity the worst I have ever known any woman guilty of. 'Oh – men! Keep them on a tight rein, that's the only way'; and she went through the motions of holding the reins in one hand and the whip in the other. She told us among other things that her husband spent every summer at her parents' country place with her and their child and the nurse, 'at my expense, you may say'. When she got back to Berlin she took two months' housekeeping money – 'his money, you understand', and spent it on the adornment of her person, to show, as she pointed out triumphantly, that she wasn't going to have him, his child and the nursemaid living on *her* money, 'what will be mine one day, anyway'. Then she heard Kessler in the next room talking to Strauss with admiration of his *Zarathustra* or *Eulenspiegel*. This put her into a furious rage. 'There they go, talking him up to write stuff no one's ever going to perform. Who wants it? Bar that lot. I know I don't. I don't understand it. He ought to write what people want to hear.'

I couldn't dispute Mahler's opinion of Strauss's marriage, but I found it harder to swallow what he had to say of Hauptmann's. I told him what Grete Hauptmann said to you (at the Hofmanns' last year). She reminded you of the verses you had written in her album when she was fifteen. They had had a profound influence on her: you had called her a sprite or wood-nymph. 'That,' she told you in Weimar, 'was the origin of the Rautendelein.' This story put Mahler in a sort of fury. Every human being, he said, was the product of generations. His character was fixed before he came into the world. Nobody should dare to dictate his own character. Everyone obeyed unalterable law. Grete would do far better to lay aside her notion of being a pixie, 'her cold-hearted egoism, in other words. Poor Gerhart – I'm sorry for him. He's far too good to her. If she were my wife she would have to sing small.' This did not go down very well with me, as you may imagine. I had already mentioned Mahler's wife and said what a wonderful impression her sunny disposition had made on us. This was accepted with pleasure, but in reply he gave as an instance of her merits that she made all the piano scores of his symphonies. That might have sounded marvellous but for the hint of making good use of her. In short, the man whom I call a genius behaves as if he were a delicate instrument to be fenced round by the barbed wire entanglement of egoism. To pass to quite another matter, he is the first Jew, except my father, to impress me as a man – one who doesn't, to put it crudely, strike me as impotent. I am glad that such a beautiful, proud, strong Christian girl has married him.

[It would seem that this intimate Diary was addressed to Frau Dehmel's husband. (D.M.)]

Splendid Isolation

1906

Mahler's life in the winter months was very different from the life he lived during the short holiday at Maiernigg, but just as strictly regulated. He got up at seven, shaved and rang his bell. The parlourmaid brought his breakfast and the newspapers. The first was rapidly disposed of and the second merely glanced at. Then he sat down at once at his writing-table, which no one was allowed to touch, and revised or orchestrated the summer's work. The sheets lay ready to his hand and he worked on them whenever he had a moment to spare. Shortly before nine he came into my room; then after paying the children a visit he hurried off to be in time to open his correspondence at the Opera before his subordinates arrived.

After lunch the newspapers came into their own. They fell sheet by sheet from the sofa to the floor, which was soon littered knee-deep.

This winter Mahler put the finishing touches to his Seventh Symphony in the mornings and made a fair copy of the score; and on 29th January *Seraglio* was produced, again with Roller's towers, which, however, were made better use of this time. It was an excellent performance. Immediately after it, Mahler took a few days' holiday, which we spent at Semmering. There was deep snow and we went driving in sledges, drank rum and indefatigably sang the great Quartet from *Seraglio*. I still remember a talk we had about Mozart during a sledge-drive. Mahler talking a lot about 'Constanzerl', whose speedy remarriage he could not forgive, and about Mozart's wretched life. He loved him as a human being more than anyone who ever lived.

The Marriage of Figaro was given on 30th March, in Mahler's edition. It was one of his finest productions and, with *Don Giovanni*, *Fidelio* and *Tristan*, one of the sacred few he kept under his own hand and eye.

Mahler went to Breslau this winter where he conducted his Third Symphony in response to the invitation of Albert Neisser, president of the Music Society. He was very fond of Neisser and his wife, who welcomed all persons of distinction to their cultured house. While he was away D'Albert came to Vienna with his umpteenth wife and played and sang me his *Flauto Solo* in the hope that Mahler might perform it – as he did.* D'Albert played, sang and mimed his small opus enchantingly.

In May Mahler and I went to Graz for the first performance in Austria of *Salome*.† It was our only chance of hearing it, as Mahler had not succeeded in getting the censor to pass it for Vienna. His proposal to substitute Baalschem for the name of Jochanaan was not found acceptable either; his persistence went so far as almost to make a cabinet question of it. We found Strauss awaiting us at the Elephant Hotel, and he at once proposed an expedition by motor-car that afternoon to see the Golling waterfalls. We set off immediately after lunch. It had been raining and we skidded on the wet road, but Strauss thought nothing of that. We arrived at a little inn and after refreshment walked on to the waterfalls, with which we were so delighted that we could not tear ourselves away. At last hunger drove us back to the bare wooden table at the inn, but here again it was so delightful that Strauss refused to budge. 'Bother it all, they can't start without me. Let 'em wait,' he said savagely. Dusk was falling. It began to get chilly. Mahler jumped up. 'Right. If you won't go, then I will – and conduct in your place.'

That settled it. Strauss reluctantly got to his feet. Mahler urged the chauffeur to hurry up. Strauss told him to take his time. It seemed as if the wrong one of the two had stage fright, but perhaps Strauss was not so unmoved as he wished us to believe. He may have been hiding his tremors under a show of frivolity.

The performance was a great success, and there was no disturbance on the part of the Christian-Socialists, as it had been feared there might be. Strauss joined us for breakfast next morning and started pitching into Mahler for taking everything too seriously. 'That old cow-shed of an Opera, for example. You

* Vienna première on 28th November 1906. (D.M.)
† On 16th May, Strauss conducting. (D.M.)

ought to go easy on it. No one'll thank you for it if you racket
yourself to bits. A pig-sty that won't even perform *Salome*. Not
worth it, I tell you.'

There was a lot in what he said; I had always been of the same
opinion, for however important his work for the Opera might be,
it was nothing in comparison with even a single note of his own
compositions. The one was ephemeral, the other eternal.

Mahler used to say: 'Strauss and I tunnel from opposite sides
of the mountain. One day we shall meet.'

On the journey back to Vienna we were standing in the corridor,
as we usually did. The country was green after much rain. We
were discussing success and its fallacies. An old gentleman was
standing close to us and obviously listening to every word we said.
It was Peter Rosegger. Mahler denied that there was any truth
behind any success whatever. Had we not just come from the
première of *Salome*? Tumults of applause – and yet we were
convinced that not one in a hundred really understood the music.
We ourselves, even during the performance, had grave doubts
about the whole theme and subject-matter, about the music for
the dance, which we did not like, and about a great deal else, in
spite of so much that showed the hand of a master – and yet the
public without hesitation gave a verdict of success. Whose was
the verdict and on what authority? Rosegger said the voice of
the people was the voice of God, to which we replied by asking
whether he meant the people here and now or the people as pos-
terity. He was a charming old gentleman, at peace with himself
and all the world, a complete contrast to Mahler, to whom peace
was unknown. He felt himself superior, but Mahler felt no inferiority.

One evening he and my mother and I drove from Klagenfurt
to Krumpendorf, where we were met by our servant who had
rowed over in the boat. It was a night of brilliant moonlight.
Mahler sat facing me, his overcoat buttoned up to his chin. His
long white face, his long, bronze-like forehead had a phosphorescent sheen. He looked frightful. He looked like death masquerad-
ing as a monk. I told him so, vainly hoping to exorcise my ghostly
pang of dread. He laughed and told us that he once went to a
fancy-dress ball in Hamburg as a monk, and nobody liked to

accost him: he looked too much like the real thing. Savonarola must have looked as he did that night.

Mahler had a reading-rehearsal of his Sixth Symphony with the Philharmonic in the spring. The notes of the bass drum in the last movement were not loud enough for him; so he had an enormous chest made and stretched with hide. It was to be beaten with clubs. He had this engine brought in before the rehearsal. The members of the orchestra crowded round the monster on the lighted stage – the rest of the house was in darkness. There was the breathless silence of suspense. The drummer raised his arm and smote: the answer was a dull, subdued boom. Once more – with all his strength: the result was the same. Mahler lost patience. Seizing the bludgeon from the man's hand he whirled it aloft and brought it down with a mighty whack. The answering boom was no louder than before. Everyone laughed. And now they brought out the old bass drum again – and the true thunder came. Nevertheless, Mahler had this chest dispatched at great cost to Essen, where it was again tried out, and finally rejected as unfit for service.

There was another similar episode. Mahler was once plaguing the orchestra so unmercifully over the three opening accents of Beethoven's Fifth Symphony that some jumped up to go and some sat in stubborn fury, resolved not to play another note. Mahler seeing this shouted out: 'Gentlemen, keep your fury for the performance, then *at last* we shall have the opening played as it should be.'

The music festival of the United German Music Society was held this year at Essen. The first performance in public of Mahler's Sixth was on the programme.*

Mahler went there alone. I now had two children and was not strong enough to accompany him, as I should have liked to do. He wrote to me in great excitement over the work and the rehearsals and also over a new friend he had made. This was Ossip Gabrilovitch, to whom he seemed to grow more and more attached. I arrived for the final rehearsals. The only person there of whom Mahler took much account was Strauss; the rest were

* 27th May 1906. (D.M.)

more or less insignificant. Oskar Fried followed Mahler like his shadow.

None of his works moved him so deeply at its first hearing as this. We came to the last rehearsals, to the dress-rehearsal – to the last movement with its three great blows of fate. When it was over, Mahler walked up and down in the artists' room, sobbing, wringing his hands, unable to control himself. Fried, Gabrilovitch, Buths and I stood transfixed, not daring to look at one another. Suddenly Strauss came noisily in, noticing nothing. 'Mahler, I say, you've got to conduct some funeral overture or other tomorrow before the Sixth – their mayor has died on them. So vulgar, that sort of thing — But what's the matter? What's up with you? But —' and out he went as noisily as he had come in, quite unmoved, leaving us petrified.

On the day of the concert Mahler was so afraid that his agitation might get the better of him that out of shame and anxiety he did not conduct the symphony well. He hesitated to bring out the dark omen behind this terrible last movement.

Mengelberg came only in time for the performance. We looked in for a moment at the supper-party after the concert for the sake of appearances. Mahler was in such a state that I dared not let him go alone; but his gloom vanished when he got there. He introduced Mengelberg to me; he seemed to me like Loge. I was planted ceremoniously next to Strauss at supper. 'Why ever does Mahler smother his effect in the last movement?' he said. 'He gets his *fortissimo* and then damps it down. Can't understand that at all.' He never did understand. He spoke simply as the showman. Anyone who understands the symphony at all understands why the first blow is the strongest, the second weaker and the third – the death-blow – the weakest of all. Perhaps the momentary effect might be greater in the inverse order. But that is not the point.

We met Strauss in the street the day we arrived at Essen. Mahler had just had a great success in Vienna* with his Second Symphony, which had been repeated. Strauss came up to Mahler, bawling out: 'Hullo, you celebrity of Vienna, how do you feel

---

* I cannot trace this performance. He had, however, recently returned from a highly successful visit to Amsterdam. See Letters 91–93. (D.M.)

Gustav Mahler

Alma Maria Schindler (Alma Mahler), 1899

Alma Mahler and her daughter, Anna

Richard Strauss and his wife, Pauline, 1914

Gustav Mahler in Vienna with Max Reinhardt, Carl Moll
and Hans Pfitzner, *c.* 1905
Gerhart Hauptmann (*in foreground*) with Alban Berg and
his wife, Helene (*left*), and Countess Gravina
(*centre*), and Margarete Hauptmann

I. Verwandlung.

Saal im königlichen Pallaste. Minister, Höflinge und Diener. — König tritt auf im Schlafrock die Krone auf dem Kopfe, in der Rechten den Zepter, in der Linken den Reichsapfel.

Alle (hymnenartig)

> Herr König! Herr König!
> Wir grüssen unterthänig!
> Gott schenk' dir langes Leben
> — Gesundheit auch daneben!

König Ich danke Euch, meine lieben Unterthanen!
Ich will mich bemühen, euch immer weise und
gnädig regieren. (zu einem Diener). Ist mein
Tochter Emma schon aufgestanden?

Diener Sie ist schon in aller Frühe mit ihren
Jungfrauen in den Wald hinunter gegangen.

A page of the libretto of *Rübezahl* in Mahler's manuscript

Arnold Schoenberg (*centre*)

In Prague (1908), Bruno Walter talking to Gustav Mahler. On the
right is Alma Mahler.

now?' We were so upset that we walked on without a word. After this we saw him often in the distance, but kept out of his way.

It was a habit of his to boost quite mediocre talent, which redounded to the credit of his heart without raising up any formidable rival. For example, there was a musician called Hermann Bischoff, whose one and the same symphony Strauss got performed annually at this festival of the Music Society and of whom he said darkly: 'You wait. This year it'll come off.'* But it never did. A work does not become a work of art merely from being taken out and put away again.

He now became very scathing about Mahler as a composer; he was all right as a producer of operas.

But Pfitzner too was incapable of appreciating Mahler.

The Jewish question touched Mahler very closely. He had often suffered bitterly from it, particularly when Cosima Wagner, whom he greatly esteemed, tried to bar his appointment in Vienna because he was a Jew. He had had to be baptized before he could aspire to such a high position under the Royal and Imperial exchequer. In any case he had a strong leaning to Catholic mysticism, whereas the Jewish ritual had never meant anything to him. He could never pass a church without going in; he loved the smell of incense and Gregorian chants. But he was not a man who ever deceived himself, and he knew that people would not forget he was a Jew because he was sceptical of the Jewish religion and baptized a Christian. Nor did he wish it forgotten, even though he frequently asked me to warn him when he gesticulated too much, because he hated to see others do so and thought it ill-bred. No one dared tell him funny stories about Jews; they made him seriously angry. And how right he was in this.

His religious songs, the Second, the Eighth, and all the chorales in the symphonies are rooted in his own personality – and not brought in from outside! He never denied his Jewish origin. Rather, he emphasized it. He was a believer in Christianity, a Christian Jew, and he paid the penalty. I was a Christian Pagan and got off scot-free.

·   ·   ·   ·   ·

* Actually, the symphony received its première at Essen on 24th May, a few days before the première of Mahler's Sixth. (D.M.)

After we arrived at Maiernigg, there was the usual fortnight during which, nearly every year, he was haunted by the spectre of failing inspiration. Then one morning just as he crossed the threshold of his studio up in the wood, it came to him – '*Veni creator spiritus*'.* He composed and wrote down the whole opening chorus to the half-forgotten words. But music and words did not fit in – the music had overlapped the text. In a fever of excitement he telegraphed to Vienna and had the whole of the ancient Latin hymn telegraphed back. The complete text fitted the music exactly. Intuitively he had composed the music for the full strophes.

He worked with superhuman energy this summer, and often played some of his new compositions to me; he was boundlessly happy and exalted. Unfortunately, he had to break off and go to Salzburg to conduct *The Marriage of Figaro* at a music festival.† The performance was given with the whole company from the Opera, but Mahler kept out of the way of everyone, except Roller. Nevertheless, he ran into Lilli Lehmann in the street. She called out to him scornfully that if he wanted to hear true Mozart he must come to her *Don Giovanni*. Mahler went the same evening with Roller and was both disgusted and amused by the amateurishness of the whole affair. He said to Roller in an undertone (misquoting from *The Magic Flute*):

> Unless a man their hearts do guide,
> These cows will wander far and wide.

A woman in front of them overheard and turned round. It was Lilli Lehmann.

The following is taken from an article in the *Neue Freie Presse* by Korngold, which appeared in the summer of 1926.

'*Figaro* at Salzburg: the words conjure up an imperishable memory. Gustav Mahler came to Mozart's town in 1906. Visions of a new symphony crowded on him; but he came, happy in these premonitions, in a mood not far from exuberance. A muchthumbed volume protruded from his coat pocket: it was *Faust*. The theme of the medieval religious poet, which was to dominate

---

* The opening of the Eighth Symphony. (D.M.)
† The performance was given on 18th August 1906. (D.M.)

the first part of the symphony – it was the Eighth – had taken shape. Now the parallel passages from Goethe were waiting. In this mood the Director of the Vienna Opera caught sight of his critic in a café and he looked like a wilful cherub about to flit in through the open window. It was in this mood too that he was inspired by the tiny theatre to perform a miracle of artistic genius in perfect keeping with it. This *Figaro* of his at Salzburg was the ideal *Figaro* in its enchanting grace, its light-winged conversational tone and the incomparable balance of the whole ensemble. No one who was present on that occasion can ever forget it.'

Mahler had played and sung to me the chorus '*Alles Vergängliche ist nur ein Gleichnis*.'* I was so utterly spell-bound by it that after a few days I sent it him from memory, fully instrumented and harmonized. As he was leaving he asked me what I would like from Salzburg, and I said Salzburg marzipan. When I met him at Klagenfurt on his return, he got out dragging a large box after him. Marzipan potatoes had now to be consumed by the hundred and the whole neighbourhood rejoiced in his wild extravagance – and absence of mind.

Once back at Maiernigg he worked feverishly at the Eighth, the conclusion of which was the end of Part 2 of *Faust*.

This was our last summer of peace and beauty and content. There followed years of horror, years which swept away the very foundations on which we had built.

We had to return to Vienna at the beginning of September, as usual; and to avoid being in town he went to stay at Dornbach with a dear old lady who had been a second mother to me as a child [Frau Conrat].

Here is a quotation from a letter from Dr. R. Horn about this visit: 'The alarming guest did not make such an upset as they expected. When he found his apples for breakfast, lunch and dinner and the first volume of Bielschowsky's biography of Goethe at Dornbach and the second in Walfischgasse,† he was in heaven; Goethe and apples are two things he cannot live without.

* The closing *Chorus Mysticus* from the Eighth. (D.M.)
† Frau Conrat put a room at his disposal in her flat in Vienna as well as in her country villa. (A.M.)

'We had many philosophic walks together; it was all I could do to snatch my afternoon siesta. Mahler is a notable thinker after the pattern of his fiery spirit, a deep and often an inspired one, but usually a thinker by fits and starts, which, I may add, does not worry me in the least.'

When Mahler was alone in Vienna, he stayed as a rule with one of our friends or at my mother's. He had to be hedged about or else he felt unhappy. After conducting at the Opera he liked going to the café of the Hotel Imperial, where he foregathered with a few of his friends who had been to the Opera. Bruno Walter and Roller were almost always among them. But he ate scarcely anything and after drinking a glass of beer (in spite of pangs of conscience) he left early. As soon as I returned, the time-table he ordained came into force. And a profound solitude enclosed us both.

In October there was the première of Erlanger's *Le Juif polonais*,* the work of an eclectic, which Mahler produced only because of its use of bells in a manner recalling the opening passage of his own Fourth Symphony. I told him so after the première – an event of little significance – and he could not deny it.

Our Paris friends, Paul Painlevé, Madame Ramazotti, Georges Picquart, Paul and Sophie Clemenceau and Baron L'Allemand, all champions of Dreyfus and close friends, paid us a visit in Vienna in October. Mahler got up a galaxy of opera in their honour: *Figaro*, *Don Giovanni*, *Tristan*. He conducted every day for their benefit and all Vienna was open-mouthed at such a gala week. But no one knew the reason for it.

On the night of 19th October, just at that breathless moment when Tristan let go the helm at Isolde's bidding and the motif of destiny was heard, a man in one of the boxes got up and, with one nervous look at his watch and one last reluctant look at the stage, hurriedly left the Opera. It was General Picquart. He had had a telegram in cipher from Georges Clemenceau recalling him instantly to take over the portfolio of Minister for War. Our festivities were upset.

* On 4th October 1906. (D.M.)

On his card he wrote:

Dear Master, forgive me. I must leave for Paris immediately. My warmest thanks for your friendly welcome and the rare artistic treat you provided for me.

My kindest regards to Frau Mahler and the Molls —

3, rue Ivon, Villarceaux   GENERAL PICQUART

He, as well as Paul Painlevé, remained my friends after Mahler's death. I saw Picquart every year in Paris, whither he always came as soon as he knew I was there. And Painlevé paid Vienna several visits and always stayed with us. The last time he complained bitterly of his 'nightmare', as he called Hitler. 'Hitler,' I told him, 'was not born at Braunau, but at Versailles,' to which he replied with his abrupt: '*Oui, oui, oui – vous avez tout à fait raison.*' Only a man with a great and open mind like his could have said that.

Our elder child used to go to Mahler's studio every morning. They held long conversations there together. Nobody has ever known what about. I never disturbed them. We had a fussy English nurse who took her to his door, as clean and neat as a new pin. By the time Mahler brought her back she was usually smeared with jam from top to toe. It was my job to pacify the English nurse. But they were so happy together after their talk that I took a secret pleasure in these occasions.

She was his child entirely. Her beauty and waywardness, and her unapproachability, her black curls and large blue eyes, foretold that she would be a danger later on. But if she was allowed only a short life, she was chosen to be his joy for a few years, and that in itself is worth an eternity. It was his wish to be buried in her grave. And his wish was fulfilled.

Mahler often used to say: 'An artist shoots in the dark, not knowing whether he hits or what he hits.'

Also: 'There is only one education – example. To live by example is everything.'

He was a foe to all explanations, wranglings and gossiping.

'I must keep on the heights. I cannot let anything irritate me or drag me down. It is hard enough as it is to keep up on that level all the time.'

Sorrow and Dread

1907

This year, so blackly underlined in the calendar of our life, began like any other year. There were beautiful productions at the Opera; at home, work and our peaceful routine. Mahler and Roller, from February onwards, made new productions of the *Valkyrie* [4th February], *Lohengrin* [27th February], and Gluck's *Iphigenie* [18th March]. The last was the most successful, the most faultless of all their collaborations.

In the early spring we went with friends to Brünn [Brno], where Mahler conducted his First Symphony in the way I had always thought of it. I had noticed that in the finale he had lately passed over the first appearance of the climax and chosen its second appearance as the highlight. For me, the first remained the essential one, and on this occasion he restored the earlier interpretation by emphasizing it strongly, recognizing that this passage was indeed the more important. He turned round to me at the rehearsal when it was played for the first time. I beamed. He tapped, and had the whole passage repeated, although it had gone brilliantly, simply for me to hear.*

Nedbal, too, noticed how in the theatre one evening Mahler put his arm under mine on the marble balustrade, so that my bare forearm should not rest on the cold stone. Nedbal often told this story afterwards with tears in his eyes. Mahler began at that time to have a new and stronger feeling for me, a conscious feeling in contrast with his earlier self-absorption.

On the next day but one after the performance at Brünn he set off for St. Petersburg; and meanwhile, before coming to the tragic events in store for us, I will relate some of the more cheerful episodes of his early years, as he himself related them to me.

Bruckner had two pupils who made all the piano scores of his

* I assume that Alma Mahler must be referring here to the two big D major climaxes in the finale – cf. Figs. 34 and 56 in the score. (D.M.)

symphonies but seem to have bullied and tormented him. They
were two brothers called Schalk. Bruckner was very fond of
Mahler and entrusted the piano-duet edition of his Third Symphony to him.* When Mahler brought him the first movement
Bruckner was childishly pleased and said with a roguish smile:
'Now I shan't need the Schalks any more!' This saying became a
household word with us and was dragged in on all possible, and
impossible, occasions.

In those early days he used often to foregather with Bruckner
at midday. Bruckner stood the beer and Mahler had to pay for
his own rolls; but as he generally had no money, he had to make
his midday meal on beer alone. Bruckner was always surrounded
by large numbers of young musicians, to whom he talked with
childlike unrestraint. But if there were Jews present, he always
– if he had occasion to say anything about Jews – gave them the
courtesy title of 'the Honourable Israelites'.

Mahler had a friend whom he looked up to and admired. His
name was Hans Rott; it was he whose symphony, although the
better of the two, failed to win the prize. Rott's mother once
knocked at Bruckner's door on a hot summer day to ask how her
son was progressing. In response to a loud 'Come in!' she
entered the room. Bruckner advanced stark naked to shake her
by the hand. She fled screaming, but for a long time he could
not understand 'what was up with the woman'. When engrossed
in composition he forgot everything else, and on hot days it was his
custom to compose in his tub with the score on a stool beside him.

He was not, strictly speaking, Mahler's teacher, but he had a
regard for him as a young man of promise. Very odd stories
about his methods of teaching went the round. His methods were
simple but graphic. He used to ask his pupils: 'Know what a
suspension in music is? No? Well, look here.' He produced a
filthy bit of rag out of his trouser-pocket. 'Dirty, eh? That's a
discord.' Next he pulled out a rather cleaner one. 'There, you see
– that's better. Been resolved.' And now he displayed a snow-
white handkerchief. 'There you are – and now we're in the tonic.'

Bruckner once taught at a girls' school, but was abruptly

* This appeared in 1878 and was Mahler's first publication. He was aided in his
task by Rudolf Krzyzanowski. (D.M.)

dismissed on account of improprieties he committed. No one believed it of him for a moment. His innocence only could have been at the bottom of it.

Many years later Siegfried Ochs told me a touching story, in which he himself had played a part. Ochs was conducting a Bruckner Mass in Berlin at a music festival, and afterwards he was giving a party in Bruckner's honour. Bruckner telephoned in the afternoon to say that he must either come with his fiancée or not at all. Ochs had a presentiment that something must be very wrong and rushed off to the hotel where Bruckner was staying. He found him in despair. The chambermaid had suddenly come in the night before – and, in short, in the morning she said with tears that he had robbed her of her innocence and would have to marry her. So Bruckner promised to do so. Ochs summoned the girl at once and asked her how much she wanted. The sum was considerable. Nevertheless, Bruckner's gratitude was embarrassing in its effusiveness.

Mahler's love of Bruckner was life-long. He gave performances of all his symphonies one after the other in New York, although they had a very bad press. In Vienna he proclaimed his merits as a matter of course.

In the title-page of his copy of Bruckner's *Te Deum*, he crossed out the words: For solo voices, chorus and orchestra, organ *ad libitum*,' and wrote: 'For the tongues of angels, heaven-blest, chastened hearts, and souls purified in the fire!'

When he was twenty Mahler went to Bad Hall, where the father of Zwerenz, the *prima donna*, appointed him conductor of the summer-theatre orchestra in a sense which must be unique. His duties were to put out the music on the music-stands before each performance, to dust the piano and to collect the music again after the performance. During the intervals he had to wheel the baby, Mizzi Zwerenz, round the theatre in her pram. He drew the line, however, when he was required to deputize on the stage. He regretted later that his pride had stood in the way, as the lost opportunity would have taught him much that was never likely to come his way again.

While there he got into what – for him – was very strange company. The painter, Angeli, was surrounded by an admiring circle

of young men of fashion, who invited Mahler to join their gatherings. He was flattered by the attentions of the first persons of
birth and breeding he had encountered. He blossomed forth. They
went on long expeditions together, which of course withdrew him
more and more from his duties, until one day he was so late for
the performance that he was dismissed. His new friends escorted
him in a body to the station and he parted from them with the
promise to look them all up in Vienna. He was delighted to have
such fine fellows as friends, and as soon as he heard they were back
in Vienna he kept his promise; but every door was closed to him.
He felt at once that he was rebuffed as a Jew and, avoiding new
acquaintances for the future, fell back on his boyhood friends.
(The slight may have been not for the Jew but the holiday
acquaintance.)

'I am thrice homeless,' he used often to say. 'As a native of
Bohemia in Austria, as an Austrian among Germans, and as a
Jew throughout all the world. Everywhere an intruder, never
welcomed.'

After Hall Mahler went to Laibach, where his remarkable
personality quickly impressed both the public and his colleagues
of the theatre. He had enormous horn-rimmed spectacles made
for him so that he could see well in all directions, and got to work
in earnest, rehearsing Marguerite (in *Faust*) without the soldiers'
chorus – a single soldier marched across the stage, singing the
chorus in Act IV, and so on. Once during a rehearsal he preached
a sermon to a singer on her loose morals, whereupon she swung
herself on to the piano and slapping her thighs informed him
that the purity of his own morals aroused her utter contempt.
(The same thing happened to him in Hamburg. When the singer,
Sch.-H.* saw that her attentions were thrown away she gave them
up and talked malicious scandal about him instead.)

His position at Laibach became uncomfortable. A ring of hatred
closed round him. Reading in the newspaper that the conductor
of the orchestra at Cassel had absconded, leaving a vacancy, he
went straight to the station, without giving notice either of his
departure or of his arrival. He was interviewed at once by the
Director of the Opera at Cassel, who asked him whether he could

* The contralto, Ernestine Schumann-Heink (1861–1936). (D.M.)

undertake *Martha* without rehearsal. Mahler said yes, although he had never seen a note of it. He asked if he might have the score just to refresh his memory in the course of the afternoon. During that afternoon he learned the whole score by heart, and conducted so brilliantly at night that he was engaged on the spot.

And yet his peace and happiness soon gave out. He fell in love with two singers at the same time, who put their heads together to make fun of him. Tormented by his feelings, he wrote verses to both, not knowing they were friends and showed his verses to each other. If he finished a poem in the middle of the night, he dispatched it at once by messenger, regardless of the lateness of the hour and the fury these untimely offerings provoked. Driven to distraction at last by gossip and his divided feelings, he left Cassel hurriedly towards the end of the season, and once in the train he was a free man again.

Next he became second conductor in Leipzig, with Arthur Nikisch as his friend and supporter. It was through him he got to know Carl Maria von Weber's grandson, with whose wife – years older than himself – he fell in love. A time of tribulation and bliss began for both. Her influence set him off composing again. He had given it up in the stress of his life as a hunted and harried musician. As he had a passionate devotion to Jean Paul, he wrote a symphony, which he called *Titan* and which was given its first performance, with this title, at the Weimar music festival.*

Later when he was continually asked to give clues to the various romantic situations in the music, he became convinced of the futility of so-called programme-music. So he abolished the title and his *Titan* Symphony became what we know today as the First.

Frau von Weber returned his passion and their mutual feeling was deepened by the musical studies they pursued together. One of these was the picking out from among Weber's manuscript

---

* Alma Mahler's memory is at fault here. The symphony was not originally entitled *Titan* and the first performance was given at Budapest, under Mahler, on 20th November 1889. The Weimar performance which is referred to here took place on 3rd June 1894, by which time the work was certainly known as *Titan*. (D.M.)

remains the notes and sketches for the *Three Pintos*, out of which Mahler pieced the opera together.* Its content, however, was as much Mahler as Weber, and yet it was still a patchwork which could not hold its own on any stage.

Finally their love rose to such a pitch that they resolved on flight together. But deep as Mahler's love was, his fear of the final step was deeper. He was a poor man and he had his family to support. Hence his relief was great when the train drew out, and the woman who was to have fled in his company had not appeared.

In the summer of 1896 Brahms and Mahler were out for a walk near Ischl. They came to a bridge and stood silently gazing at the foaming mountain stream. A moment before they had been heatedly debating the future of music, and Brahms had had hard things to say of the younger generation of musicians. Now they stood fascinated by the sight of the water breaking in foam time after time over the stones. Mahler looked upstream and pointed to the endless procession of swirling eddies. 'Which is the last?' he asked with a smile.

Mahler in his own later years was a stand-by to all struggling musicians, particularly to Schoenberg, whom he did his best to protect from the brutality of the mob. Twice he took a prominent part in quelling disturbances at concerts.

The first time was when Schoenberg's String Quartet No. I, Opus 7, was performed.† The audience were quietly and by tacit agreement taking it as a great joke, until one of the critics present committed the unpardonable blunder of shouting to the performers to 'stop it'. Whereupon a howling and yelling broke out such as I have never heard before or since. One man stood up in front and hissed Schoenberg every time he came apologetically forward to make his bow, wagging his Jewish head, so like Bruckner's, from side to side in the embarrassed hope of enlisting some stray breath of sympathy or forgiveness. Mahler sprang to his feet and went up to this man. 'I must have a good look at this

---

* Mahler's reconstruction of *Die Drei Pintos* was first performed at Leipzig on 20th January 1888, Mahler conducting . (D.M.)

† On 5th February 1907. (D.M.)

fellow who's hissing,' he said sharply. The man raised his arm
to strike Mahler. Moll, who was among the audience, saw this
and in a second he forced his way through the crowd and collared
the man. Moll's superior strength sobered him and he was
hustled out of the Bösendorfersaal without much difficulty. But
at the door he plucked up his courage and shouted: 'Needn't get
so excited – I hiss Mahler *too*!'*

The second time was when Schoenberg's first Chamber Symphony was performed in the Music Society's hall.† People began
to push their chairs back noisily half-way through, and some went
out in open protest. Mahler got up angrily and enforced silence.
As soon as the performance was over, he stood at the front of the
dress-circle and applauded until the last of the demonstrators had
gone. We spent the rest of the evening discussing the Schoenberg
question. 'I don't understand his music,' he said, 'but he's young
and perhaps he's right. I am old and I dare say my ear is not
sensitive enough.'

I was rung up that night by Guido Adler, professor of the
history of music in the University of Vienna: 'Gustav made a
painful exhibition of himself today. May cost him his job. You
ought to stop him. I went home and shed tears when I thought
of the way music is going. Yes, I shed tears. . . .' Poor music!

There was undoubtedly more behind the appeal Schoenberg's
music made to Mahler, or else he would not have shown up so
prominently as his champion. He felt, even if he did not yet know,
the secret of those tortuous paths which Schoenberg's genius was
– and is – the first to tread.

I have to say 'is', because he still leads the way in music and
no one has been able to dispute his supremacy. He opens up new
paths, which Richard Strauss and others of his contemporaries
have explored in their later works.‡

Mahler's efforts had raised the Opera in Vienna to heights un-
dreamt of. It was he who discovered the conductor, Franz Schalk,

---

* Bruno Walter, in his reminiscences (London, 1947), relates this particular story
to the première of Schoenberg's *Verklärte Nacht*, first performed in Vienna in 1899.
(D.M.)
† On 8th February 1907. (D.M.)
‡ Schoenberg died in 1951. (D.M.)

and brought Bruno Walter from Germany. He esteemed Walter highly, and expected great things from the help of a young and extremely talented conductor.

Mahler gave him an engagement at the Opera soon after taking over the directorship of it. The personal and artistic relations between him and the younger musician were congenial from the first and grew into a friendship which was never clouded to the end.

Walter had a full understanding of Mahler during his lifetime as a musician and a composer; after his death, Walter's great and exalted art was at the service of his music throughout the world. He mastered its every subtlety and gave his own original interpretation, and he took the spirit of Mahler's work as the keystone of his own work as an interpretative musician.

Roller was now in sole charge of scenery and costume, and Mahler himself moved supreme as 'God over the face of the waters'. His chief devotion in the realm of opera was given to Mozart and Wagner. He always conducted *Figaro* himself, also Smetana's *Dalibor*, Gluck's *Iphigenia*, and *Tristan*. He had given up conducting the other Wagner operas.

Fidelio was his masterpiece. I have in my possession a whole production-book devoted to it. He succeeded in making a box-office success of it. When he took over the Opera in Vienna *Manon* and *Werther* were the star performances. When he left, he had put in their place the whole of Mozart, the whole of Wagner and all the masterpieces of classical music.

His conducting of the *Valkyrie* on one occasion was such that, from '*so blühe denn Wälsungenblut*' at the end of the first act onwards, no one in the audience dared to breathe. There was a tempo in the orchestra such as I never heard before or since. Bruno Walter, at first awkward and inexperienced, came very near to realizing Mahler's ideals, whereas Schalk, the more proficient of the two, never entirely pleased him.*

There was a gala performance on 11th March, 1907, in honour of the King of Saxony, and for this Mahler made a fresh study of

---

* Erwin Stein's valuable ear-witness accounts of the Vienna Opera under Mahler have been reprinted in *The Opera Bedside Book* (Ed. Harold Rosenthal, London, 1965). They should be consulted by every interested reader. (D.M.)

Lohengrin. But only the first act was given. He chose *Lohengrin* so that money should be forthcoming from the exchequer for a superb setting. The fatuous indifference of the whole royal party was a comedy to watch. Mahler sat on the podium with his eye on Prince Montenuovo, who in turn kept his eye on the large royal box, and as soon as my uncle Nepallek, the Master of Ceremonies, gave the signal with his white staff that his Majesty had entered the box, the Prince nodded at Mahler and the overture began. The Emperor talked loudly to his guests and they all noisily sat down. The audience, following high example, also made a great deal of noise, and I was so furious that I left. I told Mahler afterwards that I had a lackey for a husband.

And yet the following true tale shows how little of a lackey he was. The singer, Mizzi Günther, came to him one day with an urgent and written recommendation from the Crown Prince, Franz Ferdinand. Mahler took the note and tore it up. 'Very well,' he said, 'and now – sing!'

The Emperor also demanded the re-engagement of the singer E.B.-F., with whom he had had a passing affair, but whose voice was no longer extant. 'Good,' Mahler said, 'but I will not let her come on.' To which Prince Montenuovo replied that it was the Emperor's express wish that she should, and a long-standing promise also, and in any case her salary would come out of his Majesty's private purse. 'Then I suppose she'll have to,' Mahler replied. 'But I shall have it printed on the programme "by command of his Majesty the Emperor".' He heard no more of it. And it must be set down to the credit of the old régime that his audacity did him more good than harm.

When Mahler was required to hand *Lohengrin* over to Schalk, who had previously conducted it, he was unwilling that this fine production should fall a victim to Schalk's pedestrian style; and so he hit on a Mephistophelian plan. He called a rehearsal and sat on the stage facing Schalk while he conducted the orchestra. Schalk had orders to follow his every nuance and every movement of his baton. A more shocking way of breaking a man's pride can scarcely be imagined, and Schalk obeyed with repugnance. The orchestra hid their grins and no one regretted his humiliation. It was not Mahler's precise aim to humiliate him, but to correct his tempi; these, however, like the fishes in the fable of the fishes and the sermon, 'remained as they were'.* But Mahler had made one more active enemy at the Opera, where already he had enough.

It was Mahler's wish to hand down his own interpretations as a tradition. His notorious saying: 'Tradition is slovenliness' ['*Tradition ist Schlamperei*'] was meant in quite another sense. When anyone pointed out to him that he took a passage in some opera otherwise than was accepted as traditional, he said: 'That is how I hear it. What is called tradition is usually an excuse for slovenliness.'

When he found himself in some unpleasant situation he used to say: 'Who hath brought me into this land?' and then laughed. It must be a quotation, but I do not know its source.†

Mahler's achievement by this time was prodigious: the Fifth, the Sixth, the Seventh and Eighth Symphonies, the *Kindertotenlieder*, all his later songs, and the sketches for *Das Lied von der Erde*, the numeration of which he wished to dodge in his dread of a ninth symphony, as neither Beethoven nor Bruckner had reached a tenth. At first he wrote *Das Lied von der Erde* as the Ninth, but then crossed the number out. When later he was writing his next symphony which he called the Ninth, he said to me: 'Actually, of course, it's the Tenth, because *Das Lied von der Erde* was really the Ninth.' Finally when he was composing the Tenth he said, 'Now the danger is past.' And yet he did not live to see the Ninth performed or to finish the Tenth. Beethoven died after his Ninth Symphony and Bruckner before finishing his Ninth; hence it was a superstition of Mahler's that no great writer of symphonies got beyond his ninth.

Our holidays were devoted exclusively to his work and well-being, and his quiet: life went on tiptoe. The poor children might not laugh or cry. We were all slaves to his work – but that was right and I would not have had it otherwise.

During all the first five years of our marriage I had been paying off the load of debts, with which Justine's incredible folly had saddled us. Fifty thousand crowns – a tremendous sum, and now

* A reference to Mahler's *Wunderhorn* song, *Des Antonius von Padua Fischpredigt*. (D.M.)

† See Letters 120 and 133. (D.M.)

at last I had just come to the end of it. He took it all as a matter of course. I existed only as his shadow, paying his debts, making no noise.

One day in the summer he came running down from his hut in a perspiration and scarcely able to breathe. At last he came out with it: it was the heat, the stillness, the Panic terror. It had gripped him and he had fled. He was often overcome by this feeling of the goat-god's frightful and ebullient eye upon him in his solitude, and he had to take refuge in the house among human beings and go on with his work there. When this happened I had to hurry through the whole house, which was built in three storeys looking over the lake, and impose silence. The cook must not make a sound, the children were closeted in their nursery, I must not play the piano, or sing, or even stir. This lasted until he reached a pause in his work and emerged to join in our life, beaming, as he always did when his work was over.

I lived his life. I had none of my own. He never noticed this surrender of my existence. He was so self-engrossed that any disturbance, however slight, was unendurable. Work, exaltation, self-denial and the never-ending quest were his whole life on and on and for ever.

I cancelled my will and my being; like a tight-rope walker, I was concerned only with keeping my balance. He noticed nothing of all it cost me. He was utterly self-centred by nature, and yet he never thought of himself. His work was all in all.

I separated myself inwardly from him, though with reverence, and waited for a miracle. I was blind: the miracle was there beside me – in the shape, at least, of a pure abstraction. In spite of having children, I was still a girl. He saw in me only the comrade, the mother and housewife, and was to learn too late what he had lost. These carnivores of genius, who think they are vegetarians! I have found it so all my life. People speak of ethics, but – they hardly experience them.

His productions at the Opera were always gala performances. Mahler was bounded by no horizon. 'I can stand people who over-exaggerate, but not people who under-exaggerate.' Roller was with us every afternoon and every evening, and at last nothing was spoken of in our flat but the problems of stage-management. Alfred Roller was cold and his self-esteem was crushing; he had not a friend in the whole Opera. Mahler backed him up through thick and thin, and his power grew. When it came into his head to design a ballet and be his own choreographer, Mahler at once gave him permission and put all means at his disposal. The lean anchorite became a dancer. All the ballerinas were constantly in his office, and the legitimate ballet-master of the Royal Opera had to put up with encroachments and finally with open defiance on Roller's part. Prince Montenuovo decided to put a stop to these irregularities, of which Mahler would never have approved and was scarcely even aware. Roller, without asking the permission of the ballet-master, Hassreiter, called a ballet-rehearsal in his office; and out of fear of Mahler, who, they supposed, must be behind Roller, all the girls attended it, although the ballet-master had arranged a rehearsal of his own. He arrived to find an empty room. He went in a fury straight to Prince Montenuovo; and he sent for Mahler.

Mahler at once took Roller's part, and for the first time in the ten years they had worked together, the Lord Chamberlain expressed displeasure as he concluded the interview. 'This is the first time you have condoned an irregularity since you have directed the Opera. My sense of duty will not allow me to overlook it.'

Montenuovo did not get over his displeasure. He was only waiting for the opportunity to get rid of Mahler, and the opportunity came. Mahler was in the habit of entering his own engagements in the large engagement book of forthcoming productions at the Opera. And under the heading 'After Easter' he innocently wrote: 'Rome, three concerts.' His leave, however, was only for Easter, and he meant to apply from Rome for a brief extension to cover the third concert. The book was removed by some subordinate official who had a grudge against him and came into the Prince's hands. He sent for Mahler and began by drawing his attention to the fact that the box-office receipts always fell whenever he went on leave. Mahler was able to contradict this on the spot, but the upshot was that his resignation was regarded on both sides as a matter for consideration.

Such was the state of affairs when, half glad to be quit of the

Opera, half fearful of the unknown future, we set off for Rome. For even if we were clear of debt, we had saved nothing, and Mahler was very tired. Nobody heard a word from us from Rome.

We left on 19th March. The first breakdown occurred at Semmering. The train came to a stop. I jumped from my bunk and so did all the other passengers; there was considerable excitement, for the train had stopped with a sudden jolt. But Mahler, who now that the train was no longer in motion was at last able to fall asleep, was completely oblivious. He slept for three hours while all the rest of us were in a state of agitation. But the material world he ignored took its revenge, as it always did; for between Bologna and Rome the engine broke down for the second, and just outside Rome for the third time. Our sleeper missed the connection; we lost our trunks, which were left behind somewhere, and with them much of our money. For weeks we had to buy our linen at great expense, and Mahler, who was used to fine, soft shirts, had to endure a stiff one, in which we both agreed he looked like a candidate for confirmation.

The tragic side of this comedy was that the orchestral scores for the concerts had gone astray with our trunks and Mahler had to conduct from any copy he could get hold of.

Spiro, the historian, showed us the sights very ably. He knew every stone of the Forum by name, and so we passed happy hours between rehearsals. Mahler's favourite expedition was along the Via Appia. I noticed that he always preferred the literary and historical point of view and disregarded nature in its untutored wildness.

The first concert promised to be a sensation, but Mahler unfortunately had to wear a hired dress-suit, and the one we procured had been made for a tall man. He looked like a small boy in his grandfather's dressing-gown. The proprietor of the pension where we were staying for the sake of economy was a German; and seeing Mahler's dilemma he offered him his own dress-coat. But there was a very imposing star (the emblem of a society of gymnasts) sewn on it in front, as so frequently happens in the case of the worthy citizens of Cologne; and, however imposing in its native element, this star would have shown oddly from the podium. It was difficult to convince the German of this and he retired hurt. I was left to do what I could with the very large dress-suit. I made tucks in trousers and sleeves, but Mahler refused to let me stitch up the trousers in front, which flapped in a very unbecoming way. So I united them from within with a large gold safety-pin, which was all I could lay hands on at the moment, and warned him not to touch it until the concert was over. He went ahead, as usual, to see that the chairs and music were all properly arranged for the orchestra. I arrived just before the performance was to begin and only just in time to avert a shocking disaster: the pin no longer where it ought to have been but extremely visible. When this had been put right he went off laughing.

Queen Margherita was in her box and summoned Mahler to her presence in the interval. She jokingly offered to help him find his luggage, but neither she nor the organizer of the concert, Count di San Martino, nor the Austrian Ambassador, Count Lützow, nor anyone else could do anything about it.

Mahler in those days was an oddity, to whom everyone gave a wide berth and who owed what little awe he inspired to his position as Director of the Royal Opera. He was nervous and irritable in Rome. Possibly his imminent resignation affected him more than he cared to show. In any case, everyone we met was astonished at my patience and reproached him to his face with his caprices. For example, I had to unpack our large trunk three times before we left. His rough drafts for the Seventh Symphony were packed, at his wish, at the very bottom. Then, when the hotel porters were waiting to carry our luggage down, he decided he must have the manuscript at the top, so that he could get it out at a moment's notice if required. I had to unpack the whole trunk. We went downstairs, escorted by our friends and admirers of his, and as soon as we were in the hall he suddenly got into a state of agitation and said he must have the score in his hand. So I had to open the heavy trunk once more almost in the street, and we held the score in our hands by turns all the way to Vienna. However understandable such behaviour was, it often made him very difficult to live with.

We never went out at night to any gay party or to the theatre all these five years – only to the Opera, and only when he was conducting, which was exactly as I would have wished it to be.

There was one exception: we went to the *Merry Widow* and enjoyed it. We danced together when we got home and played Lehár's waltz from memory; but the exact run of one passage defied our utmost efforts. We were both too 'highbrow' to face buying the music. So we went to Doblinger's* and while Mahler asked about the sale of his compositions I casually turned the pages of the various piano editions of the *Merry Widow*, and found the passage I wanted. I sang it as soon as we were in the street in case it slipped my memory a second time.

Mahler loved cheerfulness and gaiety, as this and many other incidents show, but some dark principle or other held him back. He could laugh uncontrollably, but if anybody else laughed it got on his nerves. He used often to say when we were discussing somebody: 'Oh – a beautiful face – marked by suffering,' or else: 'An empty face – no suffering in it.' It was only in the last year of his life, when excess of suffering had taught him the meaning of joy, that his natural gaiety broke through the clouds.

As a rule Mahler came home from the opera in solemn mood. After lunch he lay down on our blue divan and I read aloud. It might be *Zwei Menschen* by Dehmel, *Parsifal* by Wolfram von Eschenbach, *Tristan* by Gottfried von Strassburg, or a scientific or historical book. I went to a course of lectures by Professor Siegel at the University: 'Astronomy from Aristotle to Kant.' I took notes and worked on them at home, and read them out to Mahler in the evenings; he was touching in his eagerness to explain anything I did not understand and was often driven to seek help from his philosophers. In this way we came on Giordano Bruno and Galileo. I read *Die triumphierende Bestie* and *Das Aschermittwochmahl* aloud, and also the *Geschichte des Materialismus* of Lange, and so on. Someone observed to me once: 'Alma, you have an abstraction for a husband, not a human being.' It was quite true. But I treasured every single day of my life in those days.

I arrived from Rome feeling very unwell and found that our English nurse in my absence had scalded three fingers of my younger child's hand. She did not look well, and I was anxious; it could not only be the scald. She got feverish and was sick –

* The famous music publishers and music shop in Vienna. (D.M.)

it was scarlet fever. I waited until she had recovered and then retired to a nursing home to have an operation, but my heart was with my convalescent child. The elder one was with my mother. When I was better and the child too, we all met at the station and went to Maiernigg for our annual holiday. Before this Mahler had resigned and his resignation had been accepted.

On the third day after our arrival in the country the elder of the two children developed alarming symptoms. It was scarlet fever and diphtheria, and from the first there was no hope. We passed a fortnight in an agony of dread; then there was a relapse and the danger of suffocation. It was a ghastly time, accompanied by thunderstorms and lurid skies. Mahler loved this child devotedly; he hid himself in his room every day, taking leave of her in his heart. On the last night, when tracheotomy was resorted to, I posted his servant at his door to keep him in his room if the noise disturbed him; but he slept all through this terrible night. My English nurse and I got the operation-table ready and put the poor child to sleep. While the operation was being performed I ran along the shore of the lake, where no one could hear me crying. The doctor had forbidden me to enter the room; and at five in the morning the nurse came to tell me it was over. Then I saw her. She lay choking, with her large eyes wide open. Our agony dragged on one more whole day. Then the end came.

Mahler, weeping and sobbing, went again and again to the door of my bedroom, where she was; then fled away to be out of ear-shot of any sound. It was more than he could bear. We tele-graphed to my mother, who came at once. We all three slept in his room. We could not bear being parted for an hour. We dreaded what might happen if any one of us left the room. We were like birds in a storm and feared what each moment might bring – and how right we were!

Fate had not done with us. A relation took charge of all the hateful affairs death brings in its train. On the second day Mahler asked my mother and me to go down to the edge of the lake; and there my mother suddenly had a heart attack. I contrived cold compresses with the water of the lake and put them over her heart. Then Mahler came down the path. His face was contorted and when I looked up at him I saw, on the road above, that the coffin was being placed in the hearse. I knew now what had caused my mother's sudden seizure and why his face was contorted. He and I were so helpless, so bereft, that it was almost a joy to fall into a deep faint.

The doctor came to see me. I was suffering from extreme exhaustion of the heart and he ordered me a complete rest. He could not understand how I had kept going at all with my heart in that state. Mahler, thinking to make a cheerful diversion and distract us from our gloom said: 'Come along, doctor, wouldn't you like to examine me too?' The doctor did so. He got up looking very serious. Mahler was lying on the sofa and Dr. Blumenthal had been kneeling beside him. 'Well, you've no cause to be proud of a heart like that,' he said in that cheery tone doctors often adopt after diagnosing a fatal disease. This verdict marked the beginning of the end for Mahler.

These events, on the top of his retirement from the Opera, changed our whole existence. We were homeless in feeling and in fact. The verdict pronounced by Dr. Blumenthal took frightful, almost incomprehensible effect. Mahler went to Vienna by the next train to consult Professor Kovacs, who fully confirmed the verdict of the general practitioner.

He forbade him mountain ascents, bicycling and swimming; indeed he was so blind as to order a course of training to teach him to walk; first it was to be five minutes, then ten, and so on until he was used to walking; and this for a man who was accustomed to violent exercise! And Mahler did as he was told. Watch in hand, he accustomed himself to walking – and forgot the life he had lived up to that fatal hour.

I packed the barest necessaries and we fled from Maiernigg, which was haunted now by painful memories, to Schluderbach in the Tyrol. We revived to some extent in new and beautiful surroundings and tried to imagine our life in the future. Alfred Roller remarked to me one day on a walk at Schluderbach: 'The verdict came as no surprise to me. I noticed during the *Lohengrin* rehearsals when he was livening up the chorus, motioning them forward and holding them back again, how he stopped to get his breath and involuntarily clutched at his heart.' He had thought of mentioning this to me at the time, but had kept on putting it off for fear of upsetting me.

There was an old consumptive friend of my father's, who transferred all the love he had had for him to Mahler; he found his one outlet in seeking out songs for Mahler to set to music and bringing to his notice anything that might be a stimulus to him. It was from him Mahler got hold of *The Chinese Flute*, a recent translation from the Chinese by Hans Bethge. He was delighted with it and put it aside for future use. Now, after the loss of his child and the alarming verdict on his heart, exiled from his home and his workshop, these poems came back to his mind; and their infinite melancholy answered to his own. Before we left Schulderbach he had sketched out, on our long, lonely walks, those songs for orchestra which took final shape as *Das Lied von der Erde* a year later.

Conried, the Manager of the Metropolitan Opera, wanted to get Mahler over there. Cables and letters followed one another. Mahler welcomed the proposal as a providential means of escape from Vienna, which had rejected him, to a new country and a new world. Anything to get away. Germany, too, in spite of many overtures in the past, had suddenly turned its back on him. His immediate need was to earn enough money to enable him to work on in seclusion. He had not got a great deal done this summer. The Eighth was completed and awaited a performance; the 'Ninth', which was later to become *Das Lied von der Erde*, was still in embryo.

Conried summoned him by telegram to Berlin and there he signed at once a four-months' contract for the season 1907–8. He told me by telegram how things were going. He was to undertake three new productions at the Metropolitan and conduct at two or three concerts. He returned well pleased to Vienna, and there found a note from Montenuovo asking to see him. I waited for hours in a little tea-shop that afternoon, and at last he joined me in high spirits. Montenuovo had asked him to stay on as Director of the Opera and Mahler had made use of the Prince's own words in his refusal.

Montenuovo had said in the spring that he had no use for a director who was always away on concert tours, advertising his own compositions. Mahler had replied to this that it added to the prestige of the Opera if the Director had a reputation for original work. The Prince now said he had come round to Mahler's opinion. To this Mahler replied that he too had altered his opinion. He saw now that a director of opera should confine himself strictly to his official duties and be always on the spot.

We knew that Monteuovo had had a number of refusals during the summer. Nikisch had refused, so had Schuch; even Weingartner would have nothing to do with it. Nobody liked to risk being Mahler's successor; nor to undertake such heavy responsibilities for so small a salary. Montenuovo bound Mahler to secrecy and so denied him the opportunity of clearing himself. In the eyes of the public, he had been dismissed and he was reviled accordingly.

That did not worry us. He had his contract in his pocket; and, when late in the autumn he took up his duties again at the Opera for the last time, he was a new man. He conducted farewell performances of his chosen operas, also a wonderful performance of the Second Symphony in the Music Society's Concert Hall,* and finally, on 15th October, *Fidelio*. It must be confessed that those final performances were very poorly attended. He was not spared the mortification of being deserted by the public.

Before signing his contract with Conried for New York, he inserted a clause saying that he would not in any circumstances conduct *Parsifal*, as he could not go against the interdict in Wagner's will.

Schoenberg and Zemlinsky and their friends wanted Mahler to spend an evening with them before he left Vienna, and so they all foregathered at the Schutzengel at Grinzing. I stayed at home, as I always found such gatherings a weariness. Mahler came back at midnight in great spirits, but his clothes smelt so strongly of smoke that he had to change before giving me an account of the proceedings which kept us laughing until the early hours. He said that as soon as he joined them a religious hush descended on the company; and so to liven things up he called for the bill of fare. The waiter brought the soup with both thumbs in the plate. Mahler sent it back. The waiter next brought a roll in his hand and Mahler demanded another one. The waiter retired to the sideboard, put the same roll on a plate and brought it back again. It dawned on Schoenberg's assembled pupils, who had so far watched all this with wonder and awe, that Mahler was making fun of the man; the ice was broken, and the fun became so fast and furious that no one could hear himself speak.

Mahler found the noise worse than the solemn hush and was

* On 24th November. *Fidelio* was the last performance of an *opera* to be conducted by Mahler in Vienna. (D.M.)

now eager to get home. He arranged with Schoenberg and
Zemlinsky that he would jump off the tram at the Restaurant
Zögernitz. They were to follow his example and by this means
they would be quit of the mob of students; but the students too
jumped with one accord from the swiftly speeding tram, and
there they all were again, crowded together, enveloped in smoke,
and reduced once more to an embarrassed silence, which gave
way to merciless din.

Mahler shouted out above the racket: 'What do you fellows
think about Dostoyevsky nowadays?' A chorus of youthful voices
replied: 'We don't bother with him any more. It's Strindberg
now.' This evidence of the transience of reputations gave us a
lot to think about. Mahler made a vigorous retort; but the young
have to have their god of the moment – yesterday Strindberg,
today Wedekind, tomorrow Shaw, the day after tomorrow a rediscovered Dostoyevsky and so on *ad infinitum*. It does not matter
that fashion changes their gods. The chief thing is that they have
gods of some sort.

We talked it all over while he sat on the edge of my bed,
smoking, and eating the supper I had hastily produced for him.
He had been too nauseated to eat anything all the evening.

The moment of our departure arrived. Schoenberg and
Zemlinsky marshalled their pupils and Mahler's friends on the
platform, to which they had been given private access. They were
all drawn up when we arrived, flowers in their hands and tears in
their eyes, ready to board the train and deck out our compartment
with flowers from roof to floor. When we drew slowly out it was
without regret or backward glances. We had been too hard hit.
All we wanted was to get away, the farther the better. We even
felt happy as Vienna was left behind. We did not miss our child,
who had been left with my mother. We knew now that anxious
love was of no avail against catastrophe, and that no spot on
earth gives immunity. We had been through the fire. So we
thought. But, in spite of all, one thing had us both in its grip –
the future.

'Repertory opera is done with,' Mahler observed during the
journey. 'I'm glad not to be staying on to witness its decline.

Up to the last I contrived to hide from the public that I was making bricks without straw.'

Our friend Gabrilovitch, who worshipped Mahler blindly, awaited us in Paris. He and I were alone that evening. He blurted out: 'I have a frightful confession to make. I'm on the verge of falling madly in love with you. Help me to get over it. I love Mahler. I could not bear to hurt him.' I was too dazed to speak. So I was capable of arousing love: I was not old and ugly, as I had come to think. He felt for my hand in the dark. The light was switched on and Mahler came in; he was affectionate and kindly and the spectre vanished. Nevertheless, this episode was my standby for some time in many an onset of self-depreciation.

We travelled to Cherbourg and boarded a tender by night in a choppy sea. Our boat, the *America*, was visible from far off as a great splash of light. Mahler feared the voyage, try as he might to hide his fears. Suddenly the huge ship rose up in front of us; the Marseillaise rang out, and all was forgotten. We crossed the gangway in high spirits and were conducted immediately to our state-cabins. A wonderful meal was served in the saloon, and I suddenly realized with exultation that we were moving. Mahler was angry when I drew his attention to it: he did not want to know anything about it now that the band was silent and his apprehension had come back.

There was a rough sea, and he endeavoured to avoid sea-sickness by lying rigidly on his back on his bunk like a cardinal on his tomb, neither eating nor speaking until the dread sensation passed. This, in spite of the wonder of ocean and sky, is what I remember best of that first trip.

New World

1907 - 1908

The arrival in New York – the harbour and all the sights and scenes and human bustle – so took our breath away that we forgot all our troubles. But not for long.

Mahler went to the Metropolitan the morning after we arrived and was informed that *Tristan* was the first opera he was to conduct.* I went with him and was able to return to the Hotel Majestic by myself, even going deliberately out of my way, so clear is the layout of this divine city.

We had a suite of rooms on the eleventh floor, and, of course, two pianos. So we felt at home. Andreas Dippel, who was then business-manager of the Metropolitan, took us to lunch with the super-god, Conried, who was already a cripple from tabes and showed unmistakable signs of megalomania. This first, fantastic luncheon-party, the flat itself and our hosts' utter innocence of culture, kept us in concealed mirth until we were in the street again and could burst out laughing. In Conried's smoking-room, for example, there was a suit of armour which could be illuminated from within by red lights. There was a divan in the middle of the room with a baldachino and convoluted pillars, and on it the godlike Conried reclined when he gave audience to the members of the company. All was enveloped in sombre, flounced stuffs, illuminated by the glare of coloured electric lights. And then, Conried himself, who had 'made' Sonnenthal and was now going to 'make' Mahler.

Mahler soon got down to work in earnest and found that things went more smoothly than in Vienna. Here he could devote himself exclusively to the music, which was a blessed change from Vienna in recent years, when owing to Roller's concentration on the staging, pure music had almost been put in the shade.

* Mahler made his début at the Metropolitan with *Tristan* on 1st January 1908. (D.M.)

The orchestra, the singing, the house itself – all was wonderful, and even if the settings, which Conried kept in his own hands, were often – though not always – abominable, Mahler did not care. Fremstad sang Isolde, Knote Tristan. For the first time in my life I heard the second act as pure music. Mahler swam in bliss.

His first appearance in New York had a slightly comic prelude. Just as we were entering the lift Mahler trod on the train of my dress. I had to go back and sew it on again and while I was doing so there was a ring from the Opera. Mahler was too superstitious to go without me, whatever the cost. So we did not answer the telephone. We were both – very oddly for us – quite unmoved, and when we were on our way in the automobile Mahler remarked: 'It's their fault. Why didn't they send to fetch me?'

The audience was waiting impatiently by the time he hurried on to conduct one of the finest performances I have ever heard in my life. His triumph was immediate. Americans are very critical and do not by any means receive every European celebrity with favour. They really know something about music. Mottl, for example, was a failure. He had to return to Germany after his first performances had proved a disappointment. Certainly he deserved better, but he made the mistake of not taking the American public seriously.

These days in New York might have been perfect if we had not been annihilated by the death of our child. Mahler spent half the day in bed to spare himself; the child's name had not to be mentioned in his hearing and our days were so disconsolate that often in the early morning, after spending a sleepless night walking up and down, I sat on the stairs on our eleventh floor merely to catch some sound of human life below.

Suffering estranged and separated us. Without knowing it he increased the bitterness of our loss. Moreover, he knew now that he himself was menaced and this put out the light of the sun. He was nervous, wrought up and irritable. It was a wretched winter for me, and indeed for us both. Our saddest evening of all was Christmas Eve, the first we had spent separated from our children and in a foreign country. Mahler did not want to be reminded that it was Christmas and in the desolation of loneliness I wept without ceasing all day.

Towards evening there was a knock. It was Baumfeld, that good but clumsy Samaritan, whose obsession was a German theatre for New York. He read the whole truth in my face and would not rest until we agreed to go with him where we could see a Christmas tree and children and friendly faces. It took us out of ourselves at once; but we were driven away after dinner when some actors and actresses came in. One of these was a raddled female called 'Putzi'. This renewed our grief, for Putzi was the pet name for the child we had lost.

We went out to dinner several times. The first occasion was at Mr. B.'s, the American director of the Hamburg–America Line. I left the invitation behind and got mixed up between 72 and 27 for the number of the street and so we were nearly an hour late. Our hostess did not hide her anger. At last we sat down to dinner. Mahler was opposite me on the right of our hostess. Suddenly in a momentary silence I heard him exclaim loudly: 'What is that? Wagner showed ingratitude to Liszt? And he had a bad reputation? And what does *Tristan* mean to you?' Mrs. B., anxious to calm the storm, said disarmingly that she could never sleep the whole night after hearing a performance of *Tristan*. But Mahler only went on: 'And yet you dare to measure Wagner's character with your philistine yard-stick!' Mrs. B. said no more and in complete silence everyone rose from the table. A woman came up to me and asked innocently: 'Does your husband always make a scene at dinner?'

One morning I could not rise from my bed. Mahler telephoned for a doctor, who in turn summoned another, and the two diagnosed weakness of the heart and nervous collapse, and ordered a four-weeks' rest cure. I was given strychnine and forbidden to move. At long last I was able to give way to my grief and my physical exhaustion. Mahler at once felt his own sorrow less and gave all his thoughts to speeding my recovery.

To dispose, as he did in those days, of the finest artists and singers in the world was an entirely new experience for Mahler. He had Caruso, Bonci, Scotti, Chaliapin, Gadski, Sembrich,

Farrar, Eames for Italian opera and Mozart; Burian, Knote, Burgstaller, Jörn, Goritz, Fremstad, van Rooy, etc., for German opera. He sent for six couples of dancers from Prague to rehearse the original Bohemian dances with the corps de ballet when it came to a production of the *Bartered Bride* with Destinn.* This opera, however, did not catch on and was dropped. Mahler said after a performance of *Tristan* with Fremstad and Burian: 'The stars were kind. I have never known a performance of *Tristan* to equal this.'

The whole opera migrated in a body to Boston as soon as the New York season came to an end. We saw a great deal of Van Rooy, who was Wotan in *Valkyrie*† and talked of nothing else. He bored Mahler. Speaking of Bayreuth he told a story of Cosima Wagner, with special reference, of course, to himself. By a stroke of genius she summoned him to Bayreuth, young as he was and quite unknown, and to his dismay entrusted Wotan to him. They went downstairs together and at the entrance he took leave of her. As he walked away he felt that her eyes followed him with a blessing, under the weight of which he staggered on. At length he could not help coming to a stop and turning round; Cosima had woken from her trance and was kneeling with her back to him and offering up a prayer at Wagner's grave. And Van Rooy knew that she was imploring Wagner's spirit to help him to fill his role. The best of Van Rooy was his way of regarding his parts as a mission, even if his monomania was wearisome at times. I am astonished when I look back and see how simple and sincere and 'modern' a man Mahler was among the stagey solemnities of those vanished days.

Boston itself was dull and sedate compared with other American towns. Here too we lived in isolation for the few days we were there. We had only one invitation. Mrs. Gardner (the great collector of Italian works of art) asked us to a luncheon-party at her house, and we were eager to pay a visit to her palatial museum.

---

* New York première on 19th February 1909. (D.M.)
† First New York performance under Mahler on 4th March 1908. *Siegfried* had been given on 19th February. (D.M.)

Unfortunately we failed to find the entrance. The building resembled a gigantic cistern without windows or doors. We got out of our automobile and made the complete circuit of the house, but found neither door nor bell. So we left it at that and drove back to our hotel, glad to be alone to do as we pleased. Alone or in company we were always in any case enclosed within a vacuum.

The opera company paid several visits to Philadelphia during the winter. The first time was to perform *Tristan*. I sat in the front row immediately behind Mahler and, as though a veil had fallen, I suddenly saw in his face marks of suffering I had never seen before. The dread of losing him gave me such a pang that I had a heart attack and fell into a dead faint. Professor Leon Corning, who had been observing me, got me out and carried me into Heinrich Knote's dressing-room.

Mahler, who had often turned round to look at me during the performance, now saw my seat empty, but had to go on conducting without knowing what had happened. Corning ran out to a chemist's and by the time Mahler rushed in at the end of the act I was able to sit up. But I remained behind the scenes for the rest of the performance.

It was a new experience for me to be among the singers during a performance. I was talking to Fremstad. Suddenly she became restless and alert and edged her way nearer the wings. 'Just a moment,' she said and darted on to the stage to sing the *Liebestod* with matchless perfection.

Van Rooy, on the other hand, was permanently Wotan. During the interval he strode heavily to and fro with his spear, neither speaking nor smiling – every inch a god. Gadski was the very opposite; she cleared her throat, spat, and made silly jokes while waiting for the curtain to go up. Then at the last moment she collected herself and went on as Fricka to the life.

Don Giovanni in Philadelphia* – Donna Elvira was to come on for her great aria, but she could not, because she was shut up in the little stage-property-room on the stage and the door had been forgotten. Mahler made one fermata after another, looked round

* The New York first performance of *Don Giovanni* under Mahler was given on 23rd January 1908. (D.M.)

at me with a charming smile and we both enjoyed the delightful impasse to the full. At last Gadski burst boldly from one corner of the chamber in which she was enclosed after the whole structure had heaved and quivered. For a moment the back of the stage was revealed; then the corner was hurriedly closed up behind her and the aria began. She sang it beautifully, far more beautifully than it was ever sung in our Ministry of Music, as we used to call the Opera in Vienna, with all its hundreds of rooms and corridors. Here it was different. It was a feast for the ear, not the eyes. Don Giovanni, Scotti; Donna Anna, Fremstad; Elvira, Gadski; Zerline, Farrar; Ottavio, Bonci; Leporello, Chaliapin.

Or take *Valkyrie*: Van Rooy, Fremstad, Burgstaller. Or *Siegfried*: Knote or Burgstaller or Burian. *Figaro*: Sembrich, Eames. In short, Mahler had the finest singers of the world. He never had anything of the sort in Vienna.

After this performance of *Don Giovanni* in Philadelphia, a gentleman asked us to visit his museum the following day: the fruits of diggings he had undertaken in Babylon. Room after room of Sumerian – 3000 B.C. – tiles inscribed with cuneiform characters – stock-exchange figures from ancient Babylon – remarkable Jewish – Mongolian profiles. His exposition fascinated us. A year after this he was fiercely attacked for having forged all his inscriptions. But even so, he did it so well that he led all the experts by the nose for years. In the last resort, what does the 'genuine' matter? We both got a great deal from his enthusiastic and learned discourse.

We travelled back to New York with Knote and Leon Corning. Corning, discoverer of spinal anaesthesia, was shy and reserved in spite of his great position in the medical world. He scarcely spoke, but there was a constant flicker of lightning in his face, which was the face of a fakir, with leathery furrows. He was very well known and much feared in America; and had the reputation of being close, in spite of being a millionaire and capable on occasion of sudden generosity. Knote was his brother-in-law. Corning put 200,000 dollars as a present in his child's cradle. We had made great friends with him owing to his help when I fainted; and he sent his automobile for us a few days after we all got back to New York. A gentleman whom we took for a

Gustav Mahler

servant at the door of the automobile and, as he sat beside the chauffeur, we paid him no further attention. When we arrived at Corning's house, this same gentleman leapt out and opened the door for us and then with a bow accompanied us into the house. He was a guest like ourselves, but a deaf-mute. Leon Corning received us upstairs, casually introduced us to his wife, who vanished immediately afterwards; he then took us into his study.

Just as he himself came straight out of a tale by E. T. A. Hoffman, so this was the chamber of a medieval alchemist. Wires hanging from the ceiling crossed the room in all directions; there were steps leading up and steps leading down. The latter revealed an iron gibbet and some sort of antique machine. He went ahead of us to open a narrow door and we entered an iron-plated cell in which patients were rendered insensible by breathing condensed air. There was a couch, the pillows of which still showed the impress of a human form, and an open book lay on the floor. The space was so confined that we could barely stand erect. All was ghostly. His wife clad in black weeds swept through without word or look. Her face was a death-mask with hollow eyes. He led us on into his music-room, in which three or four grand pianos stood in a row. Dr. Corning cheered up and walked up and down playing the flute. Finally the door opened and two animate beings came in – his brother with his wife. Up to now we felt we had got into some sort of bogey-house.

Dinner was served in a small, square cabinet. Tiny candles guttered on the table and had so often to be blown out that we could scarcely see one another. The fairy electric lights with difficulty penetrated the haze. On each minute plate there was deposited something equally minute and of questionable edibility. A half-bottle of champagne was opened in our honour and yielded an egg-cupful apiece. There were seven of us. His brother asked me in a whisper: 'How did you get here? He's almost pathological and never has anybody in. What's come over him?' We were touched to see that each of us had a small symbolic object made of bronze beside his plate, Mahler a conductor's desk, I a piano. It was clear that this child with greatness stamped upon his face had prepared for the occasion days before. His wife did not utter a word. If she opened her mouth to speak her husband shut it again with an angry look.

Marie Uchatius, a young art-student, paid me a visit one day in the Hotel Majestic. Hearing a confused noise, we leaned out of the window and saw a long procession in the broad street along the side of Central Park. It was the funeral cortège of a fireman, of whose heroic death we had read in the newspaper. The chief mourners were almost immediately beneath us when the procession halted, and the master of ceremonies stepped forward and gave a short address. From our eleventh-floor window we could only guess what he said. There was a brief pause and then a stroke on the muffled drum, followed by a dead silence. The procession then moved forward and all was over.

The scene brought tears to our eyes and I looked anxiously at Mahler's window. But he too was leaning out and his face was streaming with tears. The brief drum-stroke impressed him so deeply that he used it in the Tenth Symphony.*

On another occasion when I was sitting in my room and Mahler in his, working, the silence was suddenly broken by a trickle of sound from far below. It was a tremulous and superannuated Italian barrel-organ. I rang through to the office and begged them to move him on at once at my expense. The noise stopped at once. Then Mahler burst in: 'Such a lovely barrel-organ – took me straight back to my childhood – and now it's stopped!'†

Mahler in Vienna, whether as Director of the Opera or conductor of the orchestra, was intransigent in the extreme. He permitted no cuts in Wagner and imposed five or six hours' performances on the public. He was very severe with late-comers. At first he used to turn his flashing lenses on them until, wholly cowed, they reached their seats. Toscanini copied him in this. Later he kept a box expressly for these guilty ones, and no one was allowed to enter the auditorium after the performance had begun. They had to stay in the box until the interval and then hurriedly seek out their seats. When the Emperor Franz Joseph was told of

* See Introduction, p. xiv (D.M.)
† See Introduction, pp. xv-xvi (D.M.)

this by the Intendant, he remarked: 'But after all, the theatre is meant to be a pleasure.' Mahler was very different in New York. He not only introduced all the usual cuts, but invented new ones in order to abbreviate the operas. He was merely amused, too, by lapses in the settings which in Vienna would have roused him to fury. It was not because his mind was distracted by the anxiety his illness caused him, nor that he did not take the New York public seriously – on the contrary, he found the public there entirely of his own way of thinking. The reason was that his whole attitude to the world and life in general had changed. The death of our child and his own personal sorrow had set another scale to the importance of things.

Conried, who was too low-bred to know what he said or did, could commit the greatest blunders without annoying Mahler in the least. He once proposed, when a bass was not forthcoming, to let a tenor sing the part. Also, when the scene could not be changed quickly enough after the trio in *Don Giovanni*,* he suggested that the three fairly stout gentlemen should clamber on to one of the wings and simply be hauled off in one operation. These are only two of the many little incidents of which Mahler told me at the time, laughing in spite of his heavy heart.

We spent only three months over there the first winter. We got to know Dr. Joseph Fränkel at the end of that time at the house of O. H. Kahn, one of the chief financial supporters of the Metropolitan Opera. Fränkel had a great influence both on Mahler and me during the years which followed. He was a genius both as a man and a doctor, and we both fell in love with him the day we first met him. He was a complete entertainment in himself; dazzling in his wit and a daring thinker – a little splenetic perhaps, but always original. He said, for example, that he divided people into those with whom, and those on whom, he lived. Also, that Prometheus had not brought men fire to make matches of. It was in obedience to this aphorism that he left no records of his great discoveries.

He indoctrinated us so thoroughly with his theory about ears that we could never afterwards see anyone without ascertaining

* Presumably in the so-called Introduction from Act I. (D.M.)

the make of his ear. He arrived at the most surprising results by following out Lavater's *Physiognomical Contributions to the Knowledge and Love of Man*. He said that all the organs of the body except the ear were under constant control and that therefore the ear alone revealed the naked truth.

Mahler finally fell so entirely under his sway that he would unquestionably have done whatever he told him.

At first we lived almost in solitary confinement. Mahler was so shattered by the verdict on his heart that he spent the greater part of the day in bed. When he was not having a meal he was reading; and he got up only for rehearsals or for the performance at night, if he was conducting. I, for my part, suffered from hallucinations. Wherever I looked I saw my doomed child. Life for both of us was a misery.

In spite of all, however, the voyage home was better than the voyage out. Mahler had regained much of his old physical self-confidence, and at once the world was brighter for me. Our stewardess in the autumn had struck Mahler with her blooming health and youth. 'Oh – to be as young and strong as that girl,' he said with a sigh. When we asked after her, we were told that she was dead. She had died on her very next trip back to Europe.

We disembarked this time at Cuxhaven, one day in May. I saw to the baggage and the customs examination, as I always did. Mahler wanted to help me, but he looked so aged and ill that the German official said out loud: 'Your father need not bother. I can help you through.' It pained me more than Mahler, who unfortunately heard it.

We spent some days in Hamburg and did not feel at all well there. Mahler had to go on to Wiesbaden and I followed him after a few days. He conducted his First Symphony there and Mendelssohn's *Hebrides* Overture – to a completely empty hall. The public had gone on strike against an increase in the prices of seats, of which the organizers had given notice in their preliminary announcement.

Berliner and Gabrilovitch came to Wiesbaden to welcome us home and to hear the concert. We three were almost the only persons present. When we all met for supper afterwards Berliner played a practical joke which was not at all well received. Mahler was in the habit of scraping the labels off wine and beer bottles during a meal, and so Berliner told the waiter to have this done beforehand. Mahler took up one bottle after another and put it down again in surprise; and then, catching Berliner's eye, he saw that he was at the bottom of it and was thoroughly put out. He did not recover his temper for the rest of the evening.

We went on to Vienna, and Mahler stayed there while I went to Toblach with my mother. It was May, and in deep snow we looked at every available house until we found the right one, a large farmhouse outside the village. There were eleven rooms, two verandas, two bathrooms – all somewhat primitive, but in a lovely situation. We took it at once for the summer and returned to pack. It was at Toblach in the course of his last three summers that Mahler wrote *Das Lied von der Erde*, the Ninth and the fragment of his Tenth Symphony.*

* As we know now, Mahler left not a fragment but complete sketches for the Tenth. (D.M.)

Summer

1908

There was an amusing scene when it came to allotting the rooms. We followed him proudly from room to room until, after much coming and going, he had selected the two best and lightest for himself. Next, the largest bed was sought out and moved in for his use, although he was smaller than I was. His egoism was sublimely unconscious, and if he had been aware of it he would have been deeply shocked. As it was, my mother and I followed him about, rejoicing in his innocent pleasure. We had two grand pianos installed and a small upright for his studio in the garden.

And now at last there was peace, broken only by occasional visitors. Gabrilovitch, Gustav Brecher, Oscar Fried, Ernst Decsey all came at different times and there was much music. Mahler got to work once more. His studio stood in a mossy clearing surrounded by woodland; and one night after a warm rain a host of small white mushrooms came up. He returned at midday with tears of delight in his eyes – after picking his way there and back with the utmost care not to tread on a single one of these living creatures, which charmed him as much as if they had been troops of children.

He worked at white-heat all the summer on the songs for orchestra, with Hans Bethge's Chinese poems as the text. The scope of the composition grew as he worked. He linked up the separate poems and composed interludes, and so found himself drawn more and more to his true musical form – the symphony. When this was clear, the composition rapidly took shape and was completed sooner than he expected.

He did not, however, venture to call it a symphony, owing to his superstition. And thus he thought to give God the slip.

He expressed all his sorrow and dread in this work – *The Song of the Earth*. Its first title was 'The Song of the Sorrow of the Earth'.*

* 'Das Lied vom Jammer der Erde.' The opening song, however, was entitled *Das Trinklied vom Jammer der Erde* in Mahler's final version of the work. (D.M.)

One day he came into the house in a transport of fury. He told me to dismiss our servant on the spot and flung himself on his bed, almost insensible. This was the story. The representative of a large American piano firm knocked and asked for Mr. Mahler. In obedience to strict orders, the girl refused him admittance and said that the Director was working and could see nobody. The man asked where he was working and the silly girl pointed in the direction of the wood, whereupon he advanced to the fence and shouted out at the top of his voice: 'How do you do, Mr. Mahler?' Mahler, who was lost in his work, came out and sent him about his business, but the shock gave him a heart attack. He came to me sobbing and said he had felt as if he had been flung on to the pavement from the spire of St. Stephen's Cathedral.

This agitating scene had an amusing sequel. On our arrival in New York in the autumn we found six grand pianos drawn up in the hall of the hotel, which meant that two firms had to be grievously slighted. Our visitor had said nothing of his reception but merely reported to his chief that Mahler prized their make of piano above all others.

In the meanwhile I sold our villa at Maiernigg on the Wörthersee. We could never have gone there again. I returned there once in the autumn by myself to see to the removal of our possessions, including furniture belonging to Mahler's childhood – dear to him for that reason – and said goodbye to the scene of our bitterest sorrows.

This autumn too, being exhausted by visitors, it occurred to us to escape them by going away simply for a holiday – a thing we had never done during our whole married life. We decided to take the recently opened Tauerbahn and travelled by it to Salzburg, where we put up at the Hotel Nelböck in a large garden-room. We felt that we were on our honeymoon and regretted very much that I had promised to go and see Burckhard next day. Mahler stayed in Salzburg and I went out to Sankt Gilgen, where Burckhard was. I had heard that he was seriously ill. Almost his first words were: 'I must be in a very bad way for Mahler to let you come and see me.' He was right; Mahler had always been jealous of him, but only as a spiritual influence. I had always gone to him for advice during the years before I married. In temperament and attitude to life they were complete opposites. Burckhard preached Nietzsche's doctrine of the superman, and he had the right to, for he lived up to it in all his many activities. He ran the Burgtheater, he was a Privy Councillor and judge of the High Court, he loved sailing when the lake was stormy, he was a daring climber. He had no equal in strength and courage, and nothing whatever could stop him. He was a pagan and hated Christianity. He could live among brigands in Sicily, disguised as one himself, and pick up any dialect so quickly that he was at home in any company. 'Death,' he used to say, 'exists only for those who believe in it, and therefore it has no existence for me.'

It was impossible for Mahler, who saw everything from the opposite point of view, to get on with him, and Burckhard felt the same about Mahler. Whenever they met there were fierce arguments. During our last winter in Vienna I noticed that Burckhard used to open a window to cool his heated head. This alarmed me. I told Mahler that there must be something seriously the matter, and from that moment Mahler was an altered man as far as Burckhard was concerned. He avoided all controversial subjects, and the moment feeling entered a perfect understanding followed.

When I saw Burckhard at Sankt Gilgen he was in a sorry state. 'Do you know,' he said, 'I'm on the way to going blind? It takes fifteen or twenty minutes before I can open my eyes in the mornings. One day I shan't be able to and then I'll be blind.'

He spent his nights mostly in a hut in the woods. 'We ought to do as the animals do. When their end is near, they creep into the undergrowth to die.'

He had a drawbridge made for his villa at the edge of the Wolfgangsee and laid in a stock of provisions. If he did not wish to see anybody (not even his old housekeeper) he drew up the bridge and broke off all intercourse with the world.

Mahler was going to send a motor-car to fetch me back next day, but to my great joy he came in it himself; and we persuaded Burckhard to come back with us to Salzburg. Just before we got there he grew uneasy and asked to be put down there and then. This was the last time they saw each other.

We went out to many lovely places from Salzburg, to the Königssee among others; but we avoided strenuous walks owing to the ever-present anxiety about his heart. Once we knew he had valvular disease of the heart we were afraid of everything. He was always stopping on a walk to feel his own pulse; and he often asked me during the day to listen to his heart and see whether the beat was clear, or rapid, or calm. I had been alarmed for years by the creaking sound his heart made – it was particularly loud on the second beat – and I had always known that it must be diseased.

I had often implored him to give up his long bicycle rides, his climbing and also swimming under water, to which he was so passionately attached. There was nothing of that sort now. On the contrary, he had a pedometer in his pocket. His steps and pulse-beats were numbered and his life a torment.

This summer was the saddest we had ever spent or were to spend together. Every excursion, every attempt at distraction was a failure. Grief and anxiety pursued us wherever we went. Work was his one resource. He slaved at *Das Lied von der Erde* and the first drafts of the Ninth.

The first performance of the Seventh Symphony took place in Prague in September.* Mahler went ahead and I remained behind to see to all the practical arrangements for our autumn migration. There were many of Mahler's friends in Prague, Neisser, Berliner, Gabrilovitch, and also several youthful musicians, Alban Berg, Bodanzky, Keussler, Klemperer. They all helped him to revise the orchestration and to copy the parts.† Even at the final rehearsal he was aware of lack of balance and never ceased making alterations in the proofs as long as any possibility of doing so remained. On all the various occasions when his symphonies were performed for the first time, younger musicians gathered round to give him their help, as they did now.

I arrived in time for the last rehearsals; and as I was alone he sent Berliner to meet me instead of coming himself, which very

---

* On 19th September 1908. (D.M.)

† Otto Klemperer, however, in his reminiscences of Mahler, writes that he and his young colleagues would gladly have helped Mahler 'but he would not hear of it and did it all on his own'. (D.M.)

much alarmed me. I found him in bed; he was nervous and unwell. His room was littered with orchestral parts, for his alterations were incessant in those days, not of course in the composition,
but in the instrumentation. From the Fifth onwards he found it
impossible to satisfy himself; the Fifth was differently orchestrated
for practically every performance; the Sixth and Seventh were
continually in process of revision. It was a phase. His self-
assurance returned with the Eighth, and although *Das Lied von
der Erde* is posthumous I cannot imagine his altering a note in a
work so economical in its means of expression.

But now he was torn by doubts. He avoided the society of his
fellow-musicians, which as a rule he eagerly sought, and went to
bed immediately after dinner so as to save his energy for the rehearsals. On one occasion Artur Bodanzky went up to his room
with him, and I spent an hour or so with the rest. He came back
with tears in his eyes and said to me in an undertone: 'I shall never
love any woman as I love Mahler.'

Mahler's health and spirits improved as the rehearsals went on,
and his self-confidence rose.

The Seventh was scarcely understood by the public. It had a
succès d'estime. Mahler went to Munich shortly after to rehearse
and conduct it there. He asked my mother to join him. I was unable to go, as we were soon to return to America and I had to
make use of his absence to pack; and so I missed precious moments
of our common life.

We were to sail from Hamburg this time, but before we set
off there was one more unpleasant scene between Mahler and
Justine. When she married she took away a number of books and
papers with her; among them there was the libretto, *Rübezahl*,*
which Mahler had written in rivalry with Hugo Wolf. She may
have carried it off by accident or from the desire to possess anything he had written, but in any case it was not with his permission,
for he wished to destroy it. He had made a search for this and
other manuscripts which had also vanished, but found no trace
of any of them. One day when we were lunching with the Rosés
he chanced to see a manuscript of Lipiner's in Justine's bookcase.
He accused her of being in possession of other papers of his,

* See Introduction pp. xxv-xxvi and Letter 138. (D.M.)

but she swore she had nothing else whatever. But one day Roller said to us: 'Justi gave me a youthful work of Mahler's to read yesterday.' The sequel was very odd, for Mahler insisted that I should demand the return of the manuscript on the ground that he refused to speak to her until it was in his possession.

I did as I was told, but Justine took her solemn oath that she had burnt it. I told Mahler this, but he refused to believe a word of it. I had to go to her again, armed this time with the threat that unless she handed it up she would not see him again before he set off for America. Nevertheless, she swore, as she loved her husband and children, that she had burnt it and added numerous embellishments to her tale, such as that Arnold had had to tear it up to get it into the stove, it was so bulky. Mahler was obdurate and stuck to it that she was lying, and he left Vienna without having seen her. I remained behind for some days. Justine paid me a visit and I brought the matter up once more. 'Of course I didn't burn it,' she said abruptly. 'I sent it after him the moment he had left and he'll find it waiting for him at Bremen when he gets there.'

We met in Hamburg and went on board at Cuxhaven. We had been given a rousing send-off from Cherbourg to the strains of the incomparable Marseillaise, but the sentimental Germans made our departure this time a very melancholy affair. All the passengers, including ourselves, wept aloud as the band played: ''Tis God's decree that we must part, From all that's dearest to the heart, Must pa-a-art, must pa-a-art.' It was too much.

We had our three-year-old child with us for the first time and I had engaged an elderly Englishwoman as nurse, who was always inculcating the stoicism of a Samurai in her charge. When we were on the tender and the large ship loomed up, the little girl gave a cry of delight, whereupon this lady advanced, held her tightly by the hands and said sternly: 'Don't get excited – don't get excited!' Mahler heard this and instantly snatched her up and sat her on the taffrail with her feet dangling over the water. 'There you are, and now be as excited as you like. You shall be excited.' She was.

We did not go back to the Majestic but stayed this year and the next year at the Savoy, where nearly all the stars of the Metropolitan, Caruso, Sembrich, etc., stayed also.

Mahler was now in the best of health. He conducted *Figaro*, *Queen of Spades* and *Fidelio* during this winter, 1908–9, and made fresh studies of them all. It was the first performance of *Queen of Spades* in New York.* Sembrich, Farrar, Eames and Scotti sang in *Figaro*. Slezak made his début at the Metropolitan in *Queen of Spades*. For *Fidelio*, Mahler had Roller's scenery sent over from Vienna, and he played the third *Leonore* overture before the last scene as in Vienna.†

Minnie Untermeyer and Mrs. Sheldon, both leading lights in New York society, left together after one of these performances. Both were full of enthusiasm, and on their way home they had an inspiration. They determined to put an orchestra at Mahler's disposal and within a few days they collected a hundred thousand dollars. This came in very opportunely for Mahler. His relations with the Metropolitan were no longer very good. Conried was at death's door.‡ Gatti-Casazza, who had been sent for from the Scala, was now director of the Metropolitan, and he had brought Toscanini over with him. The glorious days of German supremacy were over. It is fair to say that Mahler was offered the post but declined it.

Toscanini had gone so far as to make it a condition that the first production at which he was to conduct should be *Tristan*, an opera Mahler had already studied with the company.§ Weary of conflict he gave *Tristan* up. Toscanini immediately took it in hand and rehearsed it all over again in a manner entirely different. Mahler bitterly resented this and took no further pleasure in opera in New York. We had all read the cables between the Metropolitan and Gatti-Casazza. The Metropolitan wanted Toscanini, and he made *Tristan* his supreme object and an indispensable condition. So Mahler relinquished it to him. Instead of thanking

* The New York première of the Tchaikovsky was later than Alma Mahler states. It took place on 5th March 1910. Mahler's *Figaro* was introduced to New York on 13th January 1909. (D.M.)

† Mahler introduced his legendary performance of *Fidelio* to the Metropolitan on 20th March 1908. See also footnote on p. 72. (D.M.)

‡ He died in 1909. (D.M.)

§ In fact, Toscanini made his début at the Metropolitan in *Aïda* on 16th November 1908. He did not conduct *Tristan* until 27th November 1909. (D.M.)

him, Toscanini from the first moment contemptuously ignored him. He even went so far as to hold him up to scorn during rehearsals. He was always telling the orchestra that Mahler 'could not do that' and that he had no understanding of *Tristan*. We went to the first night of this production of Toscanini's. The nuances in his Wagner were distressing. His style has been simplified since those days.*

And so Mahler joyfully welcomed another outlet. A committee was formed immediately, the active members of which were Mrs. Draper, Mrs. Untermeyer, Mrs. Sheldon and Mrs. Schelling. The contract was signed before we left for Europe and the engagement, which was to begin when we returned, was by no means exacting. He was to give a series of concerts with an orchestra of his own. This had always been his dream.

One consequence was that I was invited to a Ladies' Lunch at a club. It was a beautiful building with a swimming-bath and the costliest furnishings. All the women also were of that incredible elegance to be seen only in America, but last of all there arrived a little person in an ill-made coat and skirt which was very much the worse for wear. She was received with acclamation and nobody appeared to notice her odd attire. It was Natalie Curtis, an amazing creature, of whom I shall have more to say. Thus I got to know and to love the truly democratic America. Wealth bowed down to poverty if it clothed a creative, gifted mind.

We also met the sculptor, Bitter, who lived on the Palisades, as the cliffs on the opposite side of the Hudson are called. We crossed the Hudson and arrived – how I no longer remember – at the summit. His studio and his house, which was separated from it, overhung the abyss in a breath-taking manner. He received us dressed in white as a chef, and grilled a fish for us in the Indian fashion on an ebony slab turned to the open fire. Mahler was so charmed with this deveice and by everything he saw that it was difficult to tear him away, and before leaving it was agreed that we should return for a New Year's party in the studio.

Friedrich Hirth, the great sinologist, spent Christmas Eve with us and told us wonderful stories of China the whole night long. We felt we had stepped out of the real world.

* Toscanini died in 1957. (D.M.)

Marcella Sembrich invited us to a Christmas party. Caruso was there and others of their circle at the Opera. We liked them all, even though intercourse with them was rather superficial. Caruso had genius even as a human being. They all had an instinctive perception of Mahler's importance and treated him with the greatest respect in private life as well as on the stage. Sembrich's Christmas tree caught fire and we were within an ace of being burnt to death.

New Year's Eve came and the long expected party in Bitter's studio; but Mahler had to go alone as I was not feeling well. A terrific blizzard blew up during the evening, and I was so anxious that in spite of a high temperature I could not leave the window. Far and wide there was no one to be seen, not a vehicle, not a cat or a dog. Only at intervals a solitary man lurched across the square, holding on desperately to the bushes of Central Park, or edging his way along the face of the buildings.

Mahler arrived at last at two o'clock, utterly exhausted. He had left Bitter just after twelve. He got on to an omnibus at the ferry-boat landing-stage. Everybody in it was drunk and he was so nauseated that he got out and with much difficulty found a hansom. A few minutes later it was blown over and he had to creep from under it. While he was paying the fare his pinz-nez were blown into a snowdrift. He was blind and the cabby tipsy, but between them, in the howling gale, they fished the pince-nez out of the snow. He was now two streets away and after clawing his way along for half an hour was blown into the entrance of the hotel.

People in Europe have no idea of the force of these blizzards. It is almost impossible to make any headway against them and no one who can avoid it goes out of doors.

Thus in a foreign land we built up a world of our own which was more European than Europe itself. One evening we had five people in, all of whom had come over steerage – Bitter to evade conscription, Fränkel for lack of money, and all either destitute or in flight. They had thrilling tales to tell of their early days in America. Mahler was younger and less oppressed, his grief was dying down; and when we arrived in Paris in the spring we were able to take a certain pleasure in life.

They were days of blissful repose.

Carl Moll had had the wonderful idea of commissioning Rodin to do a bust of Mahler, and Sophie Clemenceau had contrived to represent it as Rodin's own wish to model a head which interested him so much. Mahler believed this – though with reservations – and agreed, as he never otherwise would have done. The sittings which followed were a marvellous experience.

Rodin fell in love with his model; he was really unhappy when we had to leave Paris, for he wanted to work on the bust much longer. His method was unlike that of any other sculptor I have had the opportunity of watching. He first made flat surfaces in the rough lump, and then added little pellets of clay which he rolled between his fingers while he talked. He worked by adding to the lump instead of subtracting from it. As soon as we left he smoothed it all down and next day added more. I scarcely ever saw him with a tool in his hand. He said Mahler's head was a mixture of Franklin's, Frederick the Great's and Mozart's. After Mahler's death Rodin showed me a head in marble, which he had done from memory, and pointed out how like it was. A custodian of the Rodin Museum in Paris actually labelled it 'Mozart'.

One of his mistresses was always waiting patiently in the next room while he worked. This singular arrangement held good in whichever of his numerous studios he happened to be; some girl or other with scarlet lips invariably spent long and unrewarded hours there, for he took very little notice of her and did not speak to her even during the rests. His fascination must have been powerful to induce these girls – and they were girls in what is called 'society' – to put up unabashed with such treatment. But then, his own wife waited in Meudon all her life.

He sadly showed us the sketches for his Balzac, which were never carried out. It is the same in Paris as in Vienna, those boils of a sick world.

Picquart, then Minister for War, gave us lunch in the Ministry, where he lived. His old friend, Madame Ramazotti, was hostess. Painlevé, the Clemenceaus, Baron L'Allemand and we were the guests. We first met Picquart in Strasbourg in 1905. He made a very deep impression on us. Now we heard his story from his friends.

He went to Tunis when a young officer on the General Staff. While there he received a document from Paris with an urgent minute. He read it through and finding flaws in it sent it back for correction. It soon came back, again with instructions to deal with it immediately. Again he sent it back at once without having signed it, giving as his reason that an injustice had been committed. This document was the sentence passed on Dreyfus. Colonel Henry, who was the real culprit and had the plot in hand, was now compelled to take steps against Picquart. He had a search made in the hope of finding some excuse for having him cashiered and putting an obedient tool in his place. All he could find in Picquart's desk were a few ancient and trifling love-letters to the wife of the president of the Law Court at Rennes. He sent them to the unsuspecting husband, and Picquart, in spite of the lack of incriminating evidence, went to prison. The wife was divorced, although the whole story belonged to the past. Picquart treated her as his wife in spite of her being by then an elderly woman.

Picquart had no wish at all for Dreyfus's acquaintance, eager as Dreyfus was himself. He had acted solely from humanity and a burning sense of justice. Dreyfus was nothing to him personally. As with Zola, who also was unacquainted with Dreyfus, it was a question of upholding the truth.

The rest is history: Dreyfus was declared innocent and brought back after years on Devil's Island. Colonel Henry committed suicide, and Picquart, after three years' imprisonment, was set at liberty. He and Dreyfus were rehabilitated and promoted before the whole army. Picquart added that he had not at all liked having to share the ceremony with Dreyfus.

When we drove up to the Ministry the gates opened and a guard of honour drawn up to left and right in full-dress uniform presented arms as we passed through. Picquart was standing at the top of the steps, as happy as a child over this idea of his.

'It is the rule in the case of royalty. You are the same in my eyes,' he called out to Mahler.

Each of us was given his or her favourite dish, of which Picquart had taken private note in anticipation. After lunch he showed us a small gold box. He pressed a spring, the lid flew open and a bird set with jewels sprang out of the box, sat on the lid and sang enchantingly. He gazed at this bird, which had diamonds for eyes, and said with emotion: 'It was the only music I heard during my three years of imprisonment. An American, who has remained anonymous, smuggled it in. I was not allowed to have any music or books from my friends. I might receive visits one day a month, when for ten minutes I could speak with friends or relations from behind a grill – overheard, of course. Attempts to poison me were made twice. Knowing this I made it my habit to hold up every morsel of food I ate against the light, and so I was never caught out. Another time there was ground glass in my food. Thank God, it's over.'

He carefully put the box away again in another room.

His love for Mahler was both reverent and paternal, for although he was only his elder by a year or two he was more detached and set. After the fall of the Government he commanded a division at Amiens. A thoroughbred reared with him and only great presence of mind kept him in the saddle. The same thing happened at a parade soon after, and during the last march past his horse reared for the third time and fell with him. He was fatally injured and taken to Paris, where he died in the arms of the devoted friend who had been a mother to him. His funeral procession gave rise to one of the most impressive demonstrations

Paris has ever known. Is it possible that a nation understood the greatness of a soul like his?

I happened to be in the cinema when his funeral procession was shown. It seemed incredible that the man we loved was passing by in that coffin. This was after Mahler's death.

The Chief of the Police invited us to his box at the Opéra for a gala performance of *Tristan*. General Picquart and the Clemenceaus were there too. Louise Grandjean and Van Dyck were singing. In the great scene between Tristan and Isolde in the second act, Van Dyck jumped up time after time and advanced to the prompter's box and there, embracing the audience with extended arms, he addressed to them instead of to Isolde his intimate discourse on the dear little word 'and'. This was too much for Mahler. He could not bring himself to sit it out a moment longer; so disregarding the feelings of our host and the surprised glances of General Picquart and the rest, we got up and went out.

By the time we got back to Vienna my nerves were in a critical state and I was ordered a rest-cure at Levico. I first took Mahler to Toblach and then went to Levico with my child. I was in a state of profound melancholy. I sat night after night on my balcony, weeping and looking out at the crowd of gay and happy people, whose laughter grated on my ears. I longed to plunge myself into love or life or anything that could release me from my icy constraint. We exchanged letters daily on abstract topics. He got anxious about me and at last he came to see me.

I met him at Trient, but when he got out of the train I failed to recognize him. Wishing to look his best he had gone to the barber at Toblach before he left, and he had been given a close crop while he read the newspaper without giving a thought to what was going on. The sides of his head were shorn as close as a convict's and his excessively long, thin face, deprived now of all relief, was unrecognizably ugly. I could not get used to the transformation and after two days he sadly departed again.

Mahler was quite without vanity about his personal appearance.

He grew a beard in his earlier years to give him an older look. He also had enormous horn-rimmed spectacles made for him, 'So as to see in all directions.' The lenses were round and gave him a very menacing appearance. Later on, at Maiernigg, he used to let his moustache grow because he found shaving a nuisance.

He had been working at full pressure during the summer and had finished the Ninth, but without venturing to call it so. In the winter too he had kept to his usual Vienna programme, devoting every morning to revision and orchestration.

Erich Wolfgang Korngold had played his fairy-tale cantata, *Gold*, to Mahler for the first time in June 1907. I was not present, but Mahler told me afterwards with great enthusiasm what an impression the music of this ten-year old boy had made on him.

Now, Julius Korngold, a music critic and a friend of ours, and his wife, paid us a visit and brought their son, Erich with them. He at once engrossed all our attention. At Mahler's request he played some of his own compositions and played them so perfectly that it seemed incredible he had only just begun to learn the piano. He did not welcome the attention paid to him. He slipped out to play with our little daughter on the top of a haystack. I went out to call them in to tea. 'Don't want to,' he said. 'Why not?' ''Cause I don't eat nicely.'

He was not to be persuaded and so the two children ate their cakes out of doors. They got on quite well together as both were laconic and morose. Indeed, my daughter Anna, who was five, begged him not to go but to spend the night with her.

As soon as we were alone again we talked for hours of Erich's unbelievable talent.

Happy that he could work again and, as he felt, better than ever, Mahler was in excellent spirits. The summer was interrupted only by a visit from Strauss and his wife, preceded by an exasperating exchange of telegrams from either side of the Alps. What was the weather like with us? What did the glass say? At last the omens were favourable. They arrived at Toblach and expected us to dinner. But first Mahler went down at midday. Frau Pauline greeted him in the square in front of the hotel by shouting out at the top of her voice: 'Hello, Mahler. What was it like in America? Filthy, eh? Hope you got a pile anyway.'

Mahler hurried them inside and up to their room, and leaving them as soon as possible came to meet us. He had no stomach for such situations. And besides he grudged every hour of his time.

My mother, Roller and I were included in the invitation to dinner and the Strausses had a neighbour of theirs at Garmisch with them, whom they had brought along out of gratitude for his kindness in shutting up his dogs, and himself too, while Strauss was working. We fully understood. We too had had neighbours at Maiernigg, an amiable but utterly uninteresting family, with whom we had to be on friendly terms as our only defence against their live-stock of all descriptions – poultry, geese, dogs, of course, and a brother of the lady of the house, who was a baritone and sang most execrably. In addition to all this, the master of the house was deaf, and it took the combined lungs of the whole family to arouse in him a gleam of comprehension. The massacre of Mahler's music had to be bought off with visits, theatre-tickets, boxes for the opera and, in general, at the cost of eternal vigilance. We understood very well.

This gentleman of Garmisch was a colonel and quite scatter-brained. He constantly mixed everything up. He took my mother to be Mahler's wife and Roller to be my husband.

Frau Strauss was very much wrought up that evening. Her son, who was still a boy, got first a slap on the head and next a glass of milk. We all stood awkwardly round and Strauss, to get the company seated, motioned to Mahler to sit next his wife. At this Pauline exclaimed: 'Yes, but only if he doesn't start fidgeting, because I can't put up with it.' Mahler, who was just about to sit down, went instead to the far end of the table. Strauss joined him and they both left us to deal with her. She excelled herself that evening. We trailed home exhausted in mind and body.

On 1st October we made a move. Our Vienna flat in Auen-bruggergasse was superfluous now that we spent so much of every winter in New York; and so I packed all the books and china, and all our movable possessions were stored. Mahler said goodbye to the rooms where he had spent eight years of his life and went to Moravia to put the final touches to *Das Lied von der Erde*.

I always did my utmost to save Mahler all the drudgery of life. When we moved house or went away anywhere he knew nothing of what went on behind the scenes. The only exception was our first, honeymoon journey. He said there was nothing in packing and piled everything into a trunk in a heap. As soon as the trunk was turned on one side all was confusion. From that day onwards I took sole charge.

He did not return from Moravia until my child and I had recovered from an operation on our tonsils, and after spending a few days at my mother's he went to Amsterdam to conduct his Seventh Symphony. Mengelberg's preliminary rehearsals were so thorough, on this occasion as on all others, that Mahler was able to conduct this difficult work without rehearsing it himself. He arrived in Paris the day I did.

October found us in America once more. We could no more restrain our tears now than the first time at the sight of the magnificent spectacle which the arrival in the harbour of New York unfolds. No one who was near and dear to us ever awaited us on the quay, and yet this scene, unequalled of its kind in the whole world, moved us so deeply that our knees shook as we walked down the gangway; and not even the highly unpleasant customs examination could dash the feeling of eager suspense.

This time Mahler came to conduct his own concerts and he was glad to have no more to do with the operatic stage. The arrangements made allowed him every other week in New York for the rehearsal of one or two programmes, which the week after he gave twice in New York and twice in Brooklyn. Later, when he had a number of programmes ready, there were to be longer tours to Philadelphia, Springfield, Buffalo and all the towns which looked to New York to provide their music.

He conducted once only at the Metropolitan by permission of the new committee, which was responsible for all the expenses of this year's trip. He conducted Smetana's *Bartered Bride*, with Destinn as Marie, Jörn as Hans. It was a marvellous performance. Americans, however, were no lovers of rusticity in opera. Nor were they of the starkly Germanic: they could dispense with the *Ring*. Their favourite Wagner operas were *Tristan* and *Meistersinger*.

Mahler took four particularly lovely pieces from the Bach suites and strung them together for one of his concert programmes. He worked out the figured bass and played it marvellously on the harpsichord, with his baton clipped tightly under his arm. Schirmer, the publisher, made an offer to him for this arrangement of Bach's music and Mahler took the keenest pleasure in working on it.* He played it at many of the concerts, more for us than for the audience. He altered his continuo realization according to his fancy every time and cross-examined me afterwards about the effect of each. It was hardly likely that any change would be lost on me. The critics over there did not raise the cry of sacrilege. This was reserved for the pundits of Europe.

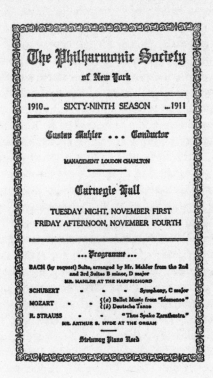

The Philharmonic Society
of New York

1910— SIXTY-NINTH SEASON —1911

Gustav Mahler ... Conductor

MANAGEMENT LOUDON CHARLTON

Carnegie Hall

TUESDAY NIGHT, NOVEMBER FIRST
FRIDAY AFTERNOON, NOVEMBER FOURTH

... Programme ...

BACH (by request) Suite, arranged by Mr. Mahler from the 2nd
and 3rd Suites B minor, D major
MR. MAHLER AT THE HARPSICHORD

SCHUBERT   •   •   Symphony, C major
MOZART   •   •   {(a) Ballet Music from "Idomeneo"
                    {(b) Deutsche Tänze
R. STRAUSS   •   •   "Thus Spake Zarathustra"
MR. ARTHUR S. HYDE AT THE ORGAN

Steinway Piano Used

When Marcella Sembrich bade farewell to the stage† every artist was eager to take part in the great occasion and so, instead of a single opera, acts and scenes from several in which she particularly shone were performed. Caruso, Bonci, Farrar, Eames, Scotti and all the conductors, including Mahler, offered their services as a tribute to this incomparable singer. Mahler conducted

* It was published in 1910. (D.M.)
† On 6th February 1909. (D.M.)

an act from *Figaro*. She herself sang all her parts for the last time with a perfection unsurpassed even in her best years. At the end, after she had been called before the curtain thirty or forty times, the curtain went up and revealed a grove of laurel overhanging the whole stage. The whole company stood in a half-circle round a table, at which the Mayor of New York was seated. He rose immediately and advanced towards Madame Sembrich, who retreated in embarrassment as he presented her with a large rope of magnificent pearls, while the audience stood and clapped. After he had made a speech in praise of her merits as an artist and a woman, all her colleagues came forward with their presents. She had invited us to a ball after the performance, and we all proceeded there laden with the costly tributes of silver and gold which were heaped upon her. The orchestra of the opera surprised her on her arrival at the hotel with a flourish of trumpets and played at the ball throughout the night, to show their gratitude for her generosity after the San Francisco earthquake; all their instruments were destroyed and she gave up her salary until they were replaced. She opened the ball by dancing a mazurka with Paderewski.

Shortly afterwards the whole opera company gave her a farewell party on her leaving New York. Everyone connected with the opera was present besides a few others, including Paderewski. It took place at the Hotel Plaza with the greatest pomp and ceremony. Caruso drew his masterly caricatures and showed them to all save the victim. They were often too telling to be borne with equanimity. He did several of Mahler and showed them to me, but could not be persuaded to let Mahler see them. 'People say beforehand they won't mind,' he said. 'Then you let them see and they're very angry. That's happened to me too often already.'

We saw a good deal in those days of the aristocratic families whose ancestors had come over in the *Mayflower*. Our circle had become so large that every day was filled up. Anglo-Americans are quite unlike the Latin Races, among whom one remains a foreigner for ever. They genuinely take you to their hearts. You are at home and share in all their pleasures. They are at your service if they see any opportunity of serving you, as I was to learn very often later on. Mahler accompanied me whenever he felt inclined and enjoyed himself more than I should ever have thought possible. He never missed a dinner-party; and they were very different, certainly, from those we knew at home. The invitation was for 7.15 or 7.30; the dinner was excellent, far better, needless to say, than in the hotel; the talk was lighter in vein than in Europe, but whether it was as trivial or as profound depended naturally, as in Europe, on whom chance placed one next to. The men retreated to the smoking-room after dinner and the ladies were left to themselves. By ten one was at home again without fatigue. New faces had been seen, new personalities encountered, and these new acquaintances did not fail to invite us in their turn, and so our engagements lengthened out in an unending chain. We used to sit up for an hour afterwards and talk over our impressions.

On 15th November, a date I noted because we enjoyed the day so much, we went out to Oyster Bay, a stretch of coast owned almost entirely by the Roosevelt family. It was a day of cloudless weather. We travelled by a little railway and were met at the station and driven in a pony-trap across sand dunes to Mrs. West-Roosevelt's house. We stopped in front of a high terrace wall, on to which we stepped from the trap, and saw in front of us a lovely old timber house standing on its terraced eminence and surrounded by the sea. The sight was so overwhelming that we forgot to greet our hostess.

The hall and every room were as perfect as the surroundings. We felt at home immediately. Mrs. Roosevelt took us to see the house of her brother-in-law Theodore Roosevelt, who was big-game shooting in Africa at the time. It too, although it had less character than the old farmhouse, was beautifully situated on rising ground, surrounded by blue sea. We could see through the house from outside because every room opened on to a veranda of glass. Mrs. Roosevelt observed that this was symbolic of Theodore, whose life was as clear and open as his house.

One evening after dining with Otto H. Kahn we went to a séance of Eusapia Palladino's. Mahler, the Kahns, an Englishman, Fränkel and I drove there in two automobiles. We got out in Broadway at a building of dreary proletarian aspect and ascended in the lift to what might be called the attic floor. There was no one to be seen. After a search we discovered Palladino's spacious room, where the séance was to take place, but she was not there. Next door a riotous drinking-party was in progress. There was a great bawling and smashing of glasses against the walls; but we were none the wiser. There was a flat opposite, vacant except for the litter of its recent occupants. Next to it, there was the shining brass plate of an agency for mechanical pianos. We heard trills and roulades, but when we looked through the keyhole there was nobody there. We began to feel very queer. Mrs. Kahn was wearing a white satin dress with white slippers and strings of pearls nearly to the floor and the sight of her finery in these surroundings added to the weird effect. At last Palladino appeared.

She had a kind of peasant's shawl round her head and a face which was red and puffy and vinous. She gave us a brief and casual greeting and went on with a reeling gait into the large and dimly lighted room. We followed. Before her arrival we had been invited by her two secretaries, who later took notes of the proceedings, to examine the room and in particular the alcove, curtained off by a black hanging, which was immediately behind her chair. Its walls were papered black. It had a window looking out on to a roof illumined by the moon and covered with snow. There was nothing whatever to arouse suspicion.

She sat down without ceremony and the two secretaries and a girl turned out the lights, leaving only a red one in front of each of the two secretaries. We sat down uneasily and held hands. Within a very short space she went into convulsions. Her face began to flicker wanly, her breath came in quick gasps. The Englishman and Fränkel sat on each side of her, gripping her hands and knees. Fränkel felt her pulse, counting out aloud at a terrific rate when she rose to a crisis. She insisted on us all repeating 'va bene' without interruption, and if any of us stopped he was angrily told to go on. The Englishman went into a trance from the perpetual repetition of 'va bene' and so was out of the running.

The rest of us all felt we were being touched: phosphorescent bodies which we saw moving about came into contact with us. I grasped at one of them and had something and then nothing in my hand. Palladino commanded Mahler to look into the alcove behind her. He drew the black curtain aside. Everything in there was bathed in phosphorescent light and everything was in movement. A mandolin flew through the air and bashed him lightly on the forehead. He let the curtain fall hastily back in his confusion and Palladino murmured that he was in danger. She summoned him almost compassionately to come and sit beside her. The table shot up to the ceiling, but if anyone of us spoke a word in an unsympathetic tone it abruptly descended. The black curtain swept the table as though waved by an unseen hand; the mandolin and light objects of wood glided about above the table, on the edge of which our hands were resting with interlinked fingers. Although warned not to, I caught at the bellying, balloon-like curtain and again I felt something palpable and impalpable.

We went away in silence, pondering deeply; and for many days after we were still pondering. After a week Mahler said: 'Perhaps there wasn't any truth in it and we only dreamt it.' This seemed to me very remarkable, since for the first two or three days he had done nothing but fish out fresh details from his memory, and now suddenly it was all a dream.

We often went to Mrs. Havemeyer's. She lived in a fairy-palace, built by Tiffany, and gave musical afternoons. We did not, however, go to hear the Haydn and Brahms quartets. We went straight to her gallery of masterpieces. She had eight Rembrandts, and a large number of Goyas; but the cream of the collection was El Greco's only landscape, Toledo, and his Cardinal. My stepfather, Moll, had so often shown us this painting of the Cardinal in photographs and described its colouring that when Mrs. Havemeyer first displayed it Mahler broke in: 'I've seen that before somewhere.' She went pale, for there is nothing so terrible to a collector's ears as the suggestion that any object in his collection, whatever its merits or beauty, is not unique. I tried in vain to recall to Mahler's memory Moll's description of the picture: he obstinately stuck to it that he must have seen the picture before. I then explained his mistake to the poor woman, who was beginning to think she had been cheated and that somewhere, unknown to her, there was a duplicate Cardinal in existence.

We spent many an hour walking up and down in this long

gallery, in which the concealed lighting fell smoothly on the pictures, while snatches of music came to our ears from far away without fatiguing or enlisting our attention. Mahler had no native feeling for painting; his mind was too much under the dominion of literature. Yet by degrees, through much looking and an exorbitant desire to know all that was to be known, he began to derive pleasure from pure painting and the ability to judge it. Moll, Klimt, Roller and Kolo Moser disputed the right to be his teacher.

One day after Mahler had got his orchestra, a card arrived from Louis Tiffany requesting permission to attend the rehearsals in concealment owing to his shyness. Shortly afterwards he invited us to his house and Mrs. Havemeyer, the link between us, took us there. We stopped before a palatial building and ascended an imposing flight of steps; thence we proceeded upstairs. Sudanese native huts with all their furnishings were let into the walls all the way up on either side. At the top we entered a room so enormous it seemed to us immeasurable. Coloured lustres shed a soft, flowerlike light through the gloom. The prelude to *Parsifal* was being played on an organ. We were told later that the organist was a grandson of Shelley. As far as we knew we were quite alone. A black fireplace in the middle of the room had four colossal hearths, in each of which a fire of a different colour was blazing. We stood stock-still in amazement.

Then a man with a remarkably fine head came up to us and murmured a few incomprehensible words. It was Tiffany, the man who spoke to no one; and before we could collect our wits, before Mahler, indeed, could have had time to make any reply, he vanished. We heard afterwards that Tiffany was a hashish addict and never quite in his right senses. Like everything there, he made the impression of being enchanted. The chimney went up and up for ever, no roof was visible, but high up in the walls panels of stained glass, designed by Tiffany, were let in, and lighted from without. We spoke in whispers and felt that these panels of flowerlike light might be the gates of Paradise. The music stopped and it was now apparent from the murmur of voices that a large company was assembled. Silent footmen perambulated with costly glasses, filled with champagne, which although on trays never clinked. Palms and sofas, beautiful women in odd shimmering robes – or did we dream? It was the thousand and one nights – in New York.

We were invited by the music publisher, Schirmer, and his wife to dine with them one day and drive with them afterwards 'down town,' into China town. The indispensable detective sat beside the chauffeur. We turned out of the busy streets into narrower ones which became by degrees quieter, narrower, darker and more uncanny. We got out, accompanied by the detective with a loaded revolver in his pocket, and went into an opium den. A creature with a sickeningly womanish face received us in an ante-room, where we had to put down a sum of money. He began at once to give us a long account of his successes with white ladies, and told us he acted female parts in the Chinese Theatre. A Chinese woman, of course, may not either act or look on in a theatre. He showed it in his face – it was the most degenerate man-woman face you could imagine. He showed us numerous photographs of American women he had – and he said the rest by gestures. Then he conducted us into several small but high rooms, empty in the middle but furnished with bunks along the sides, each of which contained a stretcher; and on each stretcher lay a doped Chinese with his head lolling into the room. Some of them raised their heads heavily as we approached, but at once let them sink again. It was a gruesomely horrible sight. They were simply dumped there to sleep off their intoxication. They might be robbed or murdered while they were in this state and know nothing about it. The whole scene resembled a baker's shop with human loaves.

On now to a house of cards higher and higher, up into a room luxuriously furnished for strangers, cushions everywhere, and beside each cushion an opium pipe. And a Chinese, for payment, was ready to smoke a pipe on the spot while we watched him slowly succumb, rolling his eyes and twisting his limbs about. We were exhorted to smoke too but declined with horror. Next the theatre. Charming, but no play was being given. If it had been, no European would have been allowed among the audience.

On again. Rats with long pigtails slunk nimbly and rapidly along the walls of the stinking street. Mahler said: 'I can hardly believe that these are my brothers.'

On again. Small shops, small hotels, but all silent. Finally, on the outskirts of this district we came on the habitat of a religious sect. There was a large hall at the far end of which sat a man with the face of a fanatic playing hymns on a harmonium in a pronouncedly whining style. The benches were occupied by a starving congregation. We were given the explanation. For listening to the hymns and joining in – a cup of coffee and a roll. What wretchedness in those faces! We pushed our way out, followed by hostile eyes, and for long afterwards we could still hear the flat notes of the hungry singers.

On again, and now the Jewish quarter. It was dark by this time. But here all was life and bustle, chaffering and shouting. The racial difference was staggering, but it was because the Jews worked day and night shifts to lose no time. The whole street was full from end to end of old clothes and rags. The air was heavy with the smell of food. I asked Mahler softly in his own words, 'Are *these* our brothers?' He shook his head in despair.

With a sigh of relief we at last turned a corner and found ourselves in a well-lighted street among our own sort of people. Can it be that there are only class and not race distinctions?

We went a lot to the opera, and the theatre too. Boxes and seats were, naturally, always at Mahler's disposal. Once we went to a play by a young and unknown playwright named MacKay. This play – *The Scarecrow* – was based on a symbolical use of fairy-tales; it was extremely talented and marvellously produced. We saw it three times and would have seen it ten times, but as we were the whole audience it was taken off.

The Manhattan Opera, for a long time superior to the Metropolitan itself, was the creation of Hammerstein, the cigar merchant. We saw Mary Garden there as Salome; she was unrivalled also as Louise and Mélisande, with Perier and Dufranne as Pelléas and Golaud. Hammerstein sent to Paris both for the scenery and for the conductor of *Louise*. A German could never have put on such a production. Mahler conducted *Louise* himself in Vienna, but I never appreciated it to the full until I heard a quite ordinary conductor conduct it in Paris. The orchestra in Vienna was too heavy-handed – the waltz predominated; Paris has its own unaccented, ever wakeful music and thereon rested the melody and drama of *Louise*.

This was the reason no doubt why Mahler always had Italian conductors for Italian operas – Spetrino and Guarnieri. It is only natural that they should have a better command of the Italian verve and the brio in rubato than the most gifted of Germans, whether of the north or the south. However polished Toscanini's conducting of *Tristan* might be, we always felt that his Wagner suffered from a surfeit of Italian nuances. Perhaps this is the key to the future of all those opera houses which wrestle in vain with their repertory of the eighty classical operas. Perhaps there will be national seasons, Italian opera companies visiting Germany, while the whole strength of German opera migrates to Paris or Milan. Thus there would be a constant interchange of genuine art between one country and another.

Storms

1910

We got to know Joseph Weiss, the pianist, through the painter, Groll, a necessitous artist who lived among Indians, spoke their language and told us a lot about them. Weiss had a square, bald skull, with the merest tuft in the middle, and brown eyes wedged in slits, which could only mean either insanity or genius. He was the greatest pianist Mahler, according to his own account, had ever heard. He played to us for the whole of New Year's night. We sat for hours without moving.

He had arranged some of the loveliest songs of Brahms for piano only and they sounded more songful than any singer could make them. Bach's Passacaglia too – and yet his strongly original interpretations did no damage to the original composition. Mahler was so enthralled that he arranged a trio in our room. He asked Reiter, who played the horn so marvellously in the Metropolitan orchestra, and Spiering, his own first violin, to come, and Weiss was to play the piano parts. Mahler and I sat on the sofa, feeling like King Ludwig of Bavaria.

The first movement was exquisite, but as soon as the second began Weiss started playing in a wilful manner, apparently from annoyance at having to subordinate himself even for a moment. This soon brought them to loggerheads and the other two declined to play with him any longer. Weiss refused to listen to reason and simply got up and left. Mahler then played the piano part himself, and Brahms's Horn Trio cannot often have been given such a perfect performance.

After the two others had gone, Weiss, who had been keeping a look-out, came back to apologize. He was very amusing in the scorn he poured on the two others. He said their faces had put him off, and he did all he could to remove the bad impression he had made. Mahler, who had promised to help him on in New

York, felt encouraged; but, as the event was to prove, he had better have left it alone.

We asked two friends of ours, Kneisel, the well-known violinist. and Bitter, the sculptor, in to hear him play. But it was a fiasco, When he was asked to play after dinner he first of all refused and then played some perfectly frightful compositions of his own for half an hour without stopping. Mahler asked him gingerly whether he would mind playing some Brahms. This was too much for Weiss. No one who slighted his compositions could possibly understand Brahms. We had to listen a little longer while he hammered away madly and then we began talking, which Weiss apparently did not notice. The whole evening was ruined, but when Weiss joined us he was so witty and entertaining that Mahler again forgave him. In spite of warnings from all sides he agreed to let him play Schumann's piano concerto at his next concert. He had a quite extraordinary urge to break in this unbridled colt.

Weiss was starving and Mahler had induced the committee to pay him a big fee. Weiss appeared to be pleased and the rehearsals passed off unexpectedly well. Then came the dress-rehearsal. He was rather more nervous than usual, but he played the first movement well, even if without his true *élan*. This and a few wilfulnesses in his tempo annoyed Mahler, whereupon Weiss made some impertinent remarks under his breath, which Mahler purposely did not hear. He wanted to help him. Weiss recovered his self-control and began the second movement. Mahler called out to him: 'Good!' This was the end of Weiss. He seized the music and hurled it on the floor at Mahler's feet. 'As good as you any day,' he shouted, raving like a lunatic. The orchestra, thinking Mahler was in need of protection, flung themselves on Weiss. Mahler begged them not to touch him, but now it had gone too far and Weiss had to leave the concert hall.*

The rehearsal was broken off and Mahler came home, half-enraged and half-amused. But his strongest feeling was pity for

---

* A long account of the episode with Weiss at the rehearsal appeared in the New York *Press* on 31st January 1910, and it is interesting that it supports most of the details of Alma Mahler's description of the affair. On the other hand, she is perhaps a little hard on the pianist who took over at such short notice (Paolo Gallico). The first choice of deputy was someone else altogether, who sprained a tendon while rehearsing to fill Weiss's place. Gallico, who only then was approached, had not looked at Schumann's concerto for months. It was clearly a doomed occasion. (D.M.)

Weiss. And now a search began for someone to play the concerto in Weiss's place. The only pianist available was a young man whose name – not to rescue it from deserved oblivion – was X, and he undertook to play it without rehearsal, and played it so badly that Mahler from anger and shame could scarcely go on conducting. The concert was unusually well attended, because the morning papers had made a headline sensation of Mahler's fight with Weiss. There were blood-curdling pictures with the caption: 'Weiss hits Mahler on the head.' Sparks were depicted flying out of it. It was all extremely unpleasant. Immediately before the concert began Weiss turned up accompanied by a lawyer, to prove that he had presented himself with the purpose of playing, but had not been allowed to, and therefore his fee would have to be paid. 'I ought to have let him and called it quits,' Mahler said later. This concluded our friendship with Weiss. He retired soon after this to a mental home, but has apparently recovered since.

Mahler, at the request of the ladies of the committee, gave a performance of his First Symphony. After thorough rehearsal he arrived with his mind at peace. He had a rude awakening. To do him honour these ladies had wreathed and also heightened the podium, distributed the strings in an outer circle around and beneath him, and massed the brass in a tight circle at his feet. He came on to the platform suspecting nothing and was so taken aback that he could only stand and gasp. The performance was a veritable martyrdom for him, and for me too. The brass was deafening and drowned all else. We were amazed at the audience who sat it out quietly and even applauded dutifully at the end, the credit for which must be divided between Mahler's prestige and their own insensibility to music.

He had invited the orchestra to a night club, the Arion, afterwards and stayed with them (seventy in all) until the small hours. He came back in a very jolly mood, and said he felt like a father among his children.

Our box at the opera was the resort of many friends and acquaintances: Kneisel, leader of the best quartet in New York, Hassmann, the loafing Viennese painter, Fränkel, the beautiful

Crosby, the Schellings – he an extremely gifted composer, she a charming woman – Prince Troubetzkoy, brother of the sculptor, a wild, handsome Russian, whom one feared to meet in the streets of New York accompanied by his two wolves, Schindler, a really gifted musician, always eager to manage us, and many others whose names have escaped me. If we made an agreeable acquaintance we took him along, and so our box acquired a special character of its own. Carlo di Fornaro, a journalist, turned up from Mexico and told us many tales of Porfirio Díaz, who was still President of Mexico at that time, his cruelties, his overbearing arrogance and his ruthless and dictatorial oppression of his fellow-citizens. For example, after a strike when the men were returning to work, he had soldiers posted in ambush inside the open gates to shoot them down. Fornaro was now travelling about the States investigating prisons in order to expose their shortcomings. He effected an entry into these closed fortresses by disguising himself or by acquiring the papers of someone convicted of a political offence and serving his sentence instead of him. Fornaro was a journalist with an excess of conscience.

There was Poultney Bigelow, too, an aristocratic Englishman, who had been brought up with Kaiser Wilhelm the Second. He was living in New York in princely style and introduced us to all the literary people there. We could not make much of this opportunity owing to the unsurmountable barrier of language; and even when we got to speaking English of a sort it did not help us to join in serious conversation; we were soon out of our depth. Bigelow had written a rather damaging book about the Kaiser.

We also knew Natalie Curtis. She was quite fearless, and lived for years among the North American Indians with her brother, camping in the open. She wrote an excellent book on their music.

All these people were friends of ours. We were more at home than in Vienna. They loved Mahler over there and – with the exception of a malignant critic named Krehbiel* – he was not

* H. E. Krehbiel, who wrote in the *World*, 18th December 1909, about Mahler's First Symphony, 'If Mr. Gustav Mahler were not the conductor of the Philharmonic Society . . . the production of his symphony, which was played at Carnegie Hall on Thursday evening and yesterday afternoon, could be disposed of with very few words indeed. . . . Mr. Mahler is a composer of programme music, and his Symphony in D is of that class. The fact does not save it from criticism, but if it were not so the condemnation which would have to be meted out would be swift, summary and, for

harried by hostile criticism as in Vienna, where up to the very last he was always being rapped on the knuckles.

The work he was called upon to do was child's play compared with his official duties in Vienna. There were rehearsals only every other morning. I often picked him up afterwards and we walked home. He performed a great deal of music merely to hear it himself and to get to know it, without bothering whether it went down with the public or not. He conducted the overture to the *Flying Dutchman* and the Paris version of the *Tannhäuser* overture six times in succession, merely because he had fallen in love with them.

I was introduced by friends to Dana Gibson, the celebrated creator of the 'Gibson girl'. His wife was a beautiful and very empty woman. She showed me portraits of her sisters, each lovelier than the last. She and her sisters had always been her husband's only models. I was shown her very sophisticated bedroom, her carved antique of a bed with a canopy lined with looking glass, and I was not at all surprised when she asked me, in her sumptuous automobile of original design, how such a beautiful girl as I had brought myself to marry such a hideous and old and altogether impossible man as Mahler. To all I said she replied merely with a contemptuous smile. She was a beauty of spun gold, untarnished and vacant. Wealth and luxury were the only setting she could imagine for beauty like hers.

The première of Strauss's *Elektra* took place at this time at the Manhattan Opera House.* Mahler disliked it so much that he wanted to go out in the middle. We sat it out, but agreed afterwards that we had seldom in our lives been so bored. The public

* On 1st February 1910. (D.M)

the sake of the art, vigorous. . . . The impression made on the writer at the first performance, and confirmed by subsequent performances, was that Mr. Mahler is by instinct a naïve though unoriginal melodist, who, had he not been drawn into the latter-day swirl by a desire to exploit new colours, new harmonies and new notions about form, would have become a true symphonist. There is no reason why he should be a prophet of the ugly, as he discloses himself in the last movement of the Symphony in D. He makes that plain in this very movement by interrupting a painfully cacophonous din with an episode built on a melody which is exquisitely lovely and profoundly moving. The symphony has no justification without a programme. . . .' (D.M.)

decided against us. It was a success and some, very characteristically, described it as 'awfully nice'. The production was a brilliant
success, as Hammerstein's always were. The youthful Labia, the
décor – all superb!

We sailed early in April and went on to Paris, where rehearsals
began for the performance of the Second Symphony at the
Trocadéro. Pierné had pledged himself without knowing the music.
General Picquart, L'Allemand, the Clemenceaus and Painlevé were
with us daily to our great joy.

The rehearsal of the symphony interested Mahler greatly. The
chorus were lazy but incredibly talented. No one came in time for
the rehearsals and they left again when they felt inclined. On the
day of the performance they sang flawlessly with a fine metallic
tone.

While the rehearsals were on, Pierné gave a party in Mahler's
honour and invited Debussy,* Dukas, Gabriel Fauré, Bruneau and
the Clemenceaus. Debussy's strong personality and the beauty of
his head were very impressive. He brought his second wife, who
was said to be very wealthy. He sat next to me at dinner, and I
noticed that he only took the minutest helping of any dish. When
Madame Pierné tried pressing him, his face took on a look of
pain. But his abstemiousness had no ill effects: he was a broad-
shouldered, ponderous man.

Dukas told me in an undertone that when they were schoolboys
together and provided by their mothers with money to buy their
mid-morning lunches, they all selected the largest confections
except Debussy; he always chose the smallest and most expensive,
for even as a child he was nauseated by bulk. That evening, too,
we were told that Debussy's ill-treatment had almost been the
death of his first wife. It was a youthful marriage on both sides
and they were very poor. She couldn't endure her life with him,
or life without him. So she took poison. Debussy came in and
found her apparently unconscious on the floor. He went up to her
very calmly and took what money she had on her before sending

* Debussy can have had little sympathy for Mahler's music. Mahler, on the other
hand, was responsible for performances in the U.S.A. of some of Debussy's late
music when it was still very new, the *Rondes de printemps* (New York, 15th November
1910) and *Ibéria* (New York, 3rd January 1911). (D.M.)

for a doctor. She heard and saw it all, for she was not unconscious but temporarily paralysed. She recovered from the poison and was cured too of her love of Debussy, from whom she was divorced. This was the story she herself put in circulation. What truth there is in it, no one will ever know.

Mahler was not happy or at ease that evening, and he had good reason. The day of the performance came. It was a matinée. I was sitting with the Clemenceaus and my mother, who had come to Paris to meet us. All eyes were on the Countess Greffühle's box, where she was to be seen with Abbé Perosi. This for the public was the one thing that mattered.

Next, I suddenly saw Debussy, Dukas and Pierné get up and go out in the middle of the second movement of Mahler's symphony. This left nothing to be said, but they did say afterwards that it was too Schubertian for them, and even Schubert they found too foreign, too Viennese – too Slav.

The success he had with the public was no consolation for the bitterness of being so misunderstood and indeed condemned by the foremost French composers.*

We had been present the night before at *Ariane et Barbe-Bleue*. Mahler was enchanted by the first act, and so he gladly acted on L'Allemand's suggestion and went behind the scenes to compliment Dukas. By the time the piece was over he was so bored that he was glad he had obeyed his impulse when he had. His generosity in expressing his appreciation met with no return from Dukas.

We went this time from Paris to Rome. Mengelberg was there, waiting to see Mahler, for his own concerts were over. In the kindness of his heart he was unwittingly responsible for an extremely unpleasant incident. He warned Mahler not to stand any nonsense from the orchestra. They were a job-lot and quite undisciplined. He was to be stern with them. Even menaces and abuse were needed to rouse them from their lethargy.

Mahler did not need telling twice. It was never, as Mengelberg

* On the other hand, Dukas greatly admired Mahler's conducting of *Fidelio*, above all his performance of the *Leonore* overture No. 3. Dukas had heard *Fidelio* in London during Mahler's season there in 1892. For an interesting general commentary on Mahler's relationships with his great French contemporaries, see Vol. II of Edward Lockspeiser's study of Debussy (London, 1965). (D.M.)

possibly was not aware, a failing of his to err on the side of gentleness. Dictionary in hand, he pitched into the orchestra in a manner not really undeserved; for it was late in the season and the good orchestra Mengelberg had had in his earlier concerts had gone on leave to South America. But undeserved or not, when it came to Mahler's saying that he was uncertain whether to describe their behaviour as '*stupidità*' or '*indolènza*', they leapt to their feet as one man and left the hall. It was only with great difficulty that Mahler could get through his concert at all, for the whole orchestra took to passive resistance. The success of the concert was accordingly very moderate, and immediately it was over he cancelled the second one. We arrived in Vienna in very bad humour to find a garbled version of the story in all the papers and everybody talking about it.

Summer

1910

I took Mahler to Toblach and then, following medical advice, I had to go to Tobelbad for a complete rest. Mahler remained at Toblach, looked after by an old and reliable manservant, and began sketching out his Tenth Symphony. I was very ill. The wear and tear of being driven on without respite by a spirit so intense as his had brought me to a complete breakdown.

I lived an utterly solitary life at Tobelbad, as I always did whenever I was by myself anywhere. I was so solitary and so melancholy that the head of the sanatorium was worried and introduced young people to me as company on my walks. There was an architect, X, whom I found particularly sympathetic, and I soon had little doubt that he was in love with me and hoping I might return his love. So I left. Mahler met me at Toblach station and was suddenly more in love with me than ever before. Perhaps the reason was that my submerged self-confidence had been brought to the surface again by the flattering attentions of the young architect. In any case, the future seemed brighter and I was happy. But I had no wish at all to exchange my old life for a new one.

After a week had gone by a letter arrived from the architect saying that he could not live without me; and therefore if I had the slightest feeling for him I must leave all and go to him. The letter was clearly meant for me, but the envelope was very distinctly addressed to Mahler. Whether the young man made a mistake in the stress of emotion or whether it was his unconscious wish that it should come to Mahler's hands, remains a mystery.

Mahler was seated at the piano when he opened the letter. 'What is this?' he asked in a choking voice and handed it to me. He was convinced at the time, and remained convinced ever after, that the architect had deliberately addressed the letter to him as his way of asking him for my hand in marriage.*

* Alma Mahler's second husband was the eminent architect, Walter Gropius. For an account of this episode, see Alma Mahler's later volume of memoirs, *And the Bridge is Love* (London, 1959). (D.M.)

And now – at last – I was able to tell him all. I told him I had longed for his love year after year and that he, in his fanatical concentration on his own life, had simply overlooked me. As I spoke, he felt for the first time that something is owed to the person with whom one's life has once been linked. He suddenly felt a sense of guilt.

We sent for my mother to come to our help, and until she came we could do nothing but walk about together all day long in tears.

After we had laid bare the causes of our division with the completest honesty, I felt as strongly as I ever had that I could never leave him. When I told him so, his face was transfigured. His love became an ecstasy. He could not be parted from me for a second.

The letters he wrote me at this time say all that I pass over here in silence. He caught me to him – but I had never really gone away. He was now jealous of everything and everybody, although he had always shown a wounding indifference to such feelings before. The door of our two rooms, which were next to each other, had to be always open. He had to hear my breathing. I often woke in the night and found him standing at my bedside in the darkness, and started as at the apparition of a departed spirit. I had to fetch him from his studio every day for meals. I did so very cautiously. He was often lying on the floor weeping in his dread that he might lose me, had lost me perhaps already. On the floor, he said, he was nearer to the earth. We spoke to each other as we had never spoken before. But the whole truth could not be spoken. My boundless love had lost by degrees some of its strength and warmth; and now that my eyes had been opened by the impetuous assaults of a youthful lover, I knew how incredibly ingenuous I was. I knew that my marriage was no marriage and that my own life was utterly unfulfilled. I concealed all this from him, and although he knew it as well as I did we played out the comedy to the end, to spare his feelings.

We were brought back to earth by an accident of a different kind. My English nurse was suffering from a severe sore throat but said nothing about it for fear of being a nuisance. But as she was always about with us we caught it one after the other. Finally

Mahler caught it too, less severely than any of us or so it seemed. He soon recovered and started to work again.

One night I awoke suddenly. I called out to Mahler. There was no answer. I ran to his bed and found it empty. I rushed on to the landing and there found him lying unconscious with a lighted candle beside him. I carried him to bed, called my mother and sent our servant on his bicycle to fetch the doctor (a friend of ours who lived at Schluderbach), and meanwhile gave Mahler what stimulants for the heart I had in the house. He came round quickly, but was cold and white for a considerable time. We wrapped him in warm blankets, massaged him, and heated water for hot water bottles and also to steep his hands and feet in. By five o'clock when the doctor came, all had been done that could be done and all he needed was rest.

One day after this when we were out driving I caught sight of X hiding beneath a bridge. He told us later that he had been lurking in the neighbourhood for some time, in the hope of coming across me and insisting on an answer to his letter. My heart stopped, but only from fright, not joy. I told Mahler at once, and he said: 'I'll go and bring him along myself.' He went straight down to Toblach and found him at once. 'Come along,' he said. Nothing more was said by either.

It was night by this time, and in silence they walked all the way up to our house, Mahler in front with a lantern and X following on behind. It was pitch dark. I was waiting in my room. Mahler came in with a very serious air. I hesitated for a long time before going to speak to X, and I broke off our interview after a few minutes from a sudden alarm on Mahler's account. I found Mahler walking up and down his room. Two candles were alight on his table. He was reading the Bible. 'Whatever you do will be right,' he said. 'Make your decision.' But I had no choice!

Next morning I drove down to Toblach, as X was to take his departure. I saw him off at the station and drove home again as fast as I could, but Mahler had come half-way to meet me in his dread lest I had gone with X after all. X sent me a telegram from every station on his return journey. They were succeeded by lengthy appeals and adjurations, and all these Mahler wove into the beautiful verses he wrote during those days.

I could never have imagined life without him, even though the feeling that my life was running to waste had often filled me with despair. Least of all could I have imagined life with another man. I had often thought of going away somewhere alone to start life afresh, but never with any thought of another person. Mahler was the hub of my existence and so he continued to be.

He, on the other hand, was churned to the very bottom. It was at this time he wrote those outcries and ejaculations addressed to me in the draft score of the Tenth Symphony.* He realized that he had lived the life of a neurotic and suddenly decided to consult Sigmund Freud (who was then on holiday at Leyden in Holland).† He gave him an account of his strange states of mind and his anxieties, and Freud apparently calmed him down. He reproached him with vehemence after hearing his confession. 'How dared a man in your state ask a young woman to be tied to him?' he asked. In conclusion, he said: 'I know your wife. She loved her father and she can only choose and love a man of his sort. Your age, of which you are so much afraid, is precisely what attracts her. You need not be anxious. You loved your mother, and you look for her in every woman. She was careworn and ailing, and unconsciously you wish your wife to be the same.'

He was right in both cases. Gustav Mahler's mother was called Marie. His first impulse was to change my name to Marie in spite of the difficulty he had in pronouncing 'r'. And when he got to know me better he wanted my face to be more 'stricken' – his very word. When he told my mother that it was a pity there had been so little sadness in my life, she replied: 'Don't worry – that will come.'

I too always looked for a small, slight man, who had wisdom and spiritual superiority, since this was what I had known and loved in my father.

Freud's diagnosis composed Mahler's mind, although he refused to acknowledge his fixation on his mother. He turned away from notions of that kind.

* See facsimile facing p. 227. (D.M.)
† See Introduction, pp. xv-xvi (D.M.)

One day during this time of emotional upsets I went for a walk with our little girl, Gucki. When we were nearly home again I heard my songs being played and sung. I stopped – I was petrified. My poor forgotten songs. I had dragged them to and fro to the country and back again for ten years, a weary load I could never get quit of. I was overwhelmed with shame and also I was angry; but Mahler came to meet me with such joy in his face that I could not say a word.

'What have I done?' he said. 'These songs are good – they're excellent. I insist on your working on them and we'll have them published. I shall never be happy until you start composing again. God, how blind and selfish I was in those days!'

He played them over again and again. I had to sit down there and then – after a ten years' interval – and fill in what was missing. And that was not all; but since he was over-estimating my talent, I suppress all he went on to say in extravagant praise of it.

When I returned to Toblach that summer after leaving the sanatorium, Mahler told me that Hertzka of Universal Edition had been to see him. He had taken over Mahler's first four symphonies from Waldheim & Eberle.* The terms of publication were that the symphonies were to earn 50,000 crowns (10,000 dollars) before yielding Mahler any royalty. They were now within 2,500 crowns of doing so, and Mahler was therefore just about to profit from them. Having made this clear, Hertzka went on to ask Mahler to forgo his profits until a second sum of 50,000 had been earned, on the grounds that Universal Edition would like to take over the works of Bruckner also and advertise them at great expense.

Mahler agreed at once. He thought it only right that he should sacrifice his profits for another fifteen years out of love of Bruckner, without of course receiving, or expecting, a penny from the sale of Bruckner's works. This was a great sacrifice to make to Bruckner's memory and shows how deeply he revered him.

Oscar Fried paid us a visit this summer, little as Mahler wished to see him. He did not want to see anyone, and the least thing

---

* Many more publishers were in fact involved in the complex publishing history of Mahler's first four symphonies. (D.M.)

upset him. He had so little control over himself that while Fried
was with us he went to bed the moment he finished working in
the morning and again when he came in at dusk. One day he
called out to me from his bed to play my songs to Fried. I did
so on compulsion, and as soon as I had played one he wanted to
know how Fried had liked it. When Fried replied in his impudent
way that it was 'very gifted' or 'very nice', Mahler flew into a
passion; and my mother, who was sitting on the edge of his bed,
had great difficulty in preventing him from jumping up and telling
Fried what he thought of him. I could plainly hear his abusive
remarks through the wall, and Fried, who was sitting beside me
at the piano, no doubt heard them too. Mahler had not recovered
his temper when I went in to see him later on. He called Fried an
idiot, who might think himself lucky if he ever composed anything half as good; there was no calming him down. That night
Fried did not venture to give Mahler his hand, and in the morning
when in consternation he asked my mother in his Berlin cockney,
'Frau Moll, I think I'd better go, eh?', she said quietly, 'I think
so too, dear Fried.'

This brief visit of Fried's was something new as well as comic.
Mahler had always liked him hitherto, for philistine though he
was he had a streak of genius; but now suddenly Mahler could
not put up with him. It had never worried him before that Fried
never opened a book, but this time he made frequent sorties from
his studio to catch him out lounging in a chair, while I with my
back turned was trying to work at my writing-table – in spite of
being continually interrupted by his desire to talk. He took him
for a walk and scolded him for not reading more, not thinking
things out, taking himself and his work seriously enough. Fried
felt that things were getting too hot for him and departed.

There was also a dispute about Hugo Wolf of whom Fried spoke
very warmly. 'Of Wolf's one thousand songs,' Mahler said in
reply, 'I know only three hundred and forty-four. Those three
hundred and forty-four I do not like.'*

From this, I remember, we went on to auricular confession. I
had been brought up as a Catholic, but in those days I was

* One should not, of course, take Mahler's mathematics seriously, nor, perhaps,
his evaluation of Wolf's songs. (D.M.)

inclined to be sceptical. Burckhard and many another had seen to that. Mahler defended the confessional, and Fried became quite lyrical in praise of it. I, a Catholic, was the only one who had mild reservations. But then, I was the only one who had so often been to confession.

One night I was awakened by an apparition by my bed. It was Mahler standing there in the darkness. 'Would it give you any pleasure if I dedicated the Eighth to you?' Any pleasure! All the same I said: 'Don't. You have never dedicated anything to any-body. You might regret it.' 'I have just written to Hertzka now – by the light of dawn,' he said.

A long correspondence with Hertzka followed. Mahler was not satisfied with the type and spacing of the page of dedication, to which he wished to have every honour done. In this, as in all else during those days, there was the same note of passion. When the time came for him to go to Munich for the rehearsals of the Eighth, we parted as if for years, although I was to follow him in a week. He took my wedding-ring and put it on his finger. I was happy – and yet not happy. I had been through too much. Old wounds ache.

He wrote poems to me daily and telegraphed them; and when I arrived at Munich I found him in a fine suite of rooms at the Hotel Continental. Every room was smothered in roses in my honour. My mother found the piano edition of the Eighth on the table in her room. The dedication ran as follows: 'To our dear mother, who has ever been all in all to us and who gave me Alma – from Gustav in undying gratitude. Munich, September 9 1910.'

He met me at the station, looking ill and run down; he had had a recurrence of his sore throat on his arrival in Munich. He had taken to his bed, and I had not been there to look after him.

This concert, the rehearsals for which Mahler so much enjoyed, would never have taken place at all but for the high-handed and unscrupulous conduct of Emil Gutmann, who organized it. He cabled to Mahler in New York, telling him that the score was already printed and that the preliminary rehearsals had long ago begun in Vienna. In fact, not a note had been printed. As soon as Mahler knew this, he wanted to cancel the performance immediately, but by this time rehearsals were actually in progress.

Numbers of friends of ours were there, but we kept mostly to ourselves.

I too found a copy of the Eighth with its dedicatory page on my table. Mahler was eager now to hear what his old friends would have to say; for, egocentric though he was, he expected his friends to enter into and share his pleasure. But his friends kept silent. He found himself alone; his feelings and his happiness were of no account; he was of importance to them only in so far as he reflected credit on themselves. Justine excited his wrath on this account. He drove her from my door when she came to pay me a visit. 'Alma has no time for you,' he told her. He gave short shrift to a certain Countess, who regarded me as her enemy for the droll reason that Mahler refused to give an audition to a certain singer. She sent a gilded basket of roses up to my room an hour later as a propitiatory offering. But he was blind no longer. On the contrary, he was ready to take offence at the slightest sign that I was not paid enough honour or not received with enough warmth.

Eighth Symphony

12th September 1910

The whole of Munich as well as all who had come there for the occasion were wrought up to the highest pitch of suspense. The final rehearsal provoked rapturous enthusiasm, but it was nothing to the performance itself. The whole audience rose to their feet as soon as Mahler took his place at the conductor's desk; and the breathless silence which followed was the most impressive homage an artist could be paid. I sat in a box almost insensible from excitement.

And then Mahler, god or demon, turned those tremendous volumes of sound into fountains of light. The experience was indescribable. Indescribable too the demonstration which followed. The whole audience surged towards the platform. I waited behind the scenes in a state of deep emotion until the outburst died down. Then, with our eyes full of tears, we drove to the hotel. Several of our friends were waiting for us in the entrance, among them Max Reinhardt, Roller, the Neissers, Erler, Berliner, the Clemenceaus, and Paul Stefan. Beyond them in the doorway a wealthy and eccentric American from New York barred our passage. 'Since–since–since Brahms, nothing has been written to equal it,' he gasped out. We pushed past him by main force. Mahler detested flattery of any sort, and to appreciation by people who understood nothing about music he was unmerciful.

A large room had been reserved, and Mahler's guests were assembled there to celebrate the occasion. He and I were just going to sit down when we found ourselves surrounded by all the members of his family. So he scribbled me a note, saying it was not a family party – I was to find a seat somewhere else and he would follow. I sat with the Neissers and Berliner; Mahler soon joined us laughing. We spent a very jolly evening and Mahler was acclaimed and honoured on all hands.

It was a lovely warm night and we ended it up by talking until morning, with Gucki, our dear child, sleeping beside us.

Next day Berliner said to me: 'Alma, everybody's paying tribute to Mahler. But you've suffered for the Eighth and you deserve something too. Now, tomorrow evening you and Gustav are to come to Frau Neisser's room at the Hotel Vier Jahreszeiten, and there'll be a surprise waiting for you.'

We did as we were told and found a large display of costly knick-knacks, all designed by Fritz Erler. I did not like any of them at all. They were much too modish. There were heads of John the Baptist carved out of ivory and strung together to form a necklace, or a head of Christ as a pendant. Out of the corner of my eye I caught sight of three baroque pearls on a gold chain, and I chose this.

Mahler and I went out for a motor-drive in the country immediately afterwards. Unfortunately, he was now in a bad humour. He grudged Berliner this idea of his and wanted to buy the pearls from him so as to give them to me himself. I said this would not do; it was Berliner's idea and a very charming one. 'Then it really does please you?' he asked me over and over again. 'Is it really such a pleasure?' It certainly was and I could not help it now. It was the first piece of jewellery I had ever received in my life.

Mahler had no notion what gave a girl pleasure. When we became engaged he said: 'Other people give each other rings. It's very bad taste and I'm sure you don't want it any more than I do.' I hastened to say that I thought it a ridiculous custom.

The wedding came but no wedding-present. He had no idea that a wife expected such a thing from her husband, and no one told him. After the children arrived such extravagances were out of the question. In any case, I was in charge of finance from the first and had my work cut out to pay off his debts. I could not think of jewellery or of any luxuries whatever. His American earnings changed all this – but now Berliner had stepped in.

A rather painful incident took place before the first full rehearsal. Mahler wanted Rosé as leader for this special occasion and so he asked the manager of the concert to make this known to the orchestra; he, however, was afraid to do so. Mahler, thinking it was all arranged, telegraphed to Rosé, who came from Vienna at once. We went to the rehearsal with him in all innocence; but as soon as he took his seat, the whole orchestra rose and deserted in a body to show their resentment of the affront to their own leader. Mahler was dumbfounded.

Rosé got up slowly and after begging Mahler not to be upset, he left the platform and walked solemnly the whole length of the hall, with his violin under his arm, to where we were sitting. This would have covered him with shame if his dignified forbearance had not at once shifted the blame on to the other side.

As soon as we were back in Vienna, Mahler saw a doctor about his throat. As he was very sensitive to pain, it was not considered advisable to remove his tonsils; and so they were cauterized, a procedure which had had good results in my own case a year before. We believed he was now safe from further attacks and Mahler himself did not want a more radical cure.

We took up our quarters with my mother, as usual. One evening we asked Zemlinsky and Schoenberg in. Schoenberg took me aside. 'I promise you,' he said, 'never to argue with Mahler again. From today on he can shout at me as hard as he likes. I shall never take offence.' I was more alarmed than pleased. 'My mind is made up,' he went on. 'And it is because I love him.'

I remember a discussion Mahler once had with Schoenberg about the possibility of creating a melody from one note played successively on different instruments. Mahler strenuously denied that it could be done.*

We met on board the boat at Cherbourg in November, 1910, for our last outward voyage, he coming from Bremen and I from Paris. The voyage had no terrors for us now. We sailed on the 15th and arrived at New York on the 25th. We used the ten days to have a complete rest. The weather was perfect, as it was on all our voyages.

I took two photographs of Mahler on the voyage, the last times he was ever photographed.† Ever since the summer he had taken the greatest care of his appearance. He wore smart waistcoats,

* It is not unlikely that Schoenberg had in mind the principle which gave rise to the third of his *Five Orchestral Pieces* Op. 16, *Der wechselnde Akkord* ('The Changing Chord'), composed in 1909 and first performed in 1912. (D.M.)
† See also illustration facing page 130. (D.M.)

beautiful suits and shoes. It was easy enough for him – with his fine face and alert, well-proportioned figure – to look well dressed.

He had taken to saying 'Spitting on the floor doesn't help you to be Beethoven.'

His American concert tours were now extended to include Seattle, Buffalo and Springfield. A week's rehearsal was followed by two weeks of concerts in New York and Brooklyn, and a third to cover these more distant places. The same programme served for all, so that a new one had only to be rehearsed every third week and more use was made of each. This would have been a relief to most conductors, but not to Mahler, who could not bear travelling.

He left with his orchestra for Springfield on 7th December, and on the 9th I joined him at Buffalo. I arrived early in the morning; he sent Spiering, the first violin, to meet me. I found Mahler at the hotel, and after a short rest we took the train to Niagara and drove from there in an antediluvian carriage to the Falls.

It was a day of wintry sunshine. Every twig was coated in ice. When we got right up to the Falls and then beneath them by the lift, the strength of the greenish light hurt our eyes. The thunder of the water beneath the roof of ice, the trees mantled far and wide in frozen foam, and the distant view over the snow-covered plain all had a dreamlike beauty.

We turned away with reluctance and looked for somewhere where we could eat. Surprisingly, there was nowhere at all inviting and we could do no better than follow the other pilgrims into a little restaurant, heated by an iron stove and smelling of galoshes and steaming clothes. An old waiter came forward. 'It is a pleasure, Mr. Mahler,' he said beaming, 'to see you here. The last time I had the privilege of waiting on you was at the Hartmann in Vienna, but that is long ago now.' We were in good hands, for the old man could not do enough for us.

It was not easy for Mahler to be one of the crowd, when he was recognized in Europe as a celebrity wherever he went. He was so used to being a well-known figure that he had forgotten the poverty and obscurity of his early years.

We got into the little carriage and into the little train and arrived at last at Buffalo with hands and feet frozen. Mahler went straight to bed, as he had to conduct that evening. He got up after an hour, completely refreshed. I did not go to the concert, as I had heard the programme four times already and, besides, had travelled all night and arrived in the early hours.

He came straight back after the concert in high spirits to a simple and belated meal. 'I have realized today,' he said, 'that articulate art is greater than inarticulate nature.' He had been conducting the *Pastoral* symphony and had found it more tremendous than all the Niagara Falls.*

Mahler had his third concert to conduct next day at a place in the neighbourhood; so I went back to New York alone, because I did not want to leave my little girl too long alone with her nurse. At his suggestion I re-read *The Brothers Karamazov* on the journey, and I telegraphed from New York: 'Splendid journey with Aliosha.' He telegraphed back at once: 'Journey with Almiosha much more splendid.' It was a habit of his to repeat for days and weeks, even months together, some thought which particularly pleased him, turning it over in his mind and introducing variations. At this period it was: 'All creation adorns itself continually for God. Everyone therefore has only one duty, to be as beautiful as possible in every way in the eyes of God and man. Ugliness is an insult to God.'

When the Committee was first formed I warned Mahler not to allow these ladies too free a hand in the choice of the programmes. He laughed and said he did not at all mind being relieved of the burden. It would give him less to do. But he was to pay dearly for this.

He had a tale-bearer at his service in the orchestra. His name was J——. He wormed his way into Mahler's confidence by describing his sufferings as a consumptive; but soon he talked more about the orchestra than his ailment and kept Mahler informed of everything that was said against him. J. was always at his elbow, and Mahler used to come back at the end of the morning feeling

* It was not until Mahler left Europe for America that he had the opportunity to conduct the *Pastoral*, which, according to Klemperer, was a 'major experience' for him. (D.M.)

thoroughly annoyed. The orchestra also were indignant when they realized that he made use of J. as a spy, and so ill-will increased on both sides. J. may have been inspired by devotion to Mahler, but the results could not have been worse. Several of the orchestra complained to the ladies of the Committee and all demanded J.'s dismissal. Mahler refused. I advised him to give his unqualified consent, but he would not listen. J., he said, was his only friend. If he lost him he would be alone among enemies, for the whole orchestra hated him.

J. had done his work well.

Mahler had a slightly septic throat before Christmas. It passed over very quickly and did not alarm us. But it might well have done.

Christmas

1910

Some days before Christmas Mahler went out with a very solemn
air, taking his cheque-book with him, a thing he never did for
fear of losing it. I knew what it was: it was the Christmas feeling,
the giving of presents, the thrill of expectation – everything I had
missed so sorely for ten long years. Christmas came and, as usual,
I had a large Christmas tree, lots of candles, and presents for him
and Gucki, which I was just going to give them when Mahler
drove me out of the room, saying he had something he wanted
to do. A moment afterwards Gucki came out and said Papa
wanted a lace cover. I was surprised but gave it her. Next they
both came in arm in arm and requested me to follow them.

I entered the bright and festal room – but what words are there
for the awful premonition, the pang of icy dread which gripped
me, when I saw, on a table all for me, that long mound of presents
covered with a white cloth and smothered in roses. I snatched
off the covering. Mahler stood sadly by. But his sadness soon
vanished and my dread premonition also, for I was touched to the
heart by all the lovely things he had thought of without any
regard for his own likes and dislikes. There was scent, for example,
which he hated and I loved. There were also two promissory
notes, which I give verbatim:

Bon
to the value of 40 dollars
for a fine spree
along the Fifth Av.
For Herr Gustav Mahler on a country ramble with his Almschili
Bon
for the purchase of a
Solitaire
worth over 1,000 dollars
Gustav Mahler
New York Christmas, 1910,

The whole room was soon full of the pink roses. We spent this Christmas – by our own choice – quite alone.

We often went for walks together arm in arm that winter, or else, as I had to spare myself fatigue, I sent him out alone with Gucki. It was good too that he should get to know his little daughter, of whom he grew more and more fond. I could see them nearly the whole time from my ninth-floor window, walking together in Central Park and snowballing each other.

He always worked on his compositions of the summer during the winter. This time it was the Ninth Symphony, for the Tenth was not completed and he had a superstitious fear of working on it. He played bits of *Das Lied von der Erde* to me almost daily during these last two years. I knew it by heart before it was first performed. One day while he was working Gucki stood beside him, watching with engrossment. He was scratching out one note after another. 'Papi,' she said, 'I wouldn't like to be a note.' 'Why not?' he asked. 'Because then you might scratch me out and blow me away.' He was so delighted that he came at once to tell me what she had said.

Our drawing-room was a corner room. It had three enormous windows, one of which was a bow-window occupying the whole corner. Immediately below there was the Plaza, but the noise of its ceaseless traffic reached us only as a murmur. In front we had a magnificent view over the vast Central Park, studded with lakes and ponds.

Fränkel was with us on New Year's Night – our last. New York stretched on out of sight in a milk-white haze. Sirens opened up at five minutes to twelve from every factory in the city and from every boat in the harbour. The bells of all the churches united in an organ-note of such awful beauty that we three who loved each other joined hands without a word and wept. Not one of us – then – knew why.

The End

1911

I saw a lot of a young American woman who tried to imbue me with the occult. She lent me books by Leadbeater and Mrs. Besant. I always went straight to Mahler the moment she left and repeated word for word all she had said. It was something new in those days and he was interested. We started shutting our eyes to see what colours we could see. We practised this – and many other rites ordained by occultists–so zealously that Gucki was once discovered walking up and down the room with her eyes shut. When we asked her what she was doing, she replied: 'I'm looking for green.'

It was at this time also that I had a visit from the singer, Alda Gatti-Casazza.* As soon as she was announced by telephone from the office I went to fetch Mahler, but she said that her visit was to me and me only. She had seen my volume of songs and wanted to sing one of them at her next recital. Mahler went up in the air at once. He urged her to sing all the five songs in the volume. This she could not do, as her programme was already settled. He got quite angry, and said she ought to leave out some of her other songs. I protested and the conclusion was that Mahler agreed to rehearse this one song with her.

A few days later we went, as arranged, to the Waldorf-Astoria, where she was staying, and Mahler rehearsed the song with her most carefully. 'Is that right?' he kept asking me from the piano. I was so nervous I could scarcely open my mouth. I begged him in a low voice not to ask me any more, as he knew better than I. We were very near together in those days.

It was a very different matter between him and his committee of ladies. Storms were brewing, although he paid no attention. They were now dictating programmes he had no wish to perform and they did not like it when he declined. J. had set the whole

* The first wife of the General Director of the Metropolitan Opera. (D.M.)

orchestra by the ears and they were so refractory that Mahler no longer felt secure in his position. His habit of shutting his eyes to what was unpleasant prevented him seeing his danger, until one day in the middle of February, he was required to attend at Mrs. Sheldon's house. She was chairman of the Executive. He found several of the male members of the Committee there and was severely taken to task. The ladies had many instances to allege of conduct which in their eyes was mistaken. He rebutted these charges, but now at a word from Mrs. Sheldon a curtain was drawn aside and a lawyer, who (as came out later) had been taking notes all the time, entered the room. A document was then drawn up in legal form, strictly defining Mahler's powers. He was so taken aback and so furious that he came back to me trembling in every limb; and it was only by degrees that he was able to take any pleasure in his work. He decided to ignore all these ladies in the future. The only exception was Mrs. Untermeyer, his guardian angel. She was away at this time; otherwise nothing of all this could have happened.

And so now J. was dismissed in the middle of the season – which Mahler took as a personal affront – in response to unanimous representation from the orchestra. Mahler went on conducting, but with rage in his heart against the orchestra and the Committee. But the ladies were in the right.

On 20th February he was suffering once more from inflammation of the throat and fever. On the 21st he was to conduct and insisted on doing so. Fränkel, he said, would pull him through. Fränkel warned him not to attempt it, but Mahler insisted that he had conducted time after time with a temperature and Fränkel had to give way. We wrapped him up carefully and drove to Carnegie Hall. Among other works he conducted that night was the first performance in public of Busoni's *Cradlesong at the Grave of my Mother*.

He felt very exhausted when the interval came, and his head was aching. But he pulled himself together and conducted the rest of the concert. His last concert. We drove back, taking all possible precautions, accompanied by Fränkel, who examined him as soon as we arrived. His temperature was normal again and Mahler was very merry about conducting himself back to health.

We all parted from each other much relieved. He was given
aspirin. Next morning he seemed better and in a few days the
inflammation of the throat had vanished. But the fever had come
back. At first it was slight, but it kept on rising in zig-zags. By
the end of a week Fränkel had no doubts left about the nature of
the disease. I called him in one evening when Mahler had a sort
of collapse. He reassured him and me too, but when he returned
in the morning his hair had gone grey. Thus Mahler and I saw
with our own eyes that hair can turn white in a few hours.
Fränkel told me years later that he had buried his dearest friend
that night.

I did not know how great the danger was. If I had, I could
never have got through the next three months. Even so, they were
terrible. His ups and downs kept us on the rack; he was often
convinced of his recovery; often again he despaired and was in
mortal dread. When he felt better he joked about his approaching
death. 'You will be in great demand when I am gone, with your
youth and looks. Now who shall it be?'

'No one,' I said. 'Don't talk of it.'

'Yes, but let's see, who is there?'

He went through his list, and always ended up with: 'It'll be
better, after all, if I stay with you.'

I had to laugh with tears in my eyes.

He entrusted his re-touched scores of Beethoven and Schumann
and other symphonies to me. 'They're valuable,' he said. 'Have
them printed.'*

Sometimes he got up and went into our large corner sitting-
room. He lay on a comfortable sofa and I read aloud to him.

When I went out, the policeman on duty in the Plaza, the most
crowded spot in New York, asked me again and again: 'How is
Mr. Mahler?' Then he took me safely across and gave me his good
wishes. Never in my whole life have I met so much genuine
warmth of heart and delicacy of feeling as in America.

One day Schindler, who was to accompany Alda Casazza, came
to ask me about the tempi of the song of mine she was going to
sing. Mahler who was in bed in the next room was enraged at

---

* These editions of Beethoven and Schumann, which included Mahler's re-scoring
(substantial in the case of Schumann), have never been published. (D.M.)

the dilettante way he went to work, and when Schindler went on to play me some Mussorgsky songs he whistled for me to come in and told me to send Schindler about his business. He said it was tactless of him to start playing something else immediately after my song, and said it so emphatically that there was no contradicting him.

I was often taken out for drives by friends as a relief from constant attendance at his bedside; and one afternoon Fränkel came for me unexpectedly. This was very opportune, as it was the afternoon of Alda Casazza's recital and I had a ticket for the back of the gallery. Mahler and I came to a secret understanding that Fränkel should take me. Fränkel was very much astonished when he found I was going to a concert, a thing I had not done for weeks. I did not say what the concert was, let alone that a song of mine was being sung, and I parted from him speedily before he had time to ask. Meanwhile, Mahler was awaiting my return in the keenest suspense. He said he had never been in such a state of excitement over any performance of his own works. When I told him it had been encored he said, 'Thank God,' over and over again. He was quite beside himself for joy.

I looked after him now just as if he were a little child. I put every bite into his mouth for him and slept in his room without taking off my clothes. We got so used to it that he said more than once: 'When I'm well again we'll go on like this. You'll feed me – it's so nice.'

Delicacies of every kind were sent to us in a constant stream, by strangers as well as friends. Every day he was delighted by some fresh surprise, and as nourishment was all-important he was fed almost every hour of the day and night. In the early stages Fränkel had suggested a blood test, and it yielded the verdict: streptococci. Neither Mahler nor I had ever heard the word before and in our innocence were not at all alarmed.

The test was done on two occasions. The first time we had a surgeon from the Montefiore Hospital, who must have been rather incompetent, for the bed, the floor and the bathroom were covered in blood. Mahler shouted to Fränkel that if another blood test had to be made, it would have to be done differently or he would throw the man downstairs. The second was carried out by a doctor from the Rockefeller Institute and there was no sign a minute after that it had been done at all.

It was remarkable that his temperature went down both times and his state of mind was better for several days after. Probably it would have been a good thing if he had been bled.

There was a weekly consultation between the leading doctors of New York. On their advice Kollargol injections were tried. Mahler joked about his little bugs, which were always either dancing or sleeping.

Fränkel often said that if it had not been a case of the celebrated Mahler, but just some ordinary person, lots of things might have been tried. Blood-transfusion, for example, or saline injections. 'But you daren't try experiments on Gustav Mahler. We must wait in the hope that nature herself will give him the strength to pull through. I could not take the responsibility.'

Finally, after a consultation at which Fränkel was present, it was decided that Mahler must be sent at all costs to Europe to some great bacteriologist in Paris or Vienna. There was talk of Metchnikov. When I heard this my strength gave out and I fell in a faint at Mahler's bedside. Fränkel and Dr. Brettauer, an eminent doctor and a friend of ours, carried me to my bed. They both insisted on my cabling at once for my mother. I did so and Mahler was delighted. He consulted the newspaper. 'She'll be here in six days,' he said. We knew she would leave Vienna the same day and take the fastest boat, undeterred by any fatigue or difficulty, as soon as she heard his cry for help. She did in fact arrive by the very boat we reckoned on.

The relation between them was very close. I used to say jokingly when I was first married that if Mahler had gone to my mother and said: 'I've had to put Alma to death,' she would simply have replied: 'I'm sure you were right, Gustav.' It was a foolish jest, because I was pleased he was always right in her eyes, even if sometimes it made things awkward for me. It was the utmost happiness when we were all three together.

Now that my mother was there I could spare myself a little, as she took part of the day-nursing. I still watched at his bedside all night as before. We tried three male nurses in turn, each of whom he dismissed at once; one's shoes squeaked, another snored. At last we tried a female nurse. He forbade her to look at him. It was more than he would endure. If she must attend on him, then she must look sideways. But this woman was a necessity. I had forty pieces of luggage to pack – without his knowledge and with dread at my heart. So every time I went out of his room I unobtrusively took an armful of things with me. He had no idea his room had been entirely emptied when the time came for him to leave it.

My mother was once stewing fruit over a spirit-stove between two open windows. There was an explosion, and instantly the curtains, window-sill and carpet were on fire. I promptly lost my head. There was Mahler in bed in one room, our daughter asleep in another, and a blazing curtain blowing out right across the room towards her door. And we were on the ninth floor. I rushed to the telephone, but could not get out the word 'fire'. The girl at the telephone, hearing the terror in my voice, at once sent some men from the office and some hotel servants, who forced the doors, which were all locked as it was last thing at night. My mother and our English nurse tore the curtains down and poured water on the flames as fast as they could. They had nearly put them out by the time the men were on the scene. When I went in to see Mahler, he was lying quietly in bed and could not not understand why I got so excited about a fire.

My mother always cooked his favourite dishes on this spirit-stove, but this time – for once – it was for herself. 'Poor Mama,' was all he said: 'Cooking all day for me. Then – for once – she thinks of herself, and has a disaster. Poor thing!'

No one in the hotel reproached us by a word or a look. All was put right next day and we had not a cent to pay for the very considerable damage we had caused, for the hotel was insured, and people over there are in any case amazingly generous.

Our cabin was booked, the packing was done, and Mahler was dressed. A stretcher was waiting, but he waved it aside. He looked as white as a sheet as he walked unsteadily to the lift, leaning on Fränkel's arm. The lift-boy kept out of the way until the last moment, to hide his tears, and then took him down for the last time. The huge hotel lounge was deserted. Mrs. Untermeyer's automobile was waiting at a side entrance; Fränkel helped him in and drove to the quay with him. I went back to the office to pay the bill and to thank the office staff for all they had done for us without a thought for themselves during those weeks. They all came out and shook hands. 'We cleared everyone out of the lounge – we knew Mr. Mahler wouldn't like to be looked at.'

Blessed America! We never met with any such proof of true sensibility during our subsequent weeks in Europe.

When I arrived on board Mahler was already in bed and Fränkel was at his side. He gave me his last instructions and warned me not to call in the ship's doctor. Then he bade Mahler a brief and sad farewell. He knew that he would never see him again.

Our cabins were heaped with presents and flowers from friends as well as from people we didn't even know.

The voyage began. My mother and I shared the nursing. He would not allow anyone else near him and we gladly, though with heavy hearts, took entire charge. What he suffered from most was the alternation of a sub-normal with a high temperature, which he reduced by violent perspiration. So our cabins had at one moment to be over-heated, the next icy cold. I had a temperature myself every evening, but I could not think of that. My bunk was under the window, and when Mahler wanted it open the ice-cold air blew straight on to me. It was the end of April.

He got up nearly every day and between us we carried rather than helped him on to the boat-deck, where the captain had had a large space screened off so that he should not be seen by the other passengers. We dressed and undressed him, lifted him up and fed him by hand; he was not obliged to make a single movement on his own.

Busoni was on board. He sent Mahler crazy specimens of counterpoint to amuse him, and also bottles of wine. Busoni had a really good heart. He and I walked on deck together one day while Mahler was sleeping. He loved him and talked of him all the time. We stopped at the taffrail and looked over the sea. 'The Germans,' he said, 'are a funny lot. Even now they have not absolutely put the stamp on Mahler's genius. They blow hot

and cold. They don't really know anything about him. But if he
– if he were taken from them, ah, then —!'

Mahler's beauty was staggering. 'Today, you're Alexander the
Great again,' I used to say. The beauty of his black shining eyes,
his white face, his black hair and blood-red mouth struck terror
into my heart.

The voyage went well, and when it came to embarking in the
tender at Cherbourg we found that the captain still had us in his
thoughts. He gave us time to board the tender and settle Mahler
down in seclusion before allowing the other passengers to leave
the ship.

There was a great stampede on the quay; and so, as we had
reserved a carriage, we sat quietly where we were until the crowd
dispersed; then we helped Mahler slowly along to the train,
which was a long way off. An official of the Hamburg–America
Line asked if he might take my place as I looked so ill. I accepted
his offer with Mahler's consent, and left my mother to accompany
them while I hurried back to the customs shed, where our forty
pieces of luggage were waiting. As soon as I said that my husband
was dangerously ill, it was all done in a moment and I hurried to
the train. But as I did not know the number of our compartment,
I had to go the whole length of the train, coach by coach, and
they were all vacant. There were two drunken porters at the end
of one of them who said they had lifted a sick man into the train.
They demanded a tip. I opened my handbag in my desperation,
and they forced me to give them all I had in it. I did not care. I
ran on and at last found Mahler lying comfortably in an improvised
bed my mother had quickly made.

Busoni had told me there was a young Austrian on board who
wished to offer his services to Mahler and me. I sent back word
that we did not need to trouble him while we were on board, but
that he might be of help when it came to landing. There was no
sign of him then, however; although in the tender he was the
only person who spied on Mahler over the barrier of our luggage.
Mahler had had to turn away to avoid his stare. Again at Cherbourg we saw him hurrying to the customs shed, and when I
got there his baggage had just been examined. Now, I thought,
he will give me his help. Not a bit of it. He vanished. I next came

on him with Gucki, telling her a fairy-story in a very loud voice. Mahler found it disturbing and asked me to tell him to stop.

We reached Paris at five in the morning. My stepfather had come from Paris to meet us and got on to our train at an intermediate station. Rooms were reserved and ready for us at the Hotel Elysée. We all went to bed, utterly worn out. When I woke at seven next morning, Mahler was sitting on the balcony. He was fully dressed. He was shaved. He rang for breakfast. I could not believe my eyes.

'I always said I should recover as soon as I set foot in Europe. I'll go for a drive this morning and in a few days, when we've got over the voyage, we two will set off for Egypt.'

I stared at him in utter astonishment. It seemed literally to be a miracle. He had not done anything for himself for months. My mother and I had had almost to carry him from the boat. And now! I sent for Mama and Moll, whose love for Mahler was nothing short of idolatry. We all laughed and wept for joy. It seemed he was saved.

He talked with great excitement about future productions during breakfast. *The Barber of Bagdad** – it would be marvellous; and he began to develop his ideas for making it go. He jumped up (a pang of dread clutched at my throat) and abruptly ordered an electric automobile. He got into it as a man recovered, and got out, after an hour's drive, as a man at death's door.

He got paler and paler from the moment we reached the Bois, athough at first the beauty of the day roused him to raptures. He leaned his head on my mother's shoulder and the drive ended without his uttering a word. We urged the chauffeur to drive as fast as possible. We were in mortal dread. At last – at last we were back in the hotel.

He was put staight to bed. He had a shivering fit. Then a collapse. A doctor was summoned by telephone. He gave him a camphor injection. And so ended our first day in Europe – after so wonderful a beginning.

I left him alone with my mother and spent the time with our little girl, who had been sadly neglected in our terrible alarm. He did not want me to hear what he said; and although my mother

* An opera by Peter Cornelius (1824–74). (D.M.)

sat by his bed and tried to rouse him from his despondency she did not suceed. He wept, and begged her if the worst came to have him buried beside his daughter at Grinzing, in a simple grave, with no pomp and ceremony, and a plain headstone with nothing but 'Mahler' on it. 'Any who come to look for me will know who I was, and the rest do not need to know. I cannot talk to Almschi about this. It would be too painful for us both.'

My mother and he wept bitterly. It was the only time during the whole of his illness that he was so utterly disconsolate. When Moll came in, he said again that he wished to be buried in the same grave as our daughter and asked him never to desert me.

As soon as I came in he fell silent. But I saw his tears. Soon he began to talk again and at length about his early associations and the companions of his youth; his complaints of them were bitter. 'They spun webs round me like spiders. They stole my life away. They kept me apart, from jealousy and envy. But I am to blame too. Why did I let it happen? My life has all been paper!' He said this again and again, as though speaking to himself: 'My life has all been paper!'

We now endeavoured to get into touch with the doctors whose names Fränkel had written down for us, but it was just before Easter and not one was available. The only bacteriologist we could get hold of was Chantemesse. When he came he insisted on instant removal to a nursing home of Dr. Dupré's in Rue Dupont. This was the best and most up to date of all the clinics in Paris at that time, but somewhat primitive compared with our hospitals in Vienna. There were wonderful rooms looking on to a garden, but no nursing to speak of. However, my mother and I needed no help in our devoted care of him.

There was no shutting our eyes now to the unmistakable signs. His growing weakness was arrested only by a feverish excitement. Yet he was glad to talk and he talked a great deal. He read works of philosophy all through his illness and up to the very end. The last book he read was *The Problem of Life* by Eduard von Hartmann. By the end it was in fragments. He tore the pages from the binding, because he had not the strength to hold more than a few pages at a time.

During his last days and while his mind was still unclouded his thoughts often went anxiously to Schoenberg. 'If I go, he will have nobody left.' I promised him to do everything in my power. Moll too promised to stand by Schoenberg.

After Mahler's death Moll told friends of ours what he had said and they resolved forthwith to collect a considerable sum and to put it at my disposal year by year for the benefit of young musicians. I chose Strauss, Busoni and Walter as trustees of the fund, and at my request the proceeds frequently went to Schoenberg. War and inflation have unfortunately made it worthless.

Chantemesse, who was a celebrated bacteriologist, now made a culture from Mahler's blood and after a few days he came to us in great delight with a microscope in his hand. I thought some miracle had happened. He placed the microscope on the table. 'Now, Madame Mahler, come and look. Even I – myself – have never seen streptococci in such a marvellous state of development. Just look at these threads – it's like seaweed.' He was eager to explain, to shine his light abroad. But I could not listen. Dumb with horror, I turned and left him. The shock it gave my mother did her serious harm.

Once when Mahler was feeling better I sat on his bed and we discussed what we should do when he had recovered. 'We'll go to Egypt and see nothing but blue sky,' he said.

'Once you are well again,' I said, 'I shall have had enough of suffering. Do you remember when you first got to know me you thought I was too happy. I've suffered enough now. I don't need any more chastening. We'll live a careless, happy life.'

He smiled tenderly and stroked my hair. 'Yes, you're right. God grant I get better and then we can still be happy.'

But he got worse, and in my anguish I telegraphed to Professor Chvostek, the most celebrated doctor in Vienna, asking him to come at once. He arrived next morning. I told him first how to behave with Mahler and then he went into the sick-room and began in a loud, jovial voice: 'Now then, Mahler, what's all this about? Working too hard, that's what it is. You'll have to knock off for six months or a year. You've brought it on yourself – you can't treat your nerves that way, you know.'

Mahler gazed at him with growing astonishment.

'Shall I ever be able to work again then?' he asked, his face lighting up with joy.

'Of course. Why not? Keep your heart up, that's all. This evening we'll be off to Vienna together.'

Chvostek told me to make preparations for leaving as soon as possible. Anything might happen and then it might be too late to move him. All the same, I did not lose all heart, and when I went back into Mahler's room the joy in his face was such as I had never seen. He cried out again and again: 'Oh, the lovely man, the lovely Chvostek! Oh, for tonight – how soon can we all start?'

And it seemed that his overwhelming joy made a new man of him. He could not endure delay. We packed madly. Moll hurried out to reserve sleepers. Mama was to follow us to Vienna with her granddaughter. Mahler was dressed long before it was time to start, blissful, transfigured.

Chvostek and I accompanied him in the ambulance and then he was carried to the train on a stretcher. His travelling-cap was awry – so helpless he was. I took it off; his beautiful face showed he understood. It was horrible to see him manipulated into the train on a stretcher along the narrow corridor. He went straight to bed, and Moll, Chvostek and I took turns in watching through the night. 'Are you there? You're an angel,' he said, and after a pause: 'We're coming home in poor trim this time. But we'll soon be on our feet again.' I was sitting on a suitcase beside him. I laid my head on his hand and kissed it.

Chvostek called me out in the middle of the night and made Moll take my place.

'No hope,' he said solemnly. 'And may the end come quickly. If he did pull through, which is not likely, he'd be condemned to a bath-chair for the rest of his life.'

'Better that than nothing,' I said. 'I can't face life without him.'

'Yes, but then the whole nervous system will go too and you don't want to wheel a senile idiot about.'

I refused to submit and asked Moll to let me return to my post. Journalists came to the door at every station in Germany and Austria for the latest bulletin, and so his last journey was like that of a dying king. They all knew his importance and had to hear how he was at half-past ten, at eleven and twelve. Mahler asked who each of them was and what paper he represented, and it seemed to do him good. He said to me over and over again: 'My madly adored Almschi.'

Vienna – and by ambulance to the Löw Sanatorium, where an enormous room with a veranda was ready for him. Not only the room but the corridor too were wreathed in flowers, and Mahler was obviously delighted. More and more flowers arrived. I had to bring them all for him to see and to arrange them with care. A white basket of flowers arrived with a card: 'From the Philharmonic.' '*My* Philharmonic,' he said again and again.

After a time he lay completely still. His mind was becoming confused. Justine paid him another visit and at the sight of her his eyes dilated unnaturally:

'Who is this lady?' he stammered. She fled.

Berliner arrived from Berlin, true to their old friendship, and Mahler recognized him and grasped his hand. 'My dear friend,' he said, and then turned to the wall, perhaps to hide his emotion.

During his last days he cried out, 'My Almschi,' hundreds of times, in a voice, a tone I had never heard before and have never heard since. 'My Almschi!' As I write it down now, I cannot keep back my tears.

When Gucki came to his bedside he put his arms round her. 'Be my good girl, my child.'

Did he know? Or not? It was impossible to tell. He lay there groaning. A large swelling came up on his knee, then on his leg. Radium was applied and the swelling immediately went down. On the evening after, he was washed and his bed made. Two attendants lifted his naked emaciated body. It was a taking down from the cross. This was the thought that came to all of us.

He had difficulty in breathing and was given oxygen. Then uraemia – and the end. Chvostek was summoned. Mahler lay with dazed eyes; one finger was conducting on the quilt. There was a smile on his lips and twice he said: 'Mozarte!' His eyes were very big. I begged Chvostek to give him a large dose of morphia so that he might feel nothing more. He replied in a loud voice. I seized his hands: 'Talk softly, he might hear you.' – 'He hears nothing now.'

How terrible the callousness of doctors is at such moments. And how did he know that he could not hear? Perhaps he was only incapable of movement?

The death-agony began. I was sent into the next room. The death-rattle lasted several hours.

That ghastly sound ceased suddenly at midnight on 18th May during a tremendous thunderstorm. With that last breath his beloved and beautiful soul had fled, and the silence was more deathly than all else. As long as he breathed he was there still. But now all was over.

I was not allowed in the death-chamber. Moll was with him to the last. I was removed that night from my room next to his. The doctors insisted. But I felt it a humiliation not to be allowed to stay near him. I could not understand it. Was I alone? Had I to live without him? It was as if I had been flung out of a train in a foreign land. I had no place on earth.

I went up to the Hohe Warte, in Heiligenstadt. The bells tolled without ceasing. I had Mahler's photograph beside me and I lay in bed and talked to him. He was still there – not yet in the earth.

Chvostek came to see me unasked. 'Your lung is touched – and badly too. If you don't look out, you'll very soon follow him.' Mama came in and for the first time for many days I smiled. It was my one hope to follow him. But – I have lived on.

I can never forget his dying hours and the greatness of his face as death drew nearer. His battle for the eternal values, his elevation above trivial things and his unflinching devotion to truth are an example of the saintly life.

Part Two

LETTERS
1901 - 1910

1901

29 November 1901 1

I have hastened, dear Fräulein Alma, to collect for you all my songs that have so far been published. My only consolation for not being able to bring them is the pleasing thought that you will now have to give me a little of your attention and will have me in your thoughts. – When I come on Monday (I count the hours till then with eager impatience) I will play any of them you want to hear.

How happy we were yesterday in spite of all; that is what I felt as soon as L. left me to go on my way home alone. Those delightful hours echoed on and on in my heart, and accompanied me even into my dreams.

In haste, dear Fräulein Alma, from

Your

GUSTAV MAHLER

Wednesday evening
4 December 1901 2

My dearest friend!

Here are the three tickets for *The Tales of Hoffmann*, accompanied, alas, by the Job's tidings (meaning myself as the luckless Job) that I have to leave for Berlin on Monday, as the first rehearsal of my symphony takes place on Tuesday.* So I can neither conduct *Tristan* on Tuesday nor pay you the now so dearly loved visit on Monday. I shall be away for about ten days and so I feel very sad and fear that the battle I fought yesterday against the clay idols of the house was fought quite in vain. Only my wounds remain. It was not at all kind of you, either, to resign yourself so patiently to the fate that banishes me for a whole week. Hero was not like that. She said, 'Come tomorrow!' So now I shall not be swimming the Hellespont, but as a modern Leander travelling by express and sleeper via Berlin to Döbling and arriving after so many fatigues and sleepless nights as a pure 'decadent'. – I send many greetings to your dear Mama and hope I may catch a glimpse of you as I flit by tomorrow morning, to take with me as a last consolation and also as provision for the journey.

The vanquished victor

PYRRHUS

* Mahler probably refers to the Berlin première of his Fourth Symphony, which he conducted himself on 16th December. (D.M.)

Dearest friend,

I hope *Hoffmann* afforded you some pleasure yesterday – although the opera gives little but the dregs of him, from which the spirit has fled. Madame Schoder brought out much that lies on the surface (unfortunately in this whole work there is only the surface to retrieve) but the triviality of poor Schrödter and his son-in-law was too leaden a weight on the wings of poetry. It is only with a struggle I can get to the end of the first two acts. But yesterday I was buoyed up by the joy of doing it for you! The third act is better. There at least I find something that helps me to evoke the demonic character of the original.

If you want to know how much the opera loses, read Hoffmann's story, *Rath Krespel*. Schoder was moving, and not far from seeing eye to eye with me. But even she left me in the lurch rather when it came to the subtleties of interpretation, for which her tendency to realism is to blame. Antonia does *not* die of consumption, as Schoder suggested by her cough – that cursed cough so beloved on the stage. It is the demonic principle of art, which pushes anybody who is possessed by it to relinquish his own personality; and in this case so penetrates a nature peculiarly disposed to give up the ghost that it snatches her out of life. One might say it is not the ghost she gives up, but the body. Or – in one of those images you love so much – she takes her way into the realm of night, from which there is no return. But these are only the elements of a powerful drama, the dark perspectives of which might be lighted up in the grisliest fashion by a composer of genius. That is how I felt it yesterday, hoping in my heart that it might come home to you. – If you will turn a sympathetic eye on Hoffmann's works, you will find a new light on the relation of music to reality; for music, mysterious as it is, often illumines our souls with a flash of lightning, and you will feel that the only true reality on earth is soul. For any one who has once grasped this, what we call reality is no more than a formula, a shadow with no substance. – And you must not, please, take this for a poetical metaphor; it is a conviction which can hold its own at the bar of sober reason. We'll discuss it when I see you again. I write rather at length on the subject because it has so close a bearing on my earnest desire, which is not, as you may think, just a piece of pedantry, to set up my God in the place of the idols of clay.

To my great sorrow, I cannot come on Saturday. I will tell you the reason when I am back from Berlin. For the moment, rather than make polite excuses, may I just say – as I find it hard to do so laconically – that I must refuse your charming invitation?

I have grown so fond of our talks in this short time – or our squabbles for that matter, or even our silences, that the dearest wish I cherish before going away is that you will still be my dear comrade and help me a little to be yours too. Don't forget our favourites: Evchen – and Hans Sachs!

Auf Wiedersehen!

G.

8 December 1901 4

Dearest Almschi,

Here is a fairy-tale belonging to my youthful days.* You were a true joy to me yesterday. You listened so charmingly and answered so charmingly too. What a pity that such an afternoon should be so short – and the coda at night almost sad. – Today brings me the evening when we shall be in the deepest sense at one – I shall think of you in every beat, and conduct for you. It shall be as it was yesterday at the piano when I spoke to you so gladly and from my heart. And sometimes I shall pause and have that mistrustful look which has so often surprised you. It is not *mistrust*, in the ordinary sense, but a *question* addressed to you and the future. Dearest, *learn to answer*. It is not an easy thing to learn – you have first to know yourself thoroughly. But to *ask* is more difficult still. Only by asking can one learn one's whole and inmost relation to others. Dearest, dear one, *learn to ask!*

Your response to me yesterday was so different and so much more mature. I feel that these last days have opened – unlocked so much for you. – How will it be when I come back again? – I shall ask you again: Are you fond of me? Fonder than yesterday? Did you know me before? And do you know me now? And now? And now, addio, my dear one, my comrade!

Your

GUSTAV

Berlin–Dresden
9 December 1901 5

Dearest,

How are you? How I should love to find a line from you on arrival at the Palast Hotel, Berlin – that's all the address you need put. For a moment your letter would make a strange room home, which now is only where you are; the least sign of you will make me forget the pain of separation.

Write to me too about *The Magic Flute*. I can well understand how a work of that kind might not go down with you. You're still too much *yourself*! I was just the same for a long time with works you describe as 'naïve'. But I treasure the least thing you say about yourself. Don't give

---

* Mahler refers to his youthful cantata, *Das klagende Lied* (see pp. 29–30). (D.M.)

a thought to your letters – write down whatever comes into your head. Imagine that I'm sitting beside you and that you're talking about everything.

I always want to know about your life day by day – every detail.

So you'll be with my sister [Justine] on Wednesday. How dearly I wish you two to get to know each other. Perhaps you will recognize in her many characteristics of mine – and at once feel more at home with them. Hurrah! Here's your letter, just come. I'll read it first before I go on.

Now I feel strong again! I needed so much to have a word from you! Only I didn't dare hope for it. But I'll confess to you now, my dearest love, that I should have been in despair if it hadn't come.

What you say of my sister goes to my heart, and now I must tell you – what I refrained from saying the other day for fear of curbing your spontaneity – she knows all and loves you already. We went straight home alone after dinner last night and talked till late about you and our future. She understands all about it and will be a true friend to us. It's too bad that I have to go away again just at this very time. It makes me very unhappy, and yet it is almost like the voice of the Master, the Teacher. (I say that to avoid saying 'God', because we have said so little on that topic, and I could not bear it if mere phrases passed between us.) The voice summons us to be brave, enduring, patient. You see, my dearest, we shall need that all our life long, and, what is more, even if the Teacher's voice is heard in thunder, we must still understand it.

Oh, God, I can write no more. There is such a noise all round me. I can't hear what I am saying – I only hear a Voice which drowns all else and will never be silenced, not in my heart, in which there is one word and one note only: my love of you, my Alma!

I'll write again at once from Berlin. All that is inexpressible and audible and comprehensible to you alone, my own, my own,

Your

GUSTAV

Palast Hotel,
Berlin, W.
11 December 1901 6
In the greatest haste!

My precious, dear girl!

Just a cry from my heart, in the tearing hurry between arrival and first rehearsal! Your dear letter of Sunday was my travelling-companion. I studied it as if it had been the New Testament. It taught me the present and the future. If I can find the time, I'll tell you, even today, all that's happened to me since I got your letter. (For me it is like the Hedschra, from which Mohammedans reckon their calendar.) My new life began there too. I can only now live, breathe, be in reference to you.

I am conducting my own work myself in Berlin. Oh, if you could only be there! But, however necessary it may be to others to be given the key to my being in my work, you, you, my Alma, starting from me, from the all-embracing present, experience it all as love's clairvoyant, you being I, I you. Astronomers recognize a star by its rays – (and yet fumble in the dark, because what they know by analysis of the spectrum is already earth-conditioned – the rays as they leave the star itself remain for ever inscrutable) – but what can the rays mean to one who inhabits the star itself? I admit the comparison doesn't quite fit. But still, it comes nearest for the moment to what I feel, and to what consoles and blesses me.

What will it be like when you share everything with me and I with you, and when this vehement and consuming longing, which is mixed with such dread and anxiety, is assuaged, and when even in separation we know everything about each other, and can love each other and be inter-penetrated without a care? (I take no account of all I shall gain through you – nor of unrest and pain – don't misunderstand what I said just now.)

Now I must be off to rehearsal. If the notes and waves of sound had as much strength as my love and longing for you, you would hear them all morning. It will all be to you and for you, all that lives in me. My beloved Alma.

> Your
>
> GUSTAV

Berlin
14 December 1901 7

Dearest,

Full rehearsals begin tomorrow. If only you were here! I find now (particularly since my thoughts have been bound up in you) that I am getting quite vulgarly ambitious in a way that is almost unworthy of a person like me!

I should like now to have success, recognition, and all those other really quite meaningless things people talk of. I want to do you honour. I have always had ambition, but I have not coveted the honours my contemporaries can confer. To be understood and esteemed by men of like mind, even if I were never to find them (and indeed they are only to be found outside space and time) has always been the goal I have striven for; and so it shall be all the more from now on. In this you must stand by me, my beloved. And to win this guerdon and to be so crowned, I must deny myself the applause of the crowd and even of the

Great and Good (even they can't always follow me). How gladly up to now I have suffered myself to be slapped in the face by the Philistine, to be scorned and hated by the immature. To my sorrow I know only too well that what little notice I have had must be put down perhaps only to misunderstanding, or at least to a dim perception of some unintelligible ideal. – I am not, of course, speaking of my activities in opera or as a conductor: they after all are of an inferior order. Please let me have your answer to this, whether, that is, *you* understand and are willing also to follow me. Alma, could you endure hardships with me, and even ignominy and shame, and gladly take up so grievous a cross? If this is to go today I must stop!

I could talk on to you for ever!

I think of you every minute, my dear, beloved Alma, and I will make use a thousand times over of the permission you give me in the post-script of your last letter.

Yours, darling girl,
GUSTAV

Palast Hotel,
Berlin, W.
14 December 1901 8
Saturday afternoon, having
thrown everyone out – to
be alone with you

My tenderly loved girl,

How I longed for your letter! It came today and has given me such a beautiful, happy day. You would know what a saint looks like if you could see my face as I walk along the streets of Berlin. Everyone, I think, sees it in my face; unless I'm imagining it, they all look at me with astonishment. A slight inversion, therefore (which ought to please you, you contrapuntist), of Goethe's 'Everyone stops in astonishment at the sight of my darling's eyes'. I have always dreamed and hoped, but never known till now, that you were my source of warmth and light. I should otherwise have given up dreaming that the happiness of being loved as I love could ever be mine. Every time a woman has crossed my path, I have been tortured afresh by having to recognize the gap between dreams of happiness and the sorry truth. I've always taken the blame and been resigned in my heart.

You know yourself, Alma, young as you are, how it has fared with you, and will be able to sympathize, when with every pulse of my heart and life and to my very depths, I feel the bliss, and can say it, too, of loving for the first time. I can never be free of the dread that this lovely dream may dissolve, and can hardly wait for the moment when your own mouth and breath will breathe into me the certainty and inmost consciousness that my life has reached port after storm. I feel that the last time we were together brought us really close for the first time, and that in spite of our apparent separation we were for the first time really united.

I read all that, you see, my darling, in your last letter. Why, Alma, can you not be with me now? I always remember your telling me one day that you loved travelling. I often feel you are here with me; I talk to you and read in your face how you enjoy it all and how you let all that is new and unknown, take you by storm.

I want to pass the dessert over to you every time it is put in front of me, knowing your love of sweets and fruit (once my weakness too). Everything recovers its value when I think of you, as I do without ceasing. Justi too has sent me news of your time together. She is positively in love with you – I am not that any longer: there is no name that I know of for what you have become to me, for that unique and deeply blissful oneness. Your good and tender feeling for my sister has relieved my heart of one of its greatest anxieties. Nothing enables me so well to estimate and recognize the value of your love. It is the same for me too. I have locked up for ever in my heart all that you hold dear. Just as mine from now on is yours, so I embrace what you possess with all my soul. Oh, God, I am talking away today from sheer suspense and longing for you, like Walther von Stolzing, and never give a thought to the other half, to poor Hans Sachs, who yet deserves your love far more.

You know, my darling, it often comes over me almost with a pang that one cannot deserve and attain the highest! What you have given me, my Alma! You have confessed to me so sweetly what you want to be to me. When I think of what I must and shall be to you, it puts me into a solemn mood. I have such a strong and deep feeling of my duties, which are at the same time my highest happiness, that I wouldn't dare – for fear of tempting providence – to take my oath, or vow a vow! And I think to myself that you feel as I do: that what fills and so unites us is a power outside and above us, a power which it is our religion to revere. If at such moments I utter the name of God, the overwhelming sense of your, of my love will enable you to grasp that this power embraces us both within itself and so achieves a unity!

Please, Alma, don't forget to say a word now and then about what I write to you. I want to know whether you understand all I mean and are willing to follow me in it. There must be no empty phrases between us – as there would be if you ever took something I said as a fine sentiment or an epistolary flourish. But I beg of you; put no constraint on yourself.

Never believe that you could be less dear to me, less beloved, if you wished to feel or to speak differently. In the same way, I shall never weary of finding out and speaking your language, if you cannot follow me in mine. I'd like too to have your answer to what I wrote in my previous letter about ambition.

What I find so eternally lovable about you is that you're so genuine, so straightforward. Empty phrases are the last thing I'd expect of you! In fact – that is the one sin against the Holy Ghost. It is the lie in itself, because in it a man belies himself. Do you remember our first talk, when Burckhard was there. I addressed every word to you. It was already God's will to make us one – only we didn't know it – but I had already had my baptism of fire! Oh, Alma, dearest, most precious girl, I want always to speak to you from the bottom of my heart, and don't get anywhere near it. Imagine telling you all that goes on around me – and yet I must do that too. We must share everything. The difficulty I find at present is not knowing where to begin. Everything is still unknown to you. You have no scale for measuring the worth or worthlessness things have for my life or yours! (Oh, how delightful it is to think every single thing has its meaning for both of us, or neither.) Just as in a modern novel. It starts in the middle and then in Chapter Two you get to work on all that's gone before.

I wrote to my sister yesterday, enclosing what I've drawn up as a very special document for the Dresden concert.* I reckoned that the letter would arrive just when you were with her. How I envy her! I've asked Justi to hand the document over to you (for whom it is actually intended), because I would not have drawn it up for the king himself, I'm so distraught now and harassed by everything that does not include you. I leave here early on Tuesday for Dresden. So from Sunday on write there, Hotel Bellevue.

Carl [Moll] will be here soon. I gave him a rendezvous here, and hope he stays on for the concert, so that a ray at least of my beloved sun will fall on me.

Greet your mother from me many, many times. I'm so used now to looking on her as mine that I shall start calling her Mama next.

Let me tell you that every day when I don't have at least two lines from your hand, Alma, is a lost day for me. I kiss it passionately, beloved.

I kiss you now, you precious, to tell you how blissful it is to be allowed to call you mine.

GUSTAV

* Mahler's Second Symphony was to be performed at Dresden on 20th December. It was conducted by Ernst von Schuch. (D.M.)

PROGRAMME OF THE SECOND SYMPHONY BY GUSTAV MAHLER

We are standing beside the coffin of a man beloved. For the last time his life, his battles, his sufferings and his purpose pass before the mind's eye. And now, at this solemn and deeply stirring moment, when we are released from the paltry distractions of everyday life, our hearts are gripped by a voice of awe-inspiring solemnity, which we seldom or never hear above the deafening traffic of mundane affairs. What next? it says. What is life – and what is death?

Have we any continuing existence?

Is it all an empty dream, or has this life of ours, and our death, a meaning?

If we are to go on living, we must answer this question.

The next three movements are conceived as intermezzi.

Second Movement. *Andante*.

A blissful moment in his life and a mournful memory of youth and lost innocence.

Third Movement. Scherzo.

The Spirit of unbelief and negation has taken possession of him. Looking into the turmoil of appearances, he loses together with the clear eyes of childhood the sure foothold which love alone gives. He despairs of himself and of God. The world and life become a witch's brew; disgust of existence in every form strikes him with iron fist and drives him to an outburst of despair.

Fourth Movement. The primal dawn. (Alto solo.)

The moving voice of ingenuous belief sounds in our ears.

'I am from God and will return to God! God will give me a candle to light me to the bliss of eternal life.'

Fifth Movement.

We are confronted once more by terrifying questions.

A voice is heard crying aloud: The end of all living beings is come – the Last Judgement is at hand and the horror of the day of days has come.

The earth quakes, the graves burst open, the dead arise and stream on in endless procession. The great and the little ones of the earth – kings and beggars, righteous and godless – all press on – the cry for mercy and forgiveness strikes fearfully on our ears. The wailing rises higher – our

senses desert us, consciousness dies at the approach of the eternal
spirit. The

'Last Trump'

is heard – the trumpets of the Apocalypse ring out; in the eerie silence
that follows we can just catch the distant, barely audible song of a
nightingale, a last tremulous echo of earthly life! A chorus of saints and
heavenly beings softly breaks forth:

'Thou shalt arise, surely thou shalt arise.' Then appears the glory of
God! A wondrous, soft light penetrates us to the heart – all is holy
calm!

And behold – it is no judgement – there are no sinners, no just. None
is great, none is small. There is no punishment and no reward.

An overwhelming love lightens our being. We know and are.

Palast Hotel,
Berlin, W.
15 December 1901 9
Sunday evening

So, dearest, now comes the best part of my day. I sit down and talk to
you. I've been tormenting and worrying the hall-porter all day. I
thought one line at least was sure to come, and so I've been hoping and
hoping all day long and now set my hopes on the first post tomorrow
morning. Yes, a man can become so greedy and exacting in eight days
that he cannot hold out for one day without a letter, and yet only eight
days ago this same man was delighted if he ever caught sight of those
blue (and then much larger) characters.

Your first letter began: Lieber Herr Direktor! Ugh, what a shudder
it gave me! Your second was charming but still very hesitant and shy,
no form of address whatever and at the end just: Alma. But in your
third you were my Alma – and now, my own, I hold you to that for
ever, and I hardly knew it before I had to go away – I almost feel without a parting, because since those lines of yours which said and gave so
much I have not been able to see you eye to eye and face to face. When
on Saturday I hold your beloved hand in mine, I shall know that you
give it me for ever. This too, like everything else between us, has come
almost suddenly.

Well then, today was the final, public rehearsal, here as great an
occasion as the concert itself, and I don't mind saying I'm frightfully
glad it went off so well. I was thinking all the time: if only my love were
down there among the audience! Mine! I would have surveyed the
scene with real pride – if it goes off so well tomorrow evening I shall
have got a foothold in Berlin. Next time perhaps you will be with me –

yes, for certain. Everything goes so fast with us, and after all the wings of love are a bit faster than the 'wings of song'! Sometimes, when I forget my cowardice (you know over what) for a moment, I feel so glad at heart and positively HOPE! I saw Carl yesterday – unfortunately W. was there too, and so my lips were sealed. It would have meant so much to me to have said something, however trivial, about you to Carl. He is staying on for the concert and leaves the same night. Heavens, suppose he doesn't like my symphony after all and then intrigues with you against me!?

You will observe from this how distraught I am! It's more than I can stand. I took refuge in the writing-room and now my fellow-guests and the waiters are incessantly in and out, and tear my nerves to pieces.

Wonderful that you have taken now to Hölderlin. He is one of my favourites among poets, and men. He is one, dearest, of the truly great. How nice it will be when we rummage round in your library and put it in order. Heavens, when I think of myself once more in the room under the roof, I feel so wild with impatience that I could get up and run about. I must think of something else if I'm not to give way.

Actually, it seems to me sometimes that we've only exchanged letters up to now – and have still to meet face to face and get to know each other.

And it is so in fact! Don't you remember that the last time I saw you we were still strangers! It is only during these last eight days that everything has taken such a wonderful turn. The letter you wrote me just after *The Magic Flute* put everything for me on a new course. Till then it was all in a way conversation between us – the forms of politeness, etc., fell away with that letter, where you, my beloved, struck for the first time the note which from now on gives the key of our living and loving. If only I had a picture of you! How I regret now not having simply stolen the photograph of you you showed me last time. Have your photo taken, Alma, full face and looking at me. I beg you too, my Alma, do write every day – if it's only one side! Otherwise, I wait in hopes all day and go to sleep unconsoled.

Write for the last time on Thursday, but early enough for the letter to reach Vienna by midday and go on by the night express for Dresden. Then I'll get it on Friday. The concert is on Friday evening.* On Saturday at four I shall make my sudden appearance in Steinfeldstrasse – with the consequence I have just described and picture to myself every day, every hour. A thousand kisses and what I had better not think of in case I die of longing! My beloved, my friend, my Alma!

Your

GUSTAV

* 20th December. (D.M.)

Dearest Almschi, don't throw out the baby with the bath-water. If, after I have struggled for fifteen years against stupidity and misunderstanding and endured all the toils and afflictions of the pioneer, a work of mine should at last be understood, particularly in Vienna, where people have come to have some idea of me without knowing it, there is no reason to mind it any more than you would mind misunderstanding and ill-will, or to feel that it would tell against my work. The point is not to take the world's opinion as a guiding star, to go one's way in life and work unerringly, neither depressed by failure nor seduced by applause. It does seem to me now that some of the seed I have sown is coming up, and, apart from all else, I rejoice that it should happen just in time to remove a few thorns from your path. Not that I would spare you them if it was a question of being true to my destiny – and yours, for they are now the same. And so we shall now support and encourage each other in facing the world with equanimity – which is the highest honour we covet.

Alma – we shall not be able to utter a word for the first hour – we shall have too much to say. Your mother knows now, doesn't she? Tell her everything before I come. I must meet her from the first moment as her son. I cannot face any formalities. Tell her everything. As you know, I did at first mean to speak to her myself – but that was before I, and still more you, had seen the whole truth. My idea was to consult her as the person who knew you best. – But now that our minds are irrevocably made up, there is nothing I could say to her except: 'Give me what is mine – let me live and breathe,' for your love is as much a condition of my life as my pulse or heart. The more I think of it, the more I feel how important for our whole future it is that at this solemn time (the true solemnity of marriage, when souls recognize their affinity and flow into one channel) we should be together not in the body but in the spirit. We should not have been able in months to say as much or to come to such a profound understanding as we have in these two (so endlessly long) weeks! – I'm so blissfully conscious that in this short time we have ripened in a sun far stronger than that blazing orb up there: it would have taken a whole summer, and we have unfolded our whole being in a couple of weeks. This would certainly never have happened if I hadn't had to go away just at that very moment

* The day on which Mahler conducted the première of his Fourth Symphony in Berlin.

when you in the true sense first opened yourself to me and gave yourself to me as my own. – We must now number our letters so as to be sure that none goes astray. – Yesterday I suddenly caught the worst cold I ever remember. Heavens, what a shock! Suppose it had happened next Saturday, or suppose it came back – I shouldn't be able to come out to you – because the renunciation I'd have to lay on myself would be beyond bearing. You see, don't you, Almschi, that I'm being funny again, because of course I should come even if I was at death's door, but to kiss you would be forbidden. But you may well believe that *seeing you, hearing you*, holding your hand would be enough to cure me. I have the feeling that you could restore me to life even if I were dead. But, heavens, I must now take proper care of myself. I'm always so distraught and imprudent on my travels. Justi takes care of me at home. – How you two must have talked on Saturday!? How I'd love to know all you said! You – in my room! How warm and cheered I'll feel when I'm there next. Now I must go out again. My own, my own – I don't know what to say. Words are so stale, because stupidity and tepid feelings have worn them down. You know, my sole good, what it means when I say, 'My dearest dear! My Alma!' May you be kept and blessed for me. May I be a blessing in your life too, which from now on is that part of the earth in which I root and still hope to flower. My beloved!

Your

GUSTAV

Hotel Bellevue,
Dresden, A.
Wednesday (?) morning
18 December 1901 11

Dearly beloved!

So – the last station (stations of suffering in our case)! I am nearer to you now, and think only of Saturday when I shall hold you in my arms. It will be the supreme moment of my life. – We start work on the Second here today. My Almschi! Justi did not tell you, then, that I only drew up the programme as a crutch for a cripple (you know whom I mean). It only gives a superficial indication, all that any programme can do for a musical work, let alone this one, which is so much all of a piece that it can no more be explained than the world itself. – I'm quite sure that if God were asked to draw up a programme of the world he had created he could never do it. – At best it would say as little about the nature of God and life as my analysis says about my C minor symphony.* In fact, as all religious dogmas do, it leads directly to misunderstanding, to a flattening and coarsening, and in the long run to such distortion that

* Mahler refers to the programme of his Second Symphony. See pp. 213–214. (D.M.)

the work, and still more its creator, is utterly unrecognizable. – I had a serious talk with Strauss in Berlin and tried to show him the blind-alley he had got into. Unfortunately, he could not quite follow what I meant. He's a charming fellow, and I'm touched by his attitude to me. And yet I can mean nothing to him – for whereas I see over his head, he sees only up to my knees. – He is coming to Vienna very soon. Perhaps I'll bring him out to see you. – Here I am, writing to you again until late at night. It is so moving, so delightful now to think over and plan our future life in every detail – with you as the centre of my whole existence – always beginning afresh from you and returning to you again – when I wake at daylight or when I go to bed – or if I get up in the night or in the early morning. I sleep little owing to an indisposition which usually afflicts me when I travel; but I don't mind, because my thoughts fly at once to you. – How I wish you could be here for the C minor. The piano-score gives no idea of it. And it is so important you should know it – for my Fourth will mean nothing to you. – It again is all humour – 'naïve', as you would say; just what you can so far understand least in me – and what in any case only the fewest of the few will ever understand to all futurity. But you, my Alma, you will be guided by love and it will light your way into the most secret places. My love and my longing, my hope and faith – a thousand thousand times yours,

Your

GUSTAV

Vienna
21 December 1901 12

My beloved Alma,

I am back in the air you breathe, my native air; and I had scarcely entered my room (how glad I am you know it now) before I saw your dear handwriting. I was touched by your affectionate welcome, even though it was written before you got my letter of yesterday. – That letter weighed on my heart when I thought of the impression it could not fail to make on you at first. For my sake and yours, I trust you read it in the light of my love and truth and recognized how strong and deep they were. For you do understand, I know, how hard and implacably truthful I am where love is concerned. – And everything must be clear between us before we hold each other in our arms – for this afternoon I could never have enough control over myself to discuss with you what all the same must be decided between us. I await the answer my servant will bring in a state of suspense and anguish such as I have never known. – What will your answer be? But do not misunderstand me. The decision rests with what you are, not what you say. The passion which literally fetters us must be momentarily overcome (and this can only be, if we do not meet face to face – and that is why I write while there is still time). Otherwise, we cannot with the inward composure and certainty of love enter those bonds which shall indissolubly unite us as long as life lasts.

'He stands the test who binds himself for ever.'

And, 'with the girdle, with the veil, the beautiful illusion is rent in two!'

No more now, for my heart overflows at the thought of our meeting again. I will come as soon as I can. But I do not know how long I may be kept at the Opera. Also I have to see the Superintendent today and often I don't get away from him before 3 o'clock.

Auf Wiedersehen, my dear, my love!

Your

GUSTAV

24 December 1901 13

My Alma!

For the first and last time I send you Christmas greetings on Christmas Eve; for in the future we shall spend Christmas together. Once united – soon, I hope – we shall need no messenger. You will be there beside me, ruling the household. The love which has ripened our happiness so quickly that it falls from the tree at our feet may have been unguarded, but it was trustful and looked with hope to the future. Today, a day that would have united us, as it does all mankind, even if we had known nothing of each other, in a children's festival, shall remain a symbol, a sign that, happy and united in our love, our hearts must be open to all others too – for a love we may call divine binds us together and links us also with all humanity.

I bless you, my beloved, my life, on this day, the children's day, in whom the seed of earthly as well as divine love strikes root wherever the seed falls. May my life be a blessing to yours, so that you become capable of recognizing the divine and of 'revering in silence the inscrutable', by growing out beyond our earthly love and out of its nature! (In essence it comes to this, that we can never be entirely happy as long as there are others who are not happy.) What I am saying to you today, understand me clearly, my Alma, is what, perhaps more clearly than anything, tells you how boundless and how sacred my love for you is. Now, when I am so close to the fulfilment of my highest aspirations and feel such inward happiness, I want to lead myself and you up into those regions where we catch a whiff of eternity and the divine. That is how I want to be yours and you to be mine.

My only one!

Your

GUSTAV

A LETTER* IN MAHLER'S OWN HAND TO THE DIRECTORS OF THE VIENNA
PHILHARMONIC ORCHESTRA

The Director of the Royal Opera
1901 14

Gentlemen,

To my sincere regret I am obliged to inform you that, owing to the
burden of work my duties lay on me, and my impaired health, I do not
feel that I am able to continue as conductor of the Philharmonic
concerts.

May I beg you to convey this to the society with the expression of
my profound regret, and my cordial thanks for the confidence they have
hitherto reposed in me.

I need not add that I shall in the future regard it as a pleasure as well
as a long-standing obligation to be at the disposal of the orchestra and
its management and to promote their welfare in any way within my
power.

GUSTAV MAHLER
Director of the Royal Opera

Vienna, April, 1901

1902

1902 15

Dearest! Lux!

It has just this moment arrived. Take it, the first!† How I wish that it
may reach your heart, as surely as it had its source in mine! Yesterday I
ascended to the fifth, or sixth heaven! The seventh will be – do you
know when?

Your

GUSTAV

Semmering
31 January 1902 16

Beloved!

Your dear little letter came just at breakfast time to my indescribable
joy. I too have been painfully awaiting the first word from you. It was

---

* Mahler wrote this letter to the Philharmonic Orchestra only when he heard that
it had made his health the excuse for engaging his successor behind his back –
Joseph Hellmesberger, that ephemeral pigmy. (A.M.)

† A copy of the just published Fourth Symphony. See p. 24, line 13.

not the parting only – I found the whole evening uncomfortable. Strauss sheds such a blight – you feel estranged from your very self. If these are the fruits, how is one to love the tree? Your comment on him hits the nail on the head. And I am very proud of your penetration. Better, by far, to eat the bread of poverty and follow one's star than sell one's soul like that. The time will come when the chaff shall be winnowed from the grain – and my day will be when his is ended. If only I might live to see it, with you at my side! But you, I hope, will see it for certain and remember the days when you discerned the sun through the mist – as on that day we were in the Park and it looked like a nasty red blot. For the moment all I think of is to get well and be yours, body and soul. I am much better already after a good night's sleep. Perhaps I may see you up here? If you came on Saturday afternoon we could go back to Vienna together on Sunday. But let your mother decide. Don't urge it on her. If I wait one more day I shall see you at any rate on Sunday evening. I am getting on now. I'll write again this evening. And, by the way, Alma, my child, do write a proper, legible address, if only for the sake of the poor postmen. How are they to make head or tail of your scrawl? I should tease you about it if you were here.

You said I did not join in the conversation the day before yesterday, and I will now tell you why. How could I take any part in his vulgar talk? I was elated by a performance which had aroused my creative energy. I was not going to be dragged down to his level and talk about royalties and percentages, of which he is for ever dreaming as though they were the food of imagination itself and part and parcel of his inspiration.

I send you a thousand kisses, in spite of Strasser who, by the way, tells me I suffer from a dilated vein, owing to a congestion of the blood-vessel, which has been going on for months – very much the same as I had last time. Never mind. Fortunately I noticed it in time and will soon be all right again.

Your

GUSTAV

1 February 1902 17

Almschi, dearest!

I am just back from the station. There was just the chance you might be coming. It is snowing hard and we shall soon be snowed under – you would love it as much as I do. I'm enchanted with it – but miss you all the more. I seem to catch sight of you everywhere I look. I have had a glorious idea – I'll come out to you for lunch on Monday – as early as I can. I'll try to be with you by one. We should have time for a little walk. I could stay until a quarter to six. You could take me to Zögernitz and I could go by train from there to the Opera, to conduct that tiresome show. Would that do? We should see more of each other than if you came to us. I feel as fit as ever now. I knew it would put me right to come up here. And so, Almschi, we set off on our travels on 10th March, if all goes well. The snow here whets my appetite for St. Petersburg.* How you will love it – that is the best of it. Do you love me a little? I can hardly bear to wait. It is only 'on grounds of health' I stay on up here. It puts new life into me. Almschi! Do you still love me?

Always your

GUSTAV

The last lines of the ballad of *Das klagende Lied* in Mahler's autograph, Vienna, 27 February 1879

1903

TO ALMA MAHLER

Wiesbaden

21 January 1903 18

So, my beloved, here I am once more for a change in a hotel room (horrible abode), writing to you as of old. How everything has altered since! And once more, oddly, after a rehearsal of the Fourth!† I felt AWFUL yesterday in the train! I wrote you a line or two and am curious to know whether you will receive them. I arrived at Frankfurt at about one in the morning and was put unfortunately into a heated room, which, air it out as I might, refused to cool down; so I woke in the morning with a slight migraine. At ten I went on to Wiesbaden and then straight from the station to rehearsal. I was awaited by the

* Mahler was to conduct three concerts there. See pp. 33–35. (D.M.)
† The performance was on the 23rd. (D.M.)

Management (I nearly said by maidens clad all in white) and the rehearsal began forthwith. *How* I thought of you all the time, and lamented that you had to stay behind for the lack of a few dibs, and are not here now – you would have quite a different feeling for my work, which I'm quite full of at the moment after not giving it a thought for so long. Oh, God, how long will it be before people are in a state to hear it! – I'd like best to escape from it. And yet what a comfort, what a joy to *remain* within my work! And a fullness of *love*! In the *Adagio*, I actually saw you as you are when your blue eyes are on me with the expression they have when you love me and are sure that I love you too. Oh, if only you were here! Then you would have heard my work and we'd now be going, after one of those meals such as only Germany goes in for, out into the beautiful world and the sunshine we've having here these days. Today before going to the station I strolled about the streets for a bit. All the people, all the shops, all the houses look just alike. Everywhere the old reliable, orderly, oppressive sameness. I stopped to look in a shop window, above which there was the promising announcement of *objets d'art* for sale. I couldn't help smiling to myself (with a slight nausea too). There you have it, and I don't know how better you could express what these Philistines look for in their theatres, concert-halls and galleries. Ha! What will they say to my *objet d'art* when I put it before them the day after tomorrow, Friday. Brrr! If only this cup had already passed from me, or if at least you were here, my Almschi, so that at least I had a human being, my human being – *the* human being in whom for me all that belongs to me and to which I belong is incorporated. – It is so sweet to have a home, and this home for me can only be *one* person, you, dearest! Now out again, for ever running round, unless nausea at these ordinary (orderly) people drives me back to my room. I embrace you and kiss you from my heart, my Almscherl!

Your

GUSTAV

Hotel Georg,
Lvov [Lemberg]
31 March 1903 19

My dearest Luxerl,

(also known as Lynx), here with my diary: well, the indispensable migraine during the journey, and on alighting, when I felt strongly inclined to vomit, there appeared, clad all in white, the whole direction of the Philharmonic Society, four-man strong, Director, conductor, first violin and secretary, how splendid! with the intention of hustling me into a fine landau. I resisted violently (rolling my eyes and groaning with pain) – thereupon all fell silent and merely offered their escort – I strode wildly on, they all at my heels. It took us about three-quarters of an hour, as the railway station is outside the town.

Arrived at the hotel, I took leave of them with all speed and went to bed. Then it all started up – you know it well from that time in Russia. The efficient Poldi* packed the aspirin so beautifully (instead of putting it in the side-pocket) that I couldn't find it. At last I fell asleep to the accompaniment of groans (my adventures meanwhile I'll tell you by word of mouth). – In the morning I was up early, hungry, and as right as a trivet. First I wired to you and then had breakfast. Rehearsal at ten. The orchestra greeted me with a tucket of drums and trumpets as I ascended the podium. You can imagine the face I made at that – like a cat in a thunderstorm. Whereupon I played my First with the orchestra, which acquitted itself admirably and was obviously well rehearsed. Sometimes it sent shivers down my spine. Damn it all, where do people keep their ears and their hearts if they can't hear *that*! Second rehearsal at four and this evening I pay my respects here to the Italian Opera – *Tosca* by Puccini. Am feeling very brisk today and in good spirits. Life here has a very odd look, all its own. But the oddest of all are the Polish Jews, who run round as dogs do elsewhere. It's the greatest lark just to look at them! My God, are these my relations!? I can't tell you how idiotic theories of race appear in the light of such examples!

I gave one solitary caper – and it was just as I was going back to the hotel to write to you after lunching out. But it was only when a boy looked at my legs with surprise that I suddenly remembered and heard you say, 'Dauthage'.†

My room is *very* dear, eleven crowns – everything else is cheap. And so I hope to keep within my budget. Judging by appearances, the public here must be very hungry for music and of sterner stuff than in Vienna. Otherwise, a Society which this year gives its hundredth orchestral concert would be unthinkable. I'm curious to know how they'll behave themselves.

Almscherl – are you being sensible and looking after yourself properly? – do make use of my absence to have a proper rest. Am curious to know what you make of the Abbazia idea. It's really comic, by the way, how well known I am. On my travels, in foreign towns – wherever I am, wherever I go, I'm addressed as Director, and every-

* Housemaid. (A.M.)

† Mahler had a tic as he walked, and we had agreed that I should always say 'Dauthage' when he gave way to this habit. I can't say now how we came on the word. (A.M.)

one's so obliging and kind that I'm often quite put to shame. I look forward to *Monday* already. You know, I don't care a bit if we spend Easter pottering quietly about the Wiener Wald and the Hinterbrühl instead of stopping at the more expensive pensions of Abbazia and Semmering. But perhaps it would *do you good*! Talk it over in any case with Mama.

A thousand kisses

from your

GUSTAV

Hotel Georg,
Lvov,
1 April 1903 20

My dear Almscherl,

Here is the card from Justi you wanted; also a clipping from the *Berliner Tagblatt*, wherein you may read what Helmholtz thinks upon a matter very puzzling to many. – Nothing better could be said in few words about all that balderdash (Maeterlinck, etc.). Oh, these people – one of them as bad as another – seeking after those things of which there are more in 'heaven and earth, Horatio', as if they were searching for lice. – And that blessed word, occultism, they have invented for them! What on earth is not occult, metaphysically speaking, I should like to know. Flat-heads! I am certain they devour the whole of Nietzsche for breakfast and follow it up with Maeterlinck for supper, and have never digested a word of sense from any source whatever.

Last night there was my visit to the Opera; *Tosca*, as I told you. An excellent production in every way; something to enthuse about, if found in a provincial town in Austria. But as for the work itself! Act I. Papal pageantry with continual chiming of bells (specially imported from Italy). Act 2. A man tortured; horrible cries. Another stabbed with a sharp bread-knife. Act 3. More of the magnificent tintinnabulations and a view over all Rome from a citadel. Followed by an entirely fresh onset of bell ringing. A man shot by a firing-party.

I got up before the shooting and went out. Needless to say, a masterly piece of trash. Nowadays any bungler orchestrates to perfection.

By the way, I was invited into his box by the Director, clad all in white; and have a dinner to get through with the same gentleman on Friday. – The rehearsals with the very undisciplined but extremely willing orchestra go quite well; so my good humour holds out, and the menu is applause-provoking on this occasion also. To judge by the rehearsals, the *Leonore* overture is still a novelty here. Why ever did you weigh Putzi again after four days? Listen, Almschl, I may probably have to spend Monday night in Vienna and only get away on Tuesday evening. For that the Lady of Bielitz,* who is once more executing her pirouettes, is to blame.

Now, all my thoughts, dearest heart, and behave yourself well. All the best to Mama, Karl, Justi!

Your

GUSTAV

Hotel Georg,
Lvov
2 April 1903 21

Dearest,

My days here are divided between sublimest contemplation and earthly tumult (due to rehearsing in primitive conditions). At intervals I read Zend-Avesta with engrossing interest; it comes home to me with the intimacy of what I have long known and seen and experienced myself.

Remarkable how close in feeling Fechner is to Rückert: they are two nearly related people and one side of my nature is linked with them as a third. How few know anything of those two!

The first concert comes off tonight. I find it hard to understand at times why I should be playing my symphony to the people of Lemberg. But as it can't be helped now, I do my best. There is no knowing where a grain of seed may fall.

And it is a thousand crowns in my pocket and brings me one step nearer to independence – although independence is merely a word unless the soul itself is free. And that freedom a man must win for himself. So help me to attain it. I went for a fine walk today, which had moments all its own (both in landscape and my inward meditation). I will tell you all about it when we meet. By the end, however, I was back in the traveller's prevailing mood; *sic transit gloria mundi! – What* a *dirty* town Lemberg is – the thought of eating anywhere except in the hotel nauseates me.

No effort of the imagination could conjure up a dirtier creature than the Polish Jew of these parts.

The weather, unfortunately, is very bad – it rains in torrents all the time and I've had to buy an umbrella. My room is excellent for sleeping in, large and airy, but for living in, frightfully uncomfortable, and I confess it costs me my utmost exertions to look on the bright side of things. What a joy it will be when I alight at half past three at the North Station and get into a cab with you and drive home, where I look forward to having a hot bath and then lunch.

* The singer, Selma Kurz, who came from Bielitz. (A.M.)

I hope you're keeping all my letters. I've written every day since I arrived here. I kiss you many times, my dear Almscherl,

Your true

GUSTAV

Hotel Georg,

Lvov

3 April 1903 22

My dearest Almscherl!

Thank God, it's nearly over. It is frightfully cold here now and I wish I had my winter clothes. I am frozen to the marrow. The symphony, yesterday, made a great impression. There was a general desire for a second hearing, and so I am giving it again at tomorrow's concert. So there's a success for you. The audience would have pleased you, they were so breathlessly still and listened so intently. I went to lunch today with the Director of the concerts. A very comical fellow, wife to match – so true to type as a provincial theatre director who has money and most ostentatiously gilds his poverty with it. – He lives in a disused theatre and has turned the foyer into his drawing-room – every pillar and alcove adorned with fans, photographs, laurel-wreaths and other trophies; all in an exaggerated profusion such as I have never seen. His wife insisted on singing to me; in the hope, I believe, of future professional contacts. To the same account is to be debited the presentation, to which I had to submit *coram publico*, of a silver – or was it even golden? I don't know – laurel wreath. You can well imagine the face I made on the occasion. – The audiences have behaved charmingly and with great respect (after maintaining at first a certain reserve).

I was much distressed yesterday, Almscherl, at having no letter from you. I nearly sent you a telegram. —

Last night was also the night on which my Second was performed at Düsseldorf.* I wonder very much how that went off.

22 May 1903† 23

My beloved Almscherl,

Just recovered (5 o'clock) from a migraine, by which I was overtaken after my departure and which with its familiar 'nuances' rose to such a pitch by 1 o'clock, that I made straight home and after various administrations and imbibings of aspirin, lay down on the sofa. – But I could not endure that for long, as my organism suddenly demanded

* On 2nd April 1903, which allows us to allot these Lvov Letters to the end of March and early April of that year. (D.M.)

† From Vienna to Göding; after Mahler's return from Göding to Vienna. (A.M.)

movement. Up I sprang, to the accompaniment of Elise's* tears and Poldi's polite but cool expressions of sympathy. And to the amusement of several very pretty maidservants rushed like mad round the Schwarzenberg garden for an hour. I was afraid by that time that I'd be prevented from writing to you – and then in the course of tommorow you would acquire the firm conviction that I no longer loved you and that you were in general born to misfortune. Naturally, as things are, I haven't seen Putzerl – and not up to now had a bite of food either. Shall go early to bed and then tomorrow out to the Hohe Warte.

True: the first moment I longed for you was in the Schwarzenberg garden, just as I was feeling a little better. I gave no tips whatever – quite forgot – please put that right. I've been very economical altogether, not spent a farthing; in that way migraine is always very advantageous.

Overjoyed at the thought of tomorrow evening. – True, the novel I took with me is a poor thing. I soon put it down. There I did myself a bad turn. Grabbe would undoubtedly have been more amusing. Anyway, I couldn't have read him either, I was feeling too bad – I must have upset myself somehow in the early morning. Well, my dear Almscherl, a thousand busses, and a wigging – you know what for. Warmest greetings to Mama and Carl and my liveliest sympathy to the married couple, R.

My dearest, addio.

Your

Gustav

Vienna-Kahlenberg
29 August 1903 24

Dearest A. Cannot run to a letter today. Only this card as a sign of life. Capital journey! Very conscious of my 70 kilos in a jolting train – on arrival, straight to theatre, changed, whereafter played hell with everybody and made myself felt, had a word in passing, too, with Arnold and Walter,† whereafter lunched with Moser at the Leidinger,‡ coffee with Roller, and then to the Leopoldsberg. Walked with Roller up the Kahlenberg, furious thirst, tea and peaches – stung by a wasp, sucked it quickly, bandaged by Roller with muslin, hurried down again to the theatre, where bound to pay due credit to playing of orchestra, then rattled up here by train at 9.30. Room very charming (only seen its windows from outside, as no time). All my — Off with Roller now!

Your

GUSTAV

---

* The cook. (A.M.)
† Arnold Rosé and Bruno Walter. (D.M.)
‡ An inn. (A.M.)

Dearest,

I only got your very, very dear letter yesterday evening. So our thoughts crossed over your birthday 'surprise', even though you expressed it rather funnily. Today, alas, will be the last I'll be able to get up to the Kahlenberg; but I'll make the best possible use of it. From tomorrow for four evenings I must be present at the performances throughout and the trains after nine have been taken off. So it would be foolish to keep the room on any longer. In any case, I go up there every afternoon. So I go about every other day to Pollak. But the poor fellow has to surrender his bed and sleep on the sofa. I cannot let that go on, although he passionately insists on it. I'll try to establish myself in my bedroom at home and borrow a sheet and pillow from Justi. The landlady will tidy up for me and it will be all right. But first I must make another attempt to find a nice room in Hietzing. That would be best. I'll let you know what happens.

Dearest Almscherl! Where are my *suits*? I can't find them; my trunk has obviously been emptied. Also, send me the letter from Chelius at once. You know, I must answer it without delay. It will be best if you telegraph the address he gives, and say too where I can find my clothes. My dear, I miss you frightfully and rejoice no end that you're coming. But, I implore you, stay on as long as you can and enjoy this lovely weather, so as to get as strong as possible, and think of our Putzerl. Why no word of her in your letter?

I haven't seen Mildenburg. I hear she is up in arms. (But she will take her salary all the same on the 1st.) There are others too I haven't seen yet, and don't wish to. Today I'm eating with Justi. I get the money today and will send it you at once. I hope I may enclose it with this. A thousand thoughts and embraces, my dear heart,

from your

GUSTAV

2 September 1903 26

My dear Almscherl,

I'm writing on the terrace of the hotel at Kahlenberg. I came up here after lunch, by the funicular, sitting by myself outside as usual, half and half hoping to find a line from you here, after vainly expecting a telegram at the theatre or something in reply to my yesterday's telegram. That's mainly why I asked you to write to the theatre, because otherwise I don't get any of your letters until just before going to bed up here. From what I hear Poldi has arrived and told her story. You come

* Addressed to Maiernigg. (A.M.)

on Sunday or Monday. Your yesterday's telegram must have been due to a momentary autumn mood. As I entered the hotel, who do you think came to meet me, smoking, whistling, in elegant summer attire, beaming with good cheer? Ernst Moll. He means to rest from his labours here for a few days. We exchanged a few words and then, smiling politely, I took my leave of him. Now I go by Hermannskogel, Hameau, Dornbach to the theatre, where a guest (Lordmann) is appearing. Tomorrow I conduct *Figaro*, the day after there is the very important guest-appearance of the tenor Bazelli as Faust. That's why I asked you not to come in any case before Friday, because it would be too sad for you to have to spend the evening alone. – The weather is too heavenly and I particularly enjoy breakfast on the terrace, followed by the walk, usually through Grinzing, to the electric railway. – How heavenly if you accompanied me! We must do that walk together without fail. I hope you'll be feeling fit and have thoroughly recovered.

I'm enclosing Schott's account for my songs. I shall ask Stritzko to produce the same from now on. I'll keep the 18 marks until you come. – The drive up here in the hotel carriage after the theatre will be a pleasure in itself, won't it? I'm relieved you're not there yet. It is so hot and oppressive in town that you'd never be able to sleep. If only I could be sure for which day to order the coupé for you. I'm so sorry you're so much alone and Grethl not with you.

Now, thank God, it won't be long till we're united once more. I'm longing for the day. I kiss you many times, my dear Almscherl!

from your

GUSTAV

27

Dearest Luxerl,

In haste, but I'll write again tonight: today I went to Hietzing and took a very nice, quiet room in the Hietzingerhof on the second floor and shall have breakfast at the Tivoli, where we've had meals together on several occasions. There's such a good connection that I can get out there quite late.

Had a meal with the Rosés today. They were very nice and not a bit upset by all those things. They seemed quite pacified by your letter and last talk. I feasted my eyes once more on those 'magic' features and remained for quite a time lost in rapt contemplation. On the subsequent walk up here – they accompanied me to Hietzing – the 'golden child' was the principal topic. It was impossible for me to take hold of anything – all meaningless. – Seats for tomorrow's gala performance are in great demand.

Please, dear Almscherl, address your letters from now to the Hietzingerhof, Hietzing.

Pollak will be in despair, but it was really too cruel to stretch the poor fellow out on a makeshift sofa. If he takes it too hard I'll spend the night with him after *Figaro* on Thursday.

A thousand busses, my dear Almscherl, from your

GUSTAV

1903–1904

Mannheim
29 January 1904 28

My dearest Almschili,

Following upon my two postcards, which I hope you received, here is a brief account of my journey. At the West Station I had an encounter with my worthy brother,* the author and book-keeper. The poor chap gave me a furtive look, half shy, half inquisitive. But we were on better terms than I expected. I was only afraid we might end by travelling in the same sleeper. Well, that was spared me – but, on the other hand, I had the pleasure of being cooped up with another man, and there was nothing else for it: the whole coach was full. However, it passed off lightly: he didn't snore beyond measure, or make much noise. He didn't stink either. But breathing the same close air with a stranger was no great joy. I lay down in my clothes and got through the night fairly well. How nice it would have been if you had been lying there. The journey came to an end at last. I made use of every stop to have a walk. I was met on arrival by Kaehler, the conductor, and rehearsed my symphony† the same evening with the orchestra. I preferred to spend the evening in the theatre, where *Romeo and Juliet* was being performed and in spite of all shortcomings put me completely under the spell of Shakespeare, greatest of poets, and, almost, of men; and my spirits were restored again. In a sense, I prefer a bad performance of a work of that kind to a just mediocre one. My imagination gets to work, and the reality, which is here unrealizable, becomes actual, and it all rises to the symbolic level.

Afterwards I joined the two conductors of the State Opera at the Bavarian Café and we talked shop until 12 o'cl. To judge from all they say, I'll find the orchestra well prepared for today's rehearsal. How good it would be if you were sitting there and I had someone for whose sake I was doing it all. – But what's Hecuba to me?

* Hans, properly Alois Mahler. (A.M.)
† Mahler's Third Symphony was performed at Mannheim and Heidelberg, at both places under Mahler himself, on 2nd and 1st February. (D.M.)

I am spending the whole time in the Mannheim hotel, as there are night trains from Heidelberg to Mannheim. So address all your letters here. How is Putzerl getting on? What advances are being made in the two opposed regions of her being, beneath and above, back and front? There's nothing between as yet! A thousand greetings and kisses from

Your

GUSTL

Mannheim
31 January 1904 29

My dear Almschli,

You must be content with a card again today. This damned rushing to and fro between Heidelberg and Mannheim takes up all my time. I was never so rushed in my life. The second rehearsal was really good already, and this evening I am going to the *Rose vom Liebesgarten*.* Yesterday, Heidelberg – lovely spot – magnificent walk up to the castle. Really quite wonderful. I have declined all invitations. Tomorrow, dress rehearsal. The boys' choir in Heidelberg is glorious. Women, all told, deadly dull. Soloists à la Crefeld.† Mannheim a ghastly spot.

No time for walks this time unfortunately. Neisser just paid me a call – I'm going with him to his lecture. He stays for both concerts; laments your absence sorely. If you had come, his wife would be there too. Not a word from you today. Thousand thoughts,

Your

GUSTL

Mannheim
1 February 1904 30

My darling,

Yesterday, as I told you, to *Liebesgarten*. A very good performance and, all told, a confirmation of my impressions on reading the score. I gained no fresh outlook and my opinion of Pfitzner remains unaltered. Great emotional appeal and very interesting in colour. Frogspawn and slime with a continual urge towards life, but the urge as continually defeated. Creation stops short at the molluscoid level. No sign of the vertebrates. It makes one wish to cry out with Calchas in Offenbach's *Hélène*: 'Flowers, nothing but flowers.' The audience, for all its good will, floundered in the stuffy air of this stagnant mist and in this mystical atmosphere.

---

* See also pp. 81–84. (D.M.)

† It was at Crefeld that the première of the Third Symphony had been given in 1902. (D.M.)

Had supper with Kähler and Wolfrum afterwards and then with the latter to Heidelberg, where I spent the night.

Nodnagel turned up suddenly with an analytic programme of the Third. Now we come to the final rehearsal.

Neisser went everywhere with me, and he stays on until I go. I like him a lot better now (he came for the symphony and only arranged his lecture to fit in with it). He has a great enthusiasm for my music and knows the Third by heart.

I hope the Neckar will prove as kind to me as the Rhine. All the auguries suggest it. There are signs of the liveliest interest on all sides and the concerts in both places are sold out (which does not occur even with Strauss, I'm told). But it shows me how important it is for me to be there in person on all occasions in the future – it is too appalling what they make of my work in my absence. Strauss is perfectly right to conduct his own works on all occasions.

And now, my deepest love, dearest. (All yesterday without news of you. I hope all is well!) How is my sweet Putzi?

Your

GUSTL

Mannheim
2 February 1904 31

Dear Almschl!

So then – Heidelberg yesterday. Went magnificently. Performance prima à la Crefeld. Wolfrum acquitted himself famously and is quite won over, I think. Today early with Neisser to Mannheim (he never leaves my side and is a very pleasant companion), another rehearsal. At midday to the Intendant. And tomorrow home again, thank God. I'm heartily tired of hotel life in a foreign town and rejoice beyond everything at the thought of you. I hope I have made a step forward this time. I have got a footing in this part of the world again; a repetition is planned this year in both towns, and next year the Second under my baton.

This cursed trailing about is a frightful bore, but it cannot be helped. I see that quite clearly.

The inevitable Nodnagel* has drawn up a ghastly analysis and enthuses like a girl. I associate with conductors and professors (between you and me, far preferable to boring women). I can quite understand your having created a furore. In your new toilette you're well up to my Third, well performed.

---

* Mahler hated analyses, but had a profound esteem for Nodnagel, one of his earliest supporters. (A.M.)

And now Auf Wiedersehen early on Friday (for you tomorrow, for me, unluckily, not for a day and a half). All my love a thousand times over,

Your

GUST

Cologne
25 [?] March 1904 32

Dear Almschl!

Well then – Fritz (Steinbach) is now quite lively with me! The orchestra enchanting, a real treat!* Chorus was there too: splendid! Only the contralto solo I haven't heard yet. I'm rehearsing now (at 6 o'clock). Best of all, I've had to promise Steinbach the first performance of my Fifth. He's going to study it all this summer with the orchestra here, and I'll come only for the last rehearsals. First performance should be on 14th October (or 15th). That would be splendid. Perhaps I may have found an artistic home here in Cologne. 'On the Rhine, the Rhine, grow our vines!' Hurrah, just for today. I'm tired out.

I eat every day with the Steinbachs; they're very kind and insist on it. He's invited the critics for tomorrow night. Very good of him.

But I rejoice already in the thought of getting out at Mattuglie!

From the depths of my heart,

Your

GUSTAV

*Hotel Disch,
Cologne*
24 March 1904 33

My dearest Almschi,

All went very well, then, yesterday. The public, they say, really warm, as to which I can't judge. I thought the audience a bit disconcerted, and no wonder if they were.

It was very pleasant at the Steinbachs' afterwards. I got back late, but had to be out of bed betimes, and off here in a sickeningly slow train where I await the local Steinbach, who takes me off to a solo rehearsal with trombones and trumpets.

Tired out today and wish I were with you. Memories here of the beautiful Crefeld time are very dear to me! I wish you were here!

* Mahler was in Cologne for a performance of his Third Symphony on 27th March. (D.M.)

I'm worried about Putzi in this weather, always wet and cold and unfriendly. Are you having the same at Abbazia? My thoughts are always with you, my Almschili. I had your first, very dear letter yesterday and was glad to have news of you at last.

Write and tell me all about your journey and how you're feeling.

All my love,

Your

GUSTAV

Hotel Disch,
Cologne
26 [?] March 1904 34

My Almschl!

So, thank God, the last letter for this trip. – Final rehearsal went splendidly. Orchestra FAR better than that time at Crefeld. The violins are nearly as good as in Vienna. – The contralto (a Frau Hertzer-Deppe) not exactly brilliant (somewhat 'theatrical') but musical and adequate. Chorus to my surprise NOT so brilliant as I should have expected on the Rhine.

All in all, however, I'm very well pleased and hope that my Fourth on its wanderings has now found a good berth. The Fifth is now booked for next year's first Gürzenich concert.* Imagine it, Steinbach wanted it for the Cologne music festival on 20th May, but I declined on account of your condition. I'm utterly fagged out by now. The Hotel Disch is not so comfortable either, draughts everywhere and an infernal racket day and night. – I have all my meals with the Steinbachs. – So, if all goes well, I'll be with you early on Wednesday. – If the weather doesn't improve, don't come to the station but wait for me in your own room. Except for the first glorious day, I haven't once seen the sun – it's mostly raining – desperate.

What gaps in my letters? I'm sure I write at least three times for your once and yet you're not satisfied. I can just see Putzi. Take care of her whatever you do.

See you soon, my Almscherl!

Your

GUSTAV

Vienna
6 June 1904 35

My beloved,

Your dear letter was a real comfort to me. It shows me you're now on the right road. When we're alone for a time we achieve a unity with

* In fact, the première of the Fifth took place at Cologne in 1904, on 18th October. (D.M.)

ourselves and nature, certainly pleasanter society than the people one sees every day. Then we become positive (instead of getting stuck fast in negation) and finally productive. The commonplace takes us farther and farther from ourselves, but we are brought back to ourselves by solitude, and from ourselves to God is only a step. Your whole temperament is steeped in this feeling and it gives me infinite joy, for I never doubted it was in you.

How petty our ordinary life, stuck fast in negation and criticism, seems to us then. – You find the same thing in your reading, don't you? Shakespeare is the positive, the productive; Ibsen merely analysis, negation, barrenness. Now you can understand why it is I strive to rescue the positive and productive mood from the clutches of the commonplace, and hence often take a bird's-eye view. – Don't be led astray when negation comes down on you again and you cannot see your way on for a time. Never believe that the positive is not there or is not the one reality. Think simply that the sun has gone behind a cloud, and is bound to emerge again.

The heat here is insufferable. Yesterday *Feuersnot*** aroused the astonishment of German critics and the envy of German operatic composers. *Der faule Hans*† then consoled them all and they wept for pain and for joy.

How I'd love to be with you and Putzerl! Today I dine with the Festival Committee, Schillings, etc., at Sacher's.

A thousand busses from

Your

GUSTL

P.S. I have found another piano quartet by Brahms, the one in C minor, which we played last year as a duet; the first two movements wonderful. Up to now the only one besides the G minor that I can accept. – Pity the last two movements fall off so sadly.

I am dropping Tolstoy for the while. You need a rest from him. I speak of the publicist and prophet. The stories and novels – that's another matter.

23 June 1904‡ 36

My dearest Almschili!

I went to bed yesterday dog-tired at half past nine and slept without a break till eight. Then had my first breakfast in the hut. – But it's odd – I always find the air here extremely relaxing. As soon as I reach Maier-

---

* Mahler refers to a revival of the opera by Richard Strauss. See pp. 27–29 for Alma Mahler's account of the Vienna première in 1902. (D.M.)

† Ballet by Oskar Nedbal. (A.M.)

‡ From Maiernigg to Vienna. (A.M.)

nigg all life and energy come to a stop, and it takes two or three weeks
before I can rouse myself at all. You know that from the last two
summers here. It's just the same this time, except that I miss you as
well and have to crawl round alone all day – God knows when I shall
be able to pull myself together a bit. I haven't felt so muted for years.
My only comfort meanwhile is that the climate is splendid for the little
ones and so they at least benefit.

There's a frightful smell of rotten glue in my room above. They say
it comes from the coating of plaster they had to put on to cover the
cracks. So I spend my time in the Böcklin room; but I have to sleep
upstairs and hope it won't do me any harm. Do ask Carl whether he has
any idea what sort of materials that kind of 'Mahler'* would use to
make such a stink.

I've given mature consideration to the play-pen. The place we chose
from memory is much too small. Putzi would scarcely be able to turn
round. But there's a place down below which might have been designed for the purpose. I've inspected it carefully and discussed it with
Theuer. I'm getting him to fence it in completely and put down 10
florins worth of fine sand. There the children will have a playground to
last them for years. I'll have it done if you agree. It's the place where we
have the bench and table and the two seats.

There can be snakes just as well higher up as lower down; and the
children will need watching wherever they are (besides, water-snakes
are *never* poisonous, and the poisonous ones are only found in particularly warm and dry spots – ask any doctor). It is the only place that
will suit. So write and tell me what you think. The place in front of the
house we first thought of is far too small in any case. To be on the safe
side, I am having all the steep places in front of the house fenced off.

The hail has now stopped and the storms are over and I'll see that
this letter goes today.

A thousand kisses from

Your

GUSTAV

23 June 1904 37

My dearest Almschili,

So the first day is over. Simply frightful! That horrible smell in my
bedroom, followed by miserable efforts to assemble the scattered fragments of my inner self (how many days will the assembling take, I
wonder), followed by confabulations with Theuer and then a bath and
lunch; read the Wagner-Wesendonck letters all day and find deep

* Mahler puns on his own name and the German for painter, '*Maler*'. (D.M.)

refreshment in them; they give an insight into an important, perhaps the most important, aspect of this unique and precious great man's life. I meant to go out for a walk over hill and dale, but a hailstorm came on which continued until night and brought all my plans to naught. So for a change I played the piano – Brahms' chamber music – but, alas, most of it utterly barren music-making, and if I had not come unexpectedly on a charming sextet in B flat major I should have given him up in despair, as I do myself at present. Then back to Wagner-Wesendonck, which after Brahms seemed all the more transcendent and superhuman. Looked occasionally into Tolstoy's *Confessions*; terrifyingly sad and savagely flagellant; a fallacy in his very way of putting the question and in consequence a withering blight on all human achievement whether of the heart or head. Occasionally I ventured out in rain and shower; I got as far as Maiernigg Café, but left the muddy coffee undrunk. Oafs to right of me, oafs to left of me, ancient, unappetizing crones knitting, and cheese-eating bald-heads soon drove me home again. Thus the day passed by at last and I tumbled into bed (still the stink of glue) and slept until half past eight. – Today I have revived slightly; your postcard in particular, dear Almscherl, refreshed my dreary existence. Now I've walked the well-known old road to Klagenfurt and am sitting in the Kaiser von Österreich, as the Café Schieder has been made odious by the introduction of waitresses – drinking coffee and chocolate and writing to you. The boat arrived today too. It looks like new. I am doing some shopping and then walking to Loretto, where Anton will pick me up with the boat.

Keep your heart up, my Almschi. I count the days until you come. Does Putzi ask for me? A thousand greetings and kisses to you all from
Your

GUSTL

Almschi, don't do any more copying! It can't be good for you.

26 June 1903 38
My love,

It is pouring down without a break – thunder and lightning, and claps so loud it's a joy to hear them. For me now the lake has nothing finer to offer – storm without and I sitting at my ease in your drawing-room with lamp, books, notes, piano, paper! But my letter won't get off now and so tomorrow you won't have one. That's the black side, but only for you. – How long will it go on? If only it were a little more possible here – more practicable and the paths less difficult. I pass my time in my own way, contemplating myself and the world, half blissful, half expectant. Unfortunately, books are giving out. And as I can't do as Quintus Fixlein did – write my own library day by day, I must buy some books next time I'm in Klagenfurt. Today is Sunday and the riff-raff down there on the lake and on the roads don't know how to make noise enough. As soon as a bubble of well-being rises in those muddy brains, it has to burst with a bang, like a gun salute for the benefit of the world at large. We've all got to know that Hans Affe and Peter Vieh are pleased with themselves.

The Wilde is very exciting but at the same time rather a hollow nut. He has got hold of a good idea and ruined it with caprice and dilettantism. You mustn't read it. Now that I've worked my way through Brahms, I've fallen back on Bruckner again. An odd pair of second-raters. The one was 'in the casting ladle'* too long, the other has not been there at all. Now I stick to Beethoven. There are only he and Richard – and after them, nobody. Mark that! You can count on enjoying the Wagner–Wesendonck letters! It was a positive necessity to disinfect the mind of those paltry 'followers of'.

I kiss you many times,

Your

GUSTAV

· 39

My dearest Almschel,

Are you being as lucky as we are? Rain all day and I sit indoors with thunderstorms on every side. Jergitsch was here today and will send an estimate tomorrow. It will all be done to your satisfaction. You'll be delighted when the little one tumbles about in the sand in the best of good air. If only the time had come! Tomorrow I'll see about the bed for her in Klagenfurt. I'm quite sure about the snakes – they are *water-snakes*, which keep near water and are NOT poisonous. Poisonous snakes need dryness and heat and shun the neighbourhood of water. You can ask any zoologist! So there's no cause for alarm.

I'm beginning by degrees to get used to my solitude, as one always does to the inevitable. But never in my whole life have I felt so *lonely*!

I have gone all through Brahms pretty well by now. All I can say of him is that he's a puny little dwarf with a rather narrow chest. Good Lord, if a breath from the lungs of *Richard Wagner* whistled about his ears he would scarcely be able to keep his feet. But I don't mean to hurt his feelings. You will be astonished when I tell you where I get more completely bogged than anywhere else – in his so-called 'developments'.

It is very seldom he can make anything whatever of his themes, beautiful as they often are. Only Beethoven and Wagner, after all, could do that.

* *Peer Gynt.* (A.M.)

Look after yourself and Putzerln. And now for Bach (with two candles). I must clear the air a bit after Brahms. Eagerly looking forward to seeing you all,

GUSTL

Saturday night
Mid-July 40

My Almschel,

I cannot bear this sultry heat any longer, so I am off to the Dolomites. One of those lightning-excursions I am so fond of. I shall drive to Toblach early – half past six – on Sunday morning, then by Schluderbach to Misurina, go for a walk there and spend the night. Next day (Monday) home again the same way, arriving at Maiernigg that evening. Then on Wednesday, God willing, I shall expect you at Klagenfurt. Be sure to write exactly when you arrive. Have had your very dear letter just in time before I start and am rejoiced to the heart by your absorption in those wonderful pages* and your comments on them. The analogies with one's own life, which continually crop up in one way or another in a correspondence of this kind, give it a peculiar fascination. On the one hand, one is able to follow the performances of the works with understanding and appreciation: on the other, there is the supreme gratification of finding oneself related in destiny and sufferings with those whose habitat is on the heights. It will always be so for you, Alma, into whosesoever life you look. Outside space and time there is a select company of solitary persons who are drawn to share an all the more intense life together. And though you find merely a poor counterfeit, still you search those effaced features for the look you understand so well, a look which only the elect can have. Your having this sympathetic insight I consider to be the most precious of blessings on your earthly course and mine.

All my love, my Almschili,

Your

GUSTAV

1904 41

My darling Almschili,

The job is done, and you'll open your eyes wide when you see what a fine playground we've made for our Putzel. It's like Columbus's egg. There's still room for a number of improvements, but they shall wait until you come. I have just been tinkering at it a bit myself. – I can hardly wait for the moment when we inspect it together for the first time and put our Putzi inside. She will have her heart's desire before

* The Wagner – Wesendonck Letters. (A.M.)

her very eyes. – And *still* I don't know when to expect you! Do write at once and tell me what the doctor's decision is. It must be insupportable now in the flat.

According to my reckoning, you will arrive at about half past three on Wednesday. If it's raining, I don't recommend the open trap and in that case I'll order a landau. What do you think? Please let me know. So now I shall only write twice more and then – I have you and need write no more letters. It's lovely here in spite of all and for the children's sake it will do very well for the time. But I see it wouldn't do for good – the air is too relaxing for us.

A thousand kisses and tenderest hugs

from your

Gustav

Frankfurt
November/December 1903 42

My dearest Almscherl,

*   *   *

Now to go on with my news. I'm staying, as I've already told you by telegram, at the Imperial, just opposite the Opera, where the concert takes place. I have a splendid room on the fourth floor, with a bath and dressing-room, a telephone and every imaginable comfort; it's only a pity I can make no use of it all as I'm never in. This morning, rehearsal! Oh, woe! What *misère* — Back to the beginning time after time, to plod through it all again. My gorge rises when that's how my Third goes. However, it made one thing very clear to me – I won't have the first performance of my Fifth with that orchestra! It is downright rough, à la Konzertverein of Vienna. I sigh all day under this *misère* and long for you beyond measure. I hope you flourish and spend a lot of time in bed, so that you'll be quite refreshed again when I come home. – For today, goodbye, my heart, and write when you can. Tell me, too, about Putzi.

I embrace you tenderly.

Your

old GUSTL

Frankfurt
1 December 1903 43

Here I am, you see, my darling Almscherl, taking a cosy quarter of an hour to talk to you over a cup of coffee, after the exhausting rehearsal (from 9.30 to 11.30) followed by a very frugal meal in an ale-house. I always take your letters to the Central Station and they go off at half past four to reach you in bed next morning.

I shall be conducting the final (public) rehearsal at the same time as you are reading this letter. It went much better today. The orchestra has got down to it now and appears to take a real interest in the business – The chorus of the Opera makes a very good job of it (no beauties amongst them, so you need not pass any sleepless nights after perusal of this letter) – and the contralto (not only alto but old [*alt*] too) is likewise quite adequate. So I hope all will go well tomorrow night. After that my hopes are set on a pleasant journey, which, thank God, will take me back to your arms. I arrive in Vienna, West Station, at 5.26 on Thursday.

I received your little letter yesterday evening and hope for another – longer one – today. I'm in excellent form, a change of air always does me good. It rains here without stopping; but I don't let it trouble me and splash cheerfully round in my spare time. So far I've been to the opera every night, but have not heard anything really good. The stars I have engaged are very feeble lights too, not a Venus, or a Mars either, among them.

Now I'm off to the station with my letter. I shall be thinking of you so hard all the way there that your ears will tingle. I kiss you from my heart. And to Putzerl, 'Ei, ei', and 'Brav, brav', many times over.

Your devoted

GUSTL

Frankfurt

2 December 1903 44

My dearest Almschi,

So this is my last day in this city, which from the look of it you would assuredly never connect with the birth of Goethe. There's nothing whatever to bring it to your mind, unless you see the name above a café. I hope you'll get this tomorrow morning and in the afternoon round about 5 o'clock we shall see each other again.

So today the final rehearsal. They behaved themselves quite gallantly. Owing to their roughness the first movement certainly came out a little too solid, but the three last will do. I took no notice of the audience and when there were a few modest attempts at applause, I at once spoke to the orchestra in a low voice.

I'll tell you by word of mouth how it goes tonight. I got both your two little letters at the same time today. They are *very dear*.

You, my Almscherl, you are always the same. It is a joy to come back to you and to Putzi! Auf Wiedersehen, my treasure.

Your old

GUSTL

FIRST PERFORMANCE OF THE FIFTH SYMPHONY

Cologne, Friday afternoon, after the first
rehearsal, 14 October 1904 45

How blessed, how blessed a cobbler to be!
With Variations [A reference to Lortzing's
opera, *Zar und Zimmermann.*]

Almschi dear,

According to my calculations, you ought to get this first post to-morrow if I take it to the station to catch the mail. And so, today was the first rehearsal!

It all went off tolerably well. The Scherzo is the very devil of a movement. I see it is in for a peck of troubles! Conductors for the next fifty years will all take it too fast and make nonsense of it; and the public – Oh, heavens, what are they to make of this chaos of which new worlds are for ever being engendered, only to crumble in ruin the moment after? What are they to say to this primeval music, this foaming, roaring, raging sea of sound, to these dancing stars, to these breath-taking, iridescent and flashing breakers? What has a flock of sheep to say but 'baaa!' to 'the singing of the rival spheres'?* How blessed, how blessed a tailor to be! Oh that I had been born a commercial traveller† and engaged as baritone at the Opera! Oh that I might give my symphony its first performance fifty years after my death!

Now I'm going for a walk along the Rhine – the only man in all Cologne who will quietly go his way after the première without pronouncing me a monster. Oh that I were 'quite the mama, quite the papa!'‡

How blessed, how blessed a locksmith§ to be and to become a tenor at the Vienna Opera. I have to go to the Opera tonight to hear the prima donna. It's *Fedora* given us by Giordano. Oh that I were an Italian roast-chestnut man!

Oh that I were a Russian police agent!

Oh that I were town councillor of Cologne with my box at the Municipal Theatre and also at the Gürzenich, and could look down upon all modern music!

Oh that I were a Professor of Music and could give lectures on Wagner and have them published.¶

* A quotation from Goethe's *Faust*. (D.M.)
† Demuth, Leopold. (A.M.)
‡ A reference to the *Sinfonia Domestica* by Richard Strauss. (A.M.)
§ Leo Slezak. (A.M.)
¶ Guido Adler. (A.M.)

I expect you without fail on Sunday. I must have one person anyway to whom my symphony will be a pleasure. If you were here now we should take a taxi and drive along the Rhine; as it is, I must go on foot in case you should be envious. The weather is glorious. A thousand greetings from your Oh, so blessed

GUSTL

Cologne
14 October 1904 46

But this is horrible! My Almschl, I was really angry at the first moment and nearly hit the telegraph-boy on the head. And now – after venting my rage – I still can't give up all hope. Leave nothing undone – sweat it out – swallow brandy – gobble aspirin – you can get over a chill in two days and still travel on Monday night and be here for the concert on Tuesday! Almschili, please – do all you can. It would be too, too ghastly – to be all alone at this – the first – performance. It's enough to kill the corpse. – The rehearsal today, as far as that goes, was a great deal more reassuring. The worst of it is that on the top of all I'm worried lest there's something serious the matter with you. For what else could stop you?

Write by return. I won't give up hope. All my thoughts! I take this to the station and send it express – you may still get it tomorrow morning!

Your speechless
GUSTL

Hotel Dom,
Cologne
18 October 1904 47

Almschel dear!

Only a word! I'm in a spin! Final rehearsal yesterday went very well. An excellent performance. Audience breathlessly attentive – even if dazed by the first movements! There was even a hiss or two after the Scherzo. The *Adagietto* and Rondo seemed to get home. A whole crowd of musicians, conductors, etc., from outside. Hinrichsen is *enthusiastic* and has already booked my Sixth with the utmost eagerness, adding humorously: 'But now – don't put up your price on me' – as I certainly shall not; he's such a good fellow. Walter and Berliner, the two stalwarts, turned up; Walter, yesterday, for the final rehearsal. Berliner only this morning – he's in his room now, weeping because you haven't come. I believe he only came for your sake.

So tonight's the concert. I'll wire tomorrow and then off to Amsterdam. Write next time to Amsterdam, Concertgebouw.

That's all you need put.

Your not being here, Almschi, spoils everything. Turns it to dust and ashes, I can almost say. You would have taken a pleasure in it, a pleasure all your own!

Kiss the little angels for me. And, God above, see you get well again!

Your old

GUSTL

Cologne
19 October 1904 48

My Almschili!

Walter will be along at once and tell you all about it in detail. Hinrichsen is very enthusiastic and refuses to be put off by any opposition. I think, in any case, that the impression made was a very significant one. I'll write to you fully from Amsterdam; I'm off there at once. I have missed you so very much – it was all only half what it might have been. It was sheer spite that it had to happen just with the Fifth. If I see any notices I'll enclose them with this. Nodnagel was there too and behaved beautifully. Get Walter to tell you all about it. The conflicting judgements are marvellous: each movement has its friends and its enemies. I kiss you and the little ones a thousand times. Goodbye. Be good bye and bye, that is.

My treasure —

Your

GUSTL

Amsterdam
20 October 1904 49

Almschl dear,

In Amsterdam, as you see. The Mengelbergs met me at the station and insisted on carrying me off with them. – So here I am again – as last year. Very charming, unassuming people. Not to lose time, I rehearsed the solos with the singer here last night. Short, stout little woman, like Cilli,* but sings beautifully – voice as clear as a bell. Why are you not here? You would get so much from it.

I hope Walter has told you all about Cologne. – I think it answered all our expectations.

* Our cook. (A.M.)

I'm off now to the first rehearsal (they start at 9 here) and am only writing these few lines in a hurry, so as not to leave you without news of me. Write to me at the Concertgebouw, it's simpler and it will be brought to me at once.

A thousand kisses in haste.

Your

GUSTL

Amsterdam
20[?] October 1903 50

My darling Almscherl,

I'm staying with Mengelberg. He seemed so set on it that I couldn't refuse and I have given up my other (much finer) abode. Now I'll tell you all my adventures from the beginning. – I travelled with the King of the Belgians [Leopold II]! To my utter astonishment, I observed as I was boarding my train symptoms of the wildest excitement in the officials of the railway, not to mention a laying down of carpets and a thronging of uniforms and shakos. We ordinary travellers were herded and hustled like cattle and our tickets were examined with calculated rudeness. The rumour spread like wild-fire and there was an excited stampede to the carriage windows – I of course sat where I was, but from a sudden increase of noise (presumably due to beating hearts of blissful subjects) I deduced that the shattering event was in progress. But I was not to be left out of it. After a short time, thinking myself safe, I looked about me with composure and saw an imposing person-age, who fixed me with a piercing eye, pass the carriage window. It was His Majesty, I realized a moment later. And I regretted for the first time since starting on the journey that my Almscherl was not there; it would have thrilled her, I'm sure. And I regret it afresh at least every half-hour. The journey was not too bad. I got the packet out every two hours and ate. It seemed incredibly long. I was so frozen my teeth chattered. – Arrived at ten, and then the noble fight for my corpse began.

By half past ten I was sitting in front of Mengelberg's fire, munching Dutch cheese. Seen nothing of the town yet, as I live in the smart quarter, close to the Concertgebouw, where I have spent the whole morning rehearsing. – I tell you, when my *Third* started up, I positively couldn't see or hear.* It positively takes your breath away. The orchestra is excellent and very well trained. Am curious about the choirs, which I'm told are even better. I stole away after lunch to write to you, my dearest; then a hubbub arose! my host was waiting for me. I miss you horribly! So now I'm off to the Grachten and confidently hope to encounter Mynheer Drogstoppel.*

Take a thousand kisses, my good Almscherl, and keep your heart up! A thousand thoughts to Mama and Carl.

Your old

GUSTAV

Amsterdam
21 October 1903 51

My darling Almschili,

It is really vexatious this time how hard it is to get a letter written. I literally have to steal away.

Yesterday, then (to resume), I strolled about all afternoon with my host along the canals and streets. In many ways I am reminded of Hamburg, only that there it is so much nobler and more open. Mengelberg is very kind, and he and his wife do all they can to make life and even the very earth a cushion to me. The only part I don't like is being for ever entertained. In that way it was much better at Lemberg, where at least I was always alone. At night, thank God, I was left to myself and rummaged about in a vast accumulation of Dutch, Belgian and French scores. What a fantastic crowd, yet how sterile! Another rehearsal this morning. The orchestra were off their heads with delight. Its beauty fairly winded me. I can't tell you what I felt when I heard it again. Only, it makes me very sad that you should not be here, dear heart. It will be a fine performance. Better than at Crefeld. Final rehearsal this evening. Now I am going to have a look at the docks. And tomorrow morning, having nothing else on, to the Museum.

On Sunday, as now decided, I shall conduct *only* my First. Is that a compliment, or not? Mengelberg claims the rest of the programme. But I'm in a fix about the ham and cheese to bring back with me! I'm so terribly clumsy! And if I asked my hosts, they would take it as a hint, which would be most painful, as they provide all they possibly can. They even produced a bottle of Asti for me today. God knows where they got it from. I would rather bring you the money when I come, and then we'll have a jaunt in the town and buy something nice for you and Putzi. When all's said and done, it's a ghastly sacrifice to make to one's work – this travelling all over the place! I'm just not cut out for it. Almscherl, I kiss you many times, my beloved, and embrace you.

Your

GUSTL

---

* A character in *Max Havelaar* by Multatuli, one of the books which I had been reading aloud to Mahler in the evenings. (A.M.)

I saw the Bourse* too yesterday. It is very imposing. People here, however, don't appear to think much of it – just like in Vienna!

Zaandam
22 October 1903 52

Dearest!

A trip round the harbour early today by boat; then to Zaandam, where it's *lovely*! I enclose some views, among them one of the house in which Peter the Great lived. It makes me quite sad that you are not here to see it all. One can understand painters feeling at home in this country! The colour-washed houses, the meadows, cows, windmills, water wherever you look, sea-gulls flying and swimming, ships and woods full of masts, and above all this wonderful bath of light. One could spend weeks here just strolling about. Then there are the people, so utterly original. How often I think of Carl, who has done a little towards teaching me to 'see'. Mama would be in her element too. I'm positively *sick* for you. We must all four go abroad one day together. The final rehearsal yesterday was glorious. Two hundred youngsters, with their teachers (six strong) roaring the Bim-bam,† and a wonderful women's chorus of three hundred and thirty voices. Orchestra *glorious*. Far better than at Crefeld. The violins just as good as in Vienna. All the other performers keep on applauding and waving. If only you were here! I'm now sitting at table (very hungry after sailing and running about). The whole family are charming and let me do just as I like.

I've made the acquaintance here of a very interesting Dutch composer, named Diepenbrock, who composes very original church music.

The musical culture in this country is stupendous! The way people can just *listen*!

A thousand kisses, my sweet, incomparable Almschl – I remain

Your old

GUSTL

Amsterdam
October 1904 53

Dearest,

I enclose the notice from the *Kölnische*, which was sent on to me here. That's all I've seen so far. I can imagine how they are letting off steam. The *Neue Freie Presse* in particular will show what it can do.

I'm really delighted by the people here.

---

* A modern building by H. P. Berlage (1856–1934), in which I had interested Mahler. (A.M.)

† In the fifth movement of the Third Symphony. (D.M.)

Just imagine the programme for Sunday:

1. Fourth Symphony by G. Mahler
   Interval
2. Fourth Symphony by G. Mahler

How do you like that? They have simply put my work twice over on the same programme.* After the interval, it starts at the beginning again! I'm really curious to know whether the audience will be warmer the second time. It must be the record for a new work. I rehearsed the Fourth today and the orchestra plays it so cleanly that I'm enchanted. In Cologne too I found my chief (if not my only) supporters in the orchestra. I must go to the rehearsal.

A thousand greetings, my dearest,

Your

GUSTL

Don't worry if the critics are abusive.

Amsterdam
23 October 1903 54

My precious Almschili,

I can't understand your not having had a letter yet after four days! I write every day! – I don't waste an hour here. This morning I went for a lovely walk in the country. This Dutch countryside – enchanting roads, paved, and lined with trees, leading out in all directions, and the long undeviating canals, converging from every quarter, shining like streaks of silver, and the little green-washed houses; and, above it all, the grey-blue, cloudy sky and flocks of birds! So lovely – I think to myself all the time how you will love it next year, when you come to hear my Second and Fourth performed. Everyone here talks about you. Your beauty is renowned throughout Holland and everyone wants to know you. They're a splendid lot, now I know them better, and so hospitable you feel completely at home. I'm very glad I'm staying with the Mengelbergs. It means I make such good use of my time that I never waste an hour. I think of you always whatever I am doing, and of you all.

And now for yesterday evening. It was magnificent. – At first they were a little puzzled, but with each movement they grew warmer and when the contralto came on (I haven't told you yet that the Dutch singer was ill and Kittel was sent for and sang very well) the whole hall was gripped, and from then to the end there was the familiar rise of temperature. When the last note died away the tumult of applause was almost daunting. Everyone said nothing like it could be remembered. I have beaten Strauss, who is all the rage here, by yards. The second

* 23rd October. (D.M.)

performance comes off tonight (not a seat to be had). – This morning there was the first rehearsal of the First. – The orchestra in the utmost enthusiasm. Too bad you're not here.

This afternoon I'm going to the Museum to see the Rembrandts. Tomorrow to The Hague and Scheveningen. Day after tomorrow, Sunday morning, to the sea at Haarlem. And early on Monday, at half past six, back to you again, my one and only one.

GUSTL

Amsterdam
21 October 1904 55

So, my Almschl, life goes on here in a veritable rush of rehearsals. Everything is splendidly prepared, and I believe that in time I might have here a kind of musical island-kingdom. I'm now only curious about the chorus with which I'm going to rehearse this evening. – I've far less leisure this year than I had last, so can't go on so many fine outings.

I'm immensely relieved by your news: I must frankly confess that I was feeling more anxious every day. But I've taken my oath that if the 'cup' passes from us this time, I will be as *brave* as the heroes of ancient times.

It's a ghastly life, waiting about in a foreign place. However kindly you're treated – but in the end it's all vexation and you feel utterly forsaken. I'm inquisitive about Sunday – how the audience will respond to the repetition of the Fourth. —

Now I've got into a muddle with old Walter over the key of the office. – But you couldn't and shouldn't go on copying* now.

In a week from today I'll be in the train! Hurrah! I can't make out yet whether I'm to hang my head in shame when I arrive in Vienna, or not? Have I fallen through or won through?

A thousand kisses and greetings, my dear! Let me hear from you often. You've plenty of time to tell me about everything.

Your old
GUSTL

Amsterdam
24 October 1904 56

Dearest!

It was an astounding evening! The audience from the very start was so attentive and understanding, and the response was warmer with each movement. – The enthusiasm increased the second time, and at the end it was something like it was at Crefeld. The singer sang the solo with

---

* I copied all Mahler's works. (A.M.)

moving simplicity, and the orchestra accompanied her as though with rays of sunshine. It was a picture on a gold ground. I really believe now I shall find in Amsterdam the musical home for which I hoped in that stupid Cologne.

Today the final rehearsals of the Second begin.* There's still a hard nut to crack there. The orchestra here is as charming to me as ever! I kiss you many times, my Almschi.

Your (in great haste)
GUSTL

Amsterdam
22 October 1904 57

Almschl dear!

Enclosed is a 'photo' taken by an 'admirer' during a concert. It will amuse you, I think, and I send it as a glimpse of my present existence. (At the moment, I'm listening to a first-rate performance of Schumann's D minor symphony, Mengelberg conducting.) – Today, the final rehearsal of the Fourth. – Last night, rehearsal with chorus of the Second. – They sang magnificently, almost as well as the Basel chorus.†

I wish it was Friday and I was in the train again. I was not born to be for ever on the move – however necessary it may be. The only moments of a trip like this when I feel at ease are the rehearsals. If only conductors had grasped by now how my work ought to go, I should leave them to it and take my ease at Heiligenstadt!

I see now, anyway, what folly it was to set about the first performance of a work of mine in Cologne, where the audience gave my Third such a cool reception. – The response of the audience always affects the newspaper-scribblers, who have no more mind of their own than a weathercock. And so all the upset and fatigue of a long journey was to no purpose. I could have got it cheaper in Vienna.

I'll try and manage things more cleverly with the Sixth. I think of you with tenderness, my Almscherl. See that you're thoroughly rested by the time I come home!

Your much harried
GUSTL

Amsterdam
25 October 1904 58

Dearest!

I send you with this a critique (from the leading newspaper here) translated for you by Mrs. Mengelberg. It will give you some idea of the

---

* Performed 26th and 27th October. (D.M.)
† See p. 59. (D.M.)

reception my Fourth has had here. *Much* warmer than the Third. Mengelberg has already put it in his next programme and will repeat it several times after that. The last movement with the soprano solo made the greatest impression of all.

I'm wrestling now with the terribly exhausting rehearsal of the Second! The final rehearsal is tonight.

I couldn't go on any real sightseeing expedition up to now, because all my mornings and evenings were occupied. I went to Haarlem yesterday to look at Hals, but unfortunately the museum was only open till three. I'm hoping I may be able to cut a rehearsal tomorrow morning, and then I shall go to Zandvoort on the North Sea (you can get there in an hour by electric railway) and get out at Haarlem on the way and have better luck, I hope. Thank God, my head is turned for home. I set off early on Friday morning and shall be with you on Saturday at about 8.

Almschi – you really have been a lazy correspondent this time! I do take your state of health into account, but surely you could have written a postcard at least every day. Please, dearest Almschi, read the enclosed notice and then give it to Mama, who is a far better public for such matters and imbibes them with more understanding.

But whatever you think of them in general, you can't help being gladdened by the understanding and absence of prejudice in criticisms such as this. The other critics all adopt the same tone.

You never say a word of the children either. Putzi must have quite forgotten me and Guckerl won't even know me again.

A tender kiss to all three.

Your old
GUSTL

Amsterdam
26 October 1904 59

Dearest,

Here's another criticism for you (from the Director of the Conservatoire here – translated by Diepenbrock, the well-known composer I mentioned to you the other day). With this, thank God, our very *one-sided* correspondence comes to an end: tomorrow evening I conduct for the last time and the day after I leave. I'm heartily sick of being on the racket, though very well in health, and will be thankful to have my legs under my own table once more. And I miss you three rogues more than a little although I must say I'm not at all pleased with the eldest of them.

Such a lazy correspondent! Almschi! The real curtain-lecture follows early on Saturday morning while I'm having my bath.

Now I'm just off to the Second. Final rehearsal yesterday went very well. All present mad with enthusiasm. A thousand kisses from

Your

Gustl

Leipzig
Saturday, 27 November 1904 60

Beloved!

Good morning! I got to bed at half past nine last night – with a warm fomentation (I don't know what the affair is called, some brew of herbs, which the hotelier's wife recommended and got ready for me) and slept till eight. Today I'm thoroughly fit except for a slight reminder in the region of my left hip, so that if I am not careful it will start up again.

I've had a fine breakfast (smoked ham) and hasten to send you a word with all my love. I've just had yours and take it with me to rehearsal where it will come to my help when the sounds emitted by the ragged wind or strings are too sadly discordant.* I hope to write again tomorrow in spite of having to pay a call on Peters and Stägemann and Nikisch.

All my thoughts, my dear, good Almscherl. What a blessing it's so short this time – only another three days.

Your

Gustl

Leipzig
Sunday, 28 November 1904 61

My Almschili!

All the rehearsals are over and here I sit, quite shattered, enjoying a little peace with nothing but the performance in front of me.† – And now, first of all: the orchestra, which yesterday was but a heap of ruins, a pile of unconnected noises, has now become an ordered structure. The stones took their places of their own accord at Arion's song, and I await today's performance with composure.

Their behaviour has been charming, poor devils. Yesterday and today I pitched into them for four hours at a stretch, and instead of taking it in bad part they bade me an enthusiastic farewell at the end of it.

The work is arousing tremendous interest throughout the town; the

* Probably the reference here is to the first Leipzig performance of the Third Symphony. (D.M.)

† The Third Symphony was performed on 24th November(D.M.)

leading critics came to both rehearsals and it is lucky I came here for the performance. Now for the details:

I gave a look round during the first rehearsal yesterday and caught sight of someone standing at the back like a worshipper. It was Herr Nodnagel! At first I was enraged, and then touched. But what an eccentric! In the afternoon I went to Stägemann's. They were as cordial to me afterwards as before, asked after you and invited me to dinner. I had to decline as I was engaged to go to Hinrichsen. When I arrived (he had already telephoned to ask if he might come and fetch me), I found him at the piano with the piano edition for four hands of a Bruckner symphony, playing one part with his hands and the second in his head. I sat down beside him and played it right through with him – secretly regarding it as my tribute of gratitude for his generosity, and some little amends for the expenses the poor fellow incurred owing to the falling through of the Fifth.

Then we were joined by Music Director Straube, a distinguished musician and charming person, and a fanatical admirer of mine.

A publisher, Kahnt, has just been in to see me. He begged me with passion for my new songs and ballads.* I shall send him the piano editions from Vienna and then he will make me an offer.

And now addio, my Almschl. Nikisch has asked me to lunch tomorrow (by telegram, as he's conducting in Berlin today) and afterwards I'm to play him my Fifth so as to initiate him into my intentions. In the evening I set off home; so early on the day after, Wednesday, I shall be with you! A thousand kisses from

Your

GUSTL

GERHART HAUPTMANN TO MAHLER   62

My dear Herr Mahler,

It is very disagreeable being banished to such a distance from you. I think of you every day and still feel the stimulus of our talks together. The greatest happiness of the children of earth lies in personality, but not only in their own. It may be that you can't help the greatness and goodness and the command of beauty with which you are endowed, but all the same I thank you for the share I am permitted to have in them – a possession I can never lose. It means that long stages of my earthly pilgrimage are cheered and illumined as otherwise they could not be. I can think of no possible reason why I should not say so. Kindest regards from us both to your wife, and also to all whom we met on the

* Among other songs of Mahler's, C. F. Kahnt published the *Kindertotenlieder*. See also Letter 70, p. 259.

evening we spent with you. For you – a shake of the hand and the expression of my lasting and devoted friendship —

GERHART HAUPTMANN

Forgive the strange shape in which this will reach you. The lack of a passable envelope left me no choice.

Hotel de la Reine,
Ospedaletti
28 February 1904 63

My dear friend Mahler,

I can now regard myself as a convalescent. I have had a life of it, I can tell you, since the end of February, no life at all, in fact, although things might have been worse. I had a temperature almost without interruption and this condemned me to pass my days in a fret of vexation. It is a bitter pill to lie in bed, to give up all that makes life worth living – worst of all, in a country where life is seen in all its glory. The thought of all you are losing is hard to shut out. I became insufferable, impatient and exacting. I could face death, I believe, with philosophy. But I am no philosopher in the case of illness – the one real affliction of mankind. That is the lesson I have learned from experience.

But now I am better and land is in sight. The doctors from Lugano gaily treated me for typhus and starved me on sops for six weary weeks. The seat of the malady was, in reality, the tip of my left lung and the proper treatment would have been super-alimentation, as I know now from the very able doctor who conducts this hospital. Following his directions, I eat as much as I can and drink a bottle of wine daily, not to mention beer, which I greatly enjoy, and lie all day long in the open air. The result is that the fever has entirely left me, I put on weight and feel my strength and my self-reliance returning. I cannot deny that even now I chafe at this passive existence, for you, my dear, dear friend, know what it means to have your head full of nonsense. Often and often I have called you in to console me, or, rather, not you but all you have had to overcome.

My dear Mahler, it seems to me quite unnatural that we should stand on ceremony with each other. Now that the joy of life returns I imagine us meeting not long hence in the fulness of health and energy and as old friends. The misfortune of not having met in our youth must not stand in the way of our intimacy in the ripeness of age; for after all we follow the same path. I have a great desire to hear your music and to know you all through.

We cherish as a dream of the future to have you and your dear wife with us here, for a whole summer if possible. (Including, of course, your children.) I believe you would be comfortable and be able to work.

Am I asking too much?
Grethe sends her love.
All our best wishes to you all.
    Ever, from the bottom of my heart,
                                Your

                                GERHART HAUPTMANN

                                Agnetendorf
                                28 September 1904 64

Dear friend Mahler,

With our heartiest greetings to you and yours, we wish you to know that we, my dear friend and I, have recently been duly registered as married persons.

The letter from your charming wife was a balm to us. We were glad to hear that she was well and lively again, not to mention all the welcome and beautiful things we hear as well. Your new symphony, we are told, is being performed in Berlin! and we are filled with happy anticipation.*

If you were able to reveal it to us with your incomparable art of presentation, dear Mahler, it would be a terrific festival.

Are you not coming to Berlin?

Wishing you all that is good, in health and every way,
                                Your

                                GERHART HAUPTMANN

ARNOLD SCHOENBERG TO MAHLER

                                12 December 1904† 65

My dear Director,

I must not speak as a musician to a musician if I am to give any idea of the incredible impression your symphony made on me: I can speak only as one human being to another. For I saw your very soul, naked, stark naked. It was revealed to me as a stretch of wild and secret country, with eerie chasms and abysses neighboured by sunlit, smiling meadows, haunts of idyllic repose. I felt it as an event of nature, which after scourging us with its terrors puts a rainbow in the sky. What does it matter that what I was told afterwards of your 'programme' did not seem to correspond altogether with what I had felt? Whether I am a good or a bad indicator of the feelings an experience arouses in me is not the point. Must I have a correct understanding of what I have lived and felt? And I believe I felt your symphony. I shared in the battling for illusion; I suffered the pangs of disillusionment; I saw the forces of

---

* The Fifth Symphony, conducted by Nikisch on 20th February 1905. (D.M.)

† This letter probably refers to Mahler's Third Symphony, twice performed in Vienna on 14th and 22nd December. Schoenberg had attended the *Generalprobe* on the 12th, at 2.30pm.

evil and good wrestling with each other; I saw a man in torment struggling towards inward harmony; I divined a personality, a drama, and *truthfulness*, the most uncompromising truthfulness.

I had to let myself go. Forgive me. I cannot feel by halves. With me it is one thing or the other!

In all devotion
ARNOLD SCHOENBERG

1904–1905

Hamburg
9 March 1905 66

My Almschi!

I am going now to the first rehearsal.* My migraine passed off by yesterday evening. I sat out two acts of *Carmen*; only singers discarded in Vienna trooped on, Fleischer-Edel, Thyssen, and Metzger, to wild ovations from the audience, and after that Demuth as lord of all – I went out. [Gustav] Brecher and Karl Wagner turned up and I supped with them. Brecher (who conducted) has developed splendidly and is a very capable fellow. What a pity you're not here with me! Hotel Streit has come down in the world rather and in spite of that my room costs 10 marks. Perhaps I'll move. A thousand thoughts from

Your
GUSTL

Hamburg
9 [?] March 1905 67

My Almschili!

Here are all the letters, and one more:

I can say no more about Zemlinsky. Frankly – I would have written just so. – What your own attitude now is, depends simply on how you feel – but go to Wydenbruck in any case. When I return, I will do what I can too. M. is a stupid fool. It seems to me, it was the publisher in him that wrote that letter, but I have no wish to let him have my songs. During today's rehearsal I kept on saying to myself: How blessed, how blessed a cobbler to be. The Fifth is an accursed work. No one understands it. At the end it began to go a little better. Well, we'll see tomorrow.

*   *   *

* For a performance of the Fifth Symphony. (D.M.)

My dearest Almschili!

Although I don't know whether or where this will find you, I want to give you a brief account of the day's events, or yesterday's, as the case may be.

Last night, then, such a wretched performance of *Undine** that I jumped up in the middle of the second act and went out. Steinbach† won't leave my side and I triumphed too soon – however, he is a very good fellow who heard my Fourth in Wiesbaden and knows nothing else of mine as yet. But it pleased him so much that he put it into his programme straight off and likes it better and better on closer acquaintance. – Rehearsal first thing this morning. Orchestra quite good and very willing, excellently rehearsed by Steinbach in four rehearsals. Singer of the soprano solo admirable, clear voice, natural production. – Lunched with Steinbach and went for another two-hour jaunt afterwards (by myself). Tomorrow after the concert there is to be a great beano at Steinbach's (at which I shall probably find consolation in a delicious supper for the drubbing I shall have had from the audience).

Steinbach will probably come with me to Cologne to make acquaintance with my Third.‡

If only I knew what you are going to do. True, Przist. keeps me posted – but all I can make out is that still no decision has been come to; and I count on your good sense, dear Almschel, not to do anything that could harm you or Putzi. – I'm going to the theatre again tonight; this time, *As You Like It.*

If only I had a line from you!

It might have come today if you had written yesterday. My tenderest love to you and I kiss you both.

Your

GUSTAV

Mainz
23 March 1904 69

My dearest Almschel,

Przist. wired me yesterday evening that he had fixed up the sleeper. You must have had my express letter, as far as I can see, at about half past five; that is, just before you left for Abbazia. As I write this, you are

* An opera by Lortzing (1801-51). (D.M.)

† Emil (not Fritz) Steinbach. (D.M.)

‡ Mahler refers to the Cologne performance of the Third Symphony, which was given on 27th March 1904. (D.M.)

delighting in the beach and Putzi opens her eyes wide and calls out, Papi, etc.

The worst is I haven't had the least word from you, not even today! Listen, Almschel, you're always telling me to write, I who always write punctually and scrupulously, and yet I have to wait so long for yours.

Today, then, there was the final rehearsal. All goes very well indeed. The soprano solo is splendidly sung by a Fräulein Becker, a concert singer from Cologne. It's a pleasure to see how the people delight in it more and more from rehearsal to rehearsal. Steinbach, who at first was very buttoned up, has now quite opened out, and so warm and cordial that it's a positive joy. I've gained in him a great and influential supporter. If only it were to go as well in Cologne too. It's a pity you can't be here. You would now be able to understand and enjoy my work quite differently.

I'm full of joy at the thought of alighting at Mattuglie on Wednesday morning after these harassing days, and being met by you with a fine two-seater (if not with bikes) and then having four whole days with nothing to do but laze and stroll about with you and Mama.

I'm not yet at all clear in my mind about the Musikverein, but I have an idea as to how it might work. We'll discuss everything at Abbazia.

*   *   *

3 [?] June 1905* 70

My Almschl!

Why have I still no sign of life from you? I was really quite sad when I saw that Mama had eight sides, while for me you could not even rise to a letter-card. I did at least hear that you had all arrived safely.

And so from this morning I am occupying your old room and will sleep in the bed you slept in as a girl. Perhaps I shall guess your thoughts, as when you take a sip from someone else's glass.

It was really nice at Graz. Mama will tell you how we passed the time. I did all I could to make life pleasant for her, only wherever we went we wished you were with us.

The most important thing is that I have an offer of 15,000 florins from Kahnt† and am now in a dilemma as to what I'm to do about Peters. I'll sleep on it for a few nights. In any case, I shan't let such a windfall slip now that it has fallen into my lap.

I lunched with Justi today and afterwards went carousing with her in the Volksgarten and then stood her a 'Comfortabel'‡ home. Now I hope she'll be reconciled.

* From the Music Festival at Graz. (A.M.)
† The publisher, who got the Sixth Symphony too. (A.M.)
‡ A one-horse cab. (A.M.)

I enclose the cheque for my salary. I'll pay Justi in full before leaving for Maiernigg and that will be a big step forward. I travelled to Graz with Strauss in a compartment to ourselves and we had a very pleasant talk, just like old times. Unfortunately, he was called away next day owing to the death of his (eighty-four-year-old) father and so did not hear my songs.*

The other gentlemen indulged in their customary bitter-sweet, super-fine extremely polite evasive manner. Honied songs with a sting in them. However, after the concert I went off alone with Mama and Walter and Adler to the hotel, where we sat very happily with Mauthner and Kolo Moser and let the Festival assembly go its way in the Schlossberg. – I don't think anyone missed me.

Now, my Almschi, my love, but I'm 'cross' with you.

Your

GUSTL

Vienna
5 June 1905 71

My Almscherl!

Lunch with Justi today. Arnold [Rosé] was back again from Graz and we discussed certain orchestra matters. He was very 'winning'. Thereafter I undressed and lay on the sofa to stew for a bit (the heat is simply murderous). Thereafter went out and drank a black coffee at the Imperial, in the course of which I fell asleep. The waiter woke me up. Pity – I was dreaming so pleasantly. But what about I've forgotten now. Now I'm in the office, inducing by degrees the appropriate state of mind for *Feuersnot*, which this evening at 7 is being lavished on its one thousand enraptured listeners.

Maddening that the Shah does not come until the 15th. I might so well have got away on Sunday!

The little ones must be darlings now. It's a shame I can't be with them to hear Putzi marvelling at everything and asking questions. Does she recognize her playground again? Has the railing been put up?

My dearest love and a hug, my Almscherl,

GUSTAV

Vienna
10 [?] June 1905 72

My Almschili,

You must forgive me. For the last few days there hasn't been a minute for writing you a letter. Such a rush owing to the Music

* Some of Mahler's songs with orchestra were performed. (D.M.)

Festival and the end of the season was never known before. One great peril was happily averted. Imagine it, I've been within an inch of having to stay on here until the 20th, because the gentleman from Persia [the Shah] does not arrive till then. After long and desperate agitation I saw a way of escape. I simply appealed to my doctor and now have leave of absence from Thursday. I set off then, God willing, on Wednesday evening and will be with you for breakfast on Thursday. I'm already longing for that breakfast.

Mengelberg is still here! Schillings and I have become quite friendly. Personally I have come to have a great sympathy for him, Mama likes him too and so does Mengelberg. No letter from you for two days. I hope nothing has happened! Your dear letters are always a refreshment for me. I thoroughly relish your saying that 'you are lost to the world'.* That is always when the real person comes out (when, of course, there is one there).

Come now, write me a proper letter. Tell me about Putzerl to buck me up.

I've bought myself a bicycle (150 florins). A thousand kisses, my beloved Almschi,

Your old

GUSTL

Vienna
13 June 1905 73

My Almschi,

Hurrah! I'm coming the day after tomorrow, early on Thursday, about half past seven, wobbling along on the bike. Please, a fine breakfast. For a start I shall simply laze. The racket is getting too idiotic. I'll telegraph tomorrow to confirm. – The business with the lamp† was a fine shock for us all. Thank God it was no worse —

A thousand

Your

GUSTL

---

* Here Mahler refers to one of the most beautiful of his late songs, *Ich bin der Welt abhanden gekommen*. (D.M.)

† I had made the fair copy of the Sixth Symphony and wanted to get a fresh sheet of music out of my writing-desk – the paraffin lamp, which was standing on the edge of the flap, fell over, and the carpet and sofa went up in flames. I shouted from the window, but by the time the servant arrived I had almost put the fire out with cushions and rugs. The two children were sleeping next door, one on each side of my music room. (A.M.)

Schluderbach
22 June 1905 74

My Almschili!

After I had with desperate efforts avoided the restaurant car at Lienz and got a seat in one of the other coaches, I was made aware by a dull sensation that an attack of migraine was irresistibly approaching and by the time I reached Schluderbach it was upon me in all its fury. In vain I tried to arrest it by lying down: it drove me from the sofa out into the street. I raced round the lake (2½ hours) and returned here, where I spent the night, more or less recovered. Even on my walk, or run (through a forest of dwarf pines) I thought all the time: If only Almschi were here! You would love it. What a pity it is – for now, just now, there is not a holiday-maker to be seen – although I must admit the country people and soldiers (from the Landro garrison) are indulging in Corpus Christi celebrations to such good effect that the whole place rocks. But go two paces from the inn and there is an end of all horror.

A thousand kisses,

Your

GUSTL

[?] August 1905 75

My Almschili!

What a day it was yesterday! All the rowing to and fro gave me another fine appetite and so I had a slice of ham at the Station Hotel. I hope you've had my card. Unluckily, I had a sleeping companion, and hardly closed my eyes. But anyway it is always a pleasure to be able to put one's feet up. I was met on arrival by Hassinger and went straight to the flat where I locked up my Seventh, got out clothes and linen and went to the theatre. There to my surprise I found (except for Wondra and Przistaupinski) only Roller, who couldn't have been more cordial; I arranged everything, and am now going to have lunch and afterwards on to Edlach, where I have taken a room by telephone. From there I shall probably wind my way slowly up on to the Schneeberg. What a shame it is you can't be with me.

Write next to Edlach, the Edlacherhof hotel. If I leave there I'll wire at once.

I kiss you tenderly, my dearest.

Tell me what the children are up to.

Your

GUSTL

My dear!

Your very dear letter, addressed to the Opera, followed me here today. I'm very glad those visitors came so à propos. They might have been only a bore to me, whereas they distracted you from a rather fatiguing routine. But don't take any notice of what Rosthorn says. If you could see me today and knew how well and rested I feel already and how exactly I know my physical strength, you would have no anxiety whatever. Your Rosthorns have not the dimmest notion of an entelechy such as mine. On the contrary, they cannot imagine the evil effects on me of *not* sticking to my work. And, as a matter of fact, there was in recent years much more cause for anxiety when I had those attacks of dizziness on going to bed – from which this year I have been entirely free. So there you have the surest indication that it fatigued me a great deal less this year.

Although it never stopped raining, I went my five hours' walk again today. The food here is positively the best I ever came across in a country hotel. Unfortunately it is pouring again today. If it doesn't mean to stop I shall go back to Vienna tomorrow. But I give you my solemn promise that I shall only idle and walk – that is to say, I shall flee to the mountains again the very first fine day.

Is there no possibility, then, of your coming any earlier? I'm horribly desolate and utterly sick of solitude and hotel life.

A thousand greetings,

Your

GUSTAV

Edlacherhof
22/23 [?] August 1905 77

Dearest!

Back again yesterday in a fine thunderstorm. I had taken Fechner's *Aesthetics* to read (extremely interesting, you'll like it immensely). It was the only book you had left on the writing-desk for me. – In the middle of the first chapter I became aware it was the second volume. So the first must be in the case. But in my desperation I simply read on. But now it occurs to me that I have left the book behind in the railway carriage. I'll write to the railway. I'm sure such a book could only be found by someone honest. Today it is still drizzling on. So nothing has come of the storm. Tomorrow, let's hope. Today I potter about on ground level.

I am not conducting *Fidelio*. I mean 'to grasp the baton' for the first time in *Tristan*. – You will be there by then and will perhaps come to it.

I miss you badly. It would be so jolly if we were pottering about together. Almost the only time in the whole year, after all, when I'm free of cares and duties. – I hope the rain is not general. In that case I must retreat to town tomorrow. However, these three days have been a wonderful refreshment and rest.

Now, many kisses, my treasure. Write about the children!

Your

GUSTL

Hochschneeberg
26 August 1905 78

My Almschl!

Here I am, after a climb somewhat overshadowed by rain and storm. Almschl! I have never seen anything to equal it for beauty and splendour. You *must* come up with me here, if only for an afternoon. You can drive up, and down again! You simply must see it – I can't think where my head and my eyes got to the last time I was here. The only explanation is that Arnold, who was with me that time, lay like heavy clouds on my ego and sealed up my breath and soul. Donkey that I am! Why didn't I come straight up here instead of going to Edlach? But now I shall stay there until I fetch you from Payerbach station. Please write and tell me once more when you are coming. – Many busses, my beloved

Your

GUSTAV

Vienna
6 September 1905 79

Dearest!

So the great moment arrived yesterday before *Tristan*. Arnold stormed in beaming with joy (like one of the thousand delighted members of the audience) and greeted me as if nothing had happened. – Within five minutes we were at each other's throats like Titschi and Tatschi.* It naturally came out – I had expected no better – that you and I were both cold self-seeking demons, and he and Justi angels of love. However, I deferred the picking of the bone to a more suitable occasion, in case I spoiled my temper for *Tristan*. He had no idea that his letter was offensive and is deeply hurt that you replied to Justi and not to him. And so it goes on. I slept in town yesterday. Frau Conrat is touchingly attentive. Today I go back to Dornbach and will stay on there.

Tomorrow the Prince arrives and then the affair will take an official turn.

* Two dogs belonging to some friends of ours, which were always fighting. (A.M.)

Today I'm sorry to say I have to go to the dentist, but that won't spoil my appetite, which will be as gigantic after as before. – The bread has arrived and I devour it slowly but surely. I have entrusted the apples to Freund. So the responsibility is on his shoulders. Woe to him if one goes rotten.

When exactly do you come? I wouldn't for the world grudge it you and the children if you stayed on a long time yet. But I'd rejoice all the same if the whole pie were here in safe keeping. Heartiest greetings to Mama.

A thousand busses to you and the children

Your

GUSTAV

Trieste
1 December 1905 80

My Almscherl!

This ghastly hotel makes my stay a torture. I'm thoroughly glad you're not here. This piggery would choke you, and there's no rest at night. At the utmost I get no more than five hours' sleep. Thank God, the concert is today and tomorrow I go.* – The orchestra makes a good job of it and I have no complaint there.

The people here are charming. Two members of the Committee even feel it their duty to act as my 'cortège' and conduct me all round the town (never leave me alone for a moment in their well-meant hospitality). This pen is typical of the hotel – I simply can't write with it. – Almscherl, had you not a word to say of our Putzerl? I conclude, then, that she is well and happy. Next Sunday, when I come, make sure that we can all have a fine walk together. –

All my love

Your

GUSTAV

Trieste
29/30 [?] November 1905 81

Dearest Almschi,

So the first day seems to be happily over. The orchestra is quite tolerable, excellently prepared, and full of zeal and fire. I'm hoping for a good performance. The concert is sold out. Unfortunately, it rains without stopping, and I splash round in galoshes and with an umbrella as best I can.

In the afternoon by carriage (accompanied by H. Schott) to

* I have not been able to trace any details of Mahler's Trieste concert. (D.M.)

Miramare, where we spent two hours. I was horribly sad you weren't with me. It is a beautiful place. Cypresses and bay trees. Green everywhere. Lakes with swans, etc. etc. And a heavenly peace. The hotel is ghastly (although it is the best in the place) – sluttishness and noise. Rehearsals here are from 12–2, and in the evenings from 8–11. – You have the Italian way of life here. – The concert too is not until half past eight.

So all in all I shall be frightfully glad to alight in Vienna again and to set out on the pleasure tour, first to your bed, then up to the children, then into the bathroom and finally to a Lucullan breakfast.

I kiss you tenderly, my Almschi.

Your

GUSTAV

Berlin

7 November 1905   82

How blessed, how blessed a

cobbler to be!

Dear Almschl!

I'm writing to you at the table on which I wrote you all those letters from the Palast Hotel – when I still had no inkling that I would one day envy a cobbler. – Breakfast was fine (a ray of light in this gloomy day). (You observe that I've just come from the final rehearsal.)* This evening I'll be with Strauss.

If I hadn't to be in Leipzig the day after tomorrow, I would leave here tonight. How happy, how happy, a tenor to be!

Your

GUSTAV

Berlin

8 November 1905   83

My dearest heart!

I am sitting once more at the table from which you were bombarded day in, day out four years ago; and I observe that my feelings have not changed since those days. My thoughts go to you with the same joy and love, and I rejoice now as then to tell you so. I am in a mad whirl today – seeing Ochs, Hülsen, Muck, Gerhart Hauptmann, Fernow, rehearsal for the concert – a talk with Fried,† etc. etc. I had quite a pleasant time with Strauss yesterday; but there is always with him that frigid, blasé feeling. However, he made me a present of his latest

---

* The Second Symphony, conducted by Oscar Fried, was performed on 8th November. (D.M.)

† Fried conducted brilliantly on this occasion. (A.M.)

publication (Berlioz's *Traité d'Instrumentation* with comments of his own), which all the same will be of great interest to you and from which you will learn a great deal. I'll give it you for your library. He promised me further a score of *Salome*, which I likewise dedicate to you, so now you will be the object of the wildest envy on the part of all composers.

But, as I said before, a little more warmth would be preferable to all this.

We are all going to Frau Wolff's tonight. Oh God, what motto shall I find to murmur there? But Fried is very docile and knows how to take a hint. (In any case, the occasion will tell me whether he has talent; yesterday he took it all too fast by half!) Now a cup of tea, and then Berliner, who had lunch with me too, is coming to take me to the concert. To Leipzig tomorrow at 8. The day after at 8 a.m. kisses and Putzi and Gucki, bath, breakfast, and then, with all speed, 'off to work', for there's going to be a mad rush of it.

A thousand greetings, and also to Mama, dear Almschili.

> Your
>
> GUSTAV

> *Breslau*
> 18 [?] December 1905 84

My dearest Almschili!

Only a few lines for today. I'm living in fine style here. The Neissers are splendid hosts and live in a beautiful house – I rehearse to extinction – a portrait of me is being done after lunch (Erler pleases me very much, as a man, anyway – very serious and unaffected). – Berliner never leaves me and his every tenth word is you.

Unfortunately I have unpleasant news from the Opera which destroys my peace of mind. More when I get back. I go to bed at 11 and get up at 8. I am looked after here like a prince.

A thousand thoughts, my Almschili. Auf Wiedersehen early Thursday.

> Your
>
> GUSTAV

COSIMA WAGNER TO MAHLER

> *Bayreuth*
> 8 June 1905 85

My dear Director,

May I trespass on your kindness to ask you two questions?

The first relates to Fräulein von Mildenburg, whom you were once so good as to recommend to me for the part of Kundry. I hear very different, in fact contradictory, opinions expressed about the achievements of this gifted singer. Some praise her unreservedly, others say she is very unequal, and explain it by her poor health.

I should like to take your verdict as final, and if you will be so kind as to give it me you may rely on our silence as implicitly as I rely on you to regard this letter as confidential.

My second question is likewise of a confidential nature. It concerns my son's new opera *Bruder Lustig*, which Director Simons would like to perform at the Kaiser-Jubiläums Theater, as he did with *Kobold*.

My son told me that it might be troubling you to no purpose to send you his opera after the rejection of *Kobold*, but that at the same time it might seem discourteous not to ask whether the Direction of the Royal Opera would like to consider his work, before he entered into negotiation with Director Simons.

I undertook to put this question and told him that there was nothing importunate in submitting his opera; for you had given sufficient proof of your good opinion of his work by the fine production of his *Bärenhäuter*,* and although the season's programme or other reasons had prevented you from accepting *Kobold*, you were certainly acquainted with the score and had presumably taken note of the performance, and were well aware of his merits as a playwright and composer. Therefore you would certainly tell me, without previous acquaintance with the score, whether you wished to see *Bruder Lustig* or not. May I request a reply by telegram? This will spare you the need to give your reasons and allow my son to communicate his decision to Director Simons without delay.

With my best thanks in advance for your replies to both my questions, I am,

> Yours most sincerely,
> C. WAGNER

Bayreuth
13 June 1905 86

My dear Director,

My best thanks for your sympathetic and early reply to my questions. I will see whether the roles which Fräulein von Mildenburg undertakes can be understudied in such a way as to spare her excessive fatigue and to guard against all eventualities. In the first place it would be a question of Kundry. I have very pleasant memories of Fräulein von Mildenburg. I recollect the study of Isolde, which I went through very carefully with

* On 27th March 1899. (D.M.)

her (especially the first act), and was glad to hear from my son that this performance had been a significant one.

Your opinion, dear Herr Mahler, has decisive weight with me and I will see now whether we have success with the alternative casting.

I thank you also very cordially for your reply to my second question, for which perhaps I am even more indebted.

I did certainly assume that the achievements of my son as conductor, as dramatist and composer, and as producer of the Bayreuth Festivals* made it natural that his works, apart from the impression they made on any one person, should (as in the case of more than one opera house) be given to the public, which could then express its own opinion of them.

Your answer to this assumption of mine, shows me, dear Herr Mahler, that you take no account of such circumstances in the case of a composer; you wish in the first place to gain a thorough knowledge of each work, so that if you accept it you can take its part, even against opposition, if necessary.

I find this not merely comprehensible but greatly to your credit. But the present case has an aspect of its own, and I crave your indulgence while I explain it to you.

After the performance of the *Bärenhäuter* in Vienna, and in consequence of it, you expressed to my son a wish to have his next opera (without having any knowledge of it). Unfortunately Siegfried was already committed to Munich; but in consideration of the honour you did him in the case of *Herzog Wildfang* he sent his *Kobold* to you in the first place. You kept it, dear Herr Mahler, for a very considerable length of time, owing no doubt to the innumerable demands made upon you, and when you were asked for your decision you declined the work without giving any reasons for doing so. Thus a new situation came into being. It is difficult, I might say impossible, for my son to subject you, and himself, to the risk of another refusal, and you would not be the artist you are if you did not understand and esteem pride and sensibility in another artist. Now, however, we are gladdened by the good news that you look forward to his new work with great interest.

Will you not give rein to this feeling of yours and decide on the production without more ado, as you did for *Wildfang*?† Even though *Kobold*, whether owing to its matter or form, its libretto or music, did not appeal to you and did not seem to you suitable for the Royal Opera, you cannot have thought it unworthy of performance, for in that case you would not have been able to feel any interest in its successor. It is

---

* One has to remind oneself of the ironic fact that Mahler, the greatest Wagnerian conductor of his day, never performed at Bayreuth. (D.M.)

† Evidently Mahler wanted *Herzog Wildfang* for Vienna, but the work was already destined for Munich, where it was first performed in 1901. (D.M.)

to this interest I appeal. I ask it to stir up the warm-hearted, trustful artist and to conquer the cautious and critical Director. If it responds to my appeal, I ask again for a reply by telegram; but if the interest you feel is overborne, I shall take silence as a sufficient reply, reproaching myself, however, in advance, for having trespassed so long on your time, already so fully occupied. – Whether I have the happiness to persuade you, dear Herr Mahler, or whether you hold to your previous opinion, you may be sure that my son and I will accept your decision with sympathy, and that I remain with renewed warmth of esteem.*

Yours, etc.,

C. WAGNER

RICHARD DEHMEL TO MAHLER

Blankenese bei Hamburg
10 September 1905 87

Dear Herr Mahler!

I am sending you by the same post as this letter a package addressed to your office, containing the score of the comic opera *Fitzebutze*, which my wife told you about. It includes a complete piano version (prelude, overture and five short acts) as well as the orchestra score of the prelude and the first act; that, I think, will enable you to form an opinion of the talent of the composer. So far as I can judge as a layman in music and from hearing the piano score only, Zilcher acquitted himself of his task perfectly, both artistically and dramatically. I am including also my libretto separately from the score. Zilcher has written it in between the staves almost throughout (including the merely scenic and pantomimic directions), but owing to the way it changes from sung passages to dumb show, you might find it advisable first to give a quick glance at the whole plot.

I shall be in Vienna at the end of October and I should be very glad if you could come to a decision by then as to whether you could have the work performed. The best time for the première in my view would be during the first half of February (before the Carnival). The staging need not give much trouble. Décor (scenery) would all be at hand in your stock, and the costumes (the simpler the better) will likewise call for little time and expense.

The one feature which might exceed the normal outlay is the lighting effects and the balloon. They would, however, present little difficulty. I have gone into it all myself.

Also, I think the staging of it would be a welcome task for Roller.

* *Bruder Lustig* was not performed at Vienna, however, but at Hamburg, in 1905. (D.M.)

I need not say how glad I should be if you were to give the work its first performance.*

I can only, *nolens volens*, beg forgiveness for the robbery you will probably suffer at the hands of the holy customs officials.

With my best greetings, and also my wife's,

Your

DEHMEL

1906–1909

Antwerp

2/3 [?] March 1906 88

My dear Almschili!

That was a charming idea of yours! I had to laugh as well as rejoice while unpacking the picture. – Now it stands on the bedside-table and I have fine talks with you and the little one. Accommodation magnifique. A very large, pleasant room, with *two beds side by side*! (What an irony!) Next door a very large, light bathroom, in which there is hot water at a touch. I bath for an hour every day. That is one of the great pleasures of life. The bad side, unfortunately, is the orchestra!† Enough to make you take to your heels! It will be music in hell. I would gladly go dirty if only they would play cleanly. Van Dyck does me the honours most kindly. He's a very good fellow. If only he would not sing! I'm asked in every day; they're very comfortable, rich, simple people. My journey was very pleasant. A sleeper to myself. Too sad you aren't here with me. It would all have been so comfortable this time.

For today a thousand thoughts and kisses, my dear; do you soon dip your pen?

Greet Mama and Karl

Your

GUSTAV

Antwerp

4 March 1906 89

My Almscherl!

So the final rehearsal too is over. I might say, as is told of Bach: 'First he whipped the boys, and afterwards the noise was dreadful.'

---

* Mahler did not accept this opera for performance. (D.M.)

† Mahler was in Antwerp for a performance of his Fifth Symphony. (D.M.)

Yesterday Clemenceau and Picquart arrived from Paris (just for the symphony) and we sighed for you during the whole of a breakfast. Picquart shook his head dolefully for minutes on end (you know, that is no joke with him), and Clemenceau assured me that he loved you! I'm jolly glad you don't have to endure the fiendish noise. Apart from that, people are most kind and do all they can. If it's like that in Amsterdam too, I'll run away. Hoping for a line from you at least by tomorrow. I'm alone a lot here, keep out of the way when I can. I have tomorrow free and will take a look round. A thousand thoughts, my Luxi.

Your old

GUSTL

Amsterdam
26 September 1909 90

My Almscherl!
Diary in brief!

Met at station by Mengelberg. As kind and hospitable as ever. Long talk and tired to bed. Little sleep though. Next morning at half past nine, rehearsal. All brilliantly rehearsed in advance.* Result magnificent. Afternoon, a drive, walks interspersed. Six o'clock, dinner. To bed at nine and slept beautifully until six. Today at nine, second rehearsal. Holland again delights me beyond measure. Consoling and characteristic above all is the note of cleanliness everywhere. The shining kitchen is only the symbol of all else. When you have had a meal here, you think with shuddering of the pig-sties in less favoured lands. Diepenbrock was already on the spot for the first rehearsal. There's a fine fellow for you. Not a moment passes but I wish you were here. I sleep in a large room with two beds side by side and, leading out of it (the door between has been removed), there is a small room with a cot. You see how thoughtfully it was all arranged for us. Mengelberg too is set on having the first performance of the Eighth, and Bodanzky and Hagemann from Mannheim have also put in a word.

The orchestra is splendid and quite infatuated with me. It's a pleasure this time instead of hard work. They sent a deputation to me yesterday asking me to conduct the other items as well at one of the concerts (this was done at the first by Mengelberg). They said they wanted so much to learn Beethoven and Wagner from me. Isn't that charming?

---

* The Seventh Symphony, performed on 3rd and 7th October. (D.M.)

For it means that instead of two free mornings they have two rehearsals. *'Tout comme chez nous!'*

I embrace you many times, my dear. Do write!

Your

GUSTAV

Amsterdam
1906 91

My dearest!

I am now installed here and have got through the first rehearsal also. *'Welch anderer Geist!'* The orchestra *splendidly rehearsed in advance* and a performance equal to any in Vienna. The chorus (in the *Klagende Lied*) very well rehearsed and trained. Mengelberg is a capital fellow! There's no one else I could entrust a work of mine to with entire confidence. The symphony* is already on the programme for next week at The Hague, Rotterdam, Haarlem, Utrecht, and Arnhem, where Mengelberg is giving concerts with the orchestra from here. I am rehearsing the *Kindertotenlieder* today. I don't know the singer yet. Am curious.

I had a marked *succès* in Antwerp. Excellent notices. I got your letters here. Putzi's drawing is simply incredible! What an eye she has! I shall be at home early on *Monday*! Heavens how glad I am! For today, my dear, all my love. Everyone here is indignant that you are not with me. The Mengelbergs would not hear of my going to the hotel. They are very warm-hearted and genuine people, and he is a man you can *rely* on. Diepenbrock was there too. I have true friends here.

Your

GUSTL

Amsterdam
9 March 1906 92

My dearest Almschili,

In spite of your 'sharp' letter. Yesterday, then, the symphony, a fine performance of the *Kindertotenlieder* except for the singer, who sang with no depth. This evening, final rehearsal of the *Klagende Lied*; tomorrow, performance; the day after I leave. Thank God, I shall be with you all again on Monday. One feels quite desolate, although they are all so kind and spare themselves no pains. I have a stout following here in Amsterdam – the young people in particular are very enthusiastic. The audience *very attentive*, the press positively glowing.

And, most important of all, Mengelberg puts me constantly in his programmes. Within the next fortnight, he is giving the Fifth again at

---

* Mahler's Fifth and the *Kindertotenlieder* were performed on 8th March, and *Das klagende Lied* on 10th and 11th March. (D.M.)

The Hague, Rotterdam and Arnhem – and it is being repeated at two concerts here.

Meanwhile, there is something very tiresome going on in Vienna between Roller and the chorus. I fear it may have far-reaching consequences. I may easily be drawn in myself, out of sympathy with him.

You wretch, are you not ever going to write to me? Are you always on the spree until two in the morning? Servus!

Your

GUST

Amsterdam

1 October 1909 93

Dearest!

At last the first lines I've had from you! I'm glad to hear of twenty cases packed. It shows that your liver is making no fuss. *But do be careful not to tire yourself out.* Tomorrow, then, off to The Hague and I'm treating myself to an automobile as a slight relaxation after very harassing days. – I have a dread, dread, you may well call it, of the days when the crowd gathers here. Then there'll be another hurly-burly and I can see myself having my meals in bed again. I can't stand so many people, nice as they all are. It's no joke to sit eight hours in a railway carriage to hear a work of mine. Such admirers nowadays are rather rare. (Although just now things seem to be moving again.) Please, Almscherl, get Carl to attend to this order at once. I want to make some return to Mengelberg for his self-sacrificing hospitality. He's been noticing my cigars with filter tips and asked me for the address of the firm.

A thousand greetings

from your

GUSTAV

I played a few passages from my Eighth to Mengelberg and Diepenbrock yesterday. Funny, this work always makes the typical, strong appeal. It would be an odd thing if my most important work should be the most easily understood.

Essen

21 May 1906 94

How blessed, how blessed –
a composer to be!

My Almschili,

Very pleased with the *first* rehearsal!* Orchestra behaves splendidly and makes it all sound just as I wish. I feel I have done well this time. The journey was madly tedious – an hour behind time. Hotel excellent, room on the first floor, so that my Almschi won't have to climb. Very

* Mahler was preparing the première of his Sixth Symphony, performed at Essen on 27th May. (D.M.)

pretty room and good food. Very CLEAN! Arrived at seven; corrected score until eleven, then ate bread and butter and worked again this morning from seven to nine.

The first rehearsal from half past nine to half past twelve. Second rehearsal at half past four. Now I'm going to have a good sleep for an hour. The telegram was a great relief. I found it on arrival. I'll write again early tomorrow.

Best love, my Almschl, and write soon! Your train starts Thursday [24 May] at half past eight.

Your

GUSTAV

Essen
22 May 1906 95

My dearest Almschl!

What a toil it was yesterday, five hours rehearsal, seven hours going over the score. Feeling fine, all the same. Your letters have been *very* dear. We talk everything over. Rehearsal again at nine today. I'm writing a few lines in haste so that you won't be without news. Very difficult to get rooms here. Impossible at the Essenerhof. Have done the best I could for Mama. You'll like the hotel very much.

I am delighted by a young Russian (the well-known pianist and conductor, Gabrilovitch) who has come here for my rehearsals and shares my table at the hotel. He tells me of my admirers among the young brigade in St. Petersburg. The rehearsals console me greatly. I hope I am not mistaken. So far I have taken them through the first three movements. I come to the last movement today. I was much interested by what you said about *Salome*. I told you so long ago. But now you under-value what is, after all, a very significant work and, as you rightly feel, a work of 'virtuosity' in a bad sense. In that respect Wagner is quite another story. The longer you live and the more you learn, the more clearly you will feel the difference between the few who are *truly* great and the mere 'virtuosi'. I am glad you see to the bottom of it so quickly. The coldness of Strauss's temperament, which is not a matter of his talent but of his nature as a man, does not escape you, and you are repelled by it. How is Putzerl? Don't ever forget to put in a word about her. All my love, my dear, and come on Friday. You are in for a treat.

Your old

GUSTL

My Almschili!

In a ghastly turmoil! I am quite battered. I was met yesterday by Roller, Stoll and Hassinger, the last representing the Festival Committee (of maidens robed in white there was none). Took steps to get rid of all but Roller, who took me to the hotel and stayed on with me. Misurina was on a visit to Burckhard. We went for a stroll in the town and fell in at once with Strauss, who joined us. I went and had supper with him in the hotel, while Roller went to the station to meet Schluderbach, I mean Misurina. Strauss left at eight-thirty to attend a Festival gathering; by this time Roller returned with Toblach, I mean to say, Schluderbach, and we spent a short time together. Whereafter, Tre Croci went to bed and Strauss came in elated from the party, accompanied by a journalist. We then discoursed for an hour about fees and royalties, etc., after which I went to bed. But not to sleep – the devil only knows why. Got up at six, breakfasted substantially, and now await the Munich impresario [Gutmann]. Rehearsal at ten. I shall then make my escape and see about throwing myself headlong from a height, or performing some other sensational feat. Then perhaps I shall have peace.

May the devil run off with this accursed tribe. Strauss has already composed a few scenes of *Elektra* (Hofmannsthal). He will not part with it for less than 10% a night and 100,000 marks down. (This, I confess, is only a supposition of mine.) As he made no further enquiry I told him nothing of the antiquated life I led in the summer. I don't think he would be greatly impressed to hear what old-fashioned rubbish I was busy on. Oh blessed, oh blessed a modern to be!

I kiss you a thousand times, my Almschi. It would be better, though, if you were here. I'm going up to my room at ten. Twenty letters, fifty invitations confront me. A reception at half past four on Friday – Archduke Eugen. The entire art world (a thousand in all) are invited. Frock-coats obligatory. I don't know what I do about that.

Write soon to your
GUSTAV

---

* Alfred Roller's wife was called Milewa. Mahler was always calling her by other names, including names of places. (A.M.)

Salzburg
17 August 1906 97

My Almschili!

What a dear letter today. Your notation was perfectly right in feeling. I have corrected only a few trifling details. (The texture is at present not quite 'clean'.) It is astonishing what a memory for music you have. I'm alone in the hotel, thank God. Roller is staying with Cortina next door. You would be astonished at Roller. He walks for hours with me. They are very nice to each other, but beyond that as unattached as if they were not married at all. We have all our meals together. Afterwards she goes up to her room and he attaches himself to me. Strauss too is now always with us and in general very charming, as he always is when alone with me. But his being will always remain alien to me. That way of thinking and feeling is worlds apart from mine. I wonder whether one of these days we shall meet on the same star. The rehearsal was excellent. I went straight down among the orchestra and saluted the soloists from below.

I went to *Don Giovanni* with Strauss yesterday (a box had been reserved for you and me). It was such an unspeakably bad performance that we left in outrage after the second scene. We supped quite alone in the hotel. Thank God, you could send such a good report of Gucki. A thousand greetings, my dear; it will not be long now.

Your

GUSTL

P.S. – Once again – your musicality really surprises me.

Salzburg
18 August 1906 98

My dear Almschili!

Yesterday was distinguished by torrents of rain. I went to a concert in the morning (conducted by Richard Strauss) in honour of Mozart. Bruckner's Ninth was performed (as was, the day before, Beethoven's Fifth). Salzburg all agog with enthusiasm. It was an orgy. Anyway, a great quantity of lager was drunk afterwards. Then lunch with Strauss and Roller. Specht,* pale and somewhat uncertain, came in with the dessert. Strauss departed and I spent an hour over a quiet talk with Specht. Then donned a borrowed frock-coat and betook myself to the reception. After having been honoured by a few words from his Highness, I retired weak with excitement to the buffet, had a drink, ate a piece of bread and butter, and evaporated to the theatre, where at six there began a most accomplished dress rehearsal of *Figaro* (with closed

---

* Richard Specht (1870–1932), writer and critic, was one of Mahler's early biographers and an enthusiastic student of his music. (A.M., D.M.)

doors).* Supped afterwards in the hotel with H., Dr. B., Roller and Specht. Specht took train joyfully for Vienna. Strauss (this is truth) keeps on insisting that I should write an opera. He says I have great talent for it. Tuesday evening – hurrah – I shall be with you. Oh, had I never left you!

A thousand greetings.

Your

GUSTL

Munich
November 1906 99

My Almschili,

I couldn't find time to write all day yesterday. Rehearsal, ten to half past twelve,† then lunch with Gutmann‡ and Stavenhagen,§ who is really a very good fellow. After that, left cards on the Management, Mottl and the Austrian ambassador, who invited me to lunch today. Needless to say, I declined. At four, second rehearsal. P. was present both morning and afternoon and again dealt with the cow-bells in the most virtuoso style. As a special enhancement the State Theatre lent a specially large single cow-bell, which P. struck single-handed and which quite unmistakably symbolized the yodel. This gave the symphony, and likewise P., a stamp all their own, which would probably move you, if you were present, to another of those doleful shakings of the head. – In consequence, I must set my face against all programmatic explanations. After the rehearsal, P. was just as before and took me to his parents, who live in a palatial house, where I drank tea and got on very well with those very charming and cultivated people.

After which I went, alone, to the Residenz Theater and saw an immensely entertaining play by Wilde and felt cross you weren't there. You'd have enjoyed it so much. Today at ten, third rehearsal. The orchestra are coming together well. As it is a charity concert, all the best people are attending. (Even the Archduchess Gisela is expected.) – The concert management insists on the cow-bells being struck in full view, and not behind the scenes. P. has to have his large one hung round his neck and to run to and fro with it, because in no other way will the local colour be produced. Otherwise it will not sound natural. This will give the finishing touch and certainly bring the feminine part of the house down. No doubt Stavenhagen will repeat the cow-bells part in a popular concert.

* Under Mahler's direction. See also pp. 102–103. (D.M.)
† Of the Sixth Symphony, performed on 8th November. (D.M.)
‡ Emil Gutmann, the impresario, who was responsible for mounting the première of the Eighth Symphony at Munich in 1910. (D.M.)
§ Bernhard Stavenhagen (1862–1914), conductor and pianist, was to direct a repeat performance of the symphony. (D.M.)

Now, my treasure, goodbye and a thousand wishes. I hope you'll be as charming when I arrive as when I left.

Your

GUSTL

ARNOLD SCHOENBERG TO GUSTAV MAHLER

Vienna
4 [?] June 1907   100

My dear Director,

I am not quite sure yet whether the engagement at the Opera refers to Zemlinsky,* or myself. However, that is a matter of indifference and was not really what I wanted to say at all. What I did want to say was how deeply impressed I was by the magnificence of the work I heard today.† I cannot forbear telling you that such music could come from only one man in the world and that man is: Mahler. I have always held you very, very dear – only you have perhaps not known it – but today I know why.

I kiss your hands a thousand times.

Yours

ARNOLD SCHOENBERG

Rottach-Egern No. 46, am Tegernsee
Upper Bavaria
18 July 1906   101

My dear Director,

I am just finishing my Chamber Symphony [No. 1], and so have only today found time to answer your letter. Do not, please, take my delay amiss.

Your letter gave me extraordinary pleasure. Nothing could please me more than your saying that we had come nearer together. It gave me more pleasure and made me prouder than if you had praised a work of mine – although this takes nothing from the value I put on your opinion. To me, the most important thing between people is their personal attachment: without it, nothing else can have its full weight; and, however conscious I may be of the distance between us, I hope to be not altogether unworthy of your friendship.

And now for your friendly invitation. In my first feelings of joy at your letter I was ready to face the journey without thinking twice about it. But on further reflection I was forced to give up the idea. Anxiety on my wife's account – she is going to have a child early in September –

* Mahler had given Alexander von Zemlinsky an engagement at the Opera. (A.M.)
† Probably a reference to Mahler's Sixth Symphony. (D.M.)

would take all pleasure out of the project. Moreover, there is the very great length of the journey to take into account – nearly fourteen hours. Anything might happen in that time before I could get back again.

And so, to my sorrow, I must give up all thought of it for this year. But I have another idea: you are conducting at the Salzburg Mozart Festival. That is only a few hours away and I could, at all events, come there. So, if you would let us know when you will be there and the dates of the performances, we could join you without fail for a few days. It would make me very happy if this plan were feasible. Your wife, I presume, will be there in any case? May I ask you to give her my heartiest greetings and to tell her how glad I am she has at last arrived at the knowledge that I am a 'dear fellow'. I have always maintained it, but unfortunately I am seldom believed!

I should be most grateful if you could let me know soon when the Salzburg Festival ends, so that I can plan accordingly. If we are not to meet before, I should very much like to send you my Chamber Symphony, and if too you have the time and the wish to look at it. Fortunately, it is not very long, and it is furnished with a piano-score for four hands (a very bad one, for I made it myself). I thank you again for your letter, and await your reply to my proposal of meeting at Salzburg.

Yours very sincerely and devotedly,
ARNOLD SCHOENBERG

GENERAL PICQUART TO MAHLER

In camp at Chalais
12 August 1906 102

Dear Master!

I thank you a thousand times for your friendly letter. At present my new military duties make severe demands on my time and unfortunately I hear no music, even though I have four regimental bands under my command. The oboists, for example, here in camp are mostly employed as stretcher-bearers!

In October, however, it will be quieter and I hope that no inopportune event will then get in the way of the trip to Vienna I look forward to so fervently.

My heartiest greetings to your wife and to Moll —

Yours always sincerely,
F. PICQUART

1907

My Almschili!

The first rehearsals are now over.* The orchestra is not by any means first-rate – but competent and very attentive (making an exception in my favour, as I am told), but one notices the slovenliness of the local celebrities (*tout comme chez nous*). I hope for a tolerable performance. – Wolff's are markedly cool; I don't mind that, for at least, they leave me in peace. – Fried sat open-mouthed from start to finish, and swallowed me whole, until at last he sat there incapable of movement, like a boa constrictor. Berliner joined us at night in the 'restaurang' and Fried was quite profound. Finally he confessed that my absolute certainty of aim in all I did had opened his eyes as nothing else had ever done, and that he himself was capable of little (he was quick to add, though, that the rest could do even less!).

Today I partly recovered my breath and will see if I can come down on Strauss for a ticket for today's *Salome*. I've got rid of Fried for today and tomorrow. I must be alone for a bit. Berliner enthused about you like a lover yesterday, and Fried was very sad you were not here. – Unfortunately, it rains the whole time. – This being for ever on my travels is too stupid. But, unfortunately, it has to be.

I embrace you tenderly, my dear, and do let me hear from you.

Your

GUSTAV

My dear, good Almschili,

I went to the Strauss's yesterday afternoon. *She* greeted me with: 'Sh! – sh! Richard's asleep,' and pulled me into her (very untidy) boudoir, where her old mother was sitting over coffee, and let loose a flood of nonsense about all the financial and sexual events of the last two years, rapidly interjecting questions about 'a thousand and one' things without waiting for the answers. She would not hear of my going, told me Richard had had an exhausting rehearsal yesterday

* Mahler was rehearsing in Berlin for a performance of his Third Symphony. (D.M.)

morning in Leipzig, had then returned to Berlin to conduct *Götter-dämmerung* at night, and today, being reduced to pulp, had lain down to sleep in the afternoon, while she kept strictest watch. I was quite touched. Suddenly she leapt up: 'But now to wake the brute.' Before I could stop her, she dragged me by both hands into his room, and roused him with a stentorian shout: 'Get up. Gustav's here.' I was 'Gustav' for an hour, and after that Director. Strauss got up with a patient smile, and the torrent of nonsense was resumed as a trio. Then we had tea and they took me back to the hotel in their automobile after it had been arranged that I should lunch with them on Sunday. There I found two front-row stalls for *Salome*; so I took Berliner with me. – The performance (orchestra and singers excellent – scenery utter Kitsch and Stoll*) again made an extraordinary impression on me. It is emphatically a work of genius, very powerful, and decidedly one of the most important works of our day. A Vulcan lives and labours under a heap of slag, a subterranean fire – not merely a firework! It is exactly the same with Strauss's whole personality. That is why it is so difficult in his case to sift the chaff from the grain. But I have an immense respect for the whole phenomenon he presents, and it has been confirmed afresh. This is an immense pleasure to me, for it puts me entirely at one with him. Blech conducted excellently yesterday. Strauss conducts on Saturday and I am going again! Destinn was magnificent! John the Baptist (Berger) quite good. The rest moderate. Orchestra splendid. This evening Berliner and I are going to see Frau Wolff. I promise you, my dear, I shall not fall in love with her. She is not the girl you dreamt of. Anyway, I dreamt of you last night. Your hair was done as it was when you were a girl, and I thought you so charming! Almschili, do do your hair one day as you used in those days. I like it so much better than this modern Jewish fashion. Now, at twelve, I am going to rehearse with the singer. I fear I may have a shock. These last three days I have been sleeping until ten, and for an hour, too, in the afternoon. It suits me very well and probably these idle ways do me good. I kiss you, my dear heart! Have you nothing to say of the children? Many greetings to Mamerl too and tell her to be good. Carl too.

Your old

GUSTL

I met Messchaert yesterday at the Opera. He was charming and very enthusiastic about my works.

* Mahler's 'producer' at the Vienna Opera; but when Stoll's name was on the bill, Mahler himself oversaw the production. (A.M.)

Bristol Hotel,
Berlin
11 January 1907 105

My Almschili,

I hope you've had my two long letters by now. Yesterday, dinner with Frau Wolff. There were only Oskar Bie, Fried and Berliner there. After general boredom I went back on foot with Fried and Bie to my room. Spent a quiet evening in the restaurant with Berliner and Ochs, who has trained the choirs splendidly – a very decent, good fellow besides. – To bed at 11. This afternoon there is the third rehearsal with chorus and solo, am very curious. Today I pay [Gerhart] Hauptmann a visit too. I'd be thankful to be back with you all.

Ochs wants to have the first performance of the Eighth. Vederemo! His chorus is certainly the biggest and best.

To judge by the stupid attitude of the critics, a première in Vienna is not to be thought of.

This evening I go to see a play by Wedekind,* put on by [Max] Reinhardt. I have got to take this bull by the horns. Fried enthuses, he's enchanted with it. – Berliner shudders with nausea.

Tomorrow morning I see Strauss and go to *Salome* in the evening for the second time. I regret it horribly that you're not with me. You know, Almschili, the girl I fell in love with was probably you – perhaps it was simply you I was dreaming of, as you of me. – All my love! You are *very good* this time.

Your

GUSTL

Grand Hotel,
Berlin
12 January 1907 106

My Luxi!

The last rehearsal is over now. I am very well satisfied. Wolff's have really done everything possible, quite contrary to their usual negligence. To lunch with Strauss afterwards. And besides that, a dinner-party for the Blechs. There was no one there when I arrived, but a moment later in came Frau Strauss, and began on a temperamental conversation, which fell steeply to this abysmal outburst: 'My God, for a million – well no, that's not enough – five million! And then Richard can stop manufacturing music.'

Almschili dear – I was interrupted by Hauptmann, whose dear face

* *Frühlings Erwachen* ('Spring's Awakening'). Wedekind's famous play ran into difficulties with the censorship, as did most of his works. It was eventually produced by Max Reinhardt at the Deutsches Theater, Berlin, about the time that Mahler reports having witnessed a performance. (See Mosco Carner, *Musical Times*, January, 1969, pp. 35–6, and Jack Diether, *American Record Guide*, May, 1969, p. 898.) D.M.

did a little to lighten the terrible desolation brought on by that occasion with Strauss. – Hauptmann wants me to spend tomorrow evening with him at Leistikow's, having 'sworn' he would bring me. As I cannot accept invitations, we agreed to have supper together in the hotel tomorrow without constraint. We talked of much else as well. I'll tell you all when I come. The detailed description of the dinner with the Strauss's has got stuck in my throat. I will only say that 'Ahna' filled me with a positive nausea, as also did his (Richard's) casual, absent-minded manner as he distributed the sunshine of his favour between me and Blech. The respectful and friendly consideration which I show him on such occasions awakes no echo, is not, probably, so much as noticed, is simply as though it had never been. – If I am to experience this sort of thing again, I feel I know neither myself nor the world about me. Are other men made of a different clay? It is enough to make one retreat to the wilderness, unsullied and alone, and never know another thing about the world.

I went yesterday to Reinhardt's Kammerspiel, an enchanting little theatre in incredibly good taste, and quite unique, to see *Frühlings Erwachen* by Wedekind. It is his Opus I and fifteen years old.* Well – it took my breath away – immensely powerful and talented and full of poetry. What a shame it is when you think what must have become of him all these years. Among what sort of people has he fallen – and what has happened to him?

I wished every moment you were with me.

Today to *Salome* again, and I will have another try to see to the bottom of the problem of Strauss. My Almschili, I'll write you tomorrow after the public final rehearsal. For today, tenderest greetings, my heart, and thank you for writing so much and so sweetly.

Your

old GUSTL

Grand Hotel,
Berlin
13 January 1907 107

My Almschl!

Salome, then, yesterday. The impression it made was stronger than ever and I am firmly convinced that it is one of the greatest master-pieces of our time. I cannot make out the drift of it, and can only sur-mise that it is the voice of the 'earth-spirit' speaking from the heart of genius, a spirit which does not indeed make a dwelling-place for itself to suit human taste but in accordance with its own unfathomable needs.

* Older than Mahler thought. Wedekind wrote the play in the winter of 1890/91. (D.M.)

Perhaps in time I shall gain a clearer understanding of this 'cocoon' it has spun for itself.

I met Strauss at the Opera before the performance, and being alone he was his agreeable self again and insisted on our foregathering afterwards. So we met in a restaurant, he and his wife and mother-in-law and Berliner and I; and we had an exhaustive and most agreeable discussion. I thoroughly enjoyed it apart from the temperamental intermezzi contributed by the eternal feminine. However, she was in a good humour and on the 'Gustav' footing with me. – This morning Hauptmann descended again; he's staying in this hotel. We're going to pay Leistikow a visit at six and afterwards at eight to *Friedensfest*.*

In an hour's time, at twelve o'clock, there is the public and final rehearsal. My Third comes to me as a Haydn Symphony. So I dare say people will think me crazy. The whole affair interests me very little.

I had the enclosed letter from Koenen. In my alarm I told Messchaert it was off for Vienna. For where should I be if I started accompanying every singer to her concerts?

A thousand greetings. How are the little ones?

Your

GUSTL

Grand Hotel,
Berlin
14 January 1907 108

So, my Almschi, this is the last day in Berlin! Thank God! I am torn to shreds. The final rehearsal went off very well indeed yesterday. There was a tumult of clapping as soon as I appeared and enthusiastic applause after each movement as well as at the end. Wolff gave a dinner in celebration afterwards. – From there to Leistikow with Hauptmann for an hour – I still can't make out why he was so set on it. From there to *Friedensfest* at the Deutsches Theater. (Hauptmann insisted on my seeing it; otherwise I would much rather have stayed at home.) A horrible, realistic affair. If you can warm up to this sort of art, you may get something out of it. I certainly did my best to see the author's point of view and to do him justice. Hauptmann asked me to come up to his room next morning and discuss it. Reinhardt picked me up after the performance and took me to a pub and we talked it all over – the piece itself and the production. He's an extremely smart man of the theatre, with whom it's a pleasure to talk shop. – Later on Wedekind joined us, at Reinhardt's invitation. I was in good form and let myself go for once. However, they were all very attentive and understanding. Perhaps it was of some help. Wedekind did not displease me. Today first thing,

* A play by Gerhart Hauptmann. (D.M.)

just after breakfast, Hauptmann came to the door. 'Well, I've come for your verdict.' So I gave it him and we had a pleasant talk. After he had gone, in came his (charming) little boy with his English nurse. She said he would not be content until he had said good-morning to me. Wasn't that nice? I could tell from the son how the father felt towards me. 1000 greetings from

Your
GUSTAV

P.S. – Leistikow made no impression on me whatever.

*Hotel Imperial,
Frankfurt*
15 January 1907 109

My dearest!

A magnificent performance yesterday! The audience was appreciative and enthusiastic beyond all expectation. – Criticism fastened on the third movement again. In the morning, for example, I picked up the *Börsencourier* at the station; it denies me in a few words all talent whatever. I cannot even orchestrate. It was unkind of Strauss not to be present. I found the enclosed card when I got home. Now that I look at it again it seems clear that Frau Pauline put her foot down! 'You'll stop here and play your skat and then go to bed.' [Frau] Wolff, Fernow, Ochs and his wife, and Berliner joined me in the hotel after the concert. They arranged everything with the utmost care so as to spare me all worry. I was in the train at eight and arrived here at four.

I was met at the station by Rottenberg and a certain Siloti from Petersburg – who offered me an engagement there next year. Rottenberg has again been conducting rehearsals in advance and is the good old friend he always was.

Unfortunately I have to work my way through all the organizers of the Museum Concerts and have an invitation for every night. But I will see how much of it I can dodge. It seems that all the newspapers have reports from Vienna of my resignation. Does it mean that there is another outcry because of my prolonged absence?

For today – a thousand greetings. Going early to bed. My dear, farewell —

GUSTAV

*Hotel Imperial,
Frankfurt*
16 [?] January 1907* 110

My Almschl,

The first rehearsal is over. The orchestra showed a willing spirit.

---

* So dated in the German edition, but this must be an error. Letter 109 clearly refers to the Berlin performance of the day before. Letter 110 (17th January?), on the other hand, refers to rehearsals for the Frankfurt concert (see Letter 111). (D.M.)

Siloti from Petersburg has been commissioned, you must know, by the orchestra there to get me at all costs to conduct two concerts. His story is much the same as Gabrilovitch's: they can't forget my rehearsals – they learned so much from them; and I must conduct a Haydn again for them and they would like, besides, the Ninth, some Wagner, and a symphony of mine. As I am to have a thousand roubles for each concert, it is worth considering. The dates are the 21st and 28th of December! Perhaps you will come with me again? I feel I have been a year away from you already. (That is because you write to me such dear letters and they have made me homesick for you.)

I don't myself know what to make of Strauss. How is one to explain his unequalness and jumbling together of bad and good? But all the same my opinion of *Salome* holds good. (You have to think of people like Titian, or the philosopher, Bacon.)

People in Vienna seem to have gone quite crazy. The newspapers here are continually inserting telegrams from them, saying that I have sent in my resignation – that I have piled up an enormous deficit, that I have become impossible, etc., etc.

Gucki is too sweet —

I kiss you many times, my dear —

Your

GUSTAV

Hotel Imperial,
Frankfurt
17 January 1907 III

My dear heart, your letter today overwhelms me with anxiety. You see, Almschili, one does not die of it – look at Mama with her heart – one goes full speed ahead and then suddenly comes the crash.

I beseech you, take proper care of yourself. Thank God, I shall be with you in three days and then I will look after you. Today's rehearsal was really good. My symphony* was excellent and the Schumann [First Symphony] will be put right tomorrow (the violins, I confess, in the last, charming movement are more scratchious than gracious). There I have to hand it to the [Vienna] Philharmonic, but unfortunately they won't have any more to do with me.

I don't find the world very kind to me just now. I am a hunted stag, hounds in full cry. But, thank God, I am not one to sink by the wayside, and the hard knocks I have to put up with now from all sides (the Berlin critics are almost unanimously contemptuous) only stimulate me. I

* This letter and Letter 110 refer to a performance of the Fourth Symphony on 18th January. (D.M.)

brush the mud from my clothes. '*Allen Gewalten zum Trotz sich erhalten*'! How grand it is that we have 50,000 dibs and a pension of 5000 a year to fall back on, and now we must set about saving with all speed. I send you a letter I had from Mengelberg. Loyalty like his does one good. – I have a good mind, anyway, to scratch Messchaert and Berlin. What is the good of being pelted with mud time after time? The curs obviously take me for a lamp-post. The concert tomorrow, and then to Linz by night-train. There I shall already breathe our own air again and on Monday at 12.35 noon I arrive at the West Station, where you will be waiting for me, and then home. I should like to see the little ones at table. They at least are works the critics cannot dismiss as miscarriages.

A thousand kisses, my heart, from your

GUSTL

Vienna
1 [?] September 1903 112

My dearest Almscherl!

The latest is that the landlord at the Kahlenberg insists on putting his car at my disposal after the performance. And as it is so utterly glorious up there, I accepted on the spot. So I'm having my breakfast today on the terrace. There is simply nothing in the world like it. Luckily no one else gets up as early, so I have the glorious view all to myself. It is just as wonderful at night. The view from my bedroom window makes it quite impossible to go to bed. – You sleep in the purest air. So I am staying on for as long as possible! Moreover, I've had another good idea. I have Sunday and Monday free and will spend those two days at Edlach and be waiting for you at Payerbach station so that we can travel home together as last year. How's that?

Your account of your solitary life was a great joy to me, and also that you sit once more by the Castalian spring! One must be often and intensely alone. – I am enjoying it too in full measure up here, in this wonderful weather, which you are benefiting from too, and then comes the best of all: our meeting at Payerbach and all that will follow. I have nothing on at the Opera and can stay at home.

Berliner's attentiveness is charming. I'll give you the autograph to keep. Imagine it, I'm excused the stamp (because my appointment was by decree, not by contract) and so I get, for this time alone, 10 florins back!

Now, my dearest heart, I am going up into the mountains again. This evening there is a gala performance – I have to be back for that and dress up. Afterwards, a quick supper and a drive up to the Kahlenberg. Lord – if you were only with me! How nice that would be and how you'd love it!

Adieu, dearest, I kiss you many times and Putzerl too. You haven't said a solitary word about her except in your today's letter, that you're so fond of her.

Your

GUSTAV

30 August 1907 113

Dearest,

The heat here begins to be rather oppressive. I had myself inoculated yesterday. By Dr. Hamperl, who examined me too at the same time. – He found a *slight* valvular defect, which is entirely compensated, and he makes nothing of the whole affair. He tells me I can certainly carry on with my work just as I did before and in general live a normal life, apart from avoiding over-fatigue. It is funny that in substance he said just what Blumenthal said, but his whole way of saying it was somehow reassuring. Also I find I have no fear of conducting now. I am seeing Montenuovo tomorrow for the first time. – Zemlinsky has been to see me too; you will be surprised how fat in the face he is now. Marriage appears to suit him. – I should really be very glad to go up to the Schneeberg! Don't you think a little high air would be good for you too? Perhaps Roller will come too, if you come.

A thousand,

Your

GUSTAV

Berlin

5 June 1907 114

My darling Almschili!

I've been waiting for two hours to get a call through to you. I hope I succeed soon. Meanwhile, I write a word or two. I set off with a pretty fair migraine (I didn't want you to know) – Walter rushed to his flat for aspirin. – Very good night and quite recovered on arrival today. Bath (in my room), breakfast, and straight to Conried,* who is staying in the hotel. He was full of projects – all fire and fervour. First and foremost, wanted me on exactly the same footing as Caruso. – Then 8 months (180,000 crowns) – then 6. Finally we got to this: 3 months (15th January to 15th April) for which 75,000 crowns net, journey and all expenses paid (first-class hotel)! We have not yet come to an agreement about the length of the contract. He wants four years, I want one only. – As soon as I have spoken to you, I am going up to him again. I am to

---

* Conried was the manager of the Metropolitan Opera, and negotiated in Berlin the terms of Mahler's New York appointment. (D.M.)

conduct Wagner and Mozart at the Opera [New York] and about 6 concerts (to include my C Minor with chorus).

Curse the thing – nothing for the last quarter of an hour but buzzing and scraping. I shall send you a telegram and give up all hope of speaking to you. I leave tomorrow evening and the day after I'll tell you all the details.

Thousand greetings from

Your

GUSTAV

kiss   kiss

4 years à 6 months à 125,000 crowns
making ½ a million crowns
or an annual guest-visit of 6–8 weeks
50,000 crowns fee
making 200,000 crowns in four years

kiss   kiss

Auf Wiedersehen

En route, Maiernigg–Vienna
17 July 1907 115

Dearest!

We are sitting in the restaurant car – with the obligatory traveller's appetite. (Pity you're not both here. You'd revel in it!) Please, don't give way too much, now that we two are not there to see to you,* and be brave. Miss [*sic*] Turner and Kathi and Anton must do everything for you. I shall take a bath as soon as I get to Vienna and shall be careful not to touch Carl.†

I shall put up at the Imperial.

A thousand greetings,

Your

GUSTAV

Vienna
17 July 1907 116

Just to announce our safe arrival. I am going straight to the hotel to

---

* Mahler's anxiety about my mother and me. We had been left in an appalling state by the death of my child, Maria, on 5th July. (A.M.)

† Carl Moll had stayed behind in Vienna with his small child and was not to be 'touched' in case of infection by scarlet fever. (A.M.)

have a bath. – Tomorrow to Kovacs, and the day after, early on Friday, you will have a telegram. Be ready to set off at once wherever Kovacs orders.*

Don't forget, Almschili, to pack the *Oberon* things.† They are in the bookcase in my room in the lower shelves. Don't forget any of them. Please, both of you, don't lift a finger over the packing!

Devotedly

Your

GUSTAV

Vienna

18 July 1907 117

My dearest Almscherl!

Now a brief report: we got here at six. Went straight to the hotel, had a bath, and then ate some ham in a café. There I came across Karpath, who says he had it on the best authority that Prince Liechtenstein said: We shall not let Mahler go; we shall not accept his resignation. Well – vederemo.

I feel very well – if Blumenthal had not said anything, I should have gone on in the same old way – and certainly not have gone to bed before twelve last night. So you see, my dear, everything has its good side. – I shall avoid all fatigue from now on, and if I am to stay on here I shall put myself entirely in Kovacs' hands (make a practice of going up to Semmering with you, etc.) – I think of you both continually, my dears, and hope we shall be together again tomorrow or the day after. I will telegraph this evening the moment I leave Kovacs. I imagine you will both have to pass through Vienna, and that you, Almscherl, will consult Kovacs too. I will arrange it all with him.

Shocking weather here; one thunderstorm after another. In that respect we are certainly better off in Maiernigg than anywhere else.

Now I kiss you both tenderly, and *mind you behave well* – and don't *lift a hand over the packing.* Don't forget my *Oberon* stuff. Bring my bicycling suit too, also Mommsen, Beethoven's Letters. In fact, of the books, leave only Goethe and Shakespeare there. Bring Rückert.

All my thoughts, my dearest,

Your

GUSTAV

* This was the first news since the death of our child and the examination of Mahler by the doctor – after which he travelled straight to Vienna to consult Professor Kovacs, who confirmed the first diagnosis. (See p. 122.) (A.M.)

† Doubtless a reference to Mahler's work on an edition of *Oberon*. See also Brecher in the Biographical List. (D.M.)

LAST MONTHS AT THE VIENNA OPERA

27 [?] August 1907 118

My Almschili,

Slept beautifully again last night; sending you some 'documents', amongst which you will find W.'s* love-letter of chief interest. – He seems to have acquired the conviction from the *Neue Freie Presse* that there might be circumstances in which I could help or injure him. We are having superb weather here and I hope you are too, for then you can get some real pleasure from your stay. – When do you come? I have not seen anybody yet. Only Przist. and Wondra, who are behaving beautifully. I am welcomed respectfully and cordially by all at the Opera. So, all told, things are going better than we expected.

No letter from you today so far. I hope it may still come.

Devotedly your

GUSTAV

Vienna
30 August 1903 119

My dearest Almscherl,

In the first place, I am in despair. All the shops are shut and even if they weren't I shouldn't know what to buy you for your birthday. So I can only hope that my love and good wishes for tomorrow will be accepted instead of a costly birthday present. And what else really is there to give when one has given oneself? – When you are here and we take one of our happy strolls along the Kärntnerstrasse, we'll find something nice for you. How's that? I look forward to it eagerly. – And now for an account of my doings. I shall have to rack my brains. Yesterday, then, after writing the card with my hand bandaged with lint by Roller, we walked by the road I have so often walked with my Almscherl, over the Hohe Warte to the electric railway and so by train to the theatre, where I quickly convinced myself that all the uproar about bad acoustics† was only a silly newspaper scare (spread abroad, as I have reason to believe, and kept going, principally by Schalk). Pollak came in during the performance and begged me to spend the night with him. But I appeased his agitated heart and took him into the box with me, where he sat with me in judgement and agreed that there was nothing amiss with the sound. After the first act I went on to the stage, pitched into Schalk and Wondra,‡ and then turned upon some others standing by, after which Pollak and I retired to the Imperial, where I had a beefsteak and some very appetizing plum tarts. I was in the train by 9 and

* Felix Weingartner the conductor. (A.M.)
† Mahler had had the orchestra-pit lowered. (A.M.)
‡ Art-adviser at the Opera. (A.M.)

Band III. — Nr. 68   Wien–Leipzig, 19. Jänner 1907   Preis 32 Heller.

DIE MUSKETE

Humoristische Wochenschrift

Alle Rechte vorbehalten
Nachdruck verboten

Preis im Abonnement
vierteljährlich K 4.—

„Tragische Sinfonie."

(Zeichnung von Fritz Schönpflug.)

»Herrgott, daß ich die Huppe vergessen habe! Jetzt kann ich noch eine Sinfonie schreiben.«

'My God, I've forgotten the motor horn! Now I can write another
symphony.' (A satirical comment on the Sixth Symphony)

Gustav Mahler in New York, 1909

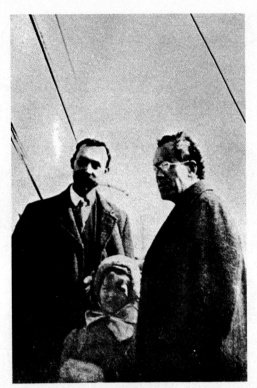

Gustav Mahler on board the *Kaiser Wilhelm II,*
with his daughter Anna and Theodore
Spiering, leader of the New York Philharmonic Orchestra

Gustav Mahler as a conductor, silhouettes by Otto Boehler

A copy, in Mahler's hand, of one of his wife's songs, 'Erntelied'

Letter from Gustav Mahler to his wife, Prague, May, 1908
   (Letter 135)

Chorus Mysticus from the Eighth Symphony in Mahler's manuscript

Page from the manuscript sketches for the Tenth Symphony

up at the Kahlenberg by 10.30. Straight to my apartments, which consist of two very dirty rooms with broken furniture covered in plush. An unbelievably beautiful view from the window of Vienna, pricked out with lights and framed by the lovely dark woods of the Wienerwald. Being tired to death I undressed without coming into contact with the furniture and slept without a break until half-past seven. Out of bed and to breakfast (dressed, of course) amidst a mob of Viennese, and on foot by Wildgrube and the Hohe Warte to the railway and so to the theatre, where a Sunday's calm! At half-past eleven to the Superintendent – most affectionately welcomed, everything arranged, and to lunch with Pollak.

Tonight *Meistersinger* with a guest singer. Up again after Act One to the Kahlenberg very happily; it was a splendid idea of Mama's.

I must append to my account of yesterday that I was not alone with Moser* for lunch; besides Hoffmann, there were three others there, with none of whom I was acquainted, which, needless to say, I did not find comforting.

The latest is my discovery on signing for my salary today that from now on I have 15 florins instead of 5 to pay in stamps. I receive my salary tomorrow morning and will send it to you at once; I hope for a line from you by that time, already much desired. – You will not, I hope, be astonished to hear that I miss you at every turn and think of you unceasingly.

If only I had a letter from you, if only a little one, in my hand at this moment! My dear heart, it is a terrible nuisance not being able to write to you from the Opera – for it is hard to find a moment on the way there and back. Don't forget that I sometimes do the journey from the Kahlenberg to town twice a day. A thousand greetings and kisses, my darling Luxi, and let me hear from you.

Your

GUSTAV

Wiesbaden
7 October 1907 120

Dearest Almschi!

On arrival here, I came in for a shock at the quite decrepit Victoria Hotel; after inspecting the room, in which, for noise and bangings and racket of every sort, I could not have closed an eye, I drove on without unpacking to the Kur Hotel in search of a better room. I was shown a room, which at least was comfortable, if not very quiet, at the Nassauerhof, and there, with God's help, I will make a try. 'Who hath brought

* Kolo Moser. (A.M.)

me into this land?' I asked every quarter of an hour. I might have been spared this watering-place and its half-witted mob.

Only the indigestible noodles and garlic-ridden veal at Theuer's could have induced me to accept that telegraphed offer. – Well, my programme is 'applause-compelling'* and light. I hope it will pay me for my trouble. I am now sitting stark naked in my room waiting for my luggage, left behind at the Victoria Hotel, thus combining the practical with the pleasant. I write to you while having an air bath, and so will not lose a moment when my bags arrive before changing my clothes. For I'm looking forward to a good dinner after the disastrous one at Frankfurt. This pen and spongy paper are no great joy either. So, no more. All greetings, etc.

Your

GUSTAV

TO HERR SCHRÖDER, ROYAL PIANO MAKERS AND CONCERT AGENCY, ST. PETERSBURG-NEVSKY

Vienna
1 October 1907 121

Dear Sir,

In spite of your somewhat peremptory refusal, may I repeat the request which I telegraphed yesterday and make my position clear?

When I made the agreement with you, I thought I should be free from the autumn. But now the Management of the Royal Opera has decided that I must remain in office until the first of January.

It would have been a simple matter to fulfil my obligations towards you between 15th October and 15th November. But now I have the tedious and exhausting labours of handing over my duties in December. If you insisted on my conducting the concerts in December, I should have to wind up all my affairs here in the second half of November. This excessive exertion would, in view of a disease of the heart which set in this summer, make it very difficult for me to carry out my agreement. My doctor has absolutely forbidden me to undertake such exhausting journeys; and it is extremely probable that he may insist on the cancellation of my American contract, although a sea voyage would be far less dangerous for me than the long railway journeys to and from Russia. So the situation is simply this: if you will dispense with me in December, I will either be at your disposal between 15th October and 15th November, or else I will carry out the two engagements, and

* The amusing description of Hans Richter's red beard by the critic, Schönaich. (A.M.)

more, if you wish, at a later date and thus the connection between us, which might in the future be of importance to us both, would not be broken off. *Should you insist*, I will in any case endeavour to meet my obligations. But frankly I might be compelled by my doctor (whose advice was the reason for my telegram) *to let you down at the last moment*, which would not only be very embarrassing for me, but would put you into far greater difficulties than now, when you still have two and a half months to make other arrangements. (I am sure Fried, or Brecher, for example, would be glad to exchange dates with me.)

May I beg you to let me have as favourable a reply as possible to the request I made by telegram and now repeat? I assuredly hope to convince you in years to come that I am not unreliable, and that it is only present circumstances which compel me to put you to this inconvenience.

Believe me,

Yours very sincerely,
GUSTAV MAHLER

Petersburg
22 October 1907 122

My Almschi!

So I go on my way – I wish I could say on my way back.

I must add to my account of the journey that I had a two-hours' wait in Warsaw and thought with emotion of our similar experience there. A morose waiter in greasy 'tails' and dirty shirt gave me tea – to my great discomfort. I could not persuade myself to take anything else from the fly-ridden buffet (the Varsovites make a speciality of blue-bottles at this season). But I took out my papers and amused myself for an hour. Then I walked up and down in search of our old Jew. I did not find him, but to make up for it there were any number of young ones. (I was not tempted to bring you one as a memento.) Nevertheless, I had my reward. There is something very odd about seeing such strange types of humanity. You want to ask each one, who he is, what he does, and what he wishes and hopes for. Young and old were indistinguishable. There was a party of women which interested me very much, three generations, two old, one middle-aged (very sympathetic) and three flappers, in three sizes like organ-pipes; the eldest of the three was accompanied by a tall young man. All were Slav in type. They moved about from one part of the station to another, always forming a circle whenever they came to a stop, but did not get into the train. What on earth were they doing in the station?

After that, a twenty-four-hour journey. By day I revised my Fifth Symphony, and by night slept splendidly.

Frank is just the same dear old fogey and comes to pick me up every day at 5. Yesterday I had dinner with them. He is longing to get away and can scarcely hold out any longer. Probably he'll throw up his job, sacrifice his pension (anyway he is now an Excellency) and retire to Munich. A rehearsal early this morning.* The orchestra gave me a cordial welcome, rehearsed splendidly and were quite enthusiastic by the end.

I then went back to the hotel and was sitting down to lunch when old Abaza came along; she was very insistent that I should share her table. I declined, however, but promised I would one day. She looks very well, and seemed to feel the need of a talk with me. Although I was very hungry and not feeling very conversational, she would not be put off. She regarded me as a keeper of souls; seems to be afraid of death and would like very much to know what comes after. It seems as if something I said to her five years ago had stuck in her mind, and she had been waiting ever since to continue where we left off. – She said she had found something so original in my Second Symphony and that it had made an abiding impression on her. I asked her whether she did not remember the text. She asked was there a text to it? Yes, but the chorus sang it in such a way that it was not comprehensible. I said: Well, read it again and you will find the answer to your questions. She: I must get it. Whereupon she went out – and I'm convinced straight to a music shop to buy a copy.

Unfortunately the hotel is very bad and has become dearer in proportion. It's all so desolate and the food too is no longer good. No peace at night: my room looks on to the courtyard. – No. 18, which we occupied before, is next door. I peeped in as I passed by. The old chambermaid is still here. She recognized me at once and asked after you. – Everyone asks after you.

Walter (the leader) is not with the orchestra any longer. (He's a free-lance now.) But he came to see me and stayed on throughout the rehearsal.

Do you remember the peculiar smell there is in Russia everywhere, even on the railway? A mixture of woodsmoke and Russian leather? It always brings back the time we were here together.

Always, always

Your

GUSTAV

* Mahler performed his Fifth Symphony in St. Petersburg. Among the audience was the young Igor Stravinsky who 'was impressed by Mahler himself and the symphony' (Stravinsky/Craft, *Expositions and Developments*, London, 1962). Stravinsky also recalled that Mahler's Petersburg concert 'was a triumph. Rimsky was still alive, I believe, but he wouldn't have attended because a work by Tchaikovsky was on the programme (I think it was *Manfred*, the dullest piece imaginable). Mahler also played some Wagner fragments...' (Stravinsky/Craft, *Conversations with Igor Stravinsky*, London, 1959). (D.M.)

My Almschili!

Yesterday was my first day in Helsinki. Unfortunately there is a thaw here and I have had to discard my fine fur coat. I went to a People's Concert in the evening – and so got to know my orchestra at the same time. It is amazingly good and well trained, which speaks well for the Director of Music here – Kajanus, who has of course a great reputation in the musical world. – He paid me a visit in the afternoon and kept me company. An extremely sympathetic, serious, and modest man.

At the concert in the evening – I was having a drink of beer – Axel Gallén suddenly sat down beside me, his wife with him. And after the concert Kajanaus and his wife and a pianist from Brussels joined us. Gallén was in tremendous form and I took to him greatly. Nevertheless, I left them at eleven and went to bed, which surprised them all very much, as they keep it up here until all hours, and indeed until morning. On Saturday, the day after the concert, Gallén is going to take me for an excursion in his motor-boat. Then in the evening I return to Petersburg.

I heard some pieces of Sibelius at the concert too – the Finnish national composer, who makes a great stir not only here but throughout the world of music. In one of them, the most hackneyed clichés were served up, with harmonizations in the 'Nordic' style, as a national dish. 'Pui Kaiki!'*

This is always the way with these national geniuses. It is the same in Russia and Sweden, not to mention Italy – all those harlots and their souteneurs. Axel puts the matter in a very different light with his dozen brandies before dinner and his motor-boat; there you have the genuine article if you want vitality and race. No news from you so far.

All my thoughts, my dear Almschili,

GUSTAV

Helsinki
2 November 1907 124

Dearest,

Concert yesterday.† People came from all over Finland. Sibelius paid me a call in the morning.‡ I found him extremely sympathetic, as all

---

* This was the nearest little Gucki, our daughter, could get to 'Pfui Teufel'. (A.M.)
† Mahler conducted the Helsinki Philharmonic Orchestra in a Beethoven–Wagner programme. The date of this letter must be open to doubt if the date of Letter 123 is correct. (D.M.)
‡ It was during this visit to Helsinki that Mahler and Sibelius had their famous conversation about the symphony as a form. 'For Sibelius, it was "the severity of style and the profound logic that created an inner connection between all of the motifs". Mahler's reply was: "No, the symphony must be like the world. It must embrace everything".' (Harold Johnson, *Sibelius*, London, 1960.) (D.M.)

Finns are. Gallén too joined us after the concert. Now I am waiting for him to come and take me out to the Schären islands in his motor-boat. Unfortunately, it's raining, which I fear will dampen the pleasure a little. But wait a moment – what's this? The sun came out just as I wrote those very words. So perhaps it will be quite enjoyable after all.

The parenthesis in your letter, saying the time had come to leave Semmering, did not please me at all. But – Almschi! Is that really any reason? You ought to have stayed on up there if it was doing you good. We can raise the 100 florins somehow. Surely you know by now what a precious thing health is.

I set off for Petersburg tonight. Thank God, the time draws to an end. I am getting very tired of it all by now, although I'm in the best of hands both here and in Petersburg. [I went to the Opera here yesterday. *Onegin*. They had everything at their disposal, but the use they made of it was crude and often dilettantish – it is always the way, and will be soon even in Vienna! As you will see in due course.

Am really curious to know whether I shall have anything but telegrams from you in the course of the week. A thousand –]

GUSTAV

Petersburg
23 [?] October 1907 125

My Almschl!

I'm trying the whole time to remember what it was I promised to bring you back from Petersburg (we talked of it in Vienna) and I simply cannot remember. So please write at once and tell me.

There was the second rehearsal today. The orchestra behave splendidly. Their enthusiasm never flags. Today a deputation very charmingly came to ask whether I would conduct two concerts for them in February. Would I agree in principle? Naturally, I told them that the journey here from America would be a little too far. But some other year I would be delighted. They thanked me for the promise.

A pity you're not here. It is a real pleasure to rehearse in such conditions.

I have gone up to the upper floor in the hotel in the hope of more quiet. But it's unbelievably dirty here. I pay 8 roubles a day. In Germany I get the best of rooms for that. At the Europa I hear it is even dearer.

Almschili! It is really not kind of you to leave me without news of you all this time. However busy you are, you could at least send me a letter-card.

Since coming to this floor with the view on to the fine square and the large St. Isaac's Cathedral, I like sitting the whole afternoon at the writing-table in the window, reading, sleeping, dreaming and looking out.

A thousand thoughts from

Your

GUSTAV

Petersburg
4 November 1907 126

My dear Almschili!

I've been ringing for the waiter for the past hour to come and bring me some notepaper. So I must write on this telegraph form – and so, of course, in telegraphic style.

I have been revising the orchestral parts* since yesterday morning after arrival from Finland – just done, after much tribulation. Middle finger of my right hand has a large hole in it. The day with Gallén was very pleasant. He and a very famous architect,† whose name has escaped me, busied themselves about me like two ants. They wrapped me in ʟugs and fed me on Finnish sandwiches until I was quite ill. I shivered like a greyhound (but so did they). After a three-hours' run through the Schärens with ever-changing views, we arrived at the end of our voyage where we were met by carriages and horses and driven very merrily to a charming house – quite à la Hoffmann – more of a castle really, and most hospitably welcomed.

The architect lives there with a friend (his name has not escaped me; it is Gesellius) winter and summer. It is on a lake and looks over the sea from the upper windows. The rooms are charming, à la Hohe Warte translated into Finnish. They are both architects, equally delightful and equally young, and they both married wives as young as themselves and lived a very happy life together (they were friends as boys); but about a year ago, when they had been married for a year, they came to the conclusion that life without variety was 'mere existence'. What was to be done? Well – they exchanged wives and have been living for the last year as merrily as ever, building new houses and populating their own. There's a pretty story for you. – When it got dusk, we sat in the twilight in front of the open fire, where huge logs blazed and glowed as though in a smithy. Gallén, who had kept his eyes fixed on me throughout the trip in the most singular way (as if he'd spotted a hare), suddenly set up an easel and began on my portrait. Lit up only by the fire, quite à la Rembrandt. After he had been painting away for half an

* Of the Fifth Symphony. (D.M.)

† This was probably Eliel Saarinen (1873–1950), father of Eero, and a famous architect in his own right. (D.M.)

hour I got restless, and we went for a walk in the wood. I was thankful to have made my escape and took care not to remind him of the portrait. An hour passed: I had to go, and was just bidding them all farewell when my host brought the easel along and there, to the wonder of all, was my portrait – completely finished. Very fine as a painting and also very like. You would be astonished! What a fellow he is! To look at too – you should see him at the wheel – usually very upright, his eyes like burning coals, fixed on the distance – taut and erect – like a Viking. I should think women must be tremendously taken with him! They were all of them so kind to me, too, I was quite touched; and yet in spite of their warm welcome they were never for one moment officious. I even lay down in the next room for a nap on the sofa, without a word said, and there was not a sound to disturb me.

Since returning here yesterday I am once more in the charge of Frank and Gabrilovitch. The latter particularly would pull down the sky for me.

Today I had a telegram from you: 'All well.' I hope it isn't a belated reply to my last letters. Do you know, they took four days to reach their destination? Do write at length. – But you'll have to be quick, or I'll be with you before they can arrive.

A thousand from

Your

GUSTAV

MAHLER TO THE SUPERINTENDENT, PRINCE MONTENUOVO

The Director
of the
Royal and Imperial Opera
[Early Summer, 1907.] 127

Your Highness,

Forgive me troubling you with a letter in reference to our conversation of yesterday. My future relations with the Royal Opera were clearly defined, but it did not occur to me (or, rather, I forgot) to raise the question of my personal interest; that is to say, what view your Highness takes of my future in the financial sense. As a decision on this point has become a matter of immediate concern, allow me to place before your Highness what I regard as desirable in view of the alteration in my circumstances.

1. As regards my pension:

I am entitled to retire on a pension of 5,500 florins at the end of my tenth year of service (on May 1st of this year). – Until recently, I might well have reckoned on claiming the higher pension of 7,000 florins to which a further three years' service would have entitled me.

My way of living has been planned on this basis – for I am not by any means past my work, nor has your Highness ever hinted that my retirement was other than premature – and also I have entered into commitments, which I must in any case meet, such as insurance policies for the benefit of my wife and children and the building of a house in the country It would weigh very hard on me for the rest of my life, if through unforeseen circumstances and, as I may well say, no fault of my own, I were to be deprived of advantages on which I had every reason to count; and I therefore request that I may be granted the pension of 7,000 florins assured to me by decree after thirteen years of service.

2. In order to wind up my present household and way of life with a quiet mind (I am forced to leave Vienna, at any rate for some years, for reasons I need not go into) I request the payment of 10,000 florins in final compensation; and would point out, in furtherance of this request, that for the first half-year of my appointment from 1st May to 1st November 1897 I received only 2,500 florins, although I had full responsibilities as Director, and also as conductor of the orchestra. The reason given for this at the time was that my predecessor, Jahn, was to enjoy his full remuneration during that period (and even up to the beginning of the following year). What I ask is, therefore, more or less the same as was granted at that time to my predecessor.

3. The assurance in the event of my death for my wife and two children of the pension for widows and orphans, as laid down by royal statute. (Your Highness was kind enough to draw my attention to this point.)

In expressing frankly and in full what I should desire in the event of my departure, I rely on the kindness your Highness has always shown me and which at our last meeting your Highness was good enough to express. It is not for me to champion my own cause by alluding to the manner in which I have carried out my duties during ten, one might well say, war-years.

I ask your Highness's forgiveness for the liberty I take and with the expression of my gratitude beg to remain your Highness's obedient servant,

MAHLER

PRINCE MONTENUOVO TO MAHLER

Deputy Superintendent
Prince Montenuovo
Semmering
10 August 1907 128

Dear Director,
I did not until yesterday receive the definite and official intimation

(accompanied by his own written reply) that Weingartner consented to take up the appointment on 1st January 1908.

I make haste to inform you of this, as I have been keenly aware of the suspense in which you have been kept. My only consolation is that your freedom comes within the appointed time, for you told me yourself in Vienna that difficulties on account of your American engagement would not arise until *after* 1st January. I have arranged everything satisfactorily with W. He will come to Vienna at the beginning of September. I am glad to be able to tell you also that your three requests have been put before his Majesty and that, after handing over your office on 1.1.1908, you will be granted

I. a pension of 14,000 crowns instead of the pension to which you are entitled under your contract,

II. a sum of 20,000 crowns in full compensation, and lastly

III. your wife after your death will be entitled to the pension of the widow of a Privy Councillor (although you did not rank as such) in accordance with the Statute of Court Pensions.

It gives me great pleasure to have been successful in settling all this in accordance with your wishes.

Please treat W.'s appointment as strictly confidential for the time being. I do not wish the matter to be made public until I consider that the moment has come.

Conried need now delay no longer making your engagement public. Please inform him of this.

Cordial greetings,
MONTENUOVO

FELIX WEINGARTNER TO MAHLER

Bad Kreuth
22 August 1907 129

My dear Herr Mahler,

What so lately appeared incredible has now come true: I am really to be your successor in Vienna. There is much I might say, but may I confine myself to the expression of one brief wish?

I learn from the newspapers that you are going to reside in Vienna. My wish and hope, then, are that the friendly relations which have existed between us, but seem to have lapsed for several years, may revive, and thereafter continue without interruption.

I look forward with warmth to seeing you again in Vienna, and hope it may be soon. Until then I remain, with my best wishes,

Ever most sincerely yours,
FELIX WEINGARTNER

FROM THE DIARY OF FRAU BERTHA ZUCKERKANDL   130

When we said goodbye to Mahler for the last time,* he said: 'After all, I take my home with me, my Alma and my child. And it is only now, when I am released from the crushing burden of work, that I know what will henceforth be my dearest task. Alma has sacrificed ten years of her youth to me. No one can ever know with what absolute selflessness she has subordinated her life to me and my work. It is with a light heart I go on my way with her.'

GERHART HAUPTMANN TO MAHLER
Telegram

12 December 1907   131
To Gustav Mahler, S.S. *Augusta Victoria*, Cherbourg
Dear Friend, With all my heart wish you happy voyage on the fine ship in which I myself made the return voyage some years ago. Come happily back to the Europe we love, which needs men like you as it does its daily bread. Your Gerhart Hauptmann.

1908–1909

Hotel Blauer Stern,
Prague
6–10 [?] September 1908   132

My dearest Almscherl!

There hasn't been a moment to send you a few lines before today. I have had to rehearse literally the whole day.† First, I had a rehearsal with the strings; afternoon and evening with the young people. H. turned up here too – he is here for a congress and I went out with him at six on the day before yesterday, and yesterday too. I am very unlucky in the hotel this time: I have a neighbour, who wakes me up every day at eleven and snores so frightfully at night that I jump up each time thinking some disaster has happened.

Thank God he is leaving today, and Prague, which is intolerably noisy, will be a little quieter, as these congresses and so on are drawing to an end. Yesterday evening I returned by myself to the Blauer Stern and ran into the inevitable Orlik (whom I encounter wherever I go). Naturally I sat with him and let him unburden himself. I heard all he had to say about Japan and China. But he is a muddle-headed fellow and seems to know nothing from direct observation but only from some report or other. Later, Bodanzky joined us. Then Orlik unburdened himself about his travels this year in Provence and what he had learned

* Mahler left Vienna for America on 9th December 1907. (D.M.)
† For the première of the Seventh Symphony on 19th September. (D.M.)

there as an artist, and how he now painted quite differently – the landscapes and the sun had been his masters and it had been such a revelation to explore new artistic territory. I suppose he took a few photographs there and copied some pictures by Cézanne and Van Gogh. However, he makes a good-humoured impression, what people call a good sort.

How glad I should be if you were here and more than all I rejoice in the prospect of the six peaceful weeks we are to be allowed after this.

*　　*　　*

Hotel Blauer Stern,
Prague
10 September 1908　133

My dearest Almscherl!

       Motto: How blessed, how blessed

  a barber
    waiter
    tenor
    rentier

Member of the Committee of the Universal German Music Society to be —

'Who hath brought me into this land?'

I have, needless to say, no wits left for writing the anyhow-articulate, anywhere-written, anywhen-sent-off letter. I have to revise parts and meditate on how to make a side drum out of a fish-kettle, a trumpet out of a rusty watering-can, a concert-hall out of a wine-shop. I have extracted only one bit of consolation out of all this turmoil. – One of the trumpets asked Bodanzky in despair: 'I'd just like to know what's beautiful about blowing away at a trumpet stopped up to high C sharp.' This gave me an insight at once into the lot of man, who likewise cannot understand why he must endure being stopped to the piercing agony of his own existence, cannot see what it's for, and how his screech is to be attuned to the great harmony of the universal symphony of all creation.

Bodanzky answered the unhappy man very logically: 'Wait a bit! You can't expect to understand it yet.' (I have, you see, been rehearsing the wind on its own – as in this vale of tears, where the consolation of the violins and lower strings, which form the groundwork and anchor of all the other instruments, are as yet absent.) 'When all the rest come in, you'll soon see what you're there for.' –

So let us patiently make the best of the turmoil.

Keussler is here too. A splendid fellow. I am going to have a vegetarian supper with him after the rehearsal on Saturday evening.

Servus, old Almschl, you too must make the best of the high stop. One day, after all, the mute will fall off!

Your

GUSTAV

Hotel Blauer Stern,
Prague

11 September 1908 134

Friday, 8 o'clock in the morning

Only a few words in great haste today, my dear Almschi. Your dear little note and the cards written in the train gave me enormous pleasure.* Unfortunately, this wonderful entering-into-possession-of-oneself is undone the moment one returns to the noise and confusion of everyday life. The only thing then is to *think oneself back* into that blissful state, and to make it a practice at every opportunity to look back at that other world and to draw one breath of that other air. – I have now done at last with the special rehearsals and there is the first full rehearsal at 10 in the morning. The hotel and the town are shockingly noisy. I have even had to take the room next door in case of being roused up four or five times a night by a snoring neighbour (he leaves today at last). A thousand greetings, my Almscherl. If only you were here!

Your

GUSTAV

Hotel Blauer Stern,
Prague

22 May [?] † 135

My Almscherl!

I was very glad to have your dear little letter today. Yesterday was very pleasing. The orchestra very good and willing. – I am constantly attended by a staff of young (very charming) people – not to mention Bodanzky, or Klemperer, who did the splendid piano edition of the Second for two hands.‡

I am eager to know what after all we are going to make of the summer. I leave it entirely in your hands. Today we have the second rehearsal.

---

* I had written to him about Novalis whom I had discovered for myself and was reading for the first time. (A.M.)

† Mahler was in Prague in May 1908, when he conducted the Czech Philharmonic Orchestra in music by Beethoven, Smetana and Wagner on 23rd May. It would seem possible to allot this letter to that month, all the more so in view of Mahler's reference to plans for the summer. (D.M.)

‡ Unpublished (D.M.)

The conductor of the Czech orchestra here, a Dr. Zemanek, who had a rousing success with my Fourth this year, pleases me personally very much. From what Bodanzky and others tell me of the performance it must have been grand. A thousand kisses, my Almschi, and here's to our speedy re-union!

Your

GUSTAV

Hotel Vierjahreszeiten
Munich
October 1908 136

My dearest Almscherl!

I feel now, after today's rehearsal with the incredibly willing orchestra, that it is really a pleasure to be the composer of a successful symphony.* They have, as you know, broken with Kaim† and set up on their own. And it is really a joy to see the fervour and cheerfulness of these poor fellows, who are having a hard struggle and yet blow and fiddle away in shabby coats with undimmed enthusiasm. At this rate these few days will be simply a rest-cure for me.

N.B. Munich, which is situated at a height of 600 metres has, as I've always noticed, a superb climate; and I always feel at the top of my form here, unless circumstances beyond the control of the weather lay me low. For example, I very well remember kicking my heels here about twenty years ago without money or any prospect of an engagement, and later again, fifteen years ago, when cholera broke out in Hamburg and I had to fall back on Pollini.

The more I think of it the more the idea of perhaps settling eventually in Munich grows on me. What do you think? You can buy a castle in a park here for 3,000 marks, and life is actually twice as cheap as in Vienna. With our income we could live here like princes. In the middle of Europe – with first-rate communications in all directions.

My room, too, in this hotel is most charming and far from dear. I'd like you to see how well-off I am, bathroom included. I hope you can make out this scribble.

All my thoughts,

Your

GUSTAV

---

* Mahler refers to his Seventh Symphony, performed on 27th October.

† Franz Kaim (1856–1935), the German impresario. He founded an orchestra in Munich which bore his name and which Mahler conducted in the first performance of his Fourth Symphony in 1901 (25th November). The Kaim Orchestra was dissolved in 1908. (D.M.)

BEFORE THE VOYAGE TO AMERICA

Hamburg 137

My dearest Almscherl!   7 November 1908

Splendid journey in an excellent train. Mama will have told you
already: you have a treat to look forward to. Berliner met us in Berlin. –
Two hours automobile drive in the Grunewald. Delightful but very
cold. So put on furs and bring rugs. Have made all necessary arrangements with Berliner.

On arrival here, we were met by [Gustav] Brecher in splendour with
automobile. Unpacked and changed. As Brecher was conducting I
drove (in Brecher's automobile, of course) to Behn's and dined there at
seven. At nine I went in a droshky (I can only say 'went' after being
'driven' by Brecher) now back to the hotel, lay down and slept until
7 o'clock in the morning. We have delightful quarters. Pity you aren't
here for longer. *In every way*, it is nicer and more comfortable than in
Vienna. Everyone asks for you and laments your absence. – Now
Brecher in his automobile to take me to the rehearsal.* More, I hope,
this afternoon.

A thousand thoughts from

Your

GUSTL

7 November 1908 138

Dearest Almscherl!

*   *   *

The porter has just brought me the parcel.† I read it for half an hour,
as though bewitched. Now I must go out to rehearse! I blush like a
child! So *this* is what that — stole from me and exposed to a stranger's
eye.

Well, forget it!

A thousand thoughts

Your

GUSTAV

MAHLER TO A PUBLISHER

Villa Alt-Schluderbach,
Toblach in Tyrol
Summer, 1908 139

Gentlemen,

Herr Fried, who is here at Toblach, has mentioned your publishing
house to me and I should be very glad to enter into relations with you.

* I have not been able to trace the details of this concert. (D.M.)

† Justi, as I said above, had taken possession of the libretto of *Rübezahl* and in her
thoughtless way shown it to Roller. The childhood memories of the manuscript had
not blinded Mahler to its weakness, and it touched him on the raw that Justi should
have shown this youthful work to Roller, the stern critic. (A.M.)

Assuming that it is not your principle to acquire an author's work outright (in which case I must ask you to state your terms), I would suggest an arrangement I adopted with the publisher of my first four symphonies and my songs. According to this, you would print the Eighth Symphony and undertake its entire publication, and pay me half the receipts. At the same time you would undertake to pay me a suitable advance on receipt of the manuscript. An account to be presented at the end of the business year.

I should also like to mention that my Seventh Symphony, which is to be given its first performance in Prague on 19th September, has not yet been published, and that it would suit me better to publish it first, particularly as enquiries for it are constantly reaching me from European as well as American concert societies, and as things are I cannot make any satisfactory answer.

This work has every prospect – owing to its clear and engaging character and also because it requires a comparatively small orchestra – of making an early appearance in most concert halls, and I ask whether you would not like to publish it before the Eighth. Both works would in due course be at your disposal.*

Yours sincerely,

MAHLER

N.B. The Seventh Symphony is ready to print (score and orchestral material) and could be in the hands of the concert agencies in time for this season.

Amsterdam

1 October 1909 140

Dearest Almscherl!

I am feeling very anxious. Your silence means, in any case, that your liver is not in order. And now all this packing will be the last straw.† Almschi, please, let it go as it likes. What does it matter whether a few crocks are broken or not? – And if the worst comes to the worst, don't come before the 11th. The few extra days might lighten your labours greatly. – Here all goes very well indeed. Mengelberg wants the Eighth unconditionally. The conditions in any case would be perfect in so far as I should have a well-trained chorus and orchestra, rehearsed as he only can, at my unrestricted disposal. Vederemo! Bodanzky and Hagemann, Bock and Fried have announced themselves by telegram. The Clemenceaus will be here by Sunday. So it does not look alto-

---

* The Seventh was eventually published by Bote und Bock (Berlin) and the Eighth by Universal Edition (Vienna). (D.M.)

† On giving up the flat in the Auenbruggergasse all our effects had to be packed and stored with the furniture. (A.M.)

gether like peace and seclusion. The orchestra is magnificent – balm after the experience in New York. Kreisler is giving concerts here at the moment and haunts my rehearsals. – I like him extremely both as a man and an artist.

The Mengelbergs are as warm-hearted as ever and hospitable as only the Dutch can be. Diepenbrock is a delight to me. He has great depth and truth. – If only I had some news of you, to keep me from worrying so much.

The last rehearsal today. – Probably, however, I shall conduct the whole programme at the third concert (Wagner, *Faust* Overture, *Siegfried Idyll*, *Meistersinger* Overture – and then my Seventh).

A thousand greetings, my dear, to you all.

Your

GUSTAV

Amsterdam

6 October 1909* 141

My Almscherl!

Please telegraph at once on receipt of this letter to

Mahler

c/o Mengelberg

107 van Eeghenstraat

Amsterdam

when you are coming.

Stop! That's no good now. I leave the day after tomorrow, Friday the 8th, for Paris, and will be at Hotel Bellevue, where I await news of you. I've had a frightful cold these last days and am tired of life in a strange place. I've been quite alone in the flat since yesterday. The enclosed letter from Reitter shows the man in a rather different light from the crude orchestral fanatic. He's right; my symphony has had a colossal success. As usual here, the ground is exceptionally well prepared for me. Nevertheless, I have made up my mind not to start in New York with a performance of the Seventh, but the Fourth. The Seventh is too complicated for a public which knows nothing of me.

In case the women give me no peace, they shall have their Tchaikovsky. (At least then they keep quiet.) I can well understand your

* This letter and the previous one were allotted to an incorrect year by Alma Mahler. The Seventh Symphony, mentioned in letter 139, was not performed for the first time in Amsterdam until 1909. Furthermore, Alma Mahler herself dates the move from the Vienna apartment (see her footnote to Letter 140), 1909 not 1908. This is made clear in her reminiscences, pp. 153-154. (D.M.)

fatigue. You know, dearest, when you have to work really hard, it is living.

All my love

Your

GUSTAV

Just had your letter: so then, I'll go to the Hotel Majestic (I arrive there on Friday). Please tell everyone in Vienna.

ALFRED ROLLER TO MAHLER

Vienna
22 January 1908   142

My dear Frau Mahler and dear Director,

Tomorrow we have the first performance of '*Fidelio*, 1908 model', and this is the milestone I resolved to reach before writing my first letter to America. Meanwhile, I have heard from Mottl that all goes well with you and that you like it over there, which after all is what matters most to us all here. I will not say apart from this what your departure has meant to me, as it goes against the grain, and you are both fond enough of me to take it on trust.

Weingartner treats me with great respect and friendliness, even with marked esteem, although, nauseated by universal intrigues and rivalries, I involuntarily withdraw into my shell and confine myself simply to carrying out my duties correctly and assiduously, in keeping with what I have learnt of them in the past. He is startlingly young. Of the productions of ours he has so far seen, he liked the *Barber*, then *Tristan*, the first act in particular, and best of all *Lohengrin*, the second act of which caused him raptures of delight. He is not so pleased with *Figaro*; it is too heavy for him. He said: 'It's Beaumarchais dramatized – not Mozart.' – He has not yet seen *Iphigenie*,* *The Magic Flute* or *Don Giovanni*, but asked me how we had staged the last. He means now to take *The Shrew*† in hand himself, it appears, but without any alteration other than restoring the end. He has not seen it performed, any more than he has *Fidelio*. And now a word or two about the new *Fidelio*. Act I: Prison yard. Front right –Rocco's house. In front of it, a cheerful little flower-garden. Then downstage to the right, the two towers of the prison. At the back of the stage in the middle – the large gateway with a grating over it, through which blue sky is seen. The bastion we used to have in the last act is behind the gateway. Jacquino's lodge is in a turret on the left of the gateway. Upstage left, the entrance to the garden and castle. This last is from the old scenery; everything else in the

* Gluck's *Iphigenie in Aulis* was the last of Mahler's newly studied productions for the Vienna Opera (first performance, 18th March 1907). (D.M.)
† Opera by Hermann Goetz, after Shakespeare's *The Taming of the Shrew*. (D.M.)

courtyard is new; I could not otherwise manage the lighting on Rocco's cheerful little house in contrast with the pitch-black walls. Even the walls are thus much lighter; only the gateway, recessed within a dark tunnel-like approach, is dark. 'A very fine bit of *décor*,' a 'feat' in the manner of the German theatres and not fussily suggestive or overdone. Schrödter is Jacquino, very hearty of course. Mayr is Rocco; in my opinion too weak and twaddlingly sentimental. The soldiers march on in twos and threes, taking very short steps, from lack of space. On the last note they make a right about turn. This looks rotten, owing to the unsoldierly bearing of our chorus, particularly when their bellies swing round at a right-angle on the right about turn. Pizarro – Demuth, very dignified. It is undoubtedly a calumny to say that the man has ever done anything to affront even the most middle-class morals. He is given a black instead of a red costume. After the arrest in the last scene he goes off with an air of injured innocence, slowly raising his cocked hat. The prisoners have been raised in number to forty and toned down in dress. The scene appeals as much as ever. The dungeon remains pretty much as before. Florestan – Schmedes. He sang the aria very beautifully at yesterday's full rehearsal. Mildenburg was to have been Leonore, but yesterday owing to ill-health she was represented by Weidt. I had to tone down the Fidelio-costume too, to suit the change of key in the whole production. – Weidemann not up to Mayr as the governor and more of a subordinate rôle for scenic reasons. But he sings: '. . . *Halt, – Euch edle Frau allein* . . .' with all his warmth and depth, quite affectingly. – The basket will be pulled out during the canon in Act I. But very slowly and on tiptoe to avoid causing a disturbance! – Weingartner is very sorry that the last scene is played in the courtyard again. But as he did not want any pause between Acts I and II (he has dropped that idea now), there was no helping it. The changing of the scene in Act II from the prison to the yard is done very easily during the overture. On the whole, a quite businesslike and, as it strikes me, a rather philistine production without any particular inspiration or go; it does not exactly ruin the opera but neither does it do anything to reveal its depths. Weingartner seems to have the orchestra well in hand. His conducting, certainly, seems to be rather pedestrian. I detect nothing of the bow of Ulysses. He has quite altered the seating of the orchestra. From tomorrow the instrumentalists all face the public and he himself stands right back against the balustrade of the stalls. In this way, you see nothing of the music-sheets, which is a gain; less so, to see the faces of the performers. He himself has the disagreeable habit of rising on his toes at *ff* passages. This is very painful. Perhaps he may refrain on the night of the performance.

Weingartner has taken sole charge of the production of *Fidelio*, and sensibly, I confess. Some things about it seem to me petty and after the manner of provincial theatres. I am not able to judge how much is to be traced to Stoll's influence. If ever I make any suggestion about questions of production which conflict with his own views, Weingartner always pays it attention and usually adopts it. But I don't say much. I do not want to come into competition with Stoll, whose behaviour disgusts me and who, led astray by Weingartner's amiability, positively plays the fool. But I think Weingartner has found him out by now, since he presides himself over the production meetings, at the very first of which (*Tiefland*)* Stoll showed himself up as a life-size idiot. – We shall not have such a pleasant time of it on the stage, as Weingartner has heightened the soffit (for the benefit of the gallery) by hoisting up the velvet hangings. So the company will enjoy a fine breeze from the soffit once more. There was a silly allusion to Weingartner, Blaas, and me in one of the newspapers the day before yesterday. Weingartner came up to me yesterday quite upset and assured me that it was not he – and not Blaas – and so forth. And when I only laughed outright at his earnestness, he went on to suggest that he and I should not in future pay the slightest attention to anything that might be written about our relations with each other. All very pleasant, frank and polite – not to say warm – but I cannot for the life of me imagine what is at the bottom of all his amiable and worthy demonstrations. The work goes on easily enough, but there is no joy in it after revelling, as I used, in working at full stretch.

Weingartner himself works at a speed he will not be able to keep up for long, and in spite of it does not get on very fast. – I had a talk with him the other day about *Les Troyens*,† which he means to do (but not till next year), and something he said gives me a clue to him, pending fuller knowledge. Meanwhile, I can't be sure whether it's my own stupidity, or – I don't know whether you have a very precise recollection of *Les Troyens*. In Part II, *Les Troyens à Carthage*, in the second act, there is a symphonic interlude, followed by a series of mimetic scenes on the stage: primeval forest near Carthage; bathing Naiads alarmed by the approach of the royal hunting party; a thunderstorm; huntsmen, on horse and foot, flee; rain and lightning; Dido and Aeneas take refuge in a grotto; torrents descend and veil the entrance. Nymphs and fauns next crowd the stage dancing wildly; a gigantic tree is struck by lightning, falls and catches fire; blazing fragments are scattered over the stage; the genii of the forest seize the burning brands and whirl them aloft, dancing more and more wildly. The whole scene is gradually

* Opera by Eugen d'Albert, performed at Vienna in 1908, after Mahler's departure. (D.M.)
† Opera by Berlioz. (D.M.)

enveloped in clouds of smoke. – I wanted to know what Weingartner
had to say about this scene; he said he took the whole thing to be a
dumb-show or masquerade got up by Dido in the forest for the
entertainment of her guest. I repeated my question twice or thrice,
thinking I must have misunderstood him. But – no, there was no
mistake, and I was left gaping in my first bewilderment. Can you beat
it?

Kaiser Karls Geisel has been put on in Berlin and – I believe – taken
off again. I went once, to see how they had staged it. Unfortunately, I
was unable to go to the rehearsals; there was too much to do here,
particularly over rehearsals for a Hassreiter ballet* (which fell through
after all). Brahm too was in Vienna and suggested my doing *Peer Gynt*
for him. – We are now involved in our 'homage to the Emperor'
celebrations: I have to help with the procession. My fellow-painters want
to have an exhibition in the spring. I am thoroughly sceptical and stand
aside from the whole affair. For society I confine myself to my wife (who
asks me to send her kindest regards). I am looking out for a studio and
mean to try to do some work. Burckhard pays us a visit now and then.
He looks worn out and aged. – Your dear Mama invited me to dinner
not long ago; she seemed to have quite recovered and to be thoroughly
pleased with her fine new house and in good spirits. Klimt and Hoffmann were the same as ever, or even in better form than has been usual
of late, owing perhaps to their exertions for the exhibition and the
unselfish hopes they have of it. – I saw a good deal of Gabrilovitch and
got on with him better and better. Otherwise, naturally enough, I see
scarcely any of your small circle and can't help thinking they must all
have crossed the ocean with you. The truth is that it was you who gave
me the key to them all; and now you have gone and taken the key with
you.

All my best and warmest wishes to you both —

Yours

ALFRED ROLLER

Vienna
10 [?] March 1908 143

My dear Director,

Your very welcome letter arrived yesterday, and I cabled to you today
to say that I was not coming to New York. In the light of what you tell
me, it would be no more than a pleasure-trip. Moreover, now that the
performance of the *Rote Gret*† has been postponed to April, I could not
arrive in time to return with you. I cannot imagine what is responsible

---

* Hassreiter was ballet-master at the Vienna Opera. (D.M.)
† Opera by Julius Bittner, the Austrian composer (1874–1939). (D.M.)

for the turn the affair has taken. You will have had my letter meanwhile (or was it two?), written since Mr. Cottenet's arrival in Vienna, and therewith the answers to most of your questions. I do not know whom he saw in Vienna. I don't think he saw much of anybody, as he and I were together on the afternoon of his arrival, in the evening he was at the Opera, and on the following afternoon he left for Paris. Maybe I made a bad impression on him. I can only speak English fluently on the most elementary topics, and of what he said I never understood more than a part, and sometimes nothing at all. It may also be that Dippel's more recent appearance in Vienna, of which I heard later, has something to do with it. I cannot tell you what it costs me to see this beautiful dream fade away. The summons to New York would have been particularly welcome now, when I feel that my position at the Opera is coming to an end. At the moment I am faced once more by an investigation into my conduct, which I was forced to demand myself, as the property-master put in a complaint of inhuman treatment at my hands and accuses me of a sadistic delight in torturing my subordinates, calling on Stoll, Bennier, all employees and 'others' as witnesses. I shall certainly not hunt up any witnesses in my defence, since I am the object of universal hatred, and the only person who understands what I do, and my motives in doing it, is yourself. So it may very well happen that the enquiry will go against me, and that I shall leave the Opera not of my own free will but on compulsion. I cannot now, needless to say, make any decisions until the investigation is concluded; whether, for example, to go back to the School, and still less whether to press for my contract with the Opera. But it seems evident that most of these worthy people are greatly disappointed that your departure did not bring mine with it; and now they try this way of getting rid of me. The only person whose friendliness has not changed since your departure and whose attitude is even cordial, is – Wondra. I cannot make head or tail of it. It is incredible even to me, who as you remember expected nothing else, how quick the disintegration has been, how quickly all whom I worked with tumbled to it that under Weingartner's just rule they might give free rein to their longings for emancipation, and that now was the time to throw off my galling yoke. To go back – there is one other besides Wondra who is friendly to me: Schalk! Repeatedly asks me to meals – I am almost bankrupt in excuses. What can that mean? Perhaps it is a consequence of a talk I had with Strauss about the possibility of my being called to Berlin (or rather the impossibility), which Schalk partly overheard. Weingartner is consistently very friendly, but nevertheless our relations remain obscure. I don't think he knows what to make of me or what use to put me to. That is how I explain his attitude, on the assumption that he is honest and not trying to make a fool of me. – I confess I see very little of him. We have had two old ballets dug up now. The Prince went out of his way to be affable to me at the dress-rehearsal. Next week there is to be a fresh study made of *Fra Diavolo*.*

Weingartner is taking the producer's rehearsals himself. Not very well, it seems to me. It's possible I don't understand. In any case, he does not impress the company; indeed he does not even interest them. After this, during the summer, *Meistersinger*, not *Siegfried*, is to be the task. It is one I have long wished for, and even now I take refuge in it from all these other vexations. I think I have now given you a clear enough picture of my prospects, and will add a few more details of my talk with Mr. Cottenet. It was very short. After he had broached the question I said: 'I know too little about the state of affairs in New York to be able to make any detailed reply. I can only say that I am ready to go to America on condition that only serious work is asked of me and that I have a position of complete independence in all matters of stage décor. I cannot say anything, even approximately, about the salary. I suggest that Herr Mahler might say something on this point, as he alone can properly speak for both sides. In any case, I count on something considerable. I should come over before the contract was concluded to see everything for myself on the spot.' He said I should have to be over there throughout the entire season; I should have to mount German opera in co-operation with you, and Italian in co-operation with Toscanini; further, he was raising the question merely for purposes of information and what he said was not binding. I noted this and expressed agreement. That was all. Later in the evening we talked only theatre and production in general. On parting he said 'au revoir', and thanked me for my company during the interval. I have told you already that when I asked him what Gatti-Casazza and Toscanini would have to say to my prospective engagement, he replied that they would welcome it gladly. The most likely explanation in my opinion is that the difficulties are made by Gatti-Casazza. A good deal, too, seems to have leaked out, probably via Milan; for I myself have maintained absolute silence. Spetrino at least has asked me twice already with a sly wink whether I had not another more important post in view. Winternitz also, partly because he was in Milan at the same time as Cottenet, where he was in touch with Casazza too, and partly because he has his spies everywhere, more especially in New York, is thoroughly well-informed about the whole project. I must add to the account of my talk with Cottenet that when he spoke of the vast resources deployed in New York I said: 'I have been hauled over the coals here for extravagance. Actually, however, I have not a great deal of money at my

* Opera by Auber. (D.M.)

disposal, and to spend little is not, in my opinion, always a saving. The point is to spend effectively; then money is well spent. Money spent to no effect is lost. It is the same with housekeeping.' That is what I said, or, rather, tried to say. Cottenet nodded his head and said Yes, yes; but whether he understood my broken English I really do not know. – I had been awaiting your letter of yesterday with eager suspense – but without any hopes. Your last telegram had told me already that it was all up. Pity. It would have been so easy to leave just at this time! I have seen little of Moll lately, as he has been suffering much from chills, and therefore I have heard little news of you and Frau Alma. I was all the more delighted to hear from you direct that she was in good health again, and I wish you the same with all my heart. My wife has got through the winter very well and asks me to give you her kind regards. I am rather weary myself, after nearly seven months on duty without a break, not to mention all these sickening vexations, which are, of course, depressing; physically, however, I am very well.

My best wishes to Frau Alma and affectionate salutations to you, my dear Director!

Always wholly yours,
ROLLER

MAHLER TO DIRECTOR DIPPEL*

[?] July 1908 144

Dear Director,

Allow me, in the first place, to reply to two points in your kind letter.

1. *Nozze di Figaro* on 19th December is not possible. I shall certainly keep my promise to be at the disposal of the theatre for rehearsals before the commencement of my engagement, in so far as this is practicable. I must, however, presumably devote the whole time that I reserve for this purpose, namely from 30th November to 17th December, to the piano rehearsals. As neither I, nor the personnel as an ensemble, will be continuously available, the number of rehearsals we can reckon on will, besides, be a limited one; and I shall have to rest content if rehearsal with piano, which with a whole cast is extremely difficult and tedious, can be got through before the commencement of my engagement. But then on top of that there would be the producer's rehearsals and the orchestra rehearsals, to which I must give quite as much time and care as Conried let me give last year to *Don Giovanni*.

2. It is inconceivable to me that a new production of *Tristan* should

* In answer to a long letter from the Director, Andreas Dippel, in which he made various proposals to Mahler, and in particular that Toscanini should conduct some performances of *Tristan* with the Milan *mise en scène* before Mahler's arrival. (A.M.)

be put on without my being consulted in any way, and I cannot give my consent. Further, I expressly stated when the contract was being discussed, *as you yourself can witness*, that I wished to keep in my hands for the ensuing season those works which I had already rehearsed and conducted in New York. I was given every assurance that this would be so, and it was only at your request and desire that I abstained from having it put in writing in the contract. If recently – out of consideration for the wishes of my colleague – I gave a free hand to the new Director, it was with the express exception of *Tristan*. – I took very special pains with *Tristan* last season and can well maintain that the form in which this work now appears in New York is my spiritual property. If Toscanini, for whom, though unknown to me, I have the greatest respect, and whom I consider it an honour to be able to salute as a colleague, were now to take over *Tristan* before my arrival, the work would obviously be given an entirely new character, and it would be quite out of the question for me to resume my performances in the course of the season. I must therefore urgently request that it shall be reserved for me to conduct and not be put in the reportory until after 17th December.*

I hasten to inform you by return of post of my attitude to this question and will reply to the rest of your letter in the course of a few days.

With all good wishes,

> Yours very sincerely,
> MAHLER

HANS PFITZNER TO MAHLER

> *23 St. Urban,*
> *Strasbourg*
> 18 August 1908   145

Dear and honoured friend!

As I may call you after your letter, which gave me quite unexpected pleasure. I would have replied at once, but that I could not say at once all that went through my head. I cannot any the more do so now, but I cannot bear to leave you any longer without an answer of some sort. I hope soon to make a better answer by word of mouth than I can on paper and so beg you to have patience. Lest you should be led by this to think I have something very definite in mind, I must explain that I, who am cursed with what (for me) is a fatal frankness, could not possibly lack frankness towards a person like you; and now after your letter I feel, as I never to the same extent felt before, the need to be completely honest with you, even at the risk of putting a distance between us just when you have begun to draw nearer. And naturally

* See note pp. 145-146. (D.M.)

you have the right to keep your intimacy for, or to accept the intimacy of, only those who unreservedly admire you as a composer. I have never yet been able to go into this thoroughly with you and it is not a question which can be disposed of by a yes or a no. All I mean is that supposing, after a thorough study of one of your works, I was unable to arrive at that attitude to your compositions which you seem to feel is essential to a really close personal intercourse, you must allow me on my side not to deceive you by taking shelter in evasions.

All that, of course, is self-evident, and you must please put it down to my clumsiness if I seem to labour the point; and do not take me up wrongly – I have so often got into hot water that I am always afraid lest any word I say outside the merest commonplaces may be made a rod to beat me with. But there is certainly no risk of that with you!

I have offered Rosé the first performance in public of a new piano quintet of mine, which I hope in due course to play with him myself. Please give my warmest regards to your dear wife, to whom I shall write soon. My heartiest greetings to you and my thanks for your friendship, which is an unqualified happiness to me.

HANS PFITZNER

OSCAR STRAUS* TO MAHLER

Helenenstrasse, 130,
Baden bei Wien
10 September 1908 146

My dear Director and Master,

On my return from Prague, where I spent such delightful and unforgettable hours in your company, I happened to be looking through my collection of scores and came on the piano score of Goetz's *The Shrew*, one of my favourite operas.† It is doubly dear to me since – I think it was about a year ago – hearing it given fresh life by your incomparable production. At that time and especially later, when Herr von Weingartner, 'the spirit who always denies' what you have affirmed, took the opera up again, there was much discussion about the cuts in the last act, which you had made, with, in my opinion, wholly beneficial effect, and which he restored, so that the opera ended with the redundant and weak ensemble. Now, the score I possess and bought years ago from a dealer in old music, contains to my delight and astonishment, besides the dedication to the conductor, Ernst Franck, clearly the opera's first conductor, various corrections and notes in Hermann Goetz's own hand. And it cannot fail to be of interest to you to see that the composer himself – clearly convinced of the weakness

---

* The well-known composer (1870–1954) of Viennese operettas. (D.M.)
† See also Letter 142. (D.M.)

and excessive length of the finale, indicated various cuts and the deletion of it altogether.

I feel impelled to send you this authentic document and it would give me inexpressible pleasure if you would accept this piano score as a mark of my unbounded esteem. I hope I can count on your acceptance and remain with my best wishes

Your devoted admirer

Oscar Straus

1909

*Toblach**

13 June 1909   147

Dearest Almschi!

So this is the first morning! With teeth chattering and knees knocking here I sit – the stove seems to have no resemblance to a stove – and there is no hope of that friendly warmth which by its excess invites one to discard coat and boots. The piano is installed in the hut – but so long as this grisly weather goes on I shall not venture downstairs. I tried to give Trenker the money yesterday, but he would not take it: it would be safer with me in the iron box† (which I had had taken straight up to me in this room).

If I only had a piano here I would warm myself up with music.

The enclosed letter will show you why I like to make peace now with my old companions. The joy and happiness that ensue may reflect their rays on us too – and will in fact. It gives me the deepest satisfaction to have cleared away the rubble between me and Lipiner – and 'to love as long as I still can love'.‡

A thousand thoughts —

Your

Gustav

Toblach

June 1909   148

My Almscherl!

That was a very dear letter from you today (and the second in one day, too). To gain a spiritual centre – that's the thing. From there, everything has another aspect. And it throws a light on your inner self

---

* We had rented a large farmhouse, of which the farmer and his family occupied the ground floor. (A.M.)

† There were always only MSS. in it. (A.M.)

‡ Allusion to old quarrels between Mahler and his early friends. (A.M.)

that you should have turned to Goethe. It shows that you reach up to the light, inwardly as well as outwardly. —

Your interpretation of the final stanza* is good; better, I am sure, than those offered by the learned commentators (whom, I confess, I have never read, but I know that this passage has kept them busy for the last hundred years). It is a peculiarity of the interpretation of works of art that the rational element in them (that is, what is soluble by reason) is almost never their true reality, but only a veil which hides their form. But in as far as a soul needs a body – which there is no disputing – an artist is bound to derive the means of creation from the rational world. Whenever he himself is not clear, or rather has not achieved wholeness within himself, the rational overcomes what is spontaneously artistic, and makes an undue claim on the attention. Now *Faust* is in fact a mixture of all this, and as its composition occupied the whole of a long life the stones of which it is built do not match, and have often been left simply as undressed stone. Hence, one has to approach the poem in various ways and from different sides. – But the chief thing is still the artistic conception, which no mere words can ever explain. Its truth shows a different face to each one of us – and a different one to each of us at different ages; just as Beethoven's symphonies are new and different at every hearing and never the same to one person as to another. If I am to try to tell you what my reason at its present stage has to say to these final verses – well, I'll try, but I don't know whether I shall succeed. I take those four lines, then, in the closest connection with the preceding ones – as a direct continuation, in one sense, of the lines they follow, and in another sense, as the peak of the whole tremendous pyramid, a world presented and fashioned step by step, in one situation and development after another. All point, at first dimly and then from scene to scene (particularly in the Second Part, where the poet's own powers have matured to match his task) with growing mastery, to this supreme moment, which though beyond expression, scarcely even to be surmised, touches the very heart of feeling.

It is all an allegory to convey something which, whatever form it is given, can never be adequately expressed. Only the transitory lends itself to description; but what we feel, surmise but will never reach (or know here as an actual happening), the intransitory behind all appearance, is indescribable. That which draws us by its mystic force, what every created thing, perhaps even the very stones, feels with absolute

* Alles Vergängliche ist nur ein Gleichnis;
  Das Unzulängliche, hier wird's Ereignis;
  Das Unbeschreibliche, hier ist's getan;
  Das Ewig-Weibliche zieht uns hinan.

From Goethe's *Faust*, the text which Mahler used for Part Two of his Eighth Symphony (the *Chorus Mysticus*). (D.M.)

certainty as the centre of its being, what Goethe here – again employing an image – calls the eternal feminine – that is to say, the resting-place, the goal, in opposition to the striving and struggling towards the goal (the eternal masculine) – you are quite right in calling the force of love. There are infinite representations and names for it. (You have only to think of how a child, an animal, or persons of a lower or higher development live their lives.) Goethe himself reveals it stage by stage, on and on, in image after image, more and more clearly as he draws nearer the end: in Faust's impassioned search for Helen, in the Walpurgis night, in the still inchoate Homunculus, through the manifold entelechies of lower and higher degree; he presents and expresses it with a growing clearness and certainty right on to the *mater gloriosa* – the personification of the eternal feminine!

And so in immediate relation to the final scene Goethe in person addresses his listeners. He says:

'All that is transitory (what I have presented to you here these two evenings) is nothing but images, inadequate, naturally, in their earthly manifestation; but there, freed from the body of earthly inadequacy, they will be actual, and we shall then need no paraphrase, no similitudes or images for them; there is done what here is in vain described, for it is indescribable. And what is it? Again I can only reply in imagery and say: The eternal feminine has drawn us on – we have arrived – we are at rest – we possess what on earth we could only strive and struggle for. Christians call this "eternal blessedness", and I cannot do better than employ this beautiful and sufficient mythology – the most complete conception to which at this epoch of humanity it is possible to attain.'

I hope I have expressed myself clearly. There is always the danger of an exuberance of words in such infinitely delicate and, as I said above, un-rational matters. That is why all commentary is so disgusting. No more for today.

A thousand greetings from

Your
GUSTAV

Toblach
24 June 1909 149
Thursday

My dearest Almschi,

*   *   *

But the house and the whole place are too delicious – except for the noise, which is a ceaseless torment. The farm people either whisper so that the windows rattle or go on tiptoe so that the house rocks. The two merry scions of the house twitter all day long: Bibi! Bibi! (this is their esperanto and means: everything). The dog reminds me too that I am but 'a man among men', and barks all day from peep of dawn and right on until its masters are sweetly dreaming. I wake every quarter of an hour, to rue the snore however gentle. – The devil take it – what a beautiful world it would be if one had two yokes of land fenced about, and were all alone in the middle.

Every time I come back from a walk I think that you and Guckerl must be coming to meet me. It is good, very good, to be alone all day; but in the afternoon, from tea-time onwards, I miss you dreadfully.

A thousand greetings, my Almschili,

Your
GUSTAV

Toblach
27 June 1909 150

My Almscherl!

Your letter yesterday did not come until the afternoon (I go for the second post myself) and I was very anxious by that time.

Your moods (induced this time by a dream) are very understandable to me, for I myself go through the same thing a thousand times over; this may surprise you, but it may at the same time be a consolation and even make it easier to understand yourself. Man – and probably all forms of life – are unceasingly productive. This occurs inevitably at all stages as a consequence of life itself. When the energy of production fails, then the entelechy dies; that is, it must acquire a new body. At the stage where men of a higher development are found, production (which is natural to the majority in the form of reproduction) is accompanied by an act of self-realization; and hence its creativeness is heightened on the one hand, and on the other is manifested as a challenge to the moral being. This then is where we find the source of all the restlessness of such men. In between the brief moments in the life of the man of genius when these challenges are answered, there are the long barren stretches of existence which wring the soul with unanswerable longings. And it is just this ceaseless struggle and its torments that give the life of these few its character. – Now perhaps you will guess, or know, what I think of the 'works' of this person or that. They are, properly speaking, the ephemeral and mortal part of him; but what a man makes of himself – what he becomes through the untiring effort to live and to be, is permanent. This is the meaning, my dear Almschi, of all that has happened to you, of all that has been laid on you, as a necessity of the growth of the soul and the forging of the

personality. And you still have a long life before you. Persist in exerting
this inner force (as indeed you do); claim as your very own your utmost
of beauty and power (more than this none of us can do – and only
the elect in any case); 'spread yourself abroad'; exercise yourself in
beauty, in goodness; grow unceasingly (that is the true productiveness),
and be assured of what I always preach: what we leave behind us is
only the husk, the shell. The *Meistersinger*, the Ninth, *Faust* – all of them
are only the discarded husk! No more, properly speaking, than our
bodies are! I don't of course mean that artistic creation is superfluous.
It is a necessity of man for growth and *joy*, which again is a question
of health and creative energy. – But what actual need is there of notes?
How often I see you in that joyful mood I know so well, when you
have 'opened out'.

I still haven't ventured down into the hut. It is always such an
upheaval to move in that I can't face it.

A thousand greetings, my Almschi.

GUSTAV

Tell me more of Gucki soon.

(ADDRESSED TO THE SANATORIUM LUITHLEN) *Göding*
18 September 1909 151

My dearest Almscherl,
You have behaved splendidly. I have heard all about it: 24 incisions
and without an anaesthetic.* I'm delighted for you both; and convinced that it will be of life-long *benefit*. But I was very anxious. Particularly as I had to wait from four till half-past five for the news by
telephone. I had decided to pack (with my well-known virtuosity) and
come to the sanatorium. Now keep well for Monday too. I think of
coming to Vienna on Wednesday and lunching with you both. Meanwhile, I have settled in here very comfortably. But drives are no fun
without you. – The rooms and life in general are very comfortable.
But noise from the factory and the railway all day and all night.
But this – without the factory and railway – is just what I'd like for
us, a comfortable house, a large garden and orchard, and flowers and
vegetables.

Carl says he will go on hunting until he has found us what we want
near Vienna.

All my thoughts, my brave Almscherl – and is Gucki really so delighted by a barrel-organ?!

Your
GUSTAV

* Cauterization of the tonsils. (A.M.) See p. 154. (D.M.)

with friends at Göding
19 September 1909 152

My Almschi!

I wrote yesterday. But hear from my talk on the telephone that you have not had the letter yet. I hope you have had it by now. I have spent an anxious day in spite of all. I feel marvellous here! To be able to sit working by the open window, and breathing the air, the trees and flowers all the time – this is a delight I have never known till now. I see now how perverse my life in summer has always been. On the other hand, I have avoided the truly murderous, infernal noise, which never ceases here day or night. But a place like this I must have. Carl says he won't rest until he has found it for us. All told, staying here suits me remarkably well. I feel myself getting better every minute. It's no good – human nature must have sun and warmth – I shudder now when I think of my various workshops; although I have spent the happiest hours of my life in them, it has probably been at the price of my health.

We go for two drives a day here. It is my greatest sorrow that you are not with us. The plain is so marvellous – we must have something like it – only without noise.

I hope to surprise you on the Hohe Warte on Wednesday. All my thoughts, my dear! It's wonderful you're so brave (but only what I expected).

Your

GUSTAV

ENGELBERT HUMPERDINCK TO MAHLER

Whitsun
30 May 1909 153

Confidential!
Honoured Master!

Your brother-in-law has kindly given me your present address, and I hasten to lay the following before you.

You have doubtless already learned from the newspapers of the proposal to establish a *second opera house* in Berlin in response to a long-felt need of the capital of the Empire. With this object a committee was formed a few months ago to organize the undertaking, and with it is associated a company which has raised the capital required. The purchase of a large site on the Friedrichstrasse is in contemplation, and here a building is to be erected as far as possible after the pattern of Bayreuth; negotiations have been initiated which will enable Wagner's works to be performed even before the expiry of the embargo. The building, which will be begun in October, ought to be so far advanced in eighteen months that the opening could take place in the spring of 1911.

We still, however, lack what is more important than all else: the future Director of our Richard Wagner Theatre, who must be not only a man of proved attainments and firm will, but above all a great artist; and, in short, combine all those qualities which are summed up in the name Mahler, a guarantee in itself of an artistic programme unsurpassable in its range and excellence. And as the bearer of this name is at the present time within reach, I venture, my dear Master, to ask whether you would be disposed to answer our call and to take this great work in hand. The position of general director which we have in mind would naturally in your case be furnished with the most far-reaching powers – similar to those you had at your command in Vienna. I can therefore well believe that the task of giving life to a new and unique enterprise would perhaps have a charm for you.

I scarcely need say how delighted I should be personally to know that you were at the head of it. As soon as we hear that you are not in principle disinclined to consider the proposal, our managing director, Herr Delmar, will get into touch with you personally and in due course travel to Vienna, in order to arrange all business matters with you. Meanwhile I await an early and, I hope, a favourable reply and remain, with the assurance of my lasting esteem, yours most sincerely,

E. HUMPERDINCK

I may of course rely on your kind discretion for the time being.

SCHOENBERG TO MAHLER

29 December 1909 154

My dear Director.

So many things got in the way that I was quite unable to find time to write to you immediately after the Seventh.* In earlier days I should have been in haste to say something at once while the feelings it aroused were still warm and at the full. Perhaps I feared lest the impression might fade. And in fact, I must confess it did not on previous occasions last long. But this time (and that is the main point) I knew I might wait as long as I liked: the impressions made on me by the Seventh, and before that, by the Third, are permanent. I am now really and entirely yours. I know that for a certainty. For I had less than before the feeling of that sensational intensity which excites and lashes one on, which in a word moves the listener in such a way as to make him lose his balance without giving him anything in its place. On the contrary, I had the impression of perfect repose based on artistic harmony; of something

* Presumably Schoenberg had heard the Vienna first performance of the Seventh, conducted by Ferdinand Löwe (1865–1925). (D.M.)

that set me in motion without simply upsetting my centre of gravity and leaving me to my fate; that drew me calmly and pleasingly into its orbit – as though by that force of attraction which guides the planets in their courses, which leaves them to go their own way, influencing them, certainly, but in a manner so measured and preordained that there are never any sudden jolts.

This may sound a little bombastic perhaps. Nevertheless, it seems to me to express one thing which I supremely felt: I have put you with the classical composers. But as one who to me is still a *pioneer*. I mean, there is surely a difference in being spared all extraneous excitement, being at rest and in tranquility, in the state in which beauty is enjoyed. And before it used to be quite otherwise with me; I know this for certain, even if I cannot now express the difference clearly. There used to be, as it were, moments of artistic conflict; personal feelings; extraneous matter; details of artistry; problems of orchestration. Of all that there was this time not a trace.

I had not much time to look through the score beforehand, and was only slightly acquainted with it. My request for the permission of the Konzertverein to attend the final rehearsal received no reply, although there were critics present.

And so I had this strong and perfectly clear impression from what was almost a first hearing and without any previous study of the work.

I cannot say whether the performance was good or not. On the whole I believe it was not bad, in so far as Löwe clearly took the trouble to reproduce with accuracy the directions in the score. Further than this I cannot say he went; I often thought I detected that this or that ought to have gone otherwise – but I mean, it was not bad for Löwe, and it is hard to see why he should understand this work in particular when he has been conducting for so many years without understanding any work whatever.

Which movement did I like the best? Each one! I can make no distinction. Perhaps I was somewhat hesitant at the beginning of the first movement. But in any case only for a short time. And from then onwards I grew warmer and warmer. From one minute to the next I felt better and better. And there was not a moment's relapse. I was in tune to the very end. And it was all so transparently clear to me. In short, at a first hearing I felt so many subtleties of form, and yet could follow a main line throughout. It gave me extraordinary pleasure. I simply cannot understand why I was so unresponsive before.

I should very much like to hear how you are and what you are doing over there. I did not of course believe the story of the opera *Theseus*, and at once imagined to myself the joke to which it was to be traced. Of course everyone in Vienna took it in good faith. Nobody thought to

himself: 'What does that mean – Theseus?' All I know of him myself
is his temple. He occupies no other niche in my consciousness, since I
have long ago shed whatever I gathered from history lessons. How
came it that he of all people should be your vehicle, your means of
expression? Nobody hit on the clue: Weingartner – *Orestes*;* Strauss –
Elektra; therefore: Mahler – *Theseus*. Greek too. It was left for me to see
that it was a parodistical reply of yours to some egregious interrogator,
asking: 'But how is it, Director, that you have never yet written anything for the operatic stage, when you are . . .' I should be very proud if
my guess turned out to be correct.

Of myself I can only report that there is little to be said. I have signed
an agreement with Universal Edition in terms very favourable – to
Universal Edition.

The Ansorge-Society is devoting an evening to me on 14th January:
the *Gurrelieder*, with piano; a song-cycle after Stefan George; three new
piano pieces [Op. 11]. My monodrama is to be performed in Mannheim.†

And in Paris my second quartet. If it ever comes off?!? Perhaps one
day you will send me a picture postcard with a small (very small)
picture and plenty of room for the text. With cordial greetings –

ARNOLD SCHOENBERG

And now to your wife

Dear lady,

You promised me news from New York. . . ! I have not had any.
Perhaps because I didn't write? But I did write! After the Third! Or
perhaps because I don't write about myself? But that is of no interest to
you. And, although I talk about *myself* a great deal, since I cannot write
at such length about myself, then better nothing at all. With me, it's all
or nothing. There would be no end. And you must not take it amiss
that I have not written to you – to make up for that, I have often
thought of you, and that at least has more, and better, style than it
would have in writing. And is also more legible.

And I don't get writer's cramp, or you yawner's cramp from boredom.

And I must not insult myself by the mere suspicion that anyone can
find me boring.

And so: on these four points I can take my oath.

But, now, I heard the last time I was with you in Döbling, that you

* An operatic trilogy by Weingartner. (D.M.)
† This performance of *Erwartung* did not take place. The first performance was
given in Prague in 1924. (D.M.)

thought of remaining in Vienna. Is it true? Is that still your plan? And how far has it gone? It would be wonderful.

How is the little girl? And you yourself? Perhaps after all you may write and tell me all your news. I would love to know too whether you and your husband have read my article in the *Merker*. Did you like it?

My wife wishes to be remembered to you very warmly, as I do too.

Yours very sincerely,
ARNOLD SCHOENBERG

1910

From Vienna to Tobelbad
8 June 1910 155

My dearest Almschili!

When I told you the last morning at Tobelbad how nice you looked, it was the expression of a spontaneous delight as I saw you coming to meet me and looking so sweet and charming. But you know me by this time. In art as in life I am at the mercy of spontaneity. If I had to compose, not a note would come. Four years ago, on the first day of the holidays, I went up to the hut at Maiernigg with the firm resolution of idling the holiday away (I needed to so much that year) and recruiting my strength. On the threshold of my old workshop the *Spiritus Creator* took hold of me and shook me and drove me on for the next eight weeks until my greatest work was done.* – One summer before that I made up my mind to finish the Seventh, both Andantes of which were there on my table. I plagued myself for two weeks until I sank into gloom, as you well remember; then I tore off to the Dolomites. There I was led the same dance, and at last gave it up and returned home, convinced that the whole summer was lost. You were not at Krumpendorf to meet me, because I had not let you know the time of my arrival. I got into the boat to be rowed across. At the first stroke of the oars the theme (or rather the rhythm and character) of the introduction to the first movement came into my head – and in four weeks the first, third and fifth movements were done. Do you remember? You see, my love, you know enough of me and my ways not to be wounded by me. And particularly when you can see for yourself that I live only for you and Gucki, and that nothing can ever come between you and my love. Everything else is so insipid – a bad wood-cut next to a Titian. Only get really well, my Luxerl, so that you can be at my side and

* Mahler refers to his Eighth Symphony. (D.M.)

we can enjoy life together again as good comrades. Living and loving are as the flowers of a tree which grows higher of itself, or often spreads abroad; flowers, or fruit that falls in winter – you have only to wait for the spring in the full assurance that they will bud again.

I have to go to Leipzig on Friday night (rehearsal Saturday), so cannot unfortunately pay you a visit. It would be too great a rush for one day or one night. But I come to the end in Munich on June 2nd.* A word from you and I'll come to you via Vienna, and then we can all live as we please for a time. Or else I'll go straight to Innsbruck and on to Toblach, where I'll have a little rest and fresh air after the exhausting rehearsals, and then come and fetch you. It's just as you find best for your cure. But once more: *I beg you, take this to heart* – get well, do everything for that.

Now a brief account of these last days. Rehearsal on Monday evening where the worthlessness of the Vienna Men's Choral Society (it simply didn't turn up and rehearsed at first with fourteen absentees) was obvious and so was Schalk's incompetence (he took the rehearsal at first and mistook all the tempi, as I was so angry that I refused to co-operate). Later more of them turned up and I came out of my corner like a sulky boy and took up the baton. It went better at once, but it was clear that the gentlemen had not mastered their parts. And so it still seems to me doubtful whether it will come to a performance, as I am absolutely determined *not* to put up with artistic sloppiness. The ladies, anyway, are fine and make up for the vileness of the men. Next day the W.'s called for us with their car and we drove to Pöchlarn in three hours, where there was a castle to be seen! Glorious situation but utterly desolate, and gnats!

Then we drove through the Wachau and along the Danube through avenues of trees, as though in a park, and back to Dürnstein and Weissenkirchen and on to Mautern. All delightful spots and quite unspoilt. From there we turned right and past Göttweig through hilly country of woods and meadows and came quite unexpectedly into the Neulengbach region and suddenly close past Plankenberg† in its lovely situation and where I thought of you so hard that your ears must have burned. – The whole way Carl and I were almost in tears (once I even fell asleep – but that was only because of Frau W. next to whom I was sitting) because you and Mama were not with us. But I have made up my mind: in September, when things are better, I'm going to do the whole trip again with you in an automobile.

* Widespread rehearsals were beginning now for the première of the Eighth Symphony in September, with its vast choral and orchestral forces. (D.M.)
† The castle where I spent my childhood. (A.M.)

Now goodbye, my dear, and write me a really jolly letter, otherwise I shall set off on my travels with a heavy heart.

A thousand kisses from

Your

GUSTL

Munich
June 1910 156

My Almschl,

Just so that you have something by post. Because it is really too stupid what this copyist (who at first sight made such an unpleasant impression on me) has done to me. This swine, to save himself trouble, has simply written *tacet* in all the parts where a number of pauses occur, instead of writing the pauses out in full. Now, as a result of this, not only does the orchestra not know where it is while playing, but I, poor devil, cannot when revising simply write in the bars in question without more ado, but must fill out the *tacet*, and even erase several lines, in order to make room. This means the loss of many, many hours. You may well say: 'Vienna' (as others might say 'Jew') but don't forget that in Vienna I have the best and most reliable of copyists (Forstik), who in future must do *all* my copying. It was very nice in Leipzig. The whole chorus (250) were punctually awaiting me at 8 sharp and stood up respectfully like a school when I came in. They knew their stuff perfectly and were gloriously enthusiastic without the least humbug – and stood in the street afterwards to give me a cheer. The conductor there, Dr. Göhler, a noted and furious opponent of Strauss and admirer of mine, is competent and conscientious. Senius (Dr. Marianus) was there too and sings splendidly. You will enjoy it. The orchestra is very good and in full strength and attentive. Gutmann does his job splendidly and deserves the most flattering attention in future. But I'm beginning to feel quite done up.

All my thoughts, my Almscherl!

Your

GUSTAV

Munich
June 157

My Almschi!

It worries me today to have no letter from you after your so sad one of yesterday. Are you hiding something? For I feel there must be something to be read between the lines.

Full rehearsal today – Part Two. There, too, God (Mahler) saw that it was good!

The soloists arrive tomorrow; Sunday, God willing, I shall be at Toblach, unless you perhaps decide that I shall come straight to Tobelbad. In which case, please telegraph. – But if you agree, please give the necessary orders at once so that I shall find all I need at Toblach. – If necessary, send me the keys required. I want to be able to get at the books there, and clothes too in the long run. Also tell them to get in fresh, good butter, on which I chiefly live. I've already arranged for everything else, from Vienna. I've still a lot to get through here this week. People are collecting in herds: Rosé with his quartet, R. Strauss with the Philharmonic, critics from every nation, etc. etc! Lord, what visitations threaten me! But I will put a good face on the awful business. But one thing I will do from today on: have my meals in my room. I must have rest and seclusion to get me through these exertions. You are always in my thoughts, my Almscherl; write every day, do, if only a p.c.

Your

GUSTAV

Munich
June 15 8

I send you my love, Almscherl, between two rehearsals (this is a trying day). Today was the first with orchestra and singers. It was staggering – the effect their quite inadequate numbers made. The orchestra literally raved at the end of the rehearsal.

Imagine it, Fried and Klemperer came to meet me as I entered the hall. That was pretty smart of them. On the other hand, on returning to the hotel I find Arnold's card. (He [Rosé] could surely have found out where the rehearsal was taking place.) Now I am going to have my meal in my room, as usual, and have asked Fried to join me. We start up again at six o'clock and tomorrow morning the children join in. God willing, I leave on Sunday morning for Toblach, where I shall arrive at about four. – I promise faithfully not to touch a note there, but to do nothing but eat, walk and above all *sleep*, a thing impossible to think of in Munich for the mere hooting of cars.

The publisher (Hertzka) is here too and as happy as a snow-king. But it does really sound overwhelming. . . .

Greetings, my Almschili,

Your

GUSTAV

Munich
June 159

My Almscherl,

You have hit on the salient point in Plato sure enough. In the discourses of Socrates, Plato gives his own philosophy, which, as the misunderstood 'Platonic love', has influenced thought right down the centuries to the present day. The essence of it is really Goethe's idea that all love is generative, creative, and that there is a physical and spiritual generation which is the emanation of this 'Eros'. You have it in the last scene of *Faust*, presented symbolically. What strikes one first in the *Symposium* is its imaginative force and the dramatic fire of the 'story'. When I read it as a boy, I remember being delighted most of all by the sudden irruption of Alcibiades, crowned with vine-leaves and pulsing with young blood – and then, in delightful contrast as a dying echo of it all, by the way Socrates, the only one of the company who has not fallen into a drunken sleep, gets up thoughtfully and goes out on to the market place to philosophize. It is only when youth is past that one arrives at a pleasure in the various themes, and finally at the discovery that it all draws to a head, by cunningly contrived gradations, in the wonderful discussion between Diotima and Socrates, which gives the core of Plato's thought, his whole outlook on the world. In all Plato's writings Socrates is the cask into which he pours his wine. What a man must Socrates have been to have left such a pupil with such an imperishable memory and love! The comparison between him and Christ is an obvious one and has arisen spontaneously in all ages. – The contrasts are due to their respective times and circumstances. There, you have the light of the highest culture, young men, and a 'reporter' of the highest intellectual attainments; here, the darkness of a childish and ingenuous age, and children as the vessels for the most wonderful practical wisdom, which is the product of moral personality, of a direct and intensive contemplation and grasp of facts. In each case, Eros as Creator of the world! No more for today, my dear, except my love – and do write!

Your

GUSTAV

Innsbruck
25 August 1910 160

Telegram

All good and evil powers accompany me; you sit throned in triumph. Goodnight, my lyre, I feel only joy and longing.*

---

* At this time Mahler addressed to his wife many intimate, lyrical affirmations of his love for her, some in verse. These highly personal documents are well-nigh impossible to translate effectively and we have contented ourselves here with including only a sample few from the large number that appear in the German edition. (D.M.)

Cologne

26 August 1910 161

Telegram

Still bearing up well, really normal. Drive sadly along Rhine and seek vanished happiness. Every moment spent with you here lives again. Last two words of your telegram open up new worlds.

Your

GUSTAV

Cologne

27 August 1910 162

Telegram

Changed trains here. Strolled two hours. Revisited all the places. Just as if it were yesterday. 'Is to me as though it could not be.' I live everything afresh. Hope to find a precious word early tomorrow.

Your

GUSTAV

Toblach

[On my bedside table in the morning]

163

My Almschilitzili, do stay in bed today. That will be the best rest for you. I'll stay with you and not go out all day. I'll look out something to read too.

My Almschilitzililitzililitzili! Remember what you said to me yesterday and say it again today!

Toblach

[On my bedside table in the morning]

164

My darling,

my lyre,

Come and exorcize the spirits of darkness, they claw hold of me, they throw me to the ground. Don't leave me, my staff, come soon today* so that I can rise up. I lie there and wait and ask in the silence of my heart whether I can still be saved or whether I am damned.

[On my desk at night]

165

Beloved,

I have had a wonderful sleep and yet my feelings were not for a moment interrupted. And I believe there can never now be a moment

* I always went to his hut at midday to bring him in to lunch. (A.M.)

when I do not feel the happiness of knowing: she loves me! That is the whole meaning of my life. When I cannot say that, I am dead! – When I come up here today, you are not there – how I long to see you and hold you in my arms, you dear and tenderly beloved! – Your dear songs, heralds of a godlike existence, shall be my stars until the sun of my life rises in my firmament!

> *Holdeste! Liebste!*
> *Mein Saitenspiel!*
> *Und mein Sturmlied!*
> *Du Herrliche! O könnt' ich Töne finden —*
> *mein stammelnd Seufzen Dir in Worte künden!*
> *Mein Athem ist – mein Wesen nicht mehr meins!*
> *Nicht ich mehr, ich bin von mir selbst geschieden*
> *– nicht eher kann mich Himmelsruh befrieden,*
> *als bis ich trunken Deines süßen Weins!*
>
> *Der Lenz hat mich und Dich zu sich bezwungen,*
> *Ich gab mich gleich, nicht hab ich erst gerungen.*
> *Ich starb – wie gern – und süß küßt er mich wach!*
> *Die Töne brausen – wüthen mir im Herzen —*
> *die heißen Worte flammen – Hochzeitskerzen —*
> *es strömt mein Wesen Dir in's Brautgemach!*

Munich
4 September 1910 166

So, my dearest Almscherl, the trivialities (sleeping, breakfasting, etc.) are over and now for the joy of finding words for the thoughts which circle continually about my dear one's fair head. – But not to be simply a schoolboy in love I will give myself a shaking and tell things in order. For that, my darling, is what I always ask of you, to give me a proper account of your days. Every scrap interests me. – Well then, the journey from the moment when I handed in my express letter and telegram at Innsbruck was very tedious. Till then like a capercailzie in love I had heard nothing and seen nothing. – Later I observed that I had been sitting stockstill in the train and began to warm myself up. – I was met by Gutmann here, most helpful and kind. He told me that the first concert was certainly sold out. I found the piano reduction* waiting for me with the dedication, and hope Hertzka had the sense to send one to Toblach too. It gave me a peculiar and exciting feeling to see the sweet, beloved name on the title-page for all the world to read as a joyful acknowledgement.† Oh, what joy to engrave it in all my piano

* Of the Eighth Symphony. (D.M.)
† See pp. 178–179. Mahler had dedicated the Eighth to his wife. (D.M.)

scores. But that would be calf-love once more. And I want it taken seriously, as a token meaning far more to me than a lover's extravagance. Does it not make the impression rather of a betrothal? Doesn't it seem more like the announcement of an engagement? Did not sleep very well, sorry to say – only four hours at most – and thought every minute of the fragrant bed, and missed the quiet breathing of my darling, which like a trustworthy clock enlivened the nights for me. I even heard you calling out 'Gustav' and would so gladly have jumped up. Today I have a sore throat and a slight inflammation, but will be careful, so as to be in good health to receive my saint. Almschili, all this seems so superfluous. Three words would be enough, the three words I'd like always to write and say and sing to you. My darling, if only for half an hour every Sunday afternoon you had the feeling of mingled bliss and sadness which keeps me sighing every hour of the day and night!

I have made a strange discovery, moreover. You know, it was with just the same longing that I have always sat down straightaway at the writing-table whenever I was away from you, and thought only of you. This propensity has always been latent in me. Freud is quite right* – you were always for me the light and the central point! The inner light, I mean, which rose over all; and the blissful consciousness of this – now unshadowed and unconfined – raises all my feelings to the infinite. But what torment and what pain that you can no longer respond. But as surely as love must wake to love, and faith find faith again, and so long as Eros is the ruler of men and gods, so surely will I make a fresh conquest of all, of the heart which once was mine and can only in unison with mine find its way to God and blessedness. —

Dearest – I was interrupted five minutes ago – Fried came in and is sitting here again now. But I was very good to him; don't worry. He means it so well and he'll be a great help to me at the rehearsal. The express letter from Carl has just arrived too. So my Almschili need have no worry. Like Endymion and others of the great age of love I shall stride along to the station even, and certainly to the restaurants and other resorts of pleasure. And no 'tragic catastrophes' shall any longer exact a 'manly bearing', or even a 'philosophic calm'. – And now here is Gutmann and the escort – the room is full of people.

Farewell, breath of my life – if they only knew how little all this means to me!

My love to Mama —

Your

GUSTAV

* See p. 175. (D.M.)

Munich
1910 167

But Almschilitzilitzilitzili!

How did you read the 'ominous' telegram then? Didn't you see at
once it was a joke? I couldn't mean such absurd bombast to be taken
seriously! You ought to have cut that inflated balloon adrift at once!
But now for yesterday – I must tell you that the feverish feeling I had on
arrival at the hotel increased yesterday morning (while I was writing to
you) so noticeably that I lay down at once on my bed in alarm and had a
doctor sent for (all because of next week). He examined me and found
white fur on the right side (septic) with acute inflammation of the whole
throat. –It gave me a horrible fright and I insisted at once on being
wrapped up and sweated. (He would not paint the throat but gave me
a wonderful antiseptic, which would be splendid for you too – a half
lozenge every half hour, a drug that has only been available in Germany
for the past year.) First of all, I had to put the whole hotel in a turmoil
to get the necessary blankets, etc. Meanwhile I had Gutmann in and
appointed him bath-man. I lay motionless for three hours sweating
profusely. Gutmann had to wipe my face and eyes with a towel every
now and then. Oh, how I fretted for a sign of life from my saint! But
nothing came – and at last your telegram of 'bewilderment', which
plunged me in despair at having innocently given my Almschili a bad
moment. – The second came only in the afternoon, but even then I was
none the wiser as to how my dear one was.

Gutmann was called away on business, and so I spent the afternoon
most wretchedly, alone with my very melancholy thoughts. The doctor
returned in the evening and found a slight improvement. The night
passed quietly – today I awoke with my temperature normal and a good
appetite. The doctor came, found me a great deal better and gave his
consent to the rehearsal. – My Almscherl, you need not be anxious; I
shall behave like an angel and be perfectly well when you come. But –
no sign from you – the suspense is awful – it simply is not a life when I
don't see your sweet eyes and hear your dear voice. – And you simply
don't need me, or you would have had to write to me. After all, a
message written out by some Mademoiselle of the telegraph office isn't
the same as your own living hand.

It was a joy when I woke early today (4.30) and the very first thing I
saw was the gleam of your dear little ring – I kissed it, and it was my joy
and consolation, as it has been all through these lonely days. You know,
it wouldn't give me any pleasure if you had given it me – but to wear
now and then what you have worn on your finger means such a lot to
me! Almschili, have you got over the disaster in the station yet?

Gutmann comes for me at 10: I want to hear the final rehearsal of the

Ninth.* Perhaps I may not go to the concert in the evening but go to bed at nine. Rehearsals start tomorrow. If only I had some news of you! All the love of my heart, you dear one. I hang on the hope of a dear word from my beloved.

Your

GUSTAV

Look at the enclosed! Isn't it kind of them to build the new street for us?

Munich
1910 168

My beloved, madly beloved Almschili!

Believe me, I am sick with love! Since Saturday at 1 o'clock, I live no longer! Thank God – I've just got your two dear letters. Now I can breathe again. For half an hour I was in bliss. But now I can bear up no longer. I'm a dead man if you stay away for another whole week. How dear were those delightful letters! They said something you had never said before. Oh, say it often so that I may always believe it afresh. — The first rehearsal today. Went quite well and my physique held out quite gallantly. With every beat, I looked round and thought how lovely it would be if my divinity were seated down there and I could brush her dear face with a stolen glance – then I'd know what I was alive for and why I was doing it all. The enclosed letter came just now and I send it for its oddity. What rascals they are! Do they think I have nothing to do but answer their questions? These notes come every minute and go straight into the wastepaper basket. What is the fool up to in Munich so early?

Yesterday afternoon, before I went to have a Turkish bath, Hirth came in. The poor devil looks very old and wizened. He seems to have given up his youthful pose, and he sat down so wearily that I was quite horrified. I made some observation about a dangerous infection, whereupon he went even paler and soon vanished. So I was left in peace again to think of the light of my life. – That is what I need nowadays. – When *she* is not there, I must at least be able to think of her or write to her. Almschili, if you had left me that time, I should simply have gone out like a torch deprived of air. When are you coming then – my heart? And how are you all getting on? Please, do always tell me something about that. You see, schoolboy in love though I am, there is still something left in me of the father of a family, or husband, or whatever you call the thing, and it wants to know how my dearest and my dears are getting on day by day. The most important part comes first

* Beethoven's Ninth. (D.M.)

and the three first sides keep to this – that you love me, my tenderly beloved. But on the fourth side I want you to tell me what you've been doing and how you are. I have the second rehearsal at 4. How I long, long, long!

Ever your

GUSTAV

169

My beloved!

Here I sit once more! The afternoon rehearsal is over – final scene – every note addressed to you! I was so madly excited, just as though I were sitting by your bed again, as it used to be in those old, delightful days, 'telling you all about it'! – Oh, how lovely it is to love! And only now do I know what it is! Pain has lost its power and death its thorn. Tristan speaks truth: I am immortal, for how could Tristan's love die? Now I am spending a quiet evening again – I am almost well again now. I ate with appetite and mean to be in perfect health when my treasure comes.

I think of the moment all the time: 'Is it true? Are you mine once more? Can I grasp it? At last! At last!' If I only knew when you were coming! Tomorrow is Tuesday, isn't that when you meant to come?

I've just had a card from Gustav Frank today, saying he's here and wants to see me. Do write a word to say whether you would like me to sleep in another room and you have Gucki with you, or what. Because I'd like to have our nest in order before you arrive.

Our rooms are very nice and unbelievably quiet. It's the first time in Munich I've known peace at night. The windows actually give on to a courtyard. But, to please you, Almschi, my love, I've taken a small reception room opposite, facing the street, where we can spend the day and have meals and receive people. – That's why I want to know exactly when you arrive, so as to make sure of the rooms being free.

Your letter of today was so dear, and for the first time for eight weeks – in my whole life, for that matter – I feel the blissful happiness love gives to one who, loving with all his soul, knows he is loved in return. After all, my dream has come true: 'I lost the world, but found my harbour!' But, Almschi, you must tell it me over and over again – for by tomorrow I know I shall no longer believe it! For it is happiness that knows no rest. Now, goodnight, my darling, my sweet – perhaps you laugh today at your schoolboy – telegraph when you come!

My beloved,

Your

GUSTAV

FERRUCIO BUSONI TO MAHLER

28 April [?] 1910 170

Dear Master and Friend,

I do not know at the moment what chance there is of our meeting again in America – fresh engagements prevent me from returning to New York. But I cannot let you go without taking any farewell, and it is in my heart to tell you that I honour and love you equally as a man and a musician; that I feel we have been brought nearer together by these weeks in America (thanks to our common sufferings); that I have gained much thereby; that I thank you for the masterly performance of *Turandot*,* for the pleasure it gave me, and for the repetition of it you plan in Rome.

Please take this ingenuous outburst with the same simplicity of feeling as prompts me to confide it to you.

To be in your company has a purifying influence and rejuvenates all who enter it. For this reason, I speak here almost as a child.

I should wish to include your wife in the bond of sympathy I venture to claim, and I beg her to keep a friendly feeling for me.

I myself am her devoted servant and was enriched by the brief opportunity of making her acquaintance.

I envy you the 1st of May in Rome. Time and place alike summon up the Old World or Europe at its most beautiful. But I do not grudge you the joy of it; indeed I wish you all the joys life can offer. May these wishes accompany you on your voyage and beyond, as also the affection with which I sign myself,

Yours very sincerely,

FERRUCCIO BUSONI

ARNOLD SCHOENBERG TO MAHLER

Vienna
5 July 1910 171

My dear Director,

Your fiftieth birthday gives me an excuse for telling you, what I should like to tell you many times over, how highly I honour you. And also how often I am bound to remember, and to be pained by the remembrance, that in earlier days I used to vex you so often by my contradictoriness. I feel I was wrong to obtrude my own opinions, instead of listening to what you had to say and to what is more important than opinions, namely, the resonance of a great personality. If the overtones of my own opinions could not harmonize, always at least, with what was the substance of your utterances (I know, since I am the younger, that I have the right to differ, if only from immaturity, and to

* Busoni's *Turandot Suite*, for orchestra, which Mahler had conducted. (D.M.)

learn by experience instead of taking things on trust), I ought at least to have bowed down unconditionally to the reality which emanates from greatness, that nameless quality I felt very clearly in your presence and which for me is the power of genius. Of the presence and influence of this power, my feeling can never be unaware.

Nevertheless, I contradicted you – why, I do not know. Perhaps it was blindness, perhaps self-will. Or perhaps it was love, for I had a tremendous veneration for you all the time. It was a sort of girlish passion: love vexed by hate.

I have for long wanted to write you this letter, or one that would, if possible, express better what I mean; for it has long been on my mind. I find it a matter for shame not to have understood you from the first; but to have gone on to vex you fills me with remorse.

I have only one excuse: I was not young enough; I had begun to be occupied too much with my own development. Perhaps you may find it in you to give weight to this.

And perhaps too you will set down to my credit the attitude I now have towards you and your work; how highly I honour you in every way.

And now my wish for your fiftieth birthday is that you may soon return to our hated and beloved Vienna; and that you may feel inclined to conduct here and yet not do so, because such riff-raff certainly don't deserve it; or that you may feel no inclination and yet do it for our joy, because perhaps we do deserve it. In any case, that you may be with us again. And that you, who have so much cause for bitterness, may receive honour and lay it as a plaster to the wounds which blindness (this more than malevolence) has inflicted. I know if you were in Vienna now, you would be so warmly wrapped in honour that you might forget all your earlier and fully justified resentments.

I hope and most eagerly desire that it will soon be so, and I should be happy if I could in any way help to bring it about.

With warmest esteem and devotion,

Yours,

ARNOLD SCHOENBERG

2 August 1910 172

My dear Director,

I can scarcely tell you how terrible it is to have to write this letter to you of all people. But you can have no idea of all I have done and attempted – possible and impossible, and all to no avail. I am really in great need; otherwise I could not have brought myself to it. And the fact that you offered to help me last year rather dissuades than encourages me.

I am without money and I have the rent to pay. It was, I know, very shortsighted of me to take a larger flat when I was earning less. But there are many excuses – the disappointment of hopes so near fulfilment that any one might have counted on them, not to mention me. I am compelled therefore to beg of you the loan of 300–400 crowns. I shall certainly be able to repay them next year when I am at the Conservatoire.

I cannot tell you how unhappy it makes me to have to cloud my relations with you in this way. And I must add that I would never have done it on my own account. But when a man has a wife and children, the decision no longer rests only with himself.

May I ask you to answer by cable whether you can grant my request. And, if it is not expecting too much, would you, in the event of your being able to come to my help, cable the money, or at least send it express.

I do beg you most earnestly not to be angry. All I wish is that your attitude to me will not be influenced in my disfavour.

I hope for an early reply, and am very sincerely yours,

ARNOLD SCHOENBERG

3 August 1910 173

My dear Director,

I have today received 800 crowns in your name from Miethke. This is as speedy as goodness itself, which in a good man calls for no decision, and not even for any external spur. It is the mere emanation of his being.

Can I thank you?

I ought to be able to and I should like to. But it weighs heavily on me because I wish my veneration to have no extraneous source. Not that there is any danger; but I should like to honour you independently of gratitude. It ought not even to seem that they have any connection. But indeed they have not; and when I reflect that I could not owe you thanks without already having been honoured by your friendship, my heart is lighter again. And when I reflect that, even in a step which I cannot be proud of, I am protected from the unjust suspicion of thoughtlessness by the purity of your way of thinking; and that what I can scarcely approve in itself becomes almost good in the light you throw on it; and that, on the other hand, even the good that issues from me becomes bad if it gets into the orbit of impure modes of thought – then I am reassured, for I feel there the manifestation of a spirit which it is the whole aspiration of my life to make my own.

Perhaps I am becoming bombastic again; but if you knew how continually these thoughts exercise me, and that this is simply the attempt to express them, you would put down my sin against good taste to an excessive bias towards the good.

For this excess is the fever which purges the soul of impurity. And it is my business to be as pure as you, since it is denied me to be as great.

Yours,

ARNOLD SCHOENBERG

THOMAS MANN TO MAHLER

Bad Tölz
September 1910 174

My dear Sir,

I was incapable of saying, that evening in the hotel, how deeply indebted to you I was for the impressions of 12th September.* It is an imperative necessity to make at least some small acknowledgement, and so I beg your acceptance of the book – my latest – which I send you herewith.

It is certainly a very poor return for what I received – a mere feather's weight in the hand of the man who, as I believe, expresses the art of our time in its profoundest and most sacred form.

It is but a trifle.

Perhaps it may afford you tolerable entertainment for an idle hour or two.

Yours sincerely,

THOMAS MANN

* Mann refers to the première of the Eighth, at which he was present. The gift he sent Mahler was his novel, *Royal Highness (Königliche Hoheit)*. (D.M.)

Biographical List

ADLER, Guido (1855–1941): Austrian musicologist, professor of the history of music in the University of Vienna and author of an early study of Mahler (1916).

AMIET: Probably a reference to the Swiss painter, Cuno Amiet (1868–?)

ANGELI, Heinrich von (1840–1925): A fashionable Austrian portrait painter.

ANSORGE: Probably a reference to the pianist Conrad Ansorge (1862–1930).

BAUER-LECHNER, Natalie (1858–1921): Austrian violinist and close friend of Mahler's before his marriage. Her *Erinnerungen an Gustav Mahler* (first published in Vienna in 1923) is an important biographical and musical document for students of Mahler.

BAZELLI: The tenor, Georg Bazelli.

BEHN, Hermann (1859–1927): Studied law and lived in Hamburg from 1887. He was a friend of Mahler's and the recipient of the early autograph orchestral version of the *Lieder eines fahrenden Gesellen*. He was a pupil of Bruckner's in Vienna, a composer (on a modest scale), and lectured on the history of music (at Hamburg). He arranged some of Mahler's works for two pianos, four hands.

BERGER, Rudolf (1874–1915): Opera singer. He was a famous Jokanaan, singing the role in Strauss's *Salome* seventy-nine times.

BERLINER, Arnold (1862–1942): Physicist and a close friend of Mahler's, an association that dated back to Mahler's Hamburg years. Berliner eventually moved to Berlin, where he committed suicide on hearing that he was to be deported by the Nazis.

BIE, Oskar (1864–1938): German writer on music.

BISCHOFF, Hermann (1868–1936): German composer. He wrote two symphonies.

BLECH, Leo (1871–1958): German conductor and composer of operas. *Das war ich* was produced at the Vienna Opera in February, 1905.

BODANZKY, Artur (1877–1939): Celebrated Austrian conductor, an assistant to Mahler in 1902 at the Vienna Opera. In 1912 he organized a Mahler Festival dedicated to the composer's memory.

BONCI, Alessandro (1870–1940): Distinguished Italian operatic tenor.

BRECHER, Gustav (1879–1940): Conductor. He conducted at Vienna in 1901 and collaborated with Mahler in a new performing edition of Weber's *Oberon*. This was not staged until after Mahler's death, at Cologne, on 10th April 1913.

BRUNEAU, Alfred (1857–1934): French composer of operas.

BURCKHARD, Max (1854–1912): Director of the Burgtheater, Vienna.

BURGSTALLER, Alois (1871–1945): German tenor. Engaged at Metropolitan Opera, New York, 1903–1909.

BURIAN, Karel (1870–1924): Czech tenor (also known as Carl Burrian). Appeared at the Metropolitan Opera, New York, 1906–1913.

BUTHS, Julius (1851–1920): German pianist and conductor.

CHANTEMESSE, André (1851–1919): French physician. Associated with L'Institut Pasteur until his death. Appointed Professor of Experimental Pathology at University of Paris in 1897.

CHELIUS, Oskar von (1859–1923): German composer. He wrote three operas, among other works.

CHVOSTEK, Franz (1864–1944): A notable Viennese physician, who rose high in the ranks of his profession. Best known for his work on haemoglobinuria, hyperthyroidism and anaemia secondary to pancreatic disease.

CONRAT: Probably a reference to Frau Ida Conrat, who was a member of Brahm's circle of friends in Vienna. She was responsible for the Brahms memorial gravestone in Vienna's Zentralfriedhof.

CONRIED, Heinrich (1848–1909): Manager of the Metropolitan Opera, New York, 1903–1908.

CORNING, James Leonard (1855–1923): American physician, who developed an extensive practice in nervous and mental diseases and was consultant to various hospitals in and around New York. Listed himself as 'discoverer' of spinal anaesthesia in 1885, but other physicians made more important contributions to this subject. He wrote fiction under the name of Roland Champion. 'Leon' is a Jewish form of the diminutive of Leonard.

COTTENET, Rawlins L. (?–?): A director of the Metropolitan Opera Company.

CURTIS, Natalie (1875–1921): American writer and researcher, with particular interest in the songs, legends and customs of the Indians of North America.

D'ALBERT, Eugène (1864–1932): British-born German pianist and composer. His best-known work was the opera, *Tiefland* (1903).

DECSEY, Ernst (1870–1941): German musicologist, author of studies of Hugo Wolf and Bruckner.

DEHMEL, Richard (1863–1920): Poet. Many distinguished composers of the day set Dehmel's texts. His poem *Verklärte Nacht* inspired Schoenberg's sextet of the same title.

DEMUTH, Leopold (1861–1910): Celebrated baritone. Appeared in many performances at Vienna under Mahler, who brought him from Hamburg. Member of the Vienna Opera from 1898–1910.

DESTINN, Emmy (1878–1930): Famous Czech soprano. Sang at the Metropolitan Opera, New York, 1908–1916.

DIEPENBROCK, Alfons (1862–1921): Celebrated Dutch composer.

DIPPEL, Andreas (1866–1932): Singer and impresario. Appointed administrative manager of the Metropolitan Opera in 1908.

DUFRANNE, Hector (1870–1951): Belgian dramatic baritone. Appeared at the Manhattan Opera House, 1908.

DYCK, Ernest van (1861–1923): Celebrated Belgian tenor. A famous Wagnerian singer and member of the Vienna Opera from 1888–1900. He was engaged at the Metropolitan Opera, New York, from 1898–1902.

EAMES, Emma (1865–1952): American soprano. Appeared at the Metropolitan Opera, New York, 1891–1909.

EPSTEIN, Julius (1832–1926): Austrian pianist, who taught at the Vienna Conservatoire from 1867–1901. Mahler was among his piano pupils.

ERLANGER, Camille (1863–1919): French composer of many operas.

ERLER, Fritz (1868–1940): German painter and artist-craftsman, a friend of the Berliners.

FARRAR, Geraldine (1882–1967): American soprano, resident at the Metropolitan Opera, New York, 1906–1922.

FERNOW, H. (?–1917): Member of the H. Wolff Concert Management.

FISCHER, Edwin (1886–1960): Celebrated Swiss pianist.

FLEISCHER-EDEL, Katherina (1873–1928): Soprano.

FOERSTER-LAUTERER, Bertha (1869–1936): Dramatic soprano and wife of the composer J. B. Foerster, the Czech composer (1859–1951), an old friend of Mahler's from the Hamburg days whose autobiography contains much interesting Mahler material. His wife was a member of the Vienna Opera from 1901–1913.

FÖRSTER-NIETZSCHE, Elisabeth (1846–1935): The sister of Friedrich Nietzsche (1844–1900), the philosopher.

FRAENKEL, Joseph (1867–1920): Physician. Moved to New York from Vienna in 1893. Interested in neurologic and psychiatric diseases, and a devotee of music and the fine arts.

FRANK, Gustav (?–?): The Gustav Frank mentioned in Letter 169 is the same Frank whom Mahler met in St. Petersburg in 1907 (Letters 122 and 126). A cousin of Mahler's (on his mother's side), he studied art at Prague and became a successful painter in Russia. He occupied a high official position in St. Petersburg.

FREMSTAD, Olive (1871–1951): Swedish, later American, soprano. A great Wagnerian singer and leading soprano at the Metropolitan Opera, New York, until 1914.

FRIED, Oskar (1871–1941): German conductor and composer, a notable interpreter of Mahler's symphonies, which he was said to perform in Mahlers' own tradition.

FUCHS, Robert (1847–1927): Minor Austrian composer, a noted teacher of composition at the Vienna Conservatoire from 1875 onwards. He taught Mahler harmony.

GABRILOVITCH, Ossip (1878–1936): Russian-born pianist and conductor.

GADSKI, Johanna (1872–1932): German dramatic soprano, member of the Metropolitan Opera, New York, 1907–1917, and a leading Wagnerian singer.

GALLÉN, Akseli Gall'Kallea (1865–1931): Finnish painter and etcher.

GARDEN, Mary (1877–1967): Scottish soprano, famous as the creator of Debussy's Mélisande. Appeared at the Manhattan Opera House, 1907.

GATTI-CASAZZA, Frances-Alda (1883–1952): Soprano and wife of Giulio Gatti-Casazza.

GATTI-CASAZZA, Giulio (1868–1940): Italian impresario. He was general director of the Metropolitan Opera, New York, from 1908–1935.

GESELLIUS, Hermann (1874–1916): Finnish architect, a partner of Eliel Saarinen.

GÖHLER, Georg (1874–1954): German conductor and composer. A chorus conductor in Leipzig at the time of Letter 156.

GOLDMARK, Karl (1830–1915): Prominent Austro-Hungarian composer who lived almost all his life in Vienna.

GORITZ, Otto (1873–1929): German dramatic baritone. He made his début at the Metropolitan Opera, New York, in 1903.

GRANDJEAN: Louise Grandjean, the French dramatic soprano.

GREFFÜHLE: The reference is to the Comtesse Greffühle, a distinguished member of Parisian society and the model, so Edward Lockspeiser tells us, for Proust's Duchesse de Guermantes. It was the Countess who organized the concert in Paris at which Mahler's Second Symphony was performed in April 1910.

GROLL, Albert Lorey (1866–1952): An American painter.

GROPIUS, Walter (b. 1883): Eminent architect.

GUARNIERI: Possibly the Italian conductor Antonio Guarnieri (1883–1952), who came into prominence at about the time of Mahler's engagement at the Metropolitan Opera, New York.

GÜNTHER, Mizzi (1879–1961): Soprano. She was the first Merry Widow in Lehár's operetta.

GUTHEIL-SCHODER, Marie (1874–1935): Noted German soprano, engaged by Mahler for the Vienna Opera, where she sang from 1900–1927.

GUTMANN, Emil (?–?): The impresario who organized the première of Mahler's Eighth Symphony at Munich in 1910.

HAGEMANN, Carl (1871–1945): Intendant at Mannheim.

HAMMERSTEIN, Oscar (1846–1919): Impresario, and founder of the Manhattan Opera House.

HARTMANN, Eduard von (1842–1906): German philosopher.

HASSMANN, Carl (1869–1933): Painter, and friend of the Mahlers in New York.

HASSREITER, Josef (1845–1940): Ballet master of the Vienna Opera. Bayer's *Bride of Korea* was in part choreographed by him.

HAUPTMANN, Gerhart (1862–1946): Important German dramatist.

HELLMESBERGER, Joseph (1855–1907): Austrian violinist and composer of numerous operettas and ballets. Solo violinist in the Court orchestra and a professor at the Vienna Conservatoire. He succeeded Mahler as conductor of the Philharmonic concerts in 1902.

HERTZER-DEPPE, Marie (?–?): Contralto. The soloist mentioned in Letter 32. She also took part in the performance of the Third Symphony at Leipzig in 1904 (Letter 61).

HERTZKA, Emil (1869–1932): Director of Universal Edition, the celebrated Vienna publishing house, at the height of its fame.

HINRICHSEN, Heinrich (1868–1942): Music publisher, head of C. F. Peters, the famous Leipzig publishing house.

HODLER, Ferdinand (1853–1918): The celebrated Swiss artist.

HOFFMANN, Josef (1870–1956): Austrian architect, a leading exponent of *Art Nouveau* and a founder member of the Vienna *Sezession*.

HOFMANNSTHAL, Hugo von (1874–1929): Celebrated Austrian man of letters, the best-known and most distinguished of Richard Strauss's librettists.

HÜLSEN: Georg von Hülsen-Haeseler (1858–1922), Intendant of the Royal Theatre, Berlin (1903–1918).

J.: Probably a reference to Walter Johner, a violinist in the New York Philharmonic Orchestra.

JAHN, Wilhelm (1834–1900): Conductor and musical director of the Vienna Opera at his retirement in 1897, when he was succeeded by Mahler.

JÖRN, Karl (1876–1947): Latvian tenor, a Wagnerian singer of note. Appeared at the Metropolitan Opera, New York, 1908–1911.

KÄHLER, Willibald (1866–1938): Conductor. He prepared the rehearsals for the performance of the Third Symphony at Mannheim in 1904.

KAHN, Otto Hermann (1867–1934): Banker and patron of music. From 1907 on the board of the Metropolitan Opera, New York.

KAINZ, Josef (1858–1910): Celebrated Austrian actor.

KAJANUS, Robert (1856–1933): Finnish conductor. Director of Music at Helsinki University from 1897 and conductor of the Helsinki Philharmonic Society. An early champion of Sibelius.

KARPATH, Ludwig (1866–1936): Singer and music critic of the *Neues Wiener Tagblatt*. His memoirs, *Begegnung mit dem Genius* (Vienna, 1934), contain some interesting material on Mahler.

KEUSSLER, Gerhard von (1874–1949): Composer and conductor. He conducted the *Deutsche Singverein* in Prague from 1906 to 1918.

KITTEL, Hermine (1879–1948): Contralto. Sang under Mahler at Vienna in opera and concert performances. Member of the Vienna Opera from 1901–1931.

KLEMPERER, Otto (*b.* 1885): Eminent conductor, who has also written a small book of reminiscences of Mahler, *Erinnerungen an Gustav Mahler* (Zürich, 1960: London, 1964). In 1907 he was appointed to the German National Theatre in Prague on Mahler's recommendation.

KLIMT, Gustav (1862–1918): Austrian painter, a leading member of the *Sezession*. Mahler is portrayed as a knight in his Beethoven frieze.

KLINGER, Max (1857–1920): Noted German painter, engraver and sculptor.

KNEISEL, Franz (1865–1926): Violin virtuoso and founder of the Kneisel Quartet.

KNOTE, Heinrich (1870–1953): German tenor. A famous Wagnerian singer and regular member of the Metropolitan Opera, New York, until 1914.

KOENEN, Tilly (1873–1941): Mezzo-soprano. Prominent in Germany and Austria after a successful tour in 1900.

KORNGOLD, Julius (1860–1945): Music critic and father of Erich Wolfgang Korngold, child prodigy and composer (1897–1957), by whose early talent Mahler was so much impressed.

KOVACS, Friedrich (1861–1931): A well-known Viennese physician. Of his day, a fine diagnostician and teacher.

KRAUS-OSBORNE, Adrienne (1873–1951): American contralto, wife of Felix von Kraus (1870–1937), the Austrian bass.

KREHBIEL, Henry Edward (1854–1923): Influential New York music critic.

KRZYZANOWSKI, Rudolf (1862–1911): A close friend of Mahler's in his student days, who became a conductor. He seems to have collaborated with Mahler in preparing the piano-duet version of Bruckner's Third Symphony, published in 1878. He conducted at the Hamburg Opera during the period that Mahler was engaged there.

KUBELIK, Jan (1880–1940): Famous Czech violinist and father of Rafael, the conductor.

KURZ, Selma (1874–1933): Austrian soprano. Engaged by Mahler for Vienna in 1899, where she sang until 1927.

LABIA, Maria (1880–1953): Italian soprano of noted dramatic gifts. She appeared with the Manhattan Opera Company in 1908.

LEHMANN, Lilli (1848–1929): Famous German operatic soprano. From 1905, artistic director of the Salzburg Festival.

LEISTIKOW, Walter (1865–1908): German painter and ethnologist, a co-founder of the Berlin *Sezession* movement.

LILIENCRON, Detlev von (1844–1909): Poet.

LIPINER, Siegfried (1856–1911): Philosopher, dramatist, epic and lyric poet.

LORDMANN: A singer, Peter Lordmann.

LÖWE, Ferdinand (1865–1925): Prominent Austrian conductor. An editor and ardent advocate of Bruckner's music. He held many distinguished appointments in Vienna from 1898–1908.

MAHLER: The Mahler family. Mahler's parents both died in 1889. For his brothers and sister who survived infancy (and it is thought that the total of children may well have exceeded the twelve mentioned on p. 6) only fragmentary documentation exists.

Leopoldine (married name Quittner): 1863–1889.

Justine (who married Arnold Rosé): 1868–1938.

Emma (who married Eduard Rosé): 1875–1933.

Otto: 1873–1895.

Alois (Louis): 1876–?.

MARSCHALK, Margarethe (?–?): Sister of Max Marschalk (1863–1940), the German critic and composer, and wife of Gerhart Hauptmann, the playwright. Max Marschalk composed incidental music for three of Hauptmann's plays, *Die versunkene Glocke* among them.

MARTEAU, Henri (1874–1934): Distinguished French violin virtuoso.

MAYR, Richard (1877–1935): Famous Austrian bass-baritone. The most celebrated Baron Ochs of his day. It was on Mahler's advice that he took up music, at the age of 21. He appeared at the Vienna Opera from 1902–1935.

MENGELBERG, Willem (1871–1951): Eminent Dutch conductor, an untiring advocate of Mahler's works during the composer's lifetime. He organized and conducted a great Mahler Festival in Amsterdam, May, 1920.

MESSCHAERT, Johannes Martinus (1857–1922): Dutch baritone, who lived for many years in Berlin.

METZGER (LATTERMANN), Ottilie (1878–?1943): Mezzo-soprano. She died in Auschwitz.

MILDENBURG, Anna von (1872–1947): Austrian dramatic soprano, pupil of Rosa Papier. Noted for her interpretations of the great Wagnerian roles. She was engaged at Hamburg from 1895–1898 and at Vienna from 1898–1916. Her published *Erinnerungen* (Vienna, 1921) include some material on Mahler.

MOLL, Carl (1861–1945): Austrian painter (a pupil of E. J. Schindler, Alma Mahler's father), who became Alma's stepfather.

MOLL, Ernst (?–?): Brother of Carl Moll.

MOSER, Koloman (1868–1918): Noted Austrian painter and designer, a founder member of the *Sezession*, with which Austrian *Art Nouveau* became wholly identified.

MOTTL, Felix (1856–1911): Celebrated Austrian conductor, noted for his performances of Wagner.

MUCK, Karl (1859–1940): Eminent German conductor.

NEDBAL, Oskar (1874–1930): Czech composer and conductor.

NEISSER, Albert (1855–1916): Dermatologist. After qualifying in 1877, appointed to work in University of Breslau Dermatologic Clinic, and thereafter developed a large private practice and notable reputation. He was President of the Breslau Music Society.

NIKISCH, Arthur (1855–1922): Famous conductor. He was principal conductor at the Leipzig Theatre from 1882–1889, where Mahler was his assistant from 1886.

NODNAGEL, Ernst Otto (1870–1909): Critic and writer on music, an early and enthusiastic advocate of Mahler's works.

OCHS, Siegfried (1858–1929): German conductor, of special distinction as a chorus trainer.

ORLIK, Emil (1870–1932): Artist. One of his drawings of Mahler (1902) achieved wide currency.

PAINLEVÉ, Paul (1863–1933): Twice Prime Minister of France.

PAPIER, Rosa (1858–1932): Austrian mezzo-soprano, who sang at the Vienna Opera until her retirement in 1891. She was Mildenburg's teacher and a person of influence in Vienna's musical life.

PERIER, Jean (1869–1954): French singer, the first Pelléas.

PEROSI, (Abbé) Lorenzo (1872–1956): Italian composer, predominantly of Catholic church music. Mahler conducted two performances of an oratorio by Perosi, *The Resurrection of Lazarus*, at Vienna in March, 1899.

PETERS, C. F.: Peters Edition, the Leipzig music publishers. See also Hinrichsen. Peters published Mahler's Fifth Symphony.

PFITZNER, Hans (1869–1949): Eminent German composer, a pronounced conservative in style and personality. His best-known opera is *Palestrina* (1917).

PIERNÉ, Gabriel (1863–1937): Minor French composer.

POLLAK, Theobald (?–?): A cultivated friend of the Moll family. It was Pollak who introduced Mahler to Bethge's version of the Chinese texts that Mahler used for *Das Lied von der Erde*.

POLLINI, Bernhard (1838–1897): Director of the Hamburg Opera.

REGER, Max (1873–1916): Eminent German composer. He was not in sympathy with Mahler's music but contributed a page of manuscript from his Op. 77a to a volume of tributes to Mahler's memory.

REINHARDT, Max (1873–1943): Celebrated Austrian actor, theatrical manager and director, with a gift for spectacle.

REITTER: As in Letter 141. The name is probably wrongly transcribed. It might be a reference to William RITTER, a French speaking critic, native of Neuchâtel, but resident in Paris, and a fervent admirer of Mahler's music. Another possibility is a reference to Josef REITLER (1883–1948), Austrian music critic and Director of the New Vienna Conservatoire (from 1915), with whom Mahler had some correspondence in 1908–9.

ROLLER, Alfred (1864–1935): Celebrated stage-designer and artist-craftsman, with whom Mahler created some of the most famous productions of Mozart, Beethoven and Wagner at Vienna.

ROOY, Anton van (1870–1932): Dutch bass-baritone. A great Wagnerian singer who appeared at the Metropolitan Opera, New York, 1898–1908.

RÖSCH, Friedrich (1862–1925): German composer and founder, with Richard Strauss and Hans Sommer, of the Association of German Composers.

ROSÉ, Arnold (1863–1946): Famous violinist, leader of the Vienna Philharmonic and Opera Orchestras and founder of the Rosé Quartet. He married Mahler's sister, Justine, in 1902. His 'cellist brother, Eduard (1855–1942), married another Mahler sister, Emma.

ROSEGGER, Peter (1843–1918): Austrian novelist.

ROTT, Hans (1858–1884): A gifted student friend of Mahler's and an organ pupil of Bruckner's. He died insane.

ROTTENBERG, Ludwig (1864–1932): Conductor and composer. He was engaged at the Frankfurt Opera from 1893–1926.

SCHALK, Franz (1863–1931): Distinguished Austrian conductor. He gave the first (posthumous) performance of the Adagio and *Purgatorio* movements from Mahler's Tenth Symphony in 1924 (12th October). Bruckner's remark about the Schalk brothers, as recorded by Alma Mahler on p. 107, must be treated with some scepticism in view of the youthfulness of the Schalks at the time (Franz would have been only fifteen). He conducted at the Vienna Opera from 1900–1929.

SCHALK, Josef (1857–1911): Brother of Franz. Pianist and writer on music. He was responsible for the piano-duet versions of Bruckner's symphonies.

SCHELLING, Ernest (1876–1939): American composer.

SCHILLINGS, Max von (1868–1933): German composer and conductor.

SCHINDLER, E. J. (1842–1892): Important Austrian painter and Alma Mahler's father.

SCHINDLER, Kurt (1882–1935): Conductor and editor. Assistant conductor at the Metropolitan Opera, New York (1905–1907), and from 1907 a reader for Schirmer's, the music publishers.

SCHIRMER, Ernest Charles (1865–1958): American music publisher.

SCHLEINZER, Marie (?–?): Solo dancer at the Vienna Opera from 1895–1901. She danced in *The Bride of Korea*, Bayer's ballet.

SCHMEDES, Erik (1866–1931): Danish tenor. A much admired Florestan and a prominent member of the Mahler ensemble in Vienna. He appeared there from 1898–1924.

SCHOTT: The publishers, B. Schott's Söhne, Mainz, who brought out the three volumes of Mahler's early songs with piano, the *Lieder und Gesänge aus der Jugendzeit*.

SCHRÖDTER, Fritz (1855–1924): Tenor. A frequent performer at Vienna under Mahler. A member of the Vienna Opera from 1885–1915.

SCHUCH, Ernst von (1846–1914): Austrian conductor, famous for his performances of Richard Strauss's operas, for many of the premières of which he was responsible.

SCHUMANN-HEINK, Ernestine (1861–1936): Celebrated Czech-born contralto. She sang at the Hamburg Opera from 1883–1898, and thereafter internationally, particularly in the U.S.A.

SCOTTI, Antonio (1866–1936): Italian baritone, engaged at the Metropolitan Opera, New York, 1899–1933.

SEMBRICH, Marcella (1858–1935): Polish soprano. Appeared at the Metropolitan Opera, New York, 1898–1909.

SILOTI, Alexander Ilyitch (1863–1945): Russian pianist, conductor and impresario.

SIMONS: Rainer Simons, Director of the Kaiser–Jubiläums Theater in Vienna (which housed the Volksoper) from 1903–1917.

SLEZAK, Leo (1873–1946): Celebrated Czech tenor. Appeared at the Vienna Opera from 1901–1912 and at the Metropolitan Opera, New York, 1909–1913.

SONNENTHAL: Possibly a reference to the producer, Hans Sonnenthal.

SPECHT, Richard (1870–1932): Austrian writer on music and music critic. Author of an early study of Mahler (1913, subsequently revised and enlarged and often reprinted).

SPETRINO, Francesco (1857–1948): Italian conductor, responsible for some performances at the Metropolitan Opera, New York.

SPIERING, Theodore (1871–1925): American violinist and conductor.

He was appointed leader of the New York Philharmonic Orchestra in 1909, under Mahler, and during Mahler's last illness conducted the orchestra himself (see illustration, facing p. 130).

STÄGEMANN, Max (?–?): Intendant of the Leipzig Stadttheater. (Mahler was conductor there from 1886–1888).

STEFAN, Paul (1879–1943): Writer on music and one of Mahler's early advocates and biographers.

STEINBACH, Emil (1849–1919): Conductor at Mainz from 1877–1910. From 1899 he directed the Mainz Stadttheater. Brother of Fritz.

STEINBACH, Fritz (1855–1916): Conductor at Cologne from 1902 and Director of the Conservatoire there. Brother of Emil.

STOLL, August (1854–1918): See note to Letter 104. Stoll was first a singer. He joined the Vienna Opera in 1884.

STRAUBE, Karl (1873–1950): Famous German organist and Leipzig musician. A great friend and advocate of Max Reger's music.

STREICHER, Theodor (1874–1940): Austrian composer. He wrote 36 settings of poems from *Des Knaben Wunderhorn*.

STRZYGOWSKI, Josef (1862–1941): Art-historian, noted for his studies of Oriental and early Christian art. Taught at Graz and at the Kunsthistorische Institut in Vienna. His *Origin of Christian Church Art* was to influence W. B. Yeats in writing the 'Byzantium' poems.

TIFFANY, Louis C. (1848–1933): The leading representative of *Art Nouveau* in America, famous above all for his exquisite designs in glass.

VELDE, Henry van de (1863–1957): Celebrated Belgian designer, painter and architect, a leading member of the *Art Nouveau* movement.

WALTER, Bruno (1876–1962): Eminent conductor. Close friend of Mahler's and fervent advocate of his music. He gave the first performances of the posthumous *Das Lied von der Erde* and Ninth Symphony. Assistant to Mahler at the Vienna Opera from 1901, remaining in this post after Mahler's departure. His monograph on Mahler appeared in English in 1936.

WEDEKIND, Frank (1864–1918): German dramatist. An important figure in the Expressionist movement in the theatre. Alban Berg was to use a conflation of his texts as the basis of his opera *Lulu*.

WEIDEMANN, Friedrich (1871–1919): Famous baritone. He sang often under Mahler at Vienna, both in opera and in Mahler's songs with orchestra, e.g., *Kindertotenlieder*, of which he gave the first performance. Member of the Vienna Opera from 1903–1919.

WEINGARTNER, Felix (1863–1942): Eminent conductor. He succeeded Mahler as Director of the Vienna Opera in 1908.

WEISS, Joseph (1864–?1940): Pianist.

WINTERNITZ: Letter 143. Probably a reference to the Austrian conductor Arnold WINTERNITZ (1874–1928), a widely travelling conductor of opera.

WOLFF'S: The Hermann Wolff Concert Management, Berlin.

WOLFF, Louise (1855–1935): The widow of Hermann Wolff (1845–1902), the founder of the famous H. Wolff Concert Management, Berlin. She continued to administer the agency after his death.

WOLFRUM, Philipp (1854–1919): Composer, organist and Professor of Musicology at the University of Heidelberg. He prepared the rehearsals for the performance of the Third Symphony at Heidelberg in 1904.

WYDENBRUCK: Letter 67. The reference is to Countess Misa Wydenbruck (1859–1926).

ZEMÁNEK, Vilem (1875–1922): Czech conductor. Conductor of the Czech Philharmonic Orchestra from 1902–1918.

ZEMLINSKY, Alexander von (1872–1942): Distinguished Austrian composer and conductor, from whom Schoenberg had his only lesson in composition. An intimate member of the Mahler circle.

ZICHY, Géza, Count Vasony-Teö (1849–1924): Hungarian composer and left-hand pianist. He was Intendant of the Budapest Opera from 1890–1894.

ZUCKERKANDL, Emil (1849–1910): Prominent Viennese anatomist. He and his wife, Bertha, were close friends of the Moll household. Bertha's sister, Sophie, married Paul Clemenceau, the brother of Georges.

Addenda

BURCKHARD: Add: As A.M. herself makes clear (see, for example, pp. 3–4, 17–18, etc.), B. was a major influence in her life and on her intellectual development. It was B. who introduced A.M. to Nietzsche and gave her the complete edition of his works (see pp. 18–19) to which G.M. was to take such strong exception. There is more about B. in A.M.'s later autobiography, *And the Bridge is Love*, London, 1959.

BRAHM, Otto (1856–1912): A prominent German producer in the Berlin theatre. B. was an enthusiastic advocate of the 'new' theatre, e.g., the works of Hauptmann and Ibsen (hence, no doubt, the reference to *Peer Gynt* on p. 313).

FECHNER, Gustav Theodor (1801–1887): German scientist and philosopher, and pioneer in psychophysics. F.'s philosophy conceived the world as comprehensively animated, including even plants and stars.

GRABBE, Christian Dietrich (1801–1836): German dramatist.

HIRTH, Georg (? – ?): See p. 337. An influential newspaper proprietor of liberal sympathies.

MAUTHNER: See p. 260. This is probably a reference to Fritz M. (1849–1923), the Austrian critic and dramatist.

RÜCKERT, Friedrich (1788–1866): German poet. G.M. made 5 independent settings of his poems and also based his 5 *Kindertotenlieder* on poems by R.

WEIDT, Lucie (1879–1940): Austrian soprano. Engaged at Vienna, 1903–1926. A leading member of G.M.'s ensemble.

ZILCHER, Hermann (1881–1948): German composer. His 'Traumspiel', *Fitzebutze*, Op. 19, was performed at Mannheim in 1903 according to Moser's *Musiklexikon* (Berlin, 1935). One wonders, therefore, if Letter 87 (see particularly line 1, p. 271) can be correctly dated?

D.M.

Notes and Commentaries
by Donald Mitchell and Knud Martner

Abbreviations

AST   Alma Schindler, *Tagebuch* (unpublished MS, transcribed by K.M. from the original German MS in the Charles Patterson Van Pelt Library, University of Pennsylvania, Philadelphia, USA).

DM¹   Donald Mitchell, *Gustav Mahler: The Early Years*, revised and edited by Paul Banks and Colin Matthews (London, Faber, 1980).

DM²   Donald Mitchell, *Gustav Mahler: The Wunderhorn Years* (London, Faber, 1975).

DM³   Donald Mitchell, *Gustav Mahler: Songs and Symphonies of Life and Death* (London, Faber, 1985).

ELM   Alma Mahler, *Ein Leben mit Gustav Mahler* (typescript of the original draft in the Charles Patterson Van Pelt Library – see above).

MSL   *Gustav Mahler: Selected Letters*, edited by Knud Martner (London, Faber, 1979).

HLG¹⁻³ Henry-Louis de La Grange, *Mahler*, Vols. 1-3 (Paris, Fayard, 1979, 1983, 1984).

Part One

MEMORIES

Page 3, line 2
According to *ELM* she was accompanied only by Carl Moll, her step-father.

Page 3, line 23
AST confirms that the meeting took place on 7th November.

Page 4, line 10
According to *AST*, Alma hardly exchanged more than two words with Klimt.

Page 4, line 16
On 7th November 1901, Jan Kubelik played in a concert conducted by Alexander Zemlinsky. A.M. was mistaken in thinking this occasion was a solo recital.

Page 4, line 33
The correct title is *Das gläserne Herz* ('The Heart of Glass'). This ballet, based on Hoffmannsthal's libretto *Der Triumph der Zeit* ('The Triumph of Time'), was composed during the summer and autumn of 1901, but has never been performed. A few years later Zemlinsky arranged an orchestral suite in three movements, of which Ferdinand Löwe gave the first performance at a concert in Vienna on 18th February 1903.

Page 5, line 3
The Bride of Korea, conducted by its composer, Josef Bayer, was performed thirty-eight times after its première in May 1897. From May 1901 it disappeared completely from the repertory during Mahler's tenure at the Opera.

Page 5, line 34
In *AST*, however, A.M. observed the very same evening: 'I must say – I liked him enormously – although terribly nervous. He paced about the room like a wild man. The chap consists *purely* of oxygen. One *burns* oneself if one comes close to him.'

Page 6, line 9
For 'Frank' read 'Hermann'. One of Marie Mahler's sisters married a Frank, whose son, Gustav Frank, we are to meet later (see pp. 34, 296, 300, 338, 346).

Page 6, line 13
The latest research proves that Marie Mahler gave birth to fourteen children, not twelve.

Page 6, line 19
A.M. is referring to the so-called 'October Diploma' (of 20th October 1860), which conceded to Jews elementary civil rights, among them the right to settle where they wished.

Page 6, lines 27-35
This anecdote is doubtful; cf. *HLG*[1], p. 18, n. 35.

Page 7, line 11
Ernst Mahler, born 18th March 1862, had – according to his school reports – been seriously ill since the summer of 1874; he died on 13th April 1875. Grünfeld senior did not own a music firm, but was a rich leather merchant. Three sons of his, Alfred, Heinrich and Siegmund, became musicians. Mahler studied at the *Gymnasium* in Prague from September 1871 until February 1872, when his father – probably owing to Gustav's extremely bad marks – opted to bring him back to Iglau.

Page 8, line 26
Mahler began his studies in Vienna in September 1875.

Page 8, line 31
See *DM*[1], Chapter IV, 'The Early Works', pp. 116-229, and Appendix, pp. 268-324.

Page 8, line 35
Hans Rott was committed to an asylum in October 1880 and died four years later, on 25th June 1884. See note to p. 107, line 19.

Page 9, line 5
Leopoldine (b. 1863) was married in Vienna on 4th May 1884, to a tradesman, Ludwig Elias Quittner (1858-1923). Mahler was at that time music director at Cassel. She died on 27th October 1889.

Page 9, line 10
Justine Ernestine Mahler was born on 15th December 1868, and died on 22nd August 1938 in Vienna. The anecdote to which A.M. refers no doubt took place in December 1871 when she was three years old. In that same month her two brothers, Arnold and Friedrich, had died. It was the custom at that time to light candles around the coffin or bed of the deceased.

Page 9, line 18
Otto Mahler, born on 18th June 1873, was, in fact, the younger brother. He committed suicide in Vienna on 6th February 1895, in the home of the author and translator Nina Hoffman-Matscheko.

Page 10, line 25
To the list of Mahler's appointments one should add Olmütz and Prague.

Page 10, lines 27-8
Mahler's father died on 18th February and his mother on 11th October 1889.

Page 11, line 2
The sum Mahler received when he resigned in Budapest (14th March 1891) was 25,000 Gulden.

Page 11, line 5
In fact only four brothers and sisters: Justine, Alois, Emma and Otto.

Page 11, line 9
Cf. A.M.'s remark on p. 36, line 17: 'and first of all I had to pay his three sisters [Justine, Alois and Emma] their share of the patrimony.' This statement (from 1902) no doubt refers to the dowry for Justine, and probably her share of the villa in Maiernigg.

Page 11, line 23
It was in September 1895 that Justine and Emma joined Mahler in Hamburg. At the same time Anna von Mildenburg began her career at the Hamburg Theatre.

Page 12, line 3
Mahler left Hamburg at the end of April 1897 having been appointed *Kapellmeister* at the Vienna Court Opera; six months later he became Director of the Opera. This had been his goal since his early days at Cassel, and his bad relationship with Pollini was his main reason for looking for another engagement. His new position did not allow him to retain an intimate relationship with one of the female members of the company. One should read the letter to Mildenburg from July 1897 (No. 251 in *Gustav Mahler Briefe*, edited by Herta Blaukopf, Hamburg-Vienna, Zsolnay, 1982).

Page 12, line 34
A.M. is referring to Arnold Rosé. His elder brother, the cellist Eduard Rosé, married Emma Marie Eleanor Mahler (1875-1933) in Vienna on 25th August 1898.

Page 14, line 11
On 25th February 1901, Mahler conducted a Philharmonic concert, which included Bruckner's Fifth Symphony, and in the evening a performance of *Die Zauberflöte* (not *Meistersinger*).

Page 14, line 18
Owing to Mahler's ill health, the two remaining Philharmonic concerts were taken over by Hellmesberger and Franz Schalk. For Mahler's letter of resignation to the Philharmonic Orchestra, see p. 220 (No. 14). It was, incidentally, not until 28th May 1901 that the orchestra elected Hellmesberger as their new conductor.

Page 16, line 4
If we are to believe A.M. she received the poem on 9th November, but in her diary (*AST*) it is first mentioned on the 19th, accompanied by the remark, 'From what I gather from certain turns of phrase I believe that the poem is by him [Mahler].' And the following day – in another context – she writes: 'If only the poem were by him [i.e. Zemlinsky] if only – –'

Page 16, line 31
Orpheus was performed on 18th November 1901, conducted by Bruno Walter. After the interval Josef Bayer conducted Delibes's ballet *Coppélia*.

Page 17, line 18
This would have been on 23rd November, which, however, is unlikely, because on the 20th Mahler went to Munich, where five days later he conducted the première of his Fourth Symphony. The invitation was no doubt made for the 30th (a Sunday), or it was open to Mahler to call on any day convenient to him. It is an interesting point that Alma usually had her lessons with Robert Gound on Thursdays (according to *AST*), and Mahler did in fact turn up on Thursday, 28th November; cf. p. 18, line 27.

Page 18, line 5
It is clear from Alma's entry in *AST* for 8th November that she did know about Mahler's conversation with Burckhard.

Page 18, line 27
On 28th November. Mahler returned from Munich on the 26th and conducted at the Opera the following evening while Alma went to a concert. In her diary (*AST*) she gives the right weekday (i.e. Thursday), but the wrong date (i.e. the 27th). As a result, she also misdated Mahler's first letter to her (No. 1, p. 205), a mistake we have rectified.

Page 18, line 32
According to *AST*, however, she continued to take lessons in counterpoint with Gound into the New Year, while her lessons with
Zemlinsky had already ceased during G.M.'s absence from Vienna.
Alma, it seems, had realized that it would have been inappropriate to
maintain an association that had been close, especially on Zemlinsky's
side, albeit platonic.

Page 18, line 33
At Steinfeldgasse, 8. The house was built by the famous architect Josef
Hoffmann. The removal must have taken place before her first meeting
with Mahler; cf. her remark on p. 5, line 21, where she refers to 'Hohe
Warte', the district where the house was located.

Page 19, line 19
Mahler's private telephone number was ex-directory, so he could not
look it up.

Page 19, line 20
For 'nine years' read 'six years'; it was only from September 1895 that
Justine lived with Mahler.

Page 19, line 37
According to *AST*, the entry for 2nd December 1901, it was on his
visit that day that Mahler and Alma first kissed.

Page 20, line 5
'M.' stands for a certain Felix Muhr who, according to *AST*, continued
to visit Alma, though he appears for the last time in *AST* on 9th
December 1901.

Page 20, line 33
Ludwig Karpath, too, remembers this episode in his *Erlebnisse mit
Gustav Mahler*, edited by Knud Martner (Hamburg, Karl Dieter
Wagner, 1990), but in a slightly different version. A.M.'s account of the
occasion, like Karpath's, suggests a date around Christmas 1901, but all
the evidence points in fact to a date around the first week of December.

Page 21, line 2
Goldschmidt's operatic trilogy, *Gaea*, remains unperformed and unpublished.

Page 21, line 7
According to *AST*, it was on 7th December 1901 that they became secretly engaged.

Page 21, line 23
The engagement was revealed in a newspaper on 27th December 1901.

Page 21, line 34
This performance took place on 8th December 1901, and it was, of course, a public performance; cf. Letter No. 5. Mahler had reserved three tickets for Alma and her family (cf. *MSL*, p. 257). According to *AST*, Justine and Natalie Bauer-Lechner were also present; cf. also Letter No. 5, p. 208, in which Mahler writes of his sister's response to the news of the engagement.

Page 22, line 6
A.M. refers to a recitative that Mahler composed for his Vienna production of *Figaro* in 1906. This is also mentioned by Erwin Stein in his important articles on 'Mahler and the Vienna Opera', reprinted in *The Opera Bedside Book* (London, Gollancz, 1965, p. 308), when he wrote:

'There was an extension of da Ponte's libretto in the *secco* recitative that precedes the sextet of the third act: in order to make the story more easily understandable, a court scene from Beaumarchais's original play *Le Mariage de Figaro* was inserted, with the Count presiding, Don Curzio as judge and Marcellina as plaintiff. The scene was a short *secco* recitative and led directly to Don Curzio's *E decisa la lite, o pagarla, o sposarla*. Purists complained of the insertion, as they would today, but artistically no harm had been done to the opera.'

Mahler's extra recitative appears in the vocal score of *Figaro* published by C.F. Peters under the title 'Bearbeitung der Wiener Hofoper' (Edition No. 9332), and Mahler himself refers to the edition in a letter to Karl Horwitz from Toblach, 27th June 1908 (see *MSL*, No. 370, p. 320). The edition uses a German translation by Max Kalbeck (1850-1921), and between pp. 186 and 193 may be found Mahler's recitative, which in fact is not, as Stein suggests, an exclusively *secco* recitative but also *accompagnato*, for which reason this vocal score also includes the relevant two pages of orchestral score for the conductor's use, pp. 190-1. Altogether this new recitative is quite an elaborate insertion, making brief use of the chorus as well as the principals. Stein seems not to be strictly correct in writing that Mahler's recitative 'led directly to Don Curzio's "E decisa la lite"'. The Mahler expansion in fact leads directly to Bartolo's 'Che superba sentenza!', which means that for the first nine bars of Mozart's recitative Mahler substitutes forty-eight bars or so of his own devising.

One notes, however, how ingeniously he stitches into the flow of his recitative the 'missing' nine bars of Mozart (i.e. see bars 36-44 [p. 189] in the piano reduction or bars 3-11 on the second page of the orchestral score [p. 191], where Mahler incorporates – or absorbs – bars 1-9 of the original Mozart, which of course is *secco* throughout). It is this, I think, that A.M. means when she writes, loosely, that Mahler 'used motifs of Mozart's for the recitatives he had to compose'; and Stein, too, is accurate in his description in so far as Don Curzio's 'E decisa la lite' is certainly there, motivically speaking, embedded in Mahler's re-composition of the recitative. The trial scene in Beaumarchais's play on which the dramatically clarifying recitative is based occurs in Act III. There is no attribution of the recitative to Mahler in the Peters edition of the vocal score, but *Figaro* in this 'Hofoper' edition was listed among Mahler's 'arrangements' by Paul Stefan, his early biographer. See also *DM²*, pp. 419-22.

Page 22, line 14
In fact, on 9th December 1901.

Page 22, line 22
Cf. Letter 10, p. 216.

Page 22, line 30
Letter of 19th December 1901, from Dresden. This is suppressed in the published editions, but a typed copy survives in *ELM* and has been published in *HLG²*, pp. 187-93, though in a slightly incorrect transcription (and thus, also, translation).

Page 22, line 31
A.M.'s account in *AST* differs somewhat. She received the letter on the 20th, in the afternoon, and it came, indeed, as a shock to her: 'My first thought was to write him off. I had to cry – for then I realised that I love him.'

The same evening she went to the Opera with Theobald Pollak to see Wagner's *Siegfried.* On her return she confided the matter to her mother, who read the letter (*her* reaction is not recorded). Early next morning Alma notes in her diary, 'I *forced* myself to sleep well the whole night through', and after having re-read the letter she continues, 'Yes – he is right – I must live completely for him in order to make him happy. I have this quite curious feeling that I love him deeply and genuinely. For how long? This I do not know but this is already much – much.'

Page 23, line 3
For the letter in question, see p. 218 (No. 12).

Page 23, line 12
According to *AST* this conversation took place on 22nd December 1901. According to Letter 9 (p. 215), Moll had recently attended the performance of Mahler's Fourth Symphony in Berlin.

Page 23, line 31
'...kept our secret from Justine...': as we have already demonstrated above (note to p. 21, line 34), only until 8th December 1901, and hardly out of fear of Justine's jealousy, but rather because Mahler himself was not sure of Alma's feelings. In this connection – the declaration of Mahler's feelings for Alma – one should remember the inscription Mengelberg wrote on the first page of the Adagietto in his conducting score; '*This Adagietto* was Gustav Mahler's *declaration of love* to *Alma! Instead of a letter* he confided it in this manuscript without a word of explanation. She understood and replied: *He should come*!!! (I have this from both of them!) W.M.' If true, this information has a bearing on the chronology of the symphony's composition (see also note to p. 42, line 21).

Page 23, line 34
'...to know him on the same occasion...': probably at the party at the Zuckerkandls on 7th November. According to *AST*, Justine accompanied Mahler, but Alma makes no further remarks about her.

Page 24, line 3
The visit Alma paid Justine on the 14th was, according to *AST*, a success.

Page 24, line 13
According to *AST*, this incident involving the Fourth Symphony occurred on 4th January 1902; cf. also Letter 15, p. 220. A similar episode is recorded in *AST* on 7th December 1901 (though the title of the work is not disclosed), but at that time Mahler had not yet formally asked Anna Moll for Alma's hand.

Page 24, line 26
Alma was then twenty-two (born 31st August 1879).

Page 25, lines 15-16
The two old friends referred to were Emil Freund and Fritz Löhr.

Page 25, line 32
According to *AST*, the gathering took place in January 1902, either on Friday 3rd or Sunday 5th (Alma's dates do not correspond with the actual weekdays). The following were present: Nina Spiegler (Lipiner's first wife), now married to Albert Spiegler (Lipiner's bosom friend); Anna von Mildenburg (Lipiner's current mistress, if we are to believe Alma); Clementine Lipiner (Lipiner's second wife); Arnold Rosé; Kolo Moser; and Anna and Carl Moll.

Page 27, lines 9-10
The evening edition of the *Neue Freie Presse* was the first to bring the news, on 27th December 1901. The following morning all the other newspapers repeated it. Mahler conducted at the Opera on the 29th but not on the 27th.

Page 27, line 30
It was Mahler who, in fact, conducted the première of *Feuersnot*. Strauss did not appear at the Vienna Opera until 1910.

Page 29, line 1
Cf. Letters 16 and 17, pp. 220-2.

Page 29, line 4
'... in Dresden...': i.e. in December 1901.

Page 31, line 26
A.M. is referring to the vocal score illustrated by Franz Stassen, which had just been published by Breitkopf & Härtel.

Page 34, line 15
Mahler gave three concerts in St. Petersburg, on 17th, 23rd and 27th March. None included a composition by Schubert.

Page 35, line 20
See Letter 122, pp. 295-6.

Page 35, line 25
'It was Advent ...': a puzzling remark. A.M. no doubt means Easter (27th-31st March 1902).

Page 35, lines 32-7
One wonders why Mahler had to rent a room to an officer. The house in Auenbruggergasse was newly built when Mahler moved into it in November 1898. Was it not possible to give the officer notice?

Page 36, line 11
For 'State Theatre' read 'City Theatre'.

Page 36, line 15
A.M.'s description of Mahler's financial situation is surely exaggerated: to whom did he owe 50,000 gold crowns? As Director of the Opera he earned 12,000 gold crowns annually (before tax), and it is unlikely that Alma could have paid back the debt she mentions in the course of five years as well as paying rent for the flat in Vienna, a mortgage for the house in Maiernigg, plus wages for two or three servants, not to mention buying food and clothes, etc., for a family of four.

Page 36, line 25
The 14th exhibition of the *Secession* was held from 15th April to 27th June 1902, and the celebration was in honour of Max Klinger's 50th birthday. It was G.M.'s original plan to give a complete performance of Beethoven's Ninth Symphony, but owing to disagreements with the Vienna Philharmonic the plan was abandoned. Instead, Mahler arranged part of the chorus from the finale, for six trombones. Mahler would, of course, have included in his arrangement the famous injunction 'Seid umschlungen, Millionen! Diesem Kuss der ganzen Welt' (see bars 594-654 of Beethoven's finale). This would undoubtedly have led to the impact that A.M. describes. We note too that one of Klimt's 'Beethoven' frescos, on show in the exhibition, was entitled 'Diesem Kuss der ganzen Welt'. According to contemporary accounts, the 'concert' took place on the 14th, the evening before the private view.

Pages 38-9
If we compare the draft programmes for the Third Symphony set out on these pages with the programmes documented by Paul Bekker in his *GMs Sinfonien* (Berlin, Schuster & Loeffler, 1921, p. 106), it is clear that what A.M. reproduces is virtually identical with the drafts quoted by Bekker. It occurs to us that both A.M. and Bekker may have used a

common documentary source, in which case A.M.'s transcriptions seem to be a shade less accurate than Bekker's, which make better musical sense. The English translation is faithful to A.M.'s German original, but we would advise students to consult the Bekker drafts, which seem to us to be the more authentic.

Page 39, line 9
It seems that it was not at the Cologne rehearsal of the Third Symphony that the young Edwin Fischer overlooked the score. According to the reminiscences of the pianist, this incident occurred at a rehearsal of the Second Symphony in the Cathedral at Basel. This would have been the performance in Basel in June 1903 (see p. 59). Fischer would then have been a youth of 17, scarcely A.M.'s 'small boy'.

Page 42, line 5
To understand Mahler's behaviour towards Pfitzner one should read Bruno Walter's letter to Pfitzner (6th March 1902): 'Mahler has a surprising antipathy (idiosyncrasy one could call it) against your whole manner, and we have really serious disagreements on account of the *Rose*; you must not think that he treats it *en passant*. On the contrary – he has been much preoccupied with it.' (Bruno Walter, *Brief*, Frankfurt/M, Fischer, 1969, p. 57.)

Page 42, line 21
Certainly the third (the Scherzo), and probably Part I of the symphony, i.e. the first and second movements, and the Adagietto. A complex and fascinating history and chronology surround the slow movement. See *DM*[3], p. 131, n. 23, and Paul Banks, 'Aspects of Mahler's Fifth Symphony: performance practice and interpretation', in *Musical Times*, Vol. 130, May 1989, pp. 258-65.

Page 47, lines 8-21
This episode no doubt belongs to the summer of 1907 or 1908.

Page 48, line 10
Mahler returned alone, paying a visit to Edlach to see his sister and Arnold Rosé.

Page 49, line 20
It was, in fact, Bruno Walter who had studied and rehearsed the opera, which was first given on 4th October 1902 and only twice repeated. The adaptation was the work of the noted critic, Robert Hirschfeld.

Page 50, line 3
The rehearsals for *The Queen of Spades* had, of course, begun much earlier. The première took place on 9th December 1902.

Page 50, line 10
On 4th March 1903, Strauss conducted a concert in Vienna (with the Berlin Tonkünstler-Orchester), but Pauline did not sing on this occasion. A.M. is perhaps referring to the recital at the end of January 1902, given by Strauss and his wife.

Page 53, line 3
Unterach on the Attersee: surely a slip of the pen. A.M. must have meant Pörtschach am Wörthersee, opposite Maiernigg on the north side of the lake. When G.M. arrived by train at Klagenfurt he would sometimes walk to Maiernigg on foot (which would take about an hour) but more often walked to Maria Loretto. There he was met by his servant Anton and they would proceed by rowing boat to Maiernigg. Sometimes he would continue on the train to Pörtschach and was fetched by Anton; but this routine was usually adopted when he had his family with him. Mahler's means of transport included a horse-drawn carriage (bought in the summer of 1904) and a bicycle (1905).

Page 53, line 13
The young musician is identified in *ELM* as Bruno Walter.

Page 54, line 2
Only the revised libretto of *Euryanthe* was published (Vienna, Künast, 1904).

Page 54, line 20
Roller was appointed chief stage-designer at the Vienna Opera from 1st June 1903 until 31st May 1909, and again from 1918-35.

Page 56, line 21
This episode must have happened in January 1902. Mahler signed the contract for the performance on 27th January 1902. The first rehearsals for *Louise* began in mid-February 1903.

Page 59, line 12
The performance of the Second Symphony in Basel took place on 15th June. The soloists were Maria Knüpfer-Egli and Hermine Kittel. The latter, by the way, did not come from Amsterdam, nor did G.M. (who

came from Frankfurt/M). Both, however, went to Amsterdam this same autumn (see Letters 50-2 and 54).

Page 60, line 10
Pfitzner's First String Quartet was given its first performance by the Rosé Quartet in Vienna on 13th January 1903, and it was, in fact, Bruno Walter who had introduced it to the Mahlers and Rosé, on 18th December 1902 (see Walter, *op. cit.*, pp. 59f.). The quartet was published during the spring of 1903 by Max Brockhaus in Wiesbaden, and dedicated to A.M.

Page 60, line 15
Mahler returned to Vienna at the end of August. In none of his letters to Alma, published or unpublished, does he respond to Alma's enthusiasm for Pfitzner's opera. Nevertheless, he decided to perform it, and the première took place on 6th April 1905.

Page 60, line 28
The Scherzo and the Andante.

Page 60, line 32
The manuscript of 'Liebst du um Schönheit' is dated 10th August 1902. The song was not published until March 1907, as an independent song for voice and piano. The arrangement for orchestra was the work of Max Puttmann (see *DM*³, pp. 123-4). It was not published until after Mahler's death.

Page 62, line 20
Hugo Wolf had died on 22nd February 1903. Mahler attended his funeral a few days later.

Page 63, line 4
It seems that the earlier warm relationship between G.M. and Rudolf Krzyzanowski cooled markedly during the season (1896-7) they worked together in Hamburg. One has the impression that Pollini tried to make bad blood between them, giving Krzyzanowski operas to conduct which G.M. contractually had the right to conduct himself. Krzyzanowski left Hamburg for Weimar soon after G.M. and later conducted some of Mahler's works in Weimar.

Page 63, line 29
The only job Wolf ever held was as chorus director at the theatre in Salz-

burg during the 1881-2 season. But he was a total failure and left before the season was over.

Page 64, line 13
Their meeting at Bayreuth must have taken place in the summer of 1883.

Page 64, lines 15-30
This incident took place on 18th September 1897. At the time Mahler was living at Bartensteingasse, 3. Three days later, on 21st September, Wolf was committed to an asylum.

Page 65, line 6
For some unknown reason this performance was conducted by Bruno Walter, who also conducted the last (the seventh) performance of the opera on 24th March.

Page 65, line 13
A.M. refers of course to the first German production of *Falstaff* in Vienna. Mahler had already conducted the work during his years in Hamburg.

Page 66, lines 36-7
This was during Easter, at the end of March; cf. Letters 32-4, pp. 234-5.

Page 67, line 3
Mahler came from Cologne, where, on 27th March, he had conducted a performance of his Third Symphony. Alma is unjust to Mahler, who took every care about how she travelled to Abbazia, but it seems she preferred not to publish those letters in which his concern is apparent.

Page 67, line 14
Marie Schleinzer was a member of the Vienna Opera from September 1895 until February 1901.

Page 67, line 16
Crown Prince Karl was born in 1887 and thus aged 17 in 1904. His younger brother, Maxim Eugen Ludwig, was born in 1895.

Page 67, line 18
The work Mahler took with him to Abbazia, was, presumably, the Sixth Symphony.

Page 67, line 30

According to Mahler's unpublished letters to Alma, he returned alone to Vienna (c. 2nd April), whereas Alma remained in Abbazia for about another week. In fact, Mahler's holiday was over; he had been away from the Opera since 20th March on a concert tour to Mainz and Cologne.

Page 70, line 2

Alma was not quite correct. Mahler probably composed three songs in 1901, and added two more (Nos. 2 and 5?) in 1904. See DM^2, pp. 34-6 and p. 439, n. to p. 35, DM^3, pp. 74-143, and Christopher O. Lewis, 'On the Chronology of the *Kindertotenlieder*', in *Revue Mahler Review* 1 (1987), pp. 21-37. During the summer he also composed the two 'Nachtmusik' Serenades of the Seventh Symphony.

Page 70, line 22

A.M. refers here to the Scherzo of the Sixth. Originally this movement was placed second in the sequence of four movements by Mahler, but even before the première of the work at Essen on 27th May 1906 he reversed the order of the inner movements, placing the Scherzo third (Two editions of the symphony were published in advance of the première. In the first edition of the orchestral score (March 1906), the inner movements were placed Scherzo-Andante. But in the piano-duet edition which appeared two months later in May, the sequence was reversed, i.e. Andante-Scherzo.) It seems that when Mahler conducted the work himself for the last time, in Vienna on 4th January 1907, he reverted to his original order, i.e. the Scherzo was placed second; and it is this order that was reinstated in the critical edition of the score published under the auspices of the International Gustav Mahler Society, Vienna, in 1963. It seems far from safe to assume, however, that this last performance of Mahler's should be interpreted as an expression of his final, irrevocable wishes with regard to the order. It is interesting to note that only a few months earlier, in Berlin on 8th October 1906, Mahler himself had attended a performance of the symphony under Oskar Fried in which the inner movements followed the Andante-Scherzo sequence. Perhaps this stimulated G.M. to experiment in 1907 with a return to his original conception, though in fact the decision to do so must have been very much a last-minute one. In the programme for the 1907 concert the movements appear in the order Andante-Scherzo. This question continues to be debated with much vigour. See HLG^2 p. 996, Norman Del Mar, *Mahler's Sixth Symphony: A Study*, with an introduction by Colin Matthews (London, Eulenburg, 1980); and

Donald Mitchell, 'The Only Sixth', in the programme book for 'Mahler, Vienna and the Twentieth Century', (London Symphony Orchestra, Barbican, Autumn, 1985). The story regarding 'the arhythmic games of the two children' has to be questioned. We know that the movement was composed during the summer of 1903, when the elder child was only eight months old, and the other not yet born. Mahler may later have compared the movement to children's games, but it is unlikely that he conceived it along the lines suggested by Alma.

Page 72, line 30
According to Letter 46, p. 244, Alma had caught a chill.

Page 73, line 1
Two reading-rehearsals of the Fifth Symphony took place between 17th and 26th September with the Vienna Philharmonic, shortly before he left for the première of the work in Cologne. As for A.M.'s description of Mahler's overscoring – 'madly and persistently' – of the percussion, Colin Matthews comments as follows in his *Mahler at Work: Aspects of the Creative Process* (D.Phil. Thesis, University of Sussex, 1977, p. 59):

> 'However much truth there may be in this engaging story, the evidence of the manuscript and the printed scores does not, unfortunately, bear it out. In fact the first edition of the score actually has very slightly more percussion in the first movement (to which Alma is surely referring) than the manuscript; while the second edition merely omits a mezzo-forte cymbal and two pianissimo bass drum strokes. The orchestral revisions are, however, all concerned with lightening and clarifying the texture – the first version was heavily scored, in places almost clumsily so, as if Mahler was unsure of how to deal with the middle-period change of style ushered in by this Symphony.'

The autograph fair copy of the full score of the Fifth is in the possession of the Pierpont Morgan Library, New York, while Alma Mahler's autograph copy is held by the New York Public Library. This was used by the engravers. The copy contains some corrections and additions in Mahler's hand but essentially is identical with Mahler's fair copy mentioned above. See also the revised and improved Critical Edition of the Fifth published under the auspices of the I.G.M.S. in 1989 with a Preface by Karl Heinz Füssl. All the evidence suggests that A.M. exaggerated somewhat her role as censor of her husband's percussion part.

Page 73, line 23
G.M. himself in fact conducted both performances of the Fourth. See Letter 53, p. 248, and *MSL*, p. 437.

Page 76, line 15
According to *AST* this episode took place on 15th December 1902.

Page 77, line 1
Rheingold was first given on 23rd January 1905.

Page 77, line 8
The concert took place on the 25th and included, besides Schoenberg's *Pelleas und Melisande*, the première of Zemlinsky's *Die Seejungfrau* (symphonic poem after Hans Andersen), and a song by Oscar Posa. Mahler was able to attend only the dress rehearsal, because he had to conduct at the Opera that night.

Page 77, line 25
Mr. Donald Ross, to whom we are indebted, informs us that it was probably Frau Ida Conrat, a member of the Brahms circle in Vienna, who was responsible for the Brahms memorial gravestone. As Mr. Ross writes: 'I think my mother was a first or second cousin of Ida. I know that her family was not welcome to visit the Conrats on Sunday nights – Brahms night!'

Page 77, line 26
A.M. probably refers to the performance of G.M.'s First Symphony in Vienna on 18th November 1900 (see p. 3).

Page 78, line 3
A.M. probably refers to the first performance of the Fourth Symphony in Vienna on 12th January 1902. However, Schoenberg was not living in Vienna at that time. After marrying Mathilde Zemlinsky on 18th October 1901, he had moved to Berlin in December of the same year and lived there until July 1903. We know that he was critical of Mahler's Second Symphony when he heard it in Vienna on 9th April 1899. It was no doubt the performance of the First Symphony (on 18th November 1900) that he did not want to hear, when he might indeed have said, 'How can Mahler do anything with the *First* when he has already failed to do anything with the *Second*?'

Page 78, line 8
It is worth mentioning that Mahler had given the first performance of Zemlinsky's opera *Es war einmal* on 22nd January 1900, in Vienna.

Page 79, line 2
The only time Mahler conducted *Tannhäuser* after meeting Alma was on 25th December 1901 (it was also the last time he was to conduct the work). The score to which A.M. refers is now in the Austrian National Library in Vienna (Catalogue No. Mus. HS. 3254/1-3). The title page has clearly been folded twice (not four times as stated by A.M.). In the bottom right-hand corner, Wagner has written: '*Am 7 / Februar 1847 / habe ich die 13ᵗᵉ Aufführung dieser / Oper aus dieser Partitur dirigiert. / Richard Wagner*' / . Only his surname is difficult to decipher.

Page 79, line 20
This episode no doubt belongs to the spring of 1906; cf. p. 90, line 8.

Page 80, line 9
Klaus Pringsheim was a coach at the Opera, on a voluntary basis, during the 1906-7 season. This episode no doubt belongs to the autumn of 1906.

Page 81, line 2
At the concert of G.M.'s songs, seven songs from *Des Knaben Wunderhorn*, four of the Rückert songs (excluding 'Liebst du um Schönheit') and the *Kindertotenlieder* were performed by various singers.

Page 81, line 6
The rehearsals had of course begun much earlier, according to the records of the Opera, as well as those of Bruno Walter, on 6th March. The première took place on 4th April.

Page 81, line 28
Fidelio was performed on 16th March.

Page 83, line 2
For all Pfitzner's want of sympathy and lack of contact with Mahler's music, he had in fact already (in 1905) given performances of Mahler's works and was to do so on some later occasions. The Second Symphony and the *Wunderhorn* songs, for example, were works that Pfitzner conducted.

Page 83, line 12
The première of *Rose Bernd* at the Burgtheater had taken place on 11th February 1904.

Page 83, line 19
Hauptmann had begun his novel, *Der Narr in Christo Emanuel Quint*, in 1901-2. It was published in 1910.

Page 83, line 32
According to *ELM* the friend was Alfred Roller. *Rose Bernd* was written in 1903.

Page 84, line 31
G.M. had conducted Strauss's *Sinfonia Domestica* as early as 23rd November 1904.

Page 85, line 1
The first concert of the Alsatian Music Festival took place on 20th May. At the second concert, the Brahms *Rhapsody* was conducted by Ernst Münch, the Mozart Violin Concerto (K. 216), by Strauss. At the third concert, *An die ferne Geliebte* was sung by Ludwig Hess (a tenor from Berlin) and the solo quartet in the Ninth was sung by Johanna Dietz (alto), Hess, and Adrienne (soprano) and Felix von Kraus-Osborne (bass).

Page 85, line 30
'Venezia in Vienna': this was an entertainment establishment on the Prater. Strauss had himself conducted three concerts there in June 1902.

Page 86, line 5
In March, Strauss had conducted two afternoon concerts at Wanamaker's Warehouse, for which he was paid $1000.

Page 89, line 22
With reference to the composition of the Seventh Symphony, see also Letter 155. We should, however, be wary of accepting G.M.'s own chronology too literally. The sheer physical bulk of the first and last movements alone would make it improbable that the symphony was completed quite as swiftly as he suggests. A.M. in fact, refers to the 'architect's drawings' for the work that belonged to the mid-summer of 1904, and it would have been on those doubtless substantial drafts and sketches that G.M. worked in the summer of 1905. What he meant

by writing to A.M., 'and in four weeks the first, third and fifth movements were done', was not that they were composed from start to finish during that short period, but brought, rather, to that stage of evolution in MS form which G.M. recognized as essentially complete. As almost always, the moment of final formulation of a work was a critical one for him, and it was almost certainly this stage that was accomplished in a great burst of creative energy in 1905 (at least as far as the first, third and fifth movements were concerned) and to which G.M. refers in his letter. We know that the two serenade movements, the Nocturnes ('Nachtmusiken'), were the first movements to be finished; and from what appears to be the first MS draft full score of the first movement, which is inscribed 'Maiernigg, 15th August, 1905, Septima finita', we learn that it was the great first movement that was the *last* to be completed. It is fascinating to note that the 'rhythm and character' of the introduction to the first movement must have been a very late musical idea to come to G.M., prompted, as he himself describes, by the stroke of the oars as he was rowed across the lake in the summer of 1905. (See also *HG*², pp. 1181-1213, and Donald Mitchell, programme note on the Seventh Symphony, BBC Symphony Orchestra, 9th March 1990, London, BBC.)

Page 90, line 5
Weingartner performed the Minuet from the Third Symphony in Hamburg on 7th December 1896 (when it was repeated!).

Page 90, line 8
The Dehmel night at the Ansorge-Society had taken place on 6th March 1904.

Page 90, line 21
The Fifth Symphony was performed by G.M. in Hamburg on 13th March 1905 (see also Letters 66 and 67).

Page 90, line 23
The *Requiem* by Berlioz was given in Vienna on 3rd March 1904.

Page 92, line 7
Concerning the Meier-Graefe questionnaire, it is worth noting that G.M. (along with Grieg), at almost the same time, refused to answer on principle a similar questionnaire about Bach ('What does Bach mean to me, and what does he mean to the music of our time?'). Julius Meier-Graefe (1867-1935) was a German art critic and historian.

Page 92, line 36

The performance of the Fifth in Prague was given on 2nd March 1905, under Leo Blech and in Berlin on 20th February 1905, under Nikisch.

Page 93, line 7

Oskar Fried's settings of Dehmel's *Verklärte Nacht* (Op. 10) and *Erntelied* (Op. 15). Mahler had met Fried in Vienna just before he went to Hamburg.

Page 97, line 1

The performance of the Third Symphony in Breslau took place on 24th October. The concert also included four of G.M.'s songs. In the preceding year in Breslau, on 20th December, G.M. had conducted his Fifth Symphony (see also Letter 84).

Page 97, line 6

In fact only his second wife, the singer Hermine Finck, whom, however, he divorced in 1911 after eleven years of marriage. The world première of *Flauto Solo* had taken place in Prague on 12th November 1905. The Vienna première was conducted by Franz Schalk.

Page 97, line 10

Strauss conducted three performances of *Salome* in Graz between 16th and 20th May 1906. The opera was not performed at the Vienna Opera until 1918.

Page 97, line 16

As the Golling waterfalls are some twenty miles south of Salzburg (i.e. almost 150 miles from Graz), this afternoon expedition does not sound practicable, at least not in 1906. A.M. must have got the name of the place wrong.

Page 99, line 4

Mahler had applied to the Philharmonic Orchestra for one reading-rehearsal, but was granted three, one of which took place on 1st May.

Page 100, line 4

The concert and the dress rehearsal both took place on 27th May, the latter in the morning.

Page 100, line 11

It was finally Strauss himself, who, in memory of the deceased mayor, conducted a performance of Mozart's *Maurerische Trauermusik* (K. 477), preceding Mahler's Sixth Symphony.

Page 100, line 33
There is a contradiction here; cf. A.M.'s remark on p. 99, line 7 from bottom. It is the case that Mahler went alone to Essen on 20th May, i.e. three days after he and Strauss had parted in Graz. It is more likely that the incident took place on the day the Mahlers had arrived at Strasbourg, in May 1905. At that time Mahler's Third had been given twice in succession in Vienna (which was never the case with the Second); and it was there, early in 1905, that his orchestral songs had also been performed twice with great success. With regard to the meeting in Strasbourg, Alma claims that Strauss arrived eight days after the Mahlers (see p. 85), but she must have been mistaken.

Page 102, lines 1-11
For Mahler's own description, see Letter 155, p. 328. The Mahlers had arrived at Maiernigg on 13th June, and already, by the 21st, he was asking Fritz Löhr for a translation of 'Veni creator spiritus' (see *MSL*, pp. 291-2). Incidentally, the hymn is to be found in all Austrian hymn-books as it is usually sung at services on Whit Sunday. See *DM*³, pp. 519-49.

Page 102, line 15
Figaro was repeated on the 20th.

Page 102, line 21
According to Letter 97, p. 277, it was in the company of Strauss, not Roller. Lehmann had sung the part of Donna Anna in that particular performance, in which case it is not clear how she could have overheard Mahler's sardonic comment. Perhaps, as so often, A.M. rolls together more than one memory.

Page 104, line 16
It was Bruno Walter who conducted Erlanger's opera, which was only given three performances in all. According to Karpath (*op. cit.*, p. 153), Mahler had seen the opera in Paris in June 1900.

Page 104, line 26
Between 12th and 19th October, Mahler conducted four times: *Figaro* (12th), *Seraglio* (14th), *Magic Flute* (18th), and *Tristan* (19th). *Don*

Giovanni was not performed during this unofficial 'Festival'. On 20th October, Mahler left for a concert in Breslau.

Page 106, line 5
The date for *Lohengrin* requires some amplification. Mahler had conducted Act I of the new production on 14th November 1905 for a royal gala (see note to p. 113), while Acts II and III followed on 27th February 1906. In the meantime Franz Schalk had taken over the new production, which Mahler never conducted in its entirety.

Page 106, line 9
The performance of the First Symphony in Brünn [Brno] took place on 11th November 1906.

Page 106, line 26
The tour to St. Petersburg, as the note above indicates, took place in the autumn of 1907; cf. Letters 122-6, pp. 295-300.

Page 107, line 19
A.M. is referring to Rott's Symphony in E major, the first movement of which was submitted in July 1878 for a competition but was rejected; cf. p. 8, lines 31-6. Paul Banks has edited the symphony, which was given its world première in Cincinnati on 4th March 1989 and recorded a few days later in London (Hyperion, CDA 66366, with an historical and analytical note by Dr. Banks). The story about Bruckner is open to doubt: Rott's mother had died in 1860, and his stepmother in 1872. Bauer-Lechner relates a similar story, but she refers to the mother of Rudolf Krzyzanowski in her anecdote.

Page 107, footnote
It seems as if Mahler was responsible for the arrangement of the first three movements of Bruckner's symphony and Krzyzanowski for the fourth. However, it is only Mahler's name that appears on the title page of this rare publication. See *DM*², pp. 68-9.

Page 108, line 6
The incident took place in May 1891 when Ochs conducted Bruckner's *Te Deum.*

Page 108, line 19
A.M. is mistaken. Only Bruckner's Fourth, Fifth and Sixth symphonies were included in Mahler's concert programmes, and it was only the

Fourth that was performed (30th March 1910) in New York. In Hamburg he had conducted the *Te Deum* three times and the Mass in D minor once.

Page 108, line 26

Mahler was *Kapellmeister* at the summer theatre in Bad Hall from the end of May until 18th August 1880. He was not dismissed from this post, but left it at the end of the short season.

Page 109, line 19

Mahler held the post of *Kapellmeister* at Laibach from the end of September 1881 until the beginning of April 1882, when the season closed, and he left Laibach with an excellent reputation. The Theatre had a male chorus of seven members. Mahler conducted *Faust* on 27th and 28th January and 1st February 1882. Act IV was given a separate performance on 3rd February 1882. None of the reviews connected with these performances mentions the incident involving a male chorus of one! However, when Mahler was about to produce *Carmen* at the Theatre in Olmütz a year later, he found that five members of the chorus had gone missing.

Page 109, line 34

It seems that A.M. has confused circumstances in Olmütz with those in Cassel. The permanent conductor in Olmütz, Emil Kaiser, suddenly resigned in January 1883, and through his agent in Vienna, G.M. was engaged as his replacement. He remained in this post until the end of the season (March 1883). It was again through his agent that Mahler got the job in Cassel. In the last week of May 1883 he was on probation. One of his duties was to conduct the dress rehearsal of Marschner's *Hans Heiling*, which was then unknown to him, whereas Flotow's *Martha* he knew quite well, having conducted it several times.

Page 110, line 7

G.M.'s contract with the Theatre in Cassel ran for three years, but at the end of the second season he asked to be released; when permission was granted, he left for Prague (1885-6 season). While at Cassel, Mahler fell in love with Johanna Richter, a soprano for whom he wrote the *Lieder eines fahrenden Gesellen*. A letter from her (signed 'Anna', i.e. pet name for Johanna) has survived in *ELM*, and this is probably the reason why A.M. had the idea that he had fallen in love with *two* singers.

Page 110, line 16

G.M. was engaged at the Theatre in Leipzig from July 1886 and remained there until May 1888, when he asked to be released.

Page 111, line 24 et seq.

A.M. mentions here the support that her husband gave Schoenberg, support that was both moral and financial (see Letters 171-3, pp. 339-42). Indeed, the Mahler-Schoenberg relationship is a continuous thread in the texture of this book, though it so happens that Schoenberg's activities as a painter are never mentioned. A little-known incident in this context has been revealed in recent years, one that throws fresh light on the two composers' friendship. On 13th September 1911, just after Schoenberg's 37th birthday, and after Mahler's death in the preceding May, Webern wrote to tell his teacher who it was who had purchased some of his paintings but had wished his identity to remain undisclosed. Webern decided that Mahler's death permitted him to release the information. 'Your paintings', he wrote to Schoenberg, 'were bought by GUSTAV MAHLER' [Webern's capitals]. (See H.H. Stuckenschmidt, 'Bilder und Schicksale', in *Hommage à Schönberg*, Berlin National-gallerie, 1974.) The pictures are not identified, nor is the occasion of their purchase specified. It would be fascinating to establish the details of this affair, though it is clear that Mahler's awareness of the proud, touchy, and independent character of Schoenberg led him to try to keep his role as purchaser secret, presumably because he feared that Schoenberg might suspect the buying of his paintings as a surreptitious act of charity. No doubt this was part of Mahler's intention: why, otherwise, the secrecy? Webern's letter of 1911 opens yet another window on the relationship between these two men of genius, and supplements what we have already known of that relationship from Letters 171-3. On the occasion of the first performance of Schoenberg's D minor String Quartet, the composer inscribed a copy of the miniature score of the work to G.M. in the following terms: 'To Director Gustav Mahler, As an attempt to express thanks for the *repeated help* through recommendation, and even *much more, much more*, through the shining artistic example. Arnold Schönberg, Vienna, 5th February, 1907.' (The score forms part of the Anna Mahler Collection at the University of Southampton.) See also Mahler's letter to Strauss of 6th February 1907 in *Gustav Mahler and Richard Strauss: Correspondence 1888-1911*, edited by Herta Blaukopf and translated by Edmund Jephcott (London, Faber, 1984, p. 96).

Page 112, footnote 1 (*)
The first performance of *Verklärte Nacht* was on 18th March 1902 (Mahler and Alma were then on honeymoon in Petersburg). The second performance, which they attended, took place on 1st March 1904.

Page 113, line 34
The gala performance to which A.M. refers took place on 14th November 1905, in honour of King Alfonso XII of Spain; see also note to p. 106, line 5.

Page 114, line 19
'E.B.-F.' was Ellen Brandt-Forster (1866-1921), who was engaged at the Vienna Opera from 1887 until 30th April 1906. Mizzi Günther (1879-1961) never appeared at the Opera.

Page 117, line 5
The ballet in question was *Rübezahl* (music by Delibes and Minkus, arranged by Julius Lehnert, who also conducted the ballet). The choreography was by Karl Godlewski, and Roller designed the production, which had its première on 1st June 1907. It is not clear who wrote the libretto for the ballet, probably Roller himself. In his book *Die Bildnisse Gustav Mahlers* (Vienna, E. P. Tal, 1922, p. 12) he relates how Mahler told him the plot of *his Rübezahl*, and perhaps it was in connection with this production that Justine showed Roller the libretto Mahler had sketched in the 1880s (cf. pp. 143-4, and Letter 138).

Page 117, line 29
Mahler had arranged to give only two concerts in Rome, the first on 25th March and the second on 1st April. The third concert, to which A.M. refers, took place at Trieste on 4th April and included the First Symphony. In 1907 Easter occurred between 26th and 30th March, and as usual the Opera was closed. Alma's story about Mahler's engagement book is corroborated in an article by Richard Specht, 'Mahlers Feinde' ('Mahler's Enemies') in *Musikblätter des Anbruch*, Nos. 7 and 8, 1920, p. 286.

Page 119, line 24
More likely drafts for the Eighth Symphony: the Seventh had been completed in 1905.

Page 121, line 3
Between 5th May and 4th June 1907, Mahler had rented a room at the

Hotel Imperial in Vienna because of the ill health of his family. On the last day he applied to the Opera for remuneration of his expenses. In the meantime, on 27th May, he had asked to be released from his contract, which was granted, providing a replacement could be found.

Page 121, line 23
Maria ('Putzi') died on 12th July.

Page 121, line 32
The relative was Alma's cousin, Richard Nepallek.

Page 122, line 19
Mahler went to Vienna on 17th July; cf. Letter 116, p. 290.

Page 122, line 29
According to some unpublished letters to Alma in *ELM*, the family apparently returned to Maiernigg during the second half of August.

Page 123, line 1
The 'old consumptive friend' was Theobald Pollak (1855-1912). A question mark hangs over the presentation of the Bethge volume to Mahler in the summer of 1907. According to the *Börsenblatt für den Deutschen Buchhandel*, the book was announced for publication at the end of July 1907, but only released at the beginning of October of that year. Was Pollak in possession of a set of advance proofs? See also *DM*[3], p. 165.

Page 124, line 13
According to Letter 114 (pp. 289-90) the contract was for three months. See also Zoltan Roman's important documentary volume, *Gustav Mahler's American Years, 1907-1911* (New York, Pendragon Press, 1989), which gives all the details; see in particular pp. 26-33 and pp. 39-40.

Page 124, line 31
It was finally Weingartner who became Mahler's successor (from 1st January 1908). The Opera had had serious negotiations with Felix Mottl, but he was unable to be released from his post at the Royal Opera in Munich.

Page 125, line 8
Mahler returned to Vienna (from Maiernigg) on 24th August, and

conducted six performances during the following two months, the first on 12th September and the last on 15th October (*Fidelio*). The other operas were *Don Giovanni, Die Walküre, Figaro, Die Zauberflöte*, and Gluck's *Iphigénie in Aulis*. It is perhaps unfair to claim that he was deserted by the public as the public could not have known when he was conducting: as was the custom, neither posters nor programmes revealed in advance the name of the conductor.

Page 126, line 22
The Mahlers left Vienna on 9th December.

Page 127, line 14
According to an article (22nd December) in the *Sonntagsblatt der New Yorker Staatszeitung*, the Mahlers arrived on board the *Kaiserin Augusta Victoria* (see also Letter 131) on 21st December. In the same article we learn that G.M. together with the singers Alois Burgstaller, Frau Holzmann-Weymouth and Mrs. Kath. M. Sharn, gave a concert on the boat on 18th December for the benefit of the seamen's pension fund.

Page 129, line 20
Alma is not quite correct about Felix Mottl. He came to New York in 1903-4 to conduct the first performance of *Parsifal* outside Bayreuth, but owing to protests by the Wagner family was unable to fulfil the engagement.

Page 130, line 3
Maurice Baumfeld (1868-1913), Austrian-born music critic, and Director of the German Theater in New York.

Page 131, line 1
Mahler did not conduct any operas in Italian in New York, except for Mozart's *Don Giovanni* and *Figaro*, and no Italian opera. The remark perhaps makes more sense as a general indication of the resources available to Heinrich Conried.

Page 131, line 7
The *Tristan* performance referred to here was given on 12th March 1909.

Page 131, line 10
'to Boston' = April 1908. *Valkyrie* was given on the 8th, *Don Giovanni* the following day, and *Tristan* on the 11th.

Page 132, line 8
The first trip to Philadelphia was with *Tristan* on 28th January 1908.

Page 132, line 32
Gadski did not sing Fricka but Brünnhilde, on 7th and 11th February 1908. The role of Donna Elvira in *Don Giovanni* was sung by Rita La Fornia on 18th February and not by Gadski as A.M. suggests on p. 133, line 10; and it was Marion Weed who sang Donna Anna not Fremstad.

Page 133, line 12
The première of *Valkyrie* in New York was given on 7th February 1908, in Philadelphia on the 11th, and repeated on the 13th. *Figaro* had its première in New York on 13th January 1909. The première of *Siegfried* in New York took place on 19th February 1908 (repeated on 27th February, 7th March and 16th April), and in Philadelphia on 24th March.

Page 133, line 16
The performance of *Don Giovanni* was on 12th February 1908. The gentleman in question is identified in the original German edition as 'Mr. Hilprecht', i.e. Hermann Hilprecht (1859-1925), a German-born professor.

Page 135, line 7
According to the *New York Times*, 15th February 1908, it was Deputy Fire Chief, Charles W. Kruger,

'known to all firemen as *Big-Hearted-Charley*, who went to his death [on the morning of 14 February] in the flooded sub-cellar of 215 Canal Street, while his driver ... and two men of Truck 8 clung to his arms and vainly tried to draw him back to safety ... but his weight of nearly 300 pounds, together with his equipment for fire fighting, proved too much and they could barely keep him from falling back into the pit, let alone draw him out of it.'

The same paper reports on 17th February of his funeral at St. Thomas's Church at 53rd Street and Fifth Avenue:

'outside at least 25,000 persons thronged the avenue, while other thousands walked 57th Street, swarmed in Columbus Circle, and crowded the sidewalks of Central Park West to stand with heads uncovered as the funeral passed ... The procession ... started shortly after 1 o'clock ... two troops of mounted police ... rode behind the band of the Police Department ... The band played *Nearer, My God, to Thee* ... The funeral parade after the service [in the church] was comparatively short. It traversed Fifth Avenue to 57th Street, 57th Street to Broadway, thence through Columbus Circle to Central Park West and to 72nd Street, where the carriage proceeded to Woodlawn and the parade was dismissed.'

This was what Mahler and Alma would have observed from their windows on Sunday, 16th February 1908.

Page 136, line 22
The Mahlers, in fact, spent four months in New York the first winter. They sailed from New York on 23rd April 1908 and arrived at Cuxhaven on 2nd May at 6.30 am.

Page 137, lines 29-31
Mahler went to Wiesbaden on 5th May, and at the concert on the 8th he conducted, besides his own First Symphony, Mendelssohn's *Fingal's Cave* overture and Beethoven's *Leonora* overture No. 3.

Page 138, line 7
They arrived at Vienna on 10th May, and ten days later Mahler went to Prague, where on the 23rd, he conducted a concert; cf. Letter 135, pp. 305-6. A.M.'s remark about 'deep snow' in Toblach – in *May* – is highly surprising to today's villagers. The Mahlers left Vienna for Toblach on 10th June.

Page 140, line 20
On 3rd November, Mahler gave Emil Freund, his friend and lawyer, power of attorney to sell the villa. Three days later it was sold for the sum of 52,000 gold crowns (including 10,000 crowns for furniture, etc.).

Page 140, line 29 et seq.
The Tauernbahn was not opened until July 1909. Thus the visit to Burckhard must have taken place the following summer, which is also confirmed by unpublished letters from Burckhard to the Mahlers.

Page 142, line 22
According to *MSL*, p. 326, Mahler left Toblach for Vienna in the

evening of 4th September, arrived the next morning, and continued to Prague the same day at 6 pm.

Page 142, line 33
A.M. arrived at Prague on 15th September.

Page 143, line 21
The Munich performance of the Seventh took place on 27th October; see also Letter 136, p. 306.

Page 144, line 20
Mahler conducted a concert in Hamburg on 9th November; three days later the family embarked at Cuxhaven (M/S *Amerika*).

Page 144, line 27
Anna Mahler had, as a matter of fact, turned four on 15th June.

Page 148, line 7
The Mahlers sailed from New York on 10th April, and arrived at Cherbourg ten days later. The family remained in Paris until the beginning of May, when they left for Vienna.

Page 151, line 7
According to *HLG*[3], pp. 178-9, this performance of *Tristan* took place on 11th December 1907.

Page 151, line 18
According to Mahler's unpublished letters to Alma (in *ELM*) it was, in fact, he who took her to Levico, and from there went alone to Toblach.

Page 151, line 24
Only two letters, Nos. 148 and 150, in the present volume could be described as being 'on abstract topics'. The eighteen unpublished letters G.M. wrote to A.M. this summer (in *ELM*) are certainly not abstract, but rather the opposite. The published letters, moreover, have been heavily cut.

Page 152, line 4
The autograph score of the final Adagio (recently acquired by M. de La Grange, Paris) is dated 'Toblach, 2 September, 1909'.

Page 153, line 33

Mahler had left Toblach for Vienna on 6th September and remained there until c. 18th September, when he paid a four-day visit to Prof. Fritz Redlich in Göding (Moravia). On 26th September he travelled to Amsterdam. For a detailed account of G.M.'s visit to Göding, see Kurt Blaukopf's 'Mahler in Göding', in the *Neue Zürcher Zeitung*, 14th September 1969. The article includes a photograph of the house, which is also reproduced in Prof. Blaukopf's documentary volume (*Mahler*, London, Thames and Hudson, 1976). See also note to Letter 23.

Page 154, line 5

Mahler conducted his Seventh at three concerts in Holland at the beginning of October 1909: The Hague on the 2nd, and Amsterdam on the 3rd and 7th, all three with the Concertgebouw Orchestra. After the last concert he met A.M. in Paris, and on 12th October they embarked at Cherbourg and arrived at New York on the 19th.

Page 154, line 18

With the reorganized New York Philharmonic Orchestra, Mahler gave forty-six concerts between 4th November 1909 and 2nd April 1910. Thirty-five took place in New York (subscription concerts divided into four cycles), plus an additional eleven non-subscription concerts. Five concerts took place at Brooklyn, two in Philadelphia, and one each in Boston, New Haven, Providence and Springfield. It was only during the following season that he conducted in Buffalo.

Page 154, line 28

Mahler's last opera project was Tchaikovsky's *Queen of Spades*, which he conducted four times during March 1910 (5th, 9th, 17th, and 21st). The Smetana had been performed the previous season; cf. p. 131.

Page 154, line 33

A reference to Mahler's Bach Suite, arranged from the orchestral Suites Nos. 2 and 3, first performed in New York on 10th November 1909, and again at twenty concerts in America during this and the following season, and once at a concert in Rome in 1910. See also DM^2, pp. 345-62.

Page 155, line 7

W.J. Henderson's account of the occasion in the *New York Sun* is reproduced in *Metropolitan Opera Annals*, compiled by William H. Seltsam

(New York, H. W. Wilson in association with Metropolitan Opera Guild, 1947, p. 197):

'After the curtain had fallen [on the *Traviata* excerpt] Mme. Sembrich was called before the curtain and the scene – the third act of *Le Nozze di Figaro* – was arranged for the ceremonies. A throne was placed at one side for Mme. Sembrich. Gustav Mahler took his place at the conductor's chair and began the march from *Figaro*. Mme. Sembrich, on the arm of Mr. Gatti-Casazza, entered, followed by all the artists of the company. Then Mr. Dippel read to Mme. Sembrich the resolution of the Metropolitan Opera Company which made her the first honorary member of the company. [This was followed by the presentation of numerous loving cups, wreaths, and other gifts and tokens, speeches by other members of the company, the mayor of the city, and a response by the artist, and "a final shower of rose petals which covered all the guests on the stage".]'

Page 156, line 17
The earthquake had occurred on 18th April 1906.

Page 157, line 20
Mrs. West-Roosevelt is identical with Mrs. James (Laura) Roosevelt (1858-1945), who was married to Mr. James West-Roosevelt (1858-96), physician and cousin of Theodore Roosevelt.

Page 157, line 35
Eusapia Palladino (1854-1918) had visited New York in the spring of 1908. According to the *New York Times* she made a return visit on 10th November 1909.

Page 159, line 21
Mrs. Louisine Havemeyer (d. 1929) was the widow of the millionaire Henry Osborne Havemeyer (1840-1907). El Greco's portrait of Cardinal Don Fernando Nino de Guevara is now in the Metropolitan Museum, New York.

Page 162, lines 24-31
Percy Wallace MacKaye's (1875-1956) play, *The Scarecrow* or *The Glass of Truth*, which was based on a story by Hawthorne, was first produced at the New York Garrick Theater on 11th January 1911, and was taken off three weeks later. This event therefore must belong to January of that year.

Page 163, line 8
Mahler had met Francesco Spetrino in Lemberg, in April 1903, and engaged him for the Vienna Opera. Antonio Guarnieri in fact was not appointed a conductor there until December 1912.

Page 166, line 18
The performance of the First Symphony in New York was given on 16th December 1909, and repeated on the afternoon of the 17th.

Page 166, line 35
Franz Kneisel, the violinist, had been a pupil at the Vienna Conservatoire at the same time as Mahler.

Page 167, line 2
Prince Paul Troubetzkoy (1866-1938), born in Milan, was himself a sculptor, as was his brother Vladimir.

Page 167, line 8
The journalist Carlo di Fornaro had just returned from a three-year stay in Mexico, and had published his *Diaz, Czar of Mexico*. Porfirio Diaz died in 1915.

Page 167, line 20
Poultney Bigelow (1855-1954), the American-born lawyer and journalist.

Page 168, lines 8-10
It was during the following season that Mahler conducted the overtures by Wagner (*Tannhäuser* five times; *Dutchman* seven times), though not in succession.

Page 169, line 3
Maria Labia did not sing in this performance. She was a member of the Hammerstein Opera Company only during the 1908-9 season.

Page 169, line 5
The Mahlers sailed from New York on 5th April and arrived in Paris on the 12th. The performance of the Second Symphony was given on 17th April 1910 (afternoon concert): the soloists were Povla Frisch and Hélène Demellier. Up to that time, the only works of G.M.'s performed in France had been the *Lieder eines fahrenden Gesellen* (Nos. 1, 2 and 4), in Paris in 1905. The First Symphony was heard in Paris and Lyon in

May 1909 from a German orchestra. The Fourth and Fifth Symphonies were to be performed in January 1911, in Paris.

Page 169, line 18ff.
Debussy's second wife was Emma Bardac. In *ELM* Alma describes her as 'old and ugly'. Debussy married his first wife, Lilly Texier, in 1899. He divorced her in 1905 after her attempted suicide in October 1904.

Page 170, line 27
Mengelberg had conducted a series of five concerts with the orchestra of the Accademia di Santa Cecilia. Mahler was to give three concerts, on 28th April, and 1st and 5th May, but the last was cancelled.

Page 172, line 1
It is obvious (see Letter 155, line 1, p. 328) that it was Mahler who took Alma to Tobelbad (about eight miles south-west of Graz). Mahler did not go to Toblach until the end of June, and only after having been in Leipzig and Munich for the preparation of the première of the Eighth Symphony. Just before he went to Toblach, G.M. paid Alma a short visit at Tobelbad, because he felt something was wrong. His instinct did not deceive him. With the publication of Reginald Isaac's *Walter Gropius: Der Mensch und sein Werk*, Vol. I, (Berlin, Mann, 1983) – which includes the correspondence between Alma and Gropius from this period – it is clear that the affair was much more serious and enduring than Alma cared to suggest here. The two lovers met in Munich at the première of Mahler's Eighth, and again in Paris, when Alma and Mahler returned to New York, in October 1910. After Mahler's death, Alma was to marry Gropius in 1915. They were divorced in 1920. Their daughter Manon, who tragically died in 1935, was the 'angel' to whose memory Berg dedicated his violin concerto (1936). See also note to Letter 157, p. 330.

Page 176, line 11
Five of Alma Mahler's songs were published in January 1911, by G.M.'s publishers, Universal Edition. The contract is dated 'Vienna, 12 October, 1910' and signed by Alma. A second set of Four Songs was published by the same publisher in 1915, and in 1924 she had a further set of Five Songs published by Weinberger in Vienna. All fourteen songs were recently collected in one volume and republished by Universal Edition. The first performance of the first set (excluding one song) was given in Vienna on 11th December 1910, by Thea Drill-Orridge, with Zemlinsky at the piano. Three songs from the last set were orchestrated

and given their first performance at a concert in Vienna on 22nd September 1924. See also Edward F. Kravitt, 'The *Lieder* of Alma Maria Schindler-Mahler', *Music Review*, 49/3 (August, 1988, pp. 190-204).

Page 176, line 20
The engraving firm of Waldheim-Eberle had published Mahler's first three symphonies under the imprint of Josef Weinberger, and the Fourth under the imprint of Ludwig Doblinger, both of them well-known music publishing houses in Vienna. Already in 1906 Universal Edition had published pocket scores of these symphonies as well as piano scores. Now, in June 1910, Universal Edition bought the rights to all Mahler's works, excluding the Fifth, Sixth and Seventh Symphonies, the Rückert settings and the early songs. Hertzka did not visit Mahler at Toblach, but they had met in Munich. Alma's story about the Bruckner symphonies should perhaps not be taken too literally.

Page 177, line 5
In *ELM* the song is identified as the setting of a poem by Dehmel, i.e. 'Die stille Stadt'.

Page 178, line 10
A typescript of the dedication has survived in *ELM*, and bears the date '20th August 1910'. The dedication was inserted into the second and revised edition of the vocal score, published during the summer of 1910. The first edition was prepared solely for performers participating in the première of the symphony.

Page 178, line 16
Mahler's departure from Toblach was on 4th September.

Page 178, line 34
The vocal score: the full score did not appear until 1911.

Page 179, line 14
The 'certain Countess' is identified in *ELM* as Countess Misa Wydenbruck, and the singer was Marie Gutheil-Schoder, who did not participate in the première of the symphony. It seems, by the way, that it was Bruno Walter who had chosen the soloists for Mahler.

Page 180, line 18
The 'eccentric American' is identified in *ELM* as James Loeb (1867-1933), a banker from New York.

Page 180, line 26

'All the members of his family': A.M. can only refer to Mahler's two sisters, Justine and Emma and their respective husbands, Arnold and Eduard Rosé. It seems natural that they should have wanted to congratulate Mahler.

Page 181, line 22

A.M. is unjust to her husband, who, less than a fortnight before, had presented her with a specially designed diadem (for her birthday on 31st August), ordered long before Alma's affair with Gropius began (see *MSL*, pp. 358 and 366). For reasons of her own A.M. deleted a sentence from Letter 13, p. 219, referring to a piece of jewellery that Mahler had enclosed with the letter; throughout the marriage we constantly find him mentioning gifts to A.M. in his letters to her. He was undoubtedly generous in this respect, though apparently not very imaginative in his choice.

Page 182, line 9

The Munich orchestra soon afterwards invited Arnold Rosé to appear as soloist in one of their regular concerts.

Page 182, Line 26

According to Isaac's biography of Gropius (*op. cit.*, p. 103) Alma left Vienna on 13th October on the Orient-Express, met Gropius in Munich, and then travelled with him to Paris, where they spent some days together. Mahler had some business to do in Berlin and Hamburg, embarking at Bremen on 18th October. The following day Alma joined him at Cherbourg.

Page 183, line 6

This season's first concert took place on 1st November in New York (the programme is reproduced on p. 155). A.M.'s account of Mahler's concerts is not accurate: Mahler never went to Seattle, and the tour to Springfield had taken place the previous season. The tour in question included Pittsburgh, Cleveland, Buffalo (on 7th December), Rochester, Syracuse and Utica. It began on 5th December and ended on the 10th. Beethoven's 'Pastoral' Symphony was included in all six concerts.

Page 184, line 30

In the original German edition the violinist in question is identified as 'Jonas'. His correct name was Theodor Eugen Johner, a Swiss musician, born in Basel on 25th July 1878. He joined the New York Symphony in

1905, and the Philharmonic in 1909. When he was dismissed from the orchestra, he returned to Switzerland, settled in Zürich, taught the violin, and conducted a chorus and a semi-professional orchestra. He was married and had three children.

Page 187, line 10

In a letter to Bruno Walter, dated 1st April 1910 (see *MSL*, p. 354), Mahler wrote that he had just finished making the fair copy of the Ninth Symphony; and on 21st May he signed a contract with his new publisher, Universal Edition, for both the Ninth and *Das Lied von der Erde*. During the winter of 1910-11 he proof-read the score of the Eighth and revised the published scores of the Fourth and Fifth Symphonies. He probably also amended the four songs by Alma which she was to publish in 1915, among them 'Erntelied' which is reproduced facing p. 306; two of these were composed in early spring, 1911 (see *MSL*, p. 371). Mahler's copies of the four songs have survived.

Page 188, et seq.

An interesting paper entitled 'G.M. and his illnesses' by Nicholas P. Christy, M.D., Beverly M. Christy, and Barry G. Wood, M.D., was published in the *Transactions of the American Clinical and Climatological Association*, (Vol. 82, 1970, pp. 200-17). It contains a good deal of further information about the medical treatment G.M. received in New York in 1911. A blood sample was taken, and 'after 4 or 5 days in the hospital laboratory, the Petri plates revealed numerous bacterial colonies and all the bouillon flasks were found to show a pure culture of the same organism which was subsequently identified as *streptococcus viridans* ... As this was long before the days of antibiotics, the bacterial findings sealed Mahler's doom. He insisted on being told the truth and then expressed a wish to die in Vienna. Accordingly, he and his wife left shortly thereafter for Paris, where the diagnosis and prognosis were reconfirmed, and then proceeded to Vienna.'

Page 189, line 6

A.M. is probably referring to a meeting on 1st February 1911 of the Guarantors' Committee. Excerpts from the minutes of this meeting are quoted by Roman, *op. cit.*, Document No. 526, p. 449. It was resolved at the meeting that:

'the General Committee forthwith appoint a Program Committee which shall be composed of six persons to be elected by the General Committee from among its members, and the Chairman of the

General Committee, Ex-Officio ... The Program Committee shall
supervise the selection of music to be played at the various concerts
of the Society. It shall submit the minutes of its meetings at the
regular meeting of the [General] Committee for approval by that
body.'

The Members of the Program Committee were, among others, Mrs.
Untermeyer, Mrs. Roosevelt and Miss Draper, and two representatives
from the orchestra.

Page 191, line 10
The song by A.M. which Frances Alda Casazza had included in her
recital on 3rd March 1911 at the Mendelssohn Hall, is entitled 'Laue
Sommernacht'. It is not a setting of a poem by Gustav Falke as stated in
the published edition, but of a poem, 'Gefunden', by Otto Julius Bier-
baum.

Page 194, line 16
On 8th April 1911, aboard the M/S *Amerika*, which arrived at Cherbourg on the 16th.

Page 195, line 29
According to *ELM*, the 'young Austrian' was Stefan Zweig.

Page 197, line 24
On 21st April Mahler was transferred to the clinic at Neuilly (50,
Avenue du Roule). The doctor's name was 'Defaut' not 'Dupré'. The
house no longer exists.

Page 200, line 5
In the afternoon of 11th May the Mahlers left Paris. The train arrived in
Vienna the following day, at 6 pm. The Loew Sanatorium was located at
20, Mariannengasse. It had been used frequently by the Mahlers in the
past.

Page 200, line 22
Mahler was buried on 22nd May in the little Grinzing cemetery. Alma's
state of health did not allow her to attend the funeral.

Part Two

LETTERS

[There are frequent references throughout the following annotations to the silent omission of sentences and paragraphs and collation of texts made by A.M. in her original German edition (1940), which were observed by the first English edition (1946). In many cases we indicate, comment on or explain these interventions by A.M., but for technical reasons it has not been possible to reinstate the omissions. In any event these amount to only a very small proportion of the whole. This final act of restoration must await the projected publication of the letters in their complete form.]

Page 205, Letter 1
The correct date is 29th November; cf. note above to p. 17, line 18. Up to that time Mahler had published his *Lieder und Gesänge*, Vols. 1-3 (1892), and later 'Knaben Wunderhorn' songs (1900). 'L.' is no doubt the painter Wilhelm Legler (1875-1951), a pupil of Carl Moll, and married to A.M.'s sister, Margarethe Julie ('Grethe'), born on 16th August 1880. She had married Legler on 4th September 1900, and their only child, Carl Wilhelm, was born on 26th February 1902.

Page 205, Letter 2
If it was G.M. who inscribed 'Wednesday evening' (i.e. 4th December 1901), then it must have been a slip of his pen. It was on that particular evening that he conducted *The Tales of Hoffmann*. He refers, however, to his visit to Alma's the previous day, which was on Monday the 2nd (cf. Letter 1). Carl Moll was about to make a trip to Berlin at that time, and it seems probable that Mahler had tried to persuade Alma to travel with him, but neither she nor her family went along with the idea.

Page 206, Letter 3
G.M.'s apology for not coming on Saturday (he did, however, turn up) and his reference to 'Evchen – and Hans Sachs' were crucial for their relationship. That, at least, is the impression one gets by reading the entry in A.M.'s diary (*AST*). While she hitherto had been rather luke-warm towards Mahler, she now suddenly found herself passionately in love with him, and she *had* to see him before he went on his travels. We do not know precisely what happened, but he came and they became secretly engaged, exactly one month after their first meeting, and having

met privately on only two occasions. See also note above to p. 23, line 31.

Page 207, Letter 5

The letter was written in Vienna, probably on the railway station before boarding the train for Dresden, where Mahler spent the next day rehearsing the Second Symphony. He left Dresden on the morning of the 11th.

Page 209, Letter 7

In the afternoon of 11th December, having posted Letter 6, Mahler visited his sister Emma at Dresden (probably to tell her about his engagement). He returned to Berlin the next morning and wrote the present letter of which only the second half is published here. The date attached to it is no doubt the date of delivery, of which A.M. made a note.

Pages 213-14

The programme of the Second Symphony was written especially for King Albert of Saxony, who was to attend the Dresden performance. Alma was given it when she visited Justine, and she copied the entire text into her diary.

Page 214, Letter 9

'W.' (p. 215, line 4) is identified in *ELM* as Wiener, i.e. Karl von Wiener (1863-1945), President of the *Gesellschaft der Musikfreunde* in Vienna.

Page 216, Letter 10

This was the day on which Mahler conducted the Berlin première of his Fourth Symphony, with Thila Plaichinger as soloist. It should be noted that the first part of the letter was omitted by A.M.

Page 217, Letter 11

According to Alma's diary there was a further letter from Mahler, which must have been lost or destroyed.

Page 219, Letter 12

The quotation (line 4) is from Schiller's 'Das Lied von der Glocke'.

Page 220, Letter 15

On 6th January 1902 A.M. wrote in her diary, 'Yesterday he sent me his V', though it was, in fact, the Fourth Symphony to which G.M. refers (see p. 220, footnote †). Alma gives the weekday as Saturday, but the first Saturday in the New Year in fact fell on 4th January. On the 2nd, they had for the first time made love, the stages of 'heaven' about which Mahler writes. The 'seventh' was probably their forthcoming wedding day.

Page 220, Letter 16
G.M. refers to the première of Strauss's *Feuersnot* on the 29th, after which a party was given (see pp. 27-8 above).

Page 221, Letter 17
The fragment from *Das klagende Lied* which we use as an illustration at the end of this letter (it is not of course related to the letter in any way), is a reproduction from a fair copy of the text that the youthful G.M. made for his close friend, Josef Steiner (who wrote the libretto for one of G.M.'s early operatic efforts, *Herzog Ernst von Schwaben*). The date refers to the day on which the copy was finished. The text itself had been completed almost a year earlier.

Page 222, Letter 18
The concert on 23rd January included, besides Mahler's Fourth (soloist: Grace Forbes), the *Carnaval romain* overture by Berlioz and Liszt's Piano Concerto No. 1 (soloist: Eugen d'Albert).

Page 223, Letter 19
Max Dauthage was a double-bass player, a member of the Vienna Philharmonic and the Opera Orchestra during G.M.'s ten years as Director. This probably explains Mahler's reference.

Page 225, Letter 20
The performance of *Tosca* on 31st March was conducted by Francesco Spetrino, whom Mahler was to engage for the Vienna Opera from November 1903 to September 1908. See also note to p. 163, line 8.

Page 227, Letter 23
At the end of the letter G.M. refers to a 'married couple, R.'. We are inclined to believe the reference is to Prof. Fritz Redlich (1868-1921) who lived in Göding and was often visited by G.M. (The late Prof. Hans F. Redlich was a nephew.) It is the same family that G.M. stayed with when he wrote Letters 151 and 152. See also note to p. 153, line 33.

Page 228, Letter 24

See note to Letter 119. A.M. did not publish all G.M.'s letters from this period, but those published here should be read in the following order: No. 119 (30th August); No. 25 (31st August – morning); No. 27 (31st August – evening); No. 122 (1st September); and No. 26 (2nd September).

Page 230, Letter 26, line 7

Peter Lordmann made two guest appearances in 1903, on 30th August and 2nd September as did Georg Bazelli, on 4th and 25th September. Line 23: 'Grethl' was A.M.'s sister. The songs referred to (line 17) are the early 'Lieder und Gesänge', Vols. 1-3. Stritzko was the Director of the engraving firm of Josef Eberle, which had the rights in G.M.'s first four symphonies, *Das klagende Lied* and the later 'Wunderhorn' songs.

Page 230, Letter 27

On 1st September a gala performance was given in honour of King Edward VII of England, who was on an official visit to Vienna. The opening of the letter should read, 'In haste, but I'll write again tonight'.

Page 232, Letter 29

The soloist in the performances of the Third Symphony in Mannheim and Heidelberg was Betty Kofler. The chorus had been placed behind a big screen on the platform. This was one of the innovations introduced at Heidelberg by Philipp Wolfrum (1854-1919), in the autumn of 1903.

Page 233, Letter 31

The symphony was not repeated, nor was the Second performed the following year.

Page 234, Letter 32

On 20th March 1904 Mahler left on a concert tour to Mainz and Cologne, where he conducted his Third and Fourth Symphonies respectively. Only five of the nine letters he wrote to Alma are published. They should be read in the following order: Letter 68 (22nd March); Letter 69 (23rd March); Letter 33 (24th March); Letter 32 (25th March); and Letter 34 (26th March). The contralto soloist in Cologne was Marie Hertzer-Deppe.

Page 235, Letter 35

This letter must belong to the year 1905. In June 1905 the United German Music Society held a meeting in Vienna, and it was in connection with this occasion that *Feuersnot* by Strauss was performed on 5th June. (See also Letter 71.) The postscript, enclosed within editorial square brackets, belongs to an unpublished letter from the summer of 1904, though written after Letter 39 in the present volume (cf. the remark on Brahms).

Page 236, Letter 36
According to Letter 311 in *MSL*, G.M. left for Maiernigg this summer on 22nd June. This allows us to date the present letter 23rd June, probably early in the morning, while the following letter (No. 37) was written in the evening of the same day. The Wagner-Wesendonck letters, edited by Wolfgang Golther, were published in Berlin in 1904. Theuer was an architect and G.M.'s neighbour in Maiernigg. He had designed the villa as well as Mahler's '*Häuschen*'. (See also Letter 120.) A sentence in the German edition (end of paragraph one) in which G.M. expresses his desire to sell the villa does not appear here.

Page 239, Letter 38
According to *ELM*, the Wilde (line 7) was *The Picture of Dorian Gray*.

Pages 241-2, Letters 42-44
These letters – as already pointed out – belong to an earlier date than given here. On 2nd December 1903, G.M. conducted his Third Symphony at the Frankfurt Opera House (soloist: Clara Weber) in commemoration of the centenary of Berlioz's birth. Whereas it is still not possible to be absolutely precise in the case of Letter 42, G.M.'s remark in Letter 43, 'So I hope all will go well tomorrow night', allows us to date it 1st December, i.e. the day before the concert. In the case of Letter 44, we know that the concert took place on a Wednesday and, from a remark in the preceding letter, that G.M. will return to Vienna on a Thursday. In view of this, and in the light of remarks in the present letter, e.g. '... tomorrow morning ... in the afternoon ... we shall see each other again' and 'I'll tell you ... how it goes tonight', we can assume that Letter 44 was written on the day of the concert, 2nd December.

At the beginning of Letter 42 two sentences have been omitted.

Page 242, Letter 43
The 'final (public) rehearsal' (line 3) took place during the morning of 2nd December, and the concert was given in the evening of the same day.

Page 243, Letter 45

The reference to Giordani's *Fedora* allows us to date the letter 14th October, the only time during G.M.'s stay the opera was performed a Cologne. The *prima donna* he heard was Frieda Felser, who was subse quently engaged for three appearances at the Vienna Opera in Decembe of the same year. Adler's lectures on Wagner had just been published.

Page 244, Letter 47

The 'final rehearsal' (line 1) took place on the 17th at 7 pm, the premier on the 18th. Hinrichsen was head of C.F. Peters, the publishers of th Fifth Symphony. Mahler was to receive a better offer from anothe publisher (C.F. Kahnt of Leipzig) for the Sixth, which he accepted.

Page 245, Letter 48

This letter was clearly written on the day after the concert, i.e. on th 19th. G.M. left Cologne at 2.30 pm and arrived at Amsterdam a 6.31 pm the same evening. Ernst Otto Nodnagel had written an analysi of the Fifth, which appeared in January 1905.

Page 245, Letter 49

Mahler was in Amsterdam to conduct his Fourth Symphony on 23r October and his Second on the 26th and 27th.

Page 246, Letter 50

This letter and those following it (Nos. 51, 52 and 54) belong to 1903 The Belgian King, Leopold II, was in Vienna in October 1903, and gala performance was given in his honour on 17th October at the Oper. In 1903, G.M. twice performed his Third Symphony in Amsterdam (o 22nd and 23rd October), when the soloist was Hermine Kittel.

Page 247, Letter 51

Several hints in this letter confirm that it must belong to 1903. Fc instance, G.M.'s remarks on his concert in Lemberg, the same year (se Letters 19-22). G.M. did not conduct his First Symphony in Hollanc but he did so in 1903.

Page 248, Letter 52

In his letter G.M. refers to his Third Symphony, which he conducted i Amsterdam only in 1903. It should be noted that this 'letter' originall consisted of a sequence of several postcards, one of which has been los

Page 248, Letter 53

The soloist in this 'double' performance of the Fourth Symphony was the soprano Alida Oldenboom-Luthkemann (1869-1932). G.M., however, conducted *both* performances (see p. 73).

Page 249, Letter 54

The letter belongs to October 1903. The performance 'yesterday evening' was of the Third Symphony, on the 22nd.

Page 250, Letter 55

From remarks in this letter, as well as in some of the letters that follow (Nos. 56-58), we conclude that it should be dated Friday, 21st October 1904. G.M. observes that 'In a week from today I'll be in the train!', a remark he elaborates in Letter 57 ('I wish it was Friday ...', etc.), and again in Letter 58 ('I set off early on Friday morning'). His last concert on this tour took place on Thursday 27th October, which means that he left the following day, on Friday. The Friday of the previous week was 21st October.

Page 251, Letter 57

The final rehearsal of the Fourth took place on 22nd October, which gives us the date of this letter. The 'photo' (line 1) was in fact a pencil drawing.

Page 251, Letter 58

The final rehearsal of the Second Symphony was on 25th October, which gives us the date for this letter.

Page 252, Letter 59

From the remark 'tomorrow evening I conduct for the last time' (i.e. 27th October), we may date this letter 26th October.

Page 253, Letters 60-1

In connection with his concert in Leipzig on 28th November 1904, Mahler wrote five times to A.M., but only the present two letters were published. The first should be dated Saturday, the 27th, and the second, Sunday, the 28th. The final rehearsal and the concert both took place on the same day. On 13th April 1905, G.M. was to sign a contract with Kahnt for the *Kindertotenlieder*, the four Rückert Songs (excluding 'Liebst du um Schönheit') and two songs from *Des Knaben Wunderhorn*, his last settings of texts from this source. Kahnt also published the Sixth Symphony and G.M.'s performing version of Weber's *Die drei Pintos*

(1888). Arthur Nikisch conducted Mahler's Fifth Symphony in Berlin on 20th February 1905.

Page 255, Letter 63
Hauptmann, we note, was writing on the last day of the month (line 2). Or perhaps he got the month wrong?

Page 256, Letter 64
Hauptmann and Grethe Marschalk (1875-1957) were married on 18th September.

Page 257, Letter 66
Carmen was performed in Hamburg on 8th March, which allows us to date this letter 9th March. Katharina Edel-Fleischer and Ottilie Metzger had both appeared as guests at the Vienna Opera in 1901; Josef Thyssen had sung there as late as 26th January. Demuth appeared in Hamburg for a series of three opera performances, and Gustav Brecher had been guest conductor at the Vienna Opera during the 1901-2 season.

Page 257, Letter 67
Only half of the original letter is reproduced here. It was probably written in the evening of 9th March, whereas Letter 66 was written in the morning of the same day. But this is only a guess. 'M.' (line 5) is identified in *ELM* as Max Marschalk, composer, music critic and publisher (Dreililien Verlag, Berlin). The performance of the Fifth Symphony took place on 13th March, and the final public rehearsal at noon the previous day.

Page 258, Letter 68
G.M. performed his Fourth Symphony in Mainz on 23rd March 1904, which means that this letter and the following letter belong to this year. The soprano solo was sung in Mainz by Stefanie Becker and in Wiesbaden by Grace Forbes. The performance of the Fourth in Wiesbaden to which Mahler refers had been given on 23rd January 1903.

'Przist.' (line 19): an abbreviation of 'Przistaupinski' (see also Letter 75). In 1919, Alois Przistaupinski, who was the Secretary of the Vienna Opera, published in Vienna his *50 Jahre Wiener Operntheater*.

Page 259, Letter 70
The Music Festival in Graz was held from 31st May to 4th June. On 1st June G.M. conducted his *Kindertotenlieder*, two of the Rückert Songs, and six songs from the *Wunderhorn* collection. Franz Strauss, Richard's

father, died on 31st May. This letter was written on G.M.'s return to Vienna and should be dated the beginning of June, possibly the 3rd. A few interesting lines about G.M.'s salary and expenses were in the original letter, e.g. that he paid 1,200 gold crowns to Justine (probably each month), and 40 crowns for 'the grave in Iglau', i.e. the grave of his parents. This is one of the many examples which contradict A.M.'s suggestion that Mahler did not concern himself with money, that he was isolated, unrealistic, etc. The sum he paid Justine was doubtless her share of the villa in Maiernigg. Presumably Mahler had had the use of Justine's inheritance when he built the villa and paid her back when he became sole owner after his and his sister's marriages in March 1902.

Page 260, Letter 71
As an extension of the Music Festival in Graz the United German Music Society held a meeting in Vienna from the 5th to the 7th June. Strauss's *Feursnot* was performed on the 5th, which is the date of this letter.

Page 262, Letter 74
G.M.'s reference to Corpus Christi enables us to establish the exact date of this letter. In 1905 Corpus Christi fell on 22nd June.

Page 262, Letter 75
This letter seems to be connected with Letter 76, which implies a date at the end of August 1905.

Page 263, Letter 76
Rosthorn (line 4) was the gynaecologist Alfons Rosthorn (1857-1909).

Page 263, Letter 77
Fidelio was conducted by Bruno Walter on 24th August which means that this letter must have been written a day or two before. Mahler conducted *Tristan* on 5th September.

Page 264, Letter 78
G.M. had returned to Vienna about the 21st. Two-thirds of the letter were omitted in the original published edition.

Page 264, Letter 79
The first sentence reads: 'So the great moment arrived yesterday before *Tristan*', i.e. on 5th September (see note above to Letter 77). This enables us to date this letter 6th September.

Page 265, Letter 80
On 1st December 1905, which must be the date of this letter, G.M. conducted his Fifth Symphony, Mozart's 'Jupiter' and Beethoven's *Coriolan* overture.

Page 265, Letter 81
G.M. had arrived at Trieste on the morning of 29th November 1905, so this letter was written either in the evening that day or in the morning of the 30th. 'H. Schott' stands for Herr [Enrico] Schott, who was manager of the orchestra.

Page 266, Letter 82
It was in Leipzig, on 9th November, that G.M. made his piano-rolls of 'Das himmlische Leben' from the Fourth Symphony, the 'Trauermarsch' from the Fifth, and the two songs, 'Ging heut' morgens' and 'Ich ging mit Lust', on the newly invented 'Welte-Mignon' piano. All have been re-issued on LPs and CDs. A recording of the Second Symphony under Oskar Fried (c. 1925) was issued in the U.S.A. by the American Bruno Walter Society (BWS 719) and re-issued by Opal (821-2) in 1984.

Page 267, Letter 84
On Wednesday, 20th December, G.M. performed in Breslau his Fifth Symphony and four of his songs.

Page 267, Letter 85
Anna von Mildenburg studied the part of Kundry in Bayreuth at the end of 1896, i.e. while she was engaged at the Hamburg Opera, where Mahler was first conductor. She did not appear again at Bayreuth until 1909.

Page 271, Letter 88
G.M. arrived at Antwerp on 2nd March and performed his Fifth Symphony there on the 5th, together with Weber's *Freischütz* overture and Liszt's orchestration of Schubert's 'Wanderer' Fantasy (with d'Albert as soloist).

Page 271, Letter 89
This letter was written the day before the Antwerp concert, i.e. on 4th March.

Page 273, Letter 91
This letter has to be dated 6th March 1906, because it was written just

after the concert in Antwerp but before the first concert on 8th March in Amsterdam. The Fifth Symphony was performed in the following cities: Rotterdam (12th), The Hague (14th), Arnhem (19th), Haarlem (20th) and Amsterdam (21st and 22nd). The soloist in the *Kindertotenlieder* was the Dutch singer, Gerard Zalsman. The repeat performance of *Das klagende Lied* on 11th March (Sunday) was conducted by Mengelberg.

Page 273, Letter 92

The difficulty with the chorus in Vienna (p. 274, line 3) had to do with the new production of *Lohengrin* (on 27th February 1905). A further dispute developed in the spring of 1907.

Page 274, Letter 93

The correct date for this letter must be 1st October 1909 (see Letter 90). G.M. conducted his Seventh Symphony in The Hague on 2nd October and this letter, no doubt, was written the previous day. We know that the Mahler family moved from the flat in Vienna in October 1909, a fact to which G.M. refers when he writes about 'twenty cases packed'.

Page 276, Letter 96

G.M. had arrived in Salzburg on the 14th, thus this letter should be dated the 15th. Roller had married Milewa Stoisavlievic (1866-1949) at Graz, on 21st July.

Page 277, Letter 97

'Your notation was perfectly right' (line 1): cf. p. 103. With respect to the performance of *Don Giovanni*, see note above to p. 102, line 21. It was conducted by the French conductor and composer Reynaldo Hahn (1874-1947). The letter was written early in the morning. At 11 o'clock G.M. went to a Philharmonic concert under Strauss (see next letter), and in the afternoon to the reception of Prince Eugen. A paragraph from this letter was omitted in the original published edition.

Page 277, Letter 98

Mahler's comment on Bruckner's Ninth, 'This work is the highpoint of *nonsense*', was deleted by A.M. In the previous year (June 1905) Richard Specht had published a small volume on Mahler. The two unidentified persons (p. 278, line 1) were Paul Hammerschlag (see *MSL*, pp. 450-1) and Hugo Botstiber (1875-1942), editor of the yearbook *Musikbuch aus Oesterreich*, first published in 1904.

Page 278, Letter 99

The programme included Wagner's *Meistersinger* overture, songs l
Strauss, Weingartner and Wolf, and Liszt's Piano Concerto No. 1, wit
Ernst von Dohnányi as soloist. This last item was conducted by Staver
hagen, as G.M. had to leave for Vienna. Stavenhagen repeated Mahler
Symphony on 14th November. As the result of a visit by D.M. to th
family of Thomas Mann, in Zürich, in 1971, we are able to fill out som
details of the 'P.' who is mentioned in G.M.'s letter (and confirmed i
ELM). Dr. Golo Mann, one of Mann's sons, wrote as follows in May c
that year:

> 'P ... is my mother's twin brother (Klaus Pringsheim). The "charmin
> and cultivated people" were my grandparents, and my mother an
> her brother, whose acquaintance you made, and who were preser
> at the meeting (with Mahler). Quite adult people then, in 1906
> and still quite alive today! That is something quite unbelievabl
> to me.'

(See also p. 80.)

Page 279, Letter 100

Zemlinsky was conductor at the Opera from 1st May 1907 to 15tl
February 1908. If Schoenberg was referring to a performance of th
Sixth Symphony, we can then date this letter 4th January 1907, the onl
occasion G.M. conducted the symphony in Vienna.

Page 281, Letter 103

During G.M.'s stay in Berlin, in January 1907, *Salome* was performe
twice, on the 9th and 12th, on the latter occasion conducted by Straus
himself. Thus this letter must have been written on 9th January.

Page 281, Letter 104

In the light of the performance of *Salome* the previous day, this lette
may safely be dated 10th January 1907. The postscript refers to a recita
consisting exclusively of songs by Mahler, which the Dutch baritone
Johannes Messchaert and the composer gave in Berlin a month later, o
14th February.

Page 283, Letter 105

Strauss conducted *Salome* on 12th January, so this letter must have bee
written on the 11th ('tomorrow ... I see Strauss and go to *Salome* ... fo
the second time').

Page 283, Letter 106
This letter must have been written on 12th January (see preceding note). Line 7 (p. 284): 'Ahna' was the maiden name of Strauss's wife, Pauline.

Page 284, Letter 107
Once again the performance of *Salome* means that the date of this letter must be the 13th. We may also note that the 'public final rehearsal' of the Third Symphony took place on the same day. G.M.'s remark (p. 285, line 13), 'My Third comes to me as a Haydn Symphony', should be compared with his letter of 28th November 1891 to Friedrich Löhr (*MSL*, p. 139). When he played through the first movement (then entitled 'Todtenfeier') of his Second Symphony to Hans von Bülow, the latter had used the same form of words. (A bizarre response, one might think.) Koenen (p. 285, line 15) was the Dutch singer Tilly Koenen (1873-1941), who wanted Mahler to participate in a recital she was to give in Berlin in February, which was to include the *Kindertotenlieder*. Mahler declined. (See Eduard Reeser, *Gustav Mahler in Holland*, Vienna, International Gustav Mahler Society, 1980, p. 80.)

Page 285, Letter 108
The performance of the Third Symphony took place on 14th January (see preceding note), and so this letter must be dated likewise. The soloist was the Dutch contralto, Maria Seret.

Page 286, Letter 109
Because of the Berlin performance on 14th January (see preceding note), this letter should be dated the 15th. Besides his Fourth Symphony (in which the soloist was Else Gentner-Fischer (1883-1943)), G.M. conducted Schumann's First Symphony and Beethoven's *Coriolan*. Strauss's postcard, to which Mahler refers in line 6, has been published in the Mahler/Strauss correspondence, *op. cit.*, p. 96.

Page 286, Letter 110
In view of G.M.'s remark about the first rehearsal, the 16th would be a better date for this letter.

Page 287, Letter 111
G.M. mentions Linz (p. 288) where, on 20th January at 3.30 pm, he conducted his First Symphony; three of his songs were also performed by the tenor, Gustav Kaitan, with Leopold Materna at the piano. In the evening of the same day G.M. attended a performance of Edmond Audran's (1842-1901) operetta, *Die Puppe* (*La Poupée*).

Page 288, Letter 112

G.M. mentions a gala performance. He was very possibly referring to the performance on 1st September in honour of King Edward VII of England who at the time was on an official visit to Vienna (see also note above to Letter 27).

Page 289, Letter 113

We know from A.M. that her husband's visits to the doctors mentioned here took place after the death of his elder daughter on 12th July (see p. 122 and Letters 116 and 117). From Mahler's unpublished letters to Alma (in *ELM*) we may conclude that the present letter was written as late as 30th August 1907.

Page 290, Letter 115

Some omitted remarks in this and the following letter tell us that G.M. was travelling with A.M.'s cousin, the neurologist, Richard Nepallek. He was the helpful relation to whom A.M. refers on p. 121, line 32.

Page 291, Letter 117

If Letter 116 is rightly dated (and it is likely to be so, because G.M.'s remark, 'Tomorrow to Kovacs, and the day after, early on Friday ...', is correct in that the 17th was a Wednesday!), we can date this letter 18th July.

Page 292, Letter 118

Weingartner's 'love-letter': see Letter 129, which must be the letter in question. A suppressed sentence in the original letter mentions performances of *Lohengrin* and *Othello* on 28th and 31st August respectively, hence we conclude that this letter must have been written c. 27th August.

Page 292, Letter 119

This letter, addressed to A.M. in Maiernigg, belongs to Letters 24-27 and 112, i.e. to 1903. The present letter was written on Sunday, 30th August. Cf. line 9 with Letter 24, where we have 'stung by wasp ... bandaged by Roller'. Furthermore, A.M. observes in her footnote that the pit at the Opera had been lowered, work that was carried out during the summer of 1903 (and re-established two years later). Finally, Mahler writes 'All the shops are shut' and refers to 'a Sunday's calm'; and in 1903 his wife's birthday would have fallen on Monday, 31st August. The 'guest singer' (p. 293, line 12) was Peter Lordmann.

Page 293, Letter 120
The concert in Wiesbaden to which this letter refers took place on 9th October 1907. G.M.'s 'applause-compelling' programme with the Kaim Orchestra consisted of Beethoven's *Coriolan* overture and Fifth Symphony, Wagner's overture to *Meistersinger* and the Prelude and 'Liebestod' from *Tristan*.

Page 295, Letter 122
We know from an unpublished telegram to A.M. that Mahler arrived at St. Petersburg on 21st October. Here he gave two concerts: the first took place on 26th October (Berlioz's *Carnaval romain*, Beethoven's 'Ah! Perfido', songs by Strauss, Max Fiedler (1859-1939) and Wolf, in which the soloist was Tilly Koenen, and Wagner's *Meistersinger* overture). The second concert was given (after the intervening concert in Helsinki), on 9th November (Beethoven's *Coriolan*, Wagner's 'Prelude and Liebestod' from *Tristan*, and finally Mahler's own Fifth Symphony). The perform- ance of the Second Symphony to which G.M. refers had been given by Oskar Fried in Petersburg on 10th November 1906. Thus Stravinsky, in his old age, was mistaken in thinking that he had heard G.M. conduct Tchaikovsky's *Manfred* (see footnote to p. 296) though Mahler had indeed conducted *Manfred* at one of his earlier Petersburg concerts in March 1902. It is interesting, though, that the memory of G.M.'s symphony and the 'Wagner fragments' stayed with Stravinsky. The present letter seems to have been written on the day after his arrival, i.e. on 22nd October.

Page 297, Letter 123
The concert G.M. attended took place on 29th October and included Sibelius's *Valse triste* and *Vårsång*. This allows us to date the letter 30th October. The Belgian pianist was Arthur de Greef.

Page 297, Letter 124
The concert on 1st November 1907 included Beethoven's Fifth and *Coriolan*, and Wagner's *Meistersinger* Prelude and 'Prelude and Liebestod' from *Tristan*. The last few lines of this letter, beginning 'I went to the Opera here yesterday', belong in fact to a letter written from Petersburg on 5th November, which was omitted from the original edition. We have added square brackets to this passage.

Page 298, Letter 125
Some remarks in this letter suggest that it belongs to the first part of

G.M.'s trip to Russia, i.e. before his visit to Helsinki, and therefore should follow Letter 122.

Page 299, Letter 126

In Letter 124 (Saturday, 2nd November) G.M. says 'I set off for Petersburg tonight.' It is a journey which takes only a few hours by train, and this means that he must have arrived in Petersburg early on Sunday morning (3rd November). This letter, therefore, must be dated 4th November. Gallén's 1907 portrait of G.M. is reproduced in Erik Tawaststjerna, *Jean Sibelius*, Vol. 3 (Helsinki, Otava, 1972, opp. p. 128). It is an exceptionally interesting painting and ought to be better known. See also Timo Martin and Douglas Siven, *Akseli Gallén-Kallela* (Watti-Kustannus Oy, 1984, p. 221), where the Mahler portrait is reproduced in colour.

Page 303, Letter 132

G.M. had left Vienna for Prague on 5th September, and the present letter seems to be the first he wrote to A.M. between 6th and 10th September.

Page 305, Letter 134

The only Friday in the period of G.M.'s rehearsals fell on 11th September, hence the date of this letter.

Page 305, Letter 135

Zemanek had performed G.M.'s Fourth Symphony on 3rd November 1907. When G.M. uses the term 'this year', he – like many other musicians and artists – had in mind the concert season from August to June rather that the calendar year.

Page 306, Letter 136

Mahler had arrived at Munich on 20th October, and the concert, which also included Wagner's 'Prelude and Liebestod' from *Tristan* and Beethoven's *Leonora* overture No. 3, took place on 27th October. In line 12 Mahler looks back to September 1888 when he had negotiated with the Munich Opera for an engagement. Soon after, he was engaged at Budapest. The cholera epidemic in Hamburg broke out in the summer of 1892.

Page 307, Letter 137

In Hamburg on 9th November G.M. conducted a programme consisting of works by Beethoven (*Coriolan* and the Seventh Symphony), Wagner

(*Meistersinger* overture) and Tchaikovsky (*Romeo and Juliet*). The letter was written on 7th November, the day after his arrival at Hamburg.

Page 307, Letter 138

Only the final third of this letter, addressed to A.M. in Vienna, is published. It should be dated 7th November. It seems, however, that she was wrong about the libretto of *Rübezahl*. In an undated letter to his sister, probably written on the same day, Mahler confirms that he received the parcel, the contents of which comprised another of his unfinished early works, the projected opera *Die Argonauten*, of which very little is known. (See also *DM*[1], pp. 134-9 and 196-7.) He wrote: 'But I was quite bemused – and can't pretend otherwise – when I opened the parcel. This is by no means Rübezahl, but something *quite* different – namely from the Argonauten and some purely lyrical things [i.e. poems]. Was it this you gave Roller? But he was talking about Rübezahl! And I remember this book pretty well – it has a smaller format. So, what's it all about? It's all very puzzling to me!' While the libretto of *Rübezahl* has survived (see the reproduction facing p. 119: the MS is now in the Osborn Collection of the Beinecke Library at Yale), the MS of *Die Argonauten* has disappeared.

Page 307, Letter 139

The addressee of this letter was undoubtedly the Leipzig publishing house, Lauterbach & Kuhn, who accepted the offer. In October they were to advertise the Seventh (see *MSL*, p. 335). The firm, however, was sold to the Berlin publishing house of Bote & Bock, who eventually published the symphony in November 1909.

Page 308, Letter 140

Cf. the content of this letter with that of Letters 90-3 regarding the packing. The letter must have been written in October 1909. G.M. mentions 'The last rehearsal today' (i.e. of the Seventh Symphony, performed on 2nd October in The Hague), which could mean that this letter was written on the previous day, 1st October. Herr Bock was the publisher, Hugo Bock (1848-1932), of the firm Bote & Bock (see the preceding note).

Page 309, Letter 141

G.M.'s last concert in Amsterdam took place on Thursday, 7th October. It is obvious from his remark, 'I leave the day after tomorrow, Friday the 8th, for Paris', that the present letter can only be dated Wednesday, 6th October. G.M. did not, however, perform his Fourth in New York until

January 1911. The soprano soloist in those two performances (on the 17th and 20th) was Bella Alten, and the symphony was the last work of his own that Mahler was to conduct. He never performed the Seventh in the U.S.A.

Page 316, Letter 144

For Dippel's letter, written on 8th July, see Zoltan Roman, *op. cit.*, pp. 144-51.

Pages 319-23, Letters 147-50

During June and July, 1909, Mahler wrote at least twenty-four letters to Alma at Levico, but only four were published, and except for Letter 148, they were all to some degree abridged. Alma joined G.M. at Toblach on 13th July, having been at Levico since 8th June.

Page 323, Letter 151

G.M. left for Göding (two hours' ride by train) on 17th September (cf. *MSL*, No. 402), and returned to Vienna on 22nd September. The present letter was no doubt written on 18th September, and Letter 152 the next day.

Page 324, Letter 153

The new Berlin opera house – the 'Städtische Oper' – was opened in 1912. Though we do not know Mahler's response to the proposal, we may guess that he did not flatly turn it down; a rumour of his appointment appeared in the German press, e.g. on 14th April 1910 in the *Musikalisches Wochenblatt*: 'Gustav Mahler will be engaged for five years at the new opera house in Berlin'.

Page 325, Letter 154

The Seventh Symphony was performed in Vienna on 3rd November, while the Third, to which Schoenberg refers in the postscript addressed to A.M. (p. 327), was given on 25th October under Bruno Walter. The story – false, of course – that G.M. planned to compose an opera, *Theseus*, for which he had written his own libretto, appeared in a number of newspapers and music journals in the autumn of 1909.

Page 328, Letter 155

The 'W.'s' (p. 329, line 26) stands for Josephine and Joseph Winter, a physician. The former's private diary (excerpts from which were published in 'News on Mahler Research', No. 11, Vienna, 1983) allows us to date this letter 8th June 1910. Four days earlier A.M. had met the architect Walter Gropius in Tobelbad and had immediately embarked on an affair with him. This caused her to reconsider her marriage with Mahler and write him a letter. The present letter is G.M.'s reply, which was 'edited' by A.M. before its publication. The opening of the letter has been deleted, along with a number of sentences and individual words.

Page 330, Letter 156
Before arriving at Munich on 14th June, G.M. had spent the previous two days in Leipzig, rehearsing a choir for the première of the Eighth. He remained in Munich until the 26th and wrote or cabled almost daily to A.M., but only the present letter and the three following it were published. These can only be approximately dated.

Page 330, Letter 157
The Sunday referred to was 26th June. Mahler however, did not go straight to Toblach as suggested here and in Letter 158. An unpublished letter (in *ELM*) from Vienna, dated 28th June, shows that he first went to Vienna and from there to Tobelbad on the 30th. Two days later, on 3rd July, he did finally go to Toblach, whereas A.M. was to remain at Tobelbad for another another two weeks (it seems that she went to Vienna for a short rendezvous with Gropius immediately after G.M.'s departure). The whole situation came to a head around the beginning of August, when Gropius suddenly turned up in Toblach, having written the fateful letter (see p. 172). The shock and agony which Mahler felt on learning of his wife's infidelity are clearly mirrored in the following messages and notes (see Letters 160-5, though these are only a minor part of the surviving documents: A.M. published only a small proportion of the letters and other communications Mahler wrote to her).

Page 332, Letter 160
This and the following two telegrams are both related to G.M.'s visit to Leyden to consult Freud (27th August). See *DM*[2], pp. 70-8 and *HG*[3], pp. 769-73.

Page 334, Letter 166
G.M. left Toblach on Saturday, 3rd September, and arrived at Munich the same evening. The present letter was written early in the morning of 4th September. But paragraph 3, p. 335, beginning 'Dearest – I was interrupted five minutes ago ...' and the rest of the text belong to Letter 167, whereas the last part of this letter, probably beginning 'It was a joy when I woke early today ...' (p. 336, paragraph 3), belongs to Letter

166. The rehearsal and performance of Beethoven's Ninth both took place on 4th September.

Page 336, Letters 167-9

All three letters were written on 5th September, in the morning, afternoon and evening, respectively.

Page 339, Letter 170

In the light of the remark (line 18) 'I envy you the 1st of May in Rome', we conclude that April might be the appropriate month with which to date this letter. During the preceding season Busoni had played Beethoven's Piano Concerto No. 5 at three concerts under Mahler (on 6th, 7th and 8th January), while Mahler had conducted Busoni's *Turandot Suite* on 10th and 11th March. The planned performance in Rome did not materialize.

[We are grateful to Marion Thorpe for her translations from the German.]

Index

1. MAHLER THE COMPOSER AND PERFORMER

THE SYMPHONIES

Symphony I, xvii–xix, xxi–xxiii, xxv, 3, 77–78, 106, 110, 137, 166–8, 176, 224, 226–7, 247, 250, 308

Symphony II, xviii–xix, xxi–xxii, xxv, 35, 59, 73, 100–1, 125, 169–70, 176, 212–15, 217–18, 227, 233, 249, 251–3, 266, 290, 296, 305, 308, 347

Symphony III, xvii–xix, xxi, xxv, 38–41, 59, 74, 90, 97, 176, 231–5, 241–2, 245–54, 256–8, 267, 281–6, 308, 325, 327, 347–8, 355

Symphony IV, xxv, 24, 29–30, 38, 73, 78, 104, 176, 205, 209, 218, 222–3, 235, 249–52, 258–9, 287, 306, 308–9

Symphony V, xi, xvii, 42, 47–48, 72–73, 85–86, 90–92, 115, 143, 234–5, 241, 243–5, 254, 256–7, 271–4, 295–6, 299, 351

Symphony VI, 60, 70–71, 99–101, plate opp. 114, 115, 143, 244, 251, 259, 261, 274–5, 278–9

Symphony VII, 89, 96, 115, 119, 142–3, 154, 262, 272, 303–4, 306, 308–9, 325–6, 328

Symphony VIII, 82, 101–3, 115, 124, 143, 178–82, plate opp. 322, 272, 274, 278, 283, 308, 320, 328–31, 334–8, 342, 347

Symphony IX, 115, 138, 142, 152, 187, 354

Symphony X, xiv, xvi, xix, 115, 135, 138, 172, 175, 187, plate opp. 323, 352

student symphony (see D. Mitchell, *Gustav Mahler* [London, 1958], p. 96), 8, 107

symphonies unspecified, xi, 49, 94, 101, 287, 343, 346

OTHER INSTRUMENTAL AND VOCAL WORKS

Blumine (from Symphony I), xvii–xix

Fünf Lieder nach Rückert, 60–61, 89, 115, 261

Humoresken, 84 (and see *Des Knaben Wunderhorn*)

Kindertotenlieder, 70, 81–82, 89, 115, 254, 273, 354

Das klagende Lied, xx, xxiv–xxv, 29–30, 207, 220, 222, 273

Des Knaben Wunderhorn, xxiii, xxv, 84, 93, 115, 205

Lieder eines fahrenden Gesellen, xx–xxv, 205, 343

Lieder und Gesänge aus der Jugendzeit, 205, 230, 353

Das Lied von der Erde, 115, 123–4, 138–9, 142–3, 153, 187, 251, 354

Quartettsatz (see D. Mitchell, *Gustav Mahler* [London, 1958], pp. 139–40), 63

Rübezahl, see Literary Works (below)

Songs, xi, xxiii, 82, 89, 101, 115, 205, 230, 254, 257, 260, 308, 354

Theseus (rumoured opera), 326–7

Der Trompeter von Säkkingen (incidental music), xviii–xix

LITERARY WORKS

Poems by Mahler mentioned, xxiii–xxiv, 110, 175, 178, 332; poems transcribed, xxiv, 16, 222, 334; production-book for *Fidelio*, 113; programme-note for Symphony II, 213–14, 217; texts for opera: *Euryanthe* (revision of lib.), 54; *The Marriage of Figaro* (additions to lib.), 22; *Rübezahl* (original lib.), xxv–xxvi, plate opp. 83, 64, 143–4, 307

PERFORMANCES, PRODUCTIONS AND ARRANGEMENTS BY MAHLER OF OTHER COMPOSERS' WORKS

Bach, J. S.: Orchestral Suites II and III, 154–5; works unspecified, 45, 240

Beethoven, L. van: Concerto for Piano in G major, 85; *Coriolan*, 85; *Fidelio*, 72, 81, 96, 113, 125, 145, 170, 310,

Beethoven, L. van: *continued.*
352; *Leonore* Overture III, 72, 145, 170, 225; Symphony III, 34; Symphony V, 99; Symphony VI, 184; Symphony IX, 36–37, 85, 87, 287; works unspecified, 190, 272, 297, 305

Brahms, J.: Horn Trio, 164; Piano Quartets in C minor and G minor, 236; String Sextet in B flat major, 238; chamber-works unspecified, 238–9

Bruckner, A.: Symphony III, 107, 349; symphonies unspecified, 108, 254

Busoni, F.: *Berceuse élégiaque (Cradlesong at the Grave of my Mother)*, 189; *Turandot Suite*, 339

Charpentier, G.: *Louise*, 56–57, 163

Cornelius, P.: *The Barber of Bagdad*, 196

D'Albert, E.: *Flauto Solo*, 97

Debussy, C.: *Ibéria* and *Rondes de printemps*, 169

Erlanger, C.: *Le Juif polonais*, 104

Flotow, F. von: *Martha*, 110

Gluck, C.: *Iphigenia in Aulis*, 106, 113, 310; *Orpheus and Eurydice*, 16

Goetz, H.: *The Taming of the Shrew*, 310, 318

Gounod, C.: *Faust*, 109

Haydn, J.: works unspecified, 34, 287

Mahler-Werfel, A.: *Lieder*, 176, plate opp. 306

Mendelssohn, F.: *The Hebrides*, 137

Mozart, W. A.: *Don Giovanni*, 89, 96, 104, 132–3, 136, 310, 316; German Dances, 155; *Idomeneo*, 155; *The Magic Flute*, 21–22, 310; *The Marriage of Figaro*, 22, 96, 102–104, 113, 145, 156, 230–1, 277, 310, 316; *The Seraglio*, 96; *Zaïde*, 49; operas unspecified, 113, 290, 352

Offenbach, J.: *The Tales of Hoffmann*, 5, 15, 205–6

Perosi, L.: *The Resurrection of Lazarus*, 351

Pfitzner, H.: *Die Rose vom Liebesgarten*, 60, 81–84

Rossini, G.: *The Barber of Seville*, 310

Schubert, F.: Symphony in C major, 155; works unspecified, 34

Schumann, R.: Piano Concerto 165–6; Symphony I, 287; symphonies unspecified, 190

Smetana, B.: *The Bartered Bride*, 131, 154; *Dalibor*, 113; works unspecified, 305

Strauss, R.: *Also Sprach Zarathustra*, 155; *Feuersnot*, 236, 260; *Sinfonia Domestica*, 84

Tchaikovsky, P.: *Manfred*, 296; *The Queen of Spades*, 49, 145; works unspecified, 309

Verdi, G.: *Falstaff*, 65

Wagner, R.: *Eine Faust Ouvertüre*, 309; *Der fliegende Holländer*, 168; *Götterdämmerung*, 34, 63; *Lohengrin*, 106, 114, 122, 310; *Die Meistersinger*, 14, 309; *Das Rheingold*, 77; *Siegfried*, 45, 131, 133; *Siegfried Idyll*, 309; *Tannhäuser*, 79, 168; *Tristan und Isolde*, 34, 54, 58, 62, 91, 96, 104, 113, 128–32, 145–6, 263–4, 310, 316–17; *Die Walküre*, 60–61, 106, 113, 131, 133; works unspecified, 113, 272, 287, 290, 296–7, 305, 352

Wagner, S.: *Der Bärenhäuter*, 268–9

Weber, C. M. von: *Die drei Pintos*, 110–11; *Euryanthe*, 53–54, 71; *Oberon*, 291, 344

Wolf, H.: *Der Corregidor*, 62, 65

2. INDEX OF PEOPLE AND PLACES

Note: Towns whose names have changed since the Mahlers knew them are indexed under the names they are given in the text, with the modern equivalent placed after a slant line, e.g. Abbazia/Opatija.

Abaza, Madame, 35, 296

Abbazia/Opatija (Istria), 14, 66–67, 224–5, 235, 258–9

Adler, Guido, 49, 112, 260, 343; *Gustav Mahler*, 343; *Richard Wagner*, 243

Agnetendorf/Jagniatkow (Silesia), 256

Aldeburgh (Suffolk), xvii

Alexander the Great, 195

Amiens, 150

Amiet, Cuno, 62, 343

Amsterdam, xxi–xxiii, 40, 59, 73, 100, 154, 245–53, 272–4, 308–9, 350

Angeli, Heinrich von, 108–9, 343
Ansorge, Conrad, 90–91, 327, 343
Anton (servant), 238, 290
Antwerp, 271–273
Aristotle, 120
Arnhem (Holland), 273–4
Arnim, L. A. von (with Clemens Brentano): *Des Knaben Wunderhorn*, xxiii–xxv, 38, 80, 93, 354
Assenjeff, Elsa, 37
Attersee (Upper Austria), 53
Auber, D. F.: *Fra Diavolo*, 315
Auschwitz (Poland), 350

Bach, J. S., 45, 240; Orchestral Suites II and III, 154–5; Passacaglia for Organ, 164
Bacon, Francis, 287
Baden bei Wien (Lower Austria), 318
Bad Hall (Upper Austria) 10, 63, 108–9
Bad Ischl (Upper Austria), 111
Bad Kreuth (Bavaria), 302
Bad Tölz (Bavaria), 342
Bartoš, František and Marie: ed. of Mahler's letters, xl
Basel, 59, 251
Bauer-Lechner, Natalie, xx–xxii, 13, 343; *Erinnerungen an Gustav Mahler*, xx–xxii, 343
Baumfeld, Herr, 130
Bayer, Josef: *The Bride of Korea*, 5, 347, 353
Bayreuth, 64, 131, 267–70, 324
Bazelli, Georg, 230, 343
Beaumarchais, Pierre–Augustin de: *Le Mariage de Figaro*, 310
Becker, Fräulein, 259
Beethoven, Ludwig van, 34, 36, 51, 115, 183, 239, 272, 297, 305; *An die ferne Geliebte*, 85; *Coriolan*, 85; *Fidelio*, 72, 81, 96, 113, 125, 145, 170, 263, 310–12, 352–3; *Leonore* Overture III, 72, 145, 170, 225; Piano Concerto in G major, 85; Symphony III, 34; Symphony V, 99, 277; Symphony VI, 184; Symphony IX, 36–37, 85, 87, 115, 287, 323, 337; symphonies, 190, 320; letters, 291
Behn, Hermann, xxii, 307, 343
Bennier, Herr, 314
Berg, Alban, plate opp. 82, 142; *Lulu*, 354
Berg, Helene, plate opp. 82

Berger, Rudolf, 282, 343
Berlage, H. P.: Amsterdam Stock-Exchange, 248
Berlin, xx, xxiii, 22, 66, 84, 91–92, 94, 108, 124, 200, 205–10, 214, 216, 218, 254, 256, 266–7, 281–90, 307–8, 313–14, 324–5, 348–50, 355
Berliner, Arnold, 137–8, 142, 180–1, 200, 244–5, 267, 281–3, 285–6, 288, 307, 343, 345
Berlioz, Hector: *Requiem*, 90; *Traité d'instrumentation*, 267; *Les Troyens* (Royal Hunt and Storm), 312–13
Besant, Annie, 188
Bethge, Hans: *The Chinese Flute*, 123, 139, 351
Bie, Oskar, 283, 343
Bielitz/Bielsko (Silesia), 226
Bielschowsky, Albert: *Goethe*, 103
Bigelow, Poultney, 167; *The German Emperor*, 167
Bischoff, Hermann, 343; symphonies, 101, 343
Bitter, Karl, 146–8, 165
Bittner, Julius: *Rote Gret*, 313
Bizet, Georges: *Carmen*, 257
Blaas, Herr, 312
Blankenese (Hamburg), 270
Blech, Leo, 282–4, 343; *Das war Ich*, 343; Frau Blech, 283
Blom, Eric, xi
Blumenthal, Dr., 122, 289, 291
Bock, Herr, 308
Böcklin, Arnold, 237
Bodansky, Artur, 142–3, 272, 303–6, 308, 343
Boehler, Otto: silhouettes of Mahler, plate opp. 131, 202
Bologna, 118
Bolzano (S. Tyrol), 10
Bonaparte, Marie, xv
Bonci, Alessandro, 130, 133, 155, 343
Boston (Massachusetts), 131–2
Bote und Bock (Berlin), 308
Brahm, Otto, 313
Brahms, Johannes, 4, 25, 77, 111, 165, 180, 238–40, 344; *Alto Rhapsody*, 85; Horn Trio, 164; *Lieder*, 164; Piano Quartets in C minor and G minor, 236; Sextet in B flat major, 238; string quartets, 159
Braunau (Upper Austria), 105
Brecher, Gustav, 30, 92, 139, 257, 291,

Brecher, Gustav, *continued.*
  295, 307, 344; ed. with G.M. of *Oberon* (Weber), 344
Bremen, 144, 182
Brentano, Clemens: *Gockel, Hinkel und Gackeleia*, 69; *Des Knaben Wunderhorn, see* L. A. von Arnim
Breslau/Wroclaw (Silesia), 97, 267, 351
Brettauer, Dr., 192
Britten, Benjamin, xvii; arr. of Minuet from Symphony III (Mahler), xvii–xviii
Brooklyn (New York), 154, 183
Bruckner, Anton, 47–48, 106–8, 111, 115, 176, 239, 343, 349, 352; Mass, 108; Symphony III, 107, 349; Symphony IX, 115, 277; symphonies, 108, 254, 352; *Te Deum*, 108
Bruneau, Alfred, 169, 344
Brünn/Brno (Moravia), 106
Bruno, Giordano: *Cena delle Ceneri* and *Spaccio della Bestia Trionfante*, 120
Brussels, 297
Budapest, xvii, 10–11, 36, 75, 110, 355
Buffalo (New York), 154, 183–4
Burckhard, Max, 3–4, 17–20, 46, 50, 65–66, 140–1, 178, 212, 276, 313, 344
Burgstaller, Alois, 131, 133, 344
Burian, Karel, *see* Carl Burrian
Burrian, Carl, 131, 133, 344
Busoni, Ferruccio, 85, 194–5, 198; Letter to Mahler, 339; *Berceuse élégiaque* (*Cradlesong at the Grave of my Mother*), 189; *Turandot Suite*, 339
Buths, Julius, 100, 344

Cardus, Neville, xii
Caruso, Enrico, 130, 145, 147, 155–6, 289
Casazza, *see* Gatti–Casazza
Cassel (Germany), xvi, 10, 109–10
Central Park (New York), xiv, 135, 147, 187
Cézanne, Paul, 304
Chalais (France), 280
Chaliapin, Feodor, 130, 133
Champion, Roland (J. L. Corning), 344
Chantemesse, André, 197–8, 344
Charpentier, Gustave, 56–59; *Louise*, 56–59, 162–3
Chelius, Oskar von, 229, 344
Cherbourg (France), 127, 144, 182, 195, 303

Chezy, Wilhelmina von: lib. for *Euryanthe* (Weber), 53–54
China Town (New York), 161–2
Chvostek, Franz, 198–201, 344
Cilli (cook), 245
Clemenceau, Georges, 4, 104, 355
Clemenceau, Paul, 87–88, 104, 149, 151, 169–70, 180, 272, 308, 355
Clemenceau, Sophie, 3–5, 14–15, 87–88, 104, 148–9, 151, 169–70, 180, 308, 355
Cologne, 38–39, 72–73, 118, 234–5, 241, 243–45, 249, 251, 258–9, 333, 344, 354
Columbus, Christopher, 241
Conrat, Ida, 77, 103, 264, 344
Conried, Heinrich, 124–5, 128–9, 136, 145, 289, 302, 316, 344
Cooke, Deryck: performing ed. of Symphony X (Mahler), xiv, xix
Cornelius, Peter: *The Barber of Bagdad*, 196
Corning, J. L., 132–5, 344; brother, 134; wife, 134–5
Cortina d'Ampezzo (S. Tyrol), [277]
Cossmann, Paul, 84
Cottenet, Rawlins, 314–16, 344
Craft, Robert, *see* Igor Stravinsky
Crefeld (Germany), 38–42, 232–5, 247–8, 250
Crosby, Mrs., 166–7
Curtis, Natalie, 146, 167, 344; *The Indians' Book*, 167; brother, 167
Cuxhaven (Germany), 137, 144

D'Albert, Eugène, 97, 344; *Flauto Solo*, 97; *Tiefland*, 312, 344; Frau d'Albert, 97
Debussy, Claude, 169–70; *Ibéria*, 169; *Pelléas et Mélisande*, 162, 346, 351; *Rondes de printemps*, 169; first wife (Lily Texier), 169–70; second wife (Emma Bardac), 169
Decsey, Ernst, 139, 345; *Bruckner* and *Hugo Wolf*, 345
Dehmel, Ida, xxiv–xxv, 79, 270–1; Diary-extract, 89–95
Dehmel, Richard, xxiv, 79, 89–95, 345; Letter to Mahler, 270–1; *Fitzebutze* (lib. for Zilcher), 270–1; *Verklärte Nacht*, 345; *Zwei Menschen*, 120; poems set to music, 93
Delmar, Herr, 325
Demuth, Leopold, 51, 56, 243, 257, 311, 345

Destinn, Emmy, 131, 154, 282, 345
Devil's Island (French Guiana), 150
Díaz, Porfirio, 167
Dickens, Charles: *Hard Times*, xxv–xxvi
Diepenbrock, Alfons, 248, 252, 272–4, 309, 345; church-music, 248
Dippel, Andreas, 128, 314, 316–17, 345
Döbling (Vienna), 19, 205, 327
Doblinger's (Vienna), 120
Dolomites (S. Tyrol), 240, 328
Dornbach (Vienna), 103, 230, 264
Dostoyevsky, Fyodor, 9, 20, 35, 126; *The Brothers Karamazov*, 184
Draper, Mrs., 146
Dresden, 22, 29, 207, 212, 215, 217–18
Dreyfus, Alfred, 87–88, 104, 149–50
Dufranne, Hector, 162, 345
Dukas, Paul, 169–70; *Ariane et Barbe-bleue*, 170
Dupré, Dr., 197
Dürnstein (Wachau, Lower Austria), 329
Düsseldorf, 227
Dyck, Ernest van, 151, 271, 345

Eames, Emma, 131, 133, 145, 155, 345
Edlach (Lower Austria), 262–4, 288
Eichendorff, Joseph von, 89
Elise (cook), 228
Epstein, Julius, 8, 345
Erlanger, Camille, 345; *Le Juif polonais*, 104
Erler, Fritz, 180–1, 267, 345; portrait of Mahler, 267
Eschenbach, Wolfram von: *Parsifal*, 120
Essen, 99–101, 274–5
Eugen, Archduke, 276

Farrar, Geraldine, 131, 133, 145, 155, 345
Fauré, Gabriel, 169
Fechner, Gustav, 226; *Vorschule der Aesthetik*, 263
Fernow, H., 266, 286, 345
Fischer, Edwin, 39, 345
Fleischer-Edel, Katherina, 257, 345
Flotow, Friedrich von: *Martha*, 110
Foerster, J. B., 56, 345; *Autobiography*, 345
Foerster-Lauterer, Bertha, 56, 345
Fornaro, Carlo di, 167
Förster-Nietzsche, Elizabeth, 90–91, 345

Forstik (copyist), 330
Fraenkel, *see* Fränkel
Franck, Ernst, 318
Frank, Gustav, 34, 296, 300, 338, 346
Frank, Marie, *see* Marie Mahler
Fränkel, Joseph, 56, 136–7, 148, 157–8, 166, 187, 189–94, 197, 346
Frankfurt am Main, 222, 241–2, 286–8, 294, 352
Franklin, Benjamin, 148
Franz Ferdinand, Archduke, 114
Franz Josef, Emperor, 6, 37, 114, 135–6, 302, 313
Frederick the Great, 148
Fremstad, Olive, 129, 131–3, 346
Freud, Sigmund, xv–xvi, 175, 335
Freund, Herr, 265
Fried, Oskar, 100, 139, 176–8, 266–7, 281, 283, 295, 307–8, 331, 335, 346; settings of Dehmel, 93
Fuchs, Robert, 8, 346

Gabrilovitch, Ossip, 99–100, 127, 137, 139, 142, 275, 287, 300, 313, 346
Gadski, Johanna, 130, 132–3, 346
Galileo Galilei, 120
Gallén, Akseli, 297–300, 346; portrait of Mahler, 299–300; wife, 297
Gallico, Paolo, 165–6
Garden, Mary, 162, 346
Gardner, Isabella Stewart, 131–2
Garmisch (Bavaria), 153
Gatti-Casazza, Frances-Alda, 188, 190–1, 346
Gatti-Cazazza, Giulio, 145, 188, 315, 346
Gesellius, Hermann, 299, 346
Gibson, Mr. and Mrs. Dana, 168
Giordano, Umberto: *Fedora*, 243
Gisela, Archduchess, 278
Gluck, C. W. von: *Iphigenia in Aulis*, 106, 113, 310; *Orpheus and Eurydice*, 16, 18
Göding/Hodonín (Moravia), 227, 323–4
Goethe, J. W. von, 26, 45, 88, 103, 210, 242, 291, 332; *Faust*, 82, 102–3, 243, 320–1, 323, 332
Goetz Hermann: *The Taming of the Shrew*, 310, 318–19
Gogh, Vincent van, 304
Göhler, Georg, 330, 346
Goldmark, Karl, 21, 52, 346
Goldschmidt, Adalbert von, 20–21; *Gaea*, 21

Golling (Salzkammergut), 97
Goritz, Otto, 131, 346
Göttweig (Lower Austria), 329
Gound, Robert, 17–18
Gounod, Charles: *Faust*, 109, 230
Goya, Francisco, 159
Grabbe, Christian, 228
Grandjean, Louise, 151, 347
Graz (Styria), 97–98, 259–60, 354
Greco, El: 'Cardinal Guevara' and 'View of Toledo', 159
Greffühle, Countess, 170, 347
Grinzing (Vienna), 125, 197, 230
Groll, Albert, 164, 347
Gropius, Walter, 172, 174–5, 347
Grünewald (Berlin), 307
Grünfeld's (Prague), 7
Grünfeld, Alfred, 7–8
Guarnieri, Antonio, 163, 347
Günther, Mizzi, 114, 347
Gutheil-Schoder, Marie, 15, 51, 56, 205, 347
Gutmann, Emil, 178, 276, 278, 330, 334–6, 347

Haarlem (Holland), 250, 252, 273
Hagemann, Karl, 272, 308, 347
The Hague, 250, 272–4
Hall, *see* Bad Hall
Halle (Germany), 91
Hals, Frans, 252
Hamburg, xxii–xxiii, 11–12, 36, 44, 56, 92, 98–99, 109, 137, 143–4, 234, 247, 257, 270, 306–7, 343, 350–1, 353
Hameau (Vienna), 230
Hammerstein, Oscar, 162, 169, 347
Hamperl, Dr., 289
Hartmann, Eduard von, 347; *Das Problem des Lebens*, 197
Hassinger, Herr, 262, 276, 278
Hassmann, Carl, 166, 347
Hassreiter, Josef, 117, 313, 347
Hauptmann, Gerhart, plate opp. 82, 65–66, 81, 83, 91, 93–94, 266, 283–6, 347; Letters to Mahler, 254–6, 303; *Der arme Heinrich*, 67–68; *Das Friedensfest*, 285–6; *Kaiser Karls Geisel*, 313; *Der Narr in Christo Emanuel Quint*, 83; *Rose Bernd*, 83; *Die versunkene Glocke*, 65–66, 94, 350
Hauptmann, Margarethe, plate opp. 82, 65–66, 91, 93–94, 230, 254–6, 350; son, 286

Havemeyer, Mrs. H. O., 159–60
Haydn, Joseph, 24, 34, 285, 287; string quartets, 159
Heidelberg (Germany), 231–3, 355
Heiligenstadt (Vienna), 201, 251
Hellmesberger, Joseph, 14, 220, 347
Helmholtz, Hermann von, 225
Helsinki, 297–300, 348
Henry, Hubert-Joseph, 149–50
Hermannskogel (Vienna), 230
Hertzer-Deppe, Marie, 235, 347
Hertzka, Emil, 176, 178, 331, 334, 347
Hietzing (Vienna), 31, 229–31
Hinrichsen, Heinrich, 244–5, 254, 347, 351
Hinterbruhl (Lower Austria), 225
Hirth, Friedrich, 146
Hitler, Adolf, 105
Hitz, Dora, 91
Hoch-Schneeberg, *see* Schneeberg
Hodler, Ferdinand, 62, 347
Hoffmann, E. T. A., 134, 206, 299; *Rath Krespel*, 206
Hoffmann, Josef, 293, 313, 348
Hofmann, Herr and Frau L. von, 90, 94
Hofmannsthal, Hugo von, 93, 348; *Elektra* (lib. for Strauss), 276; *Das goldene Herz* (scenario for Zemlinsky), 4
Hohe Warte (Vienna), 5, 17, 23–24, 54, 201, 228, 292–3, 299, 324
Hölderlin, Friedrich, 215
Horn, Dr. R., 103–4
Hülsen-Haeseler, Georg von, 266, 348
Humperdinck, Engelbert: Letter to Mahler, 324–5; *Hänsel and Gretel*, 64
Hyde, Arthur, 155

Ibsen, Henrik, 236; *Peer Gynt*, 239, 313
Iglau/Jihlava (Moravia), 6–10
Innsbruck (Tyrol), 329, 332
Ischl, *see* Bad Ischl

J., *see* Walter Johner
Jahn, Wilhelm, 12, 301, 348
Jean Paul, 110; *Leben des Quintus Fixlein*, 238; *Titan*, 110
Jergitsch (playpen-maker), 239
Johner, Walter, 184–5, 188–9, 348
Johnson, Harold: *Sibelius*, 297
Jones, Ernest, xv; *Sigmund Freud*, xv
Jörn, Karl, 131, 154, 348

Kahlenberg (Vienna), 228–30, 288, 293
Kähler, Willibald, 233, 348
Kahn, Otto, 136, 157, 348; Frau Kahn, 157–8
Kahnt, C. F., 254, 259
Kaim, Franz, 306
Kainz, Josef, 65, 68, 348
Kajanus, Robert, 297, 348; wife, 297
Kalischt/Kaliště (Bohemia), 6
Kant, Immanuel, 45, 68, 120
Karl, Emperor, 67
Karpath, Ludwig, 20–21, 291, 348; *Begegnung mit dem Genius*, 348
Kassel, *see* Cassel
Kathi (servant), 290
Kessler, Herr, 93–94
Keussler, Gerhard von, 142, 304, 348
Kittel, Hermine, 59, 249, 348
Klagenfurt (Wörthersee, Carinthia), 98, 103, 238–40
Klemperer, Otto, xli, 142, 184, 305, 331, 348; *Erinnerungen an Gustav Mahler*, 142, 348; piano ed. of Symphony III (Mahler), 305
Klimt, Gustav, 3–4, 50, 79, 90, 160, 313, 348; Beethoven Allegory, 36, 348
Klinger, Max, 36–37, 348; Beethoven Monument, 36
Kneisel, Franz, 165–6, 349
Knote, Heinrich, 129, 131–3, 349
Koenen, Tilly, 285, 349
Königssee (Bavaria), 142
Korngold, Erich, 152, 349; *Gold*, 152
Korngold, Julius, 102–3, 152, 349
Kovacs, Friedrich, 122, 291, 349
Kraus, Felix von, 85–86, 349
Kraus-Osborne, Adrienne, 85–86, 349
Krefeld, *see* Crefeld
Krehbiel, H. E., 167, 349; review of Symphony I (Mahler), 167–8
Kreisler, Fritz, 309
Kreuth, *see* Bad Kreuth
Krumpendorf (Wörthersee, Carinthia), 98, 328
Krzyzanowski, Rudolf, 63–64, 107, 349; piano-duet ed. with G. M. of Symphony III (Bruckner), 107, 349
Kubelík, Jan, 4, 349
Kubelík, Rafael, 349
Kurz, Selma, 51, 226, 349

Labia, Maria, 169, 349
Laibach/Ljubljana (Slovenia), 10, 109

L'Allemand, Baron, 87–88, 104, 149, 169–70
Landro (S. Tyrol), 262
Lange, Friedrich: *Geschichte des Materialismus*, 120
Lavater, Johann: *Physiognomische Fragmente*, 137
Leadbeater, C. W., 188
Lechter, Melchior, 90
Lehár, Franz: *The Merry Widow*, 120, 347
Lehmann, Lilli, 102, 349
Leipzig, 10, 110–11, 253–4, 266–7, 282, 329–30, 347, 351, 354
Leistikow, Walter, 284–6, 349
Lemberg, *see* Lvov
Leopold II, King of the Belgians, 246
Leopoldsberg (Vienna), 228
Levico (S. Tyrol), 151
Leyden (Holland), xiii, 175
Liechtenstein, Prince, 15, 291
Lienz (Tyrol), 262
Liliencron, Detlev von, 90, 349
Linz (Upper Austria), 288
Lipiner, Siegfried, 25–26, 31, 143, 319, 349; tr. of *Forefathers' Eve* (Mickiewicz), 26; wives and character, 25–26
Liszt, Franz, 130
Lockspeiser, Edward: *Debussy*, 170, 347
London, 170
Lordmann, Peter, 230, 349
Loretto, *see* Maria-Loretto
Lortzing, Albert: *Undine*, 258; *Zar und Zimmermann*, 243
Loudon–Charlton (New York), 155
Löwe, Ferdinand, 325–6, 349
Lublinsky, Samuel, 90
Ludwig of Bavaria, King, 164
Lugano (Switzerland), 255
Lützow, Count, 119
Lvov/Lemberg (Ukraine), 223–7, 247

M., *see* Mildenburg, Anna von
MacKay, Percy: *The Scarecrow*, 162
Maeterlinck, Maurice, 225
THE MAHLER FAMILY
Alma (*née* Schindler, G.M.'s wife), *passim*; *And the Bridge is Love*, 172; ed. of G.M.'s letters, xxxix, 8; *Lieder*, 5, 76, 81, 176–7, 188, 190–1, plate opp. 306

THE MAHLER FAMILY, *continued.*

Alois (=Hans, =Louis, G.M.'s brother) 9–11, 231, 350

Anna (='Gucki', G.M.'s younger daughter), 8, plate opp. 18, 46, 65–66, 68–69, 71–72, 85, 92, 99, 116, 120–1, 126, 129, plate opp. 130, 144, 151–2, 154, 176, 181, 184, 186–8, 193, 196, 199–200, 237, 241, 245, 252, 255, 260–2, 264–7, 277, 282, 285, 287–8, 297, 301, 303, 322–3, 328, 338

Bernhard (G.M.'s father), 6–8, 10; his mother, 6–7

Emma (G.M.'s sister), 350, 352

Ernst (G.M.'s brother), 7

'Gucki', *see* Anna Mahler

Gustav, *passim; see* Index I for his work as composer and performer

Hans, *see* Alois Mahler

Justine (G.M.'s sister), xxv, 3, 9–14, 21–26, 28, 31, 33, 36, 41, 44, 50, 53, 55–56, 67–69, 75, 84, 115, 143–4, 179, 200, 208, 211–12, 217, 225–6, 228–30, 259–60, 264, 307, 350, 352

Leopoldine (G.M.'s sister), 9, 11, 350; her husband (Quittner), 9

Louis, *see* Alois Mahler

Maria ('Putzi', G.M.'s elder daughter), 46, 48–49, 60, 62, 66, 69, 71–72, 85, 92, 99, 105, 116, 121–3, 129–30, 137, 181, 197, 225, 228–9, 232–3, 235–42, 245, 247, 252, 255, 258–62, 264–7, 271, 273, 275, 282, 285, 288–90, 301

Marie (G.M.'s mother), 6–8, 10, 49, 175, 345; her parents, 7

Otto (G.M.'s brother), 9–11, 350

'Putzi', *see* Maria Mahler

Maiernigg (Wörthersee, Carinthia), 36, 42–48, 59–60, 79, 84, 96, 102–3, 121–2, 140, 151–3, 229, ₀235–41, 260, 290–1, 328

Mainz (Germany), 258–9, 353–4

Mann, Thomas, 80; Letter to Mahler, 342; *Königliche Hoheit,* 342

Mannheim (Germany), 231–3, 272, 327, 347–8

Margherita, Queen, 119

Maria Josepha, Archduchess, 67

Maria-Loretto (Wörthersee, Carinthia), 238

Marschalk, Margarethe, *see* Margarethe Hauptmann

Marschalk, Max, 350; incidental music to Hauptmann's plays, 350

Marteau, Henri, 85, 350

Martino, Count di San, 119

Massenet, Jules: *Manon* and *Werther,* 113

Mattuglie/Matulji (Istria), 67, 234, 259

Mautern (Wachau, Lower Austria), 329

Mauthner, Herr, 260

Mayr, Richard, 311, 350

Mayreder, Rosa, 62; *Der Corregidor* (lib. for Wolf), 62

Mendelssohn-Bartholdy, Felix: *Hebrides Overture,* 137

Mengelberg, Willem, xxi, xli, 59, 73, 100, 154, 170–1, 245–7, 249, 251–2, 261, 272–4, 288, 308–9, 350; wife, 245, 247, 249, 251, 273, 309

Messchaert, Johannes, 282, 285, 288, 350

Metchnikov, Élie, 192

Metternich, Pauline, 38

Metzger, Ottilie, 257, 350

Meudon (France), 149

Mickiewicz, Adam: *Forefathers' Eve,* 26

Miethke, Herr, 341

Miklas, President, xli

Milan, 145, 163, 315

Mildenburg, Anna von, 11–12, 25–26, 30–31, 43–44, 51, 55, 229, 267–9, 311, 350–1; *Erinnerungen,* 350

Miramare (Trieste), 266

Misurina (S. Tyrol), 47, 240, [276]

Mitchell, Donald: *Gustav Mahler,* xix, 357

Moll, Anna (=Anna Schindler), 16–17, 19, 23, 25–26, 33, 47, 49–50, 53–54, 79, 84, 90–91, 104–5, 121–2, 126, 138–9, 143, 153–4, 170, 173–5, 177–8, 182, 192–9, 201, 205, 212, 216, 221, 225–6, 228, 247–8, 252, 259–61, 265, 267, 271, 275, 282, 287, 290, 293, 307, 313, 329, 335

Moll, Carl, 5, 17, 23, 25–26, 33, 36, 50, plate opp. 82, 53, 79, 84, 90, 105, 112, 148, 159–60, 196–9, 201, 212, 215, 226, 228, 237, 247–8, 271–4, 280, 282, 290, 316, 323–4, 329, 335, 350–1, 355; his child, 290

Moll, Ernst, 229, 350

Mommsen, Theodor: *History of Rome,* 51, 291

Montenuovo, Prince, 114, 117, 124–5, 136, 264, 289, 293, 300–1, 315; Letter to Mahler, 301–2

Montmartre (Paris), 57–58

Moser, Koloman, 20, 24–26, 40, 79, 160, 228, 293, 350

Mottl, Felix, 129, 278, 310, 350

Mozart, Constanze, 96

Mozart, W. A., 22, 51, 96, 113, 131, 148, 200, 277, 280, 290, 310, 352; *Don Giovanni*, 89, 96, 102, 104, 132–3, 136, 277, 310, 316; German Dances, 155; *Idomeneo*, 155; *The Magic Flute*, 21–22, 102, 207, 215, 310; *The Marriage of Figaro*, 22, 96, 102–3, 105, 113, 145, 156, 230–1, 277, 310, 316; *The Sera-glio*, 96; Violin Concerto in G major, 85; *Zaïde*, 49

Muck, Karl, 266, 350

Multatuli (E. D. Dekker): *Max Havelaar*, 247

Münchhausen, Herr and Frau von, 91

Munich, 30, 84, 143, 178–82, 269, 276, 278, 296, 306, 329–32, 334–8, 347

Mussorgsky, Modest: songs, 191

Nebdal, Oskar, 59, 106, 350; *Der faule Hans*, 236

Neisser, Albert, 97, 142, 180, 232–3, 267, 351; Frau Neisser, 97, 180–1, 232, 267

Nepallek (A.M.'s uncle), 114

Neuchâtel (Switzerland), 352

Neulengbach (Lower Austria), 329

New Haven (Connecticut), xvii

New York City, xi–xiv, xvi, 51, 86, 108, 124–5, 128–36, 140, 144–8, 153–69, 178, 180, 182–94, 289–90, 309, 313–17, 327, 339, 344–9, 352–4

Niagara Falls, 183–4

Nietzsche, Friedrich, 18–20, 26, 141, 225, 345

Nikisch, Arthur, 110, 124, 253–4, 256, 351

Nodnagel, Ernst, 90, 233, 245, 254, 351; analysis of Symphony III (Mahler), 233

Novalis (Friedrich von Hardenberg), 305

Ochs, Siegfried, 108, 266, 283, 286, 351; Frau Ochs, 286

Offenbach, Jacques: *La belle Hélène*, 232; *Les contes d'Hoffmann*, 5, 15, 205–6

Orlik, Emil, 303–4, 351; drawings of Mahler, 351

Osborn, Mrs. James, xvii

Ospedaletti (Liguria), 255

Ottmar, Father, 12

Otto, Archduke, 67

Oyster Bay (New York), 157

Paderewski, Ignaz, 156

Painlevé, Paul, 87–88, 104–5, 149, 169, 351

Palisades (New York), 146–7

Palladino, Eusapia, 157–9

Pankow (Berlin), 93–94

Papier, Rosa, 12, 350–1

Paris, 3, 56–59, 87, 104–5, 127, 148–51, 154, 162–3, 169–70, 182, 192, 196–7, 271, 309–10, 314, 327, 344, 347, 352

Payerbach (Lower Austria), 264, 288

Perier, Jean, 162, 351

Perosi, Lorenzo, 170, 351; *The Resurrec-tion of Lazarus*, 351

Peter the Great, 248

Peters, C. F., 253, 259, 347, 351

Pfitzner, Hans, 28, 41–42, plate opp. 82, 59–60, 81–84, 93, 101, 232, 351; Letter to Mahler, 317–18; *Lieder*, 81, 93; *Palestrina*, 351; Piano Quintet, 318; *Die Rose vom Liebesgarten*, 42, 60, 81–84, 232; String Quartet I 59–60, 81

Philadelphia (Pennsylvania), 132–3, 154

Picquart, Marie-Georges, 87–88, 104–5, 149–51, 169, 272; Letters to Mahler, 105, 280

Pierné, Gabriel, 169–70, 351; Madame Pierné, 169

Plankenberg (Lower Austria), 329

Plato, 332; *Symposium*, 25, 332

Pöchlarn, (Lower Austria), 329

Poldi (housemaid), 224, 228–9

Pollak, Theobald, 24, 50, 123, 229, 231, 292–3, 351

Pollini, Bernhard, 11, 306, 351

Prague, 7, 92, 131, 142–3, 276, 303–6, 308, 318, 327, 346, 348

Prater (Vienna), 67, 75

Pringsheim, Klaus, 80

Proust, Marcel: *À la recherche du temps perdu*, 347

Przistaupinski, Alois, 258, 262, 292

Puccini, Giacomo, 37; _La Bohème_, 37; _Madama Butterfly_, 37; _Tosca_, 224–5

Quittner, Leopoldine, _see_ Leopoldine Mahler

Ramazotti, Madame, 104, 149–50
Reger, Max, 351, 354; _Lieder_, 93; Serenade (op. 77a), 351
Reinhardt, Max, plate opp. 50, 84, 180, 283–5, 351
Reitler, Josef, _see_ Reitter
Reitter (Reitler? Ritter?), 164, 309, 351–2
Rembrandt van Rijn, 159, 250, 299
Reni, Guido, 25
Rennes (France), 149
Richter, Hans, 14, 294
Richter, J. P., _see_ Jean Paul
Rimsky-Korsakov, Nicolai, 296
Ritter, William, _see_ Reitter
Rodin, Auguste, 148–9; 'Balzac', 149; 'Mahler', xxvi, 148; Madame Rodin, 149
Roller, Alfred, 22, 53–55, 69, 77, 79, 84, 90, 102, 104, 113, 116–17, 122, 128, 144, 153, 160, 180, 228, 262, 270, 274, 276–8, 289, 292, 307, 352; Letters to Mahler, 310–16; décors for the Vienna Opera: _The Barber of Seville_ (Rossini), 310; _Der Corregidor_ (Wolf), 62; _Don Giovanni_ (Mozart), 89, 310; _Fidelio_ (Beethoven), 72, 145, 310–11; _Iphigenia in Aulis_ (Gluck), 106, 310; _Lohengrin_ (Wagner), 106, 310; _The Magic Flute_ (Mozart), 310; _The Marriage of Figaro_ (Mozart), 310; _Das Rheingold_ (Wagner), 77; _The Seraglio_ (Mozart), 96; _The Taming of the Shrew_ (Goetz), 310; _Tristan und Isolde_ (Wagner), 54–55, 91, 310; _Die Walküre_ (Wagner), 106
Roller, Milewa, 276–7, 313, 316
Rome, 117–20, 170–1, 225, 339
Roosevelt, Theodore, 157
Roosevelt, Mrs West, 157
Rooy, Anton van, 131–3, 352
Rösch, Friedrich, 87, 352
Rosé, Arnold, 12–13, 21, 24–26, 28, 33, 41, 50, 53, 57, 67–68, 79, 84, 143–4, 181–2, 228, 230, 260, 264, 318, 324, 331, 352
Rosé, Eduard, 352

Rosé, Emma, _see_ Emma Mahler
Rosé, Justine, _see_ Justine Mahler
Rosegger, Peter, 98, 352
Rosenthal, Harold (ed.): _The Opera B side Book_, 113
Rossini, Gioacchino: _The Barber Seville_, 310
Rosthorn, Herr, 263
Rothschild, Albert, 71
Rott, Hans, 8–9, 107, 352; Symphon 8, 107; mother, 107
Rottach (Tegernsee, Bavaria), 279
Rotterdam, 273–4
Rottenberg, Ludwig, 286, 352
Rückert, Friedrich, 226, 291; _Kind todtenlieder_, 70

Saarinen, Eero, 299
Saarinen, Eliel, 299, 346
Sackville-West, Edward, xii
St Gilgen (Wolfgangsee, Upper Au tria), 140–1
St Petersburg/Leningrad, 33–35, 5 106, 222, 275, 286–7, 294–300, 346
Salzburg, 102–3, 140–2, 276–8, 280, 3
San Francisco, 156
Savonarola, Girolamo, 99
Saxony, King of, 113–14
Schalk, Franz, 28, 107, 112–15, 29 314, 329, 352
Schalk, Josef, 107, 352; piano-duet ed of Bruckner's Symphonies, 352
Schären Islands (Finland), 298–9
Scheel, Fräulein von, 91
Scheffel, J. V. von: _Der Trompeter v Säkkingen_, xvi
Schelling, Ernest, 167, 352; wife, 14 167
Scheveningen (Holland), 250
Schiller, J. C. von, 20; _Ode to Joy_, 37
Schillings, Max von, 27, 87, 236, 26 352
Schindler, Alma, _see_ Alma Mahler
Schindler, Anna, _see_ Anna Moll
Schindler, E. J., 64, 123, 175, 350, 352
Schindler, Kurt, 167, 190–1, 352–3
Schirmer, E. C., 154, 161, 353; wife, 16
Schleinzer, Marie, 67, 353
Schlunderbach/Carbonin (S. Tyrol 122–3, 174, 240, 262, [276]
Schmedes, Erik, 311, 353
Schneeberg (Lower Austria), 262, 264 289

choder, Marie, *see* Marie Gutheil-Schoder

choenberg, Arnold, 28, plate opp. 98, 77–78, 80, 84, 111–12, 125–6, 182, 198, 355; Letters to Mahler, 256–7, 279–80, 325–8, 339–42; *Das Buch der hängenden Gärten* (op. 15), 327; Chamber Symphony I (op. 9), 112, 279–80; Dehmel settings (opp. 2–4 and 6), 93; *Erwartung* (op. 17), 327; Five Orchestral Pieces (op. 16), 182; *Gurrelieder*, 327; *Pelleas und Melisande* (op. 5), 77; String Quartet I (op. 7), 111; String Quartet II (op. 10), 327; Three Piano Pieces (op. 11), 327; *Verklärte Nacht* (op. 4), 93, 112, 345

choenberg, Mathilde, 279, 328, 341

chönaich, A. von, 294

chopenhauer, Arthur, 20; *Die Welt als Wille und Vorstellung*, 47

chott, B., 230, 353

chott, H., 265

chröder's (St. Petersburg), 294–5

chrödter, Fritz, 56, 206, 311, 353; son-in-law, 206

chubert, Franz, 8, 34, 170; Symphony in C major, 155

chuch, Ernst von, 90, 124, 353

chumann, Robert: Piano Concerto, 165–6; Symphony I, 287; Symphony IV, 251; symphonies, 190

chumann-Heink, Ernestine, 109, 353

cotti, Antonio, 130, 133, 145, 155, 353

eattle (Washington), 183

embrich, Marcella, 130, 133, 145, 147, 155–6, 353

emmering (Lower Austria), 29, 96, 118, 220–1, 225, 291, 298, 301

enius, Frank, 330

esenheim (Alsace), 88

hah of Persia, 260–1

hakespeare, William, 231, 236, 291; *As You Like It*, 258; *Hamlet*, 225, 231; *A Midsummer Night's Dream*, 38; *Romeo and Juliet*, 231; *The Taming of the Shrew*, 310

haw, G. B., 126

hawe-Taylor, Desmond, x

heldon, Mrs., 145–6, 189

helley, P. B., 160

ibelius, Jean, 297–8, 348

iegel, Carl, 120

iloti, Alexander, 286–7, 353

Simons, Rainer, 268, 353

Slezak, Leo, 56, 145, 243, 353

Slonimsky, Nicolas, 33

Smetana, Bedřich, 305; *The Bartered Bride*, 131, 154; *Dalibor*, 113

Socrates, 4, 332

Sommer, Hans, 352

Sonnenthal, Hans, 128, 353

Specht, Richard, 54, 277–8, 353; *Gustav Mahler*, 277, 353

Spetrino, Francesco, 163, 315, 353

Spiering, Theodore, plate opp. 130, 164, 183, 353–4

Spiro, Friedrich, 118

Springfield (Massachusetts), 154, 183

Stägemann, Max, 253–4, 354

Stavenhagen, Bernhard, 278

Stefan, Paul, 180, 354; *Gustav Mahler*, xviii–xix, xxiii, 354

Stein, Erwin, 84, 113

Steinbach (Attersee, Upper Austria), 234

Steinbach, Emil, 258–9, 354

Steinbach, Fritz, 234–5, 258, 354; Frau Steinbach, 234–5

Steinitzer, Max, xvi

Steinway's (New York), 155

Stoll, August, 276, 282, 311, 314, 354

Strasbourg (France), 85–88, 149, 317

Strassburg, Gottfried von: *Tristan*, 120

Strasser, Dr., 221

Stratz: illustrations to *Tristan und Isolde* (Wagner), 31

Straube, Karl, 254, 354

Straus, Oskar: Letter to Mahler, 318–19

Strauss, Pauline, plate opp. 19, 27–28, 50–51, 86, 93–94, 152–3, 281–6; mother, 281, 285; son, 153

Strauss, Richard, xli, plate opp. 19, 27–28, 41, 50–51, 85–86, 88–90, 93–94, 97–101, 112, 152–3, 198, 218, 221, 233, 249, 260, 266–7, 275–8, 281–7, 314, 330–1, 348, 352–3; *Also Sprach Zarathustra*, 94, 155; *Elektra*, 51, 168–9, 276, 327; *Feuersnot*, 27–29, 236, 260; *Josephslegende*, 15; *Der Rosenkavalier*, 350; *Salome*, 88–89, 97–98, 162, 267, 275, 281–5, 287, 343; *Sinfonia Domestica*, 84–86, 243; *Till Eulenspiegel*, 94; edition of Berlioz's *Traité d'instrumentation*, 267; settings of Dehmel, 93; father, 260; neighbour at Garmisch, 153; son, 153

Stravinsky, Igor, 296; *Conversations* and *Expositions and Developments* (with Robert Craft), 296

Streicher, Theodor, 79–80, 354; *Wunderhornlieder*, 80, 354; Frau Streicher, 80

Strindberg, August, 126

Stritzko, Josef, 126

Strzygowski, Josef, 50, 354; *The Origin of Christian Church Art*, 354

Tchaikovsky, Peter, xxvi–xxvii, 309; *Eugene Onegin*, 35, 298; *Manfred*, 296; *The Queen of Spades*, 50, 145

Theuer, Alfred, 237

Thyssen, Josef, 257

Tiffany, Louis, 159–61, 354

Titian, 287, 328

Tobelbad (Styria), 172, 328, 331

Toblach/Dobbiaco (S. Tyrol), 138–40, 151–2, 172–6, 240, [276], 307, 319, 321–3, 329, 331, 333–4

Tolstoy, Leo, 236; *Confessions*, 238

Tölz, *see* Bad Tölz

Toscanini, Arturo, 72, 135, 145–6, 163, 315–17

Tre Croci (Verona), [276]

Trenker, Herr, 319

Treumann, Herr, 67

Trient/Trento (S. Tyrol), 151

Trieste, 265–6

Troubetzkoy, Prince, 167

Tunis, 149

Turner, Miss, 290

Uchatius, Marie, 135

Universal Edition (Vienna), 176, 308, 327, 347

Unterach (Attersee, Upper Austria), 53

Untermeyer, Minnie, 145–6, 189, 194

Utrecht (Holland), 273

Velde, Henry van de, 91, 354; wife, 91

Verdi, Giuseppe: *Aida*, 65, 145; *Falstaff*, 65

Versailles, 105

Vienna, xiii, xli, 3–6, 8, 10–39, 44, 47–58, 60, 62–69, 72–85, 90, 92, 96–106, 108–9, 112–20, 122, 124–6, 128, 133, 135–6, 138, 140–1, 144, 149, 151–4, 163, 167–8, 171, 178, 181–3, 192, 197–201, 215–16, 218–22, 224–30, 235–6, 241–3, 248, 250–1, 254, 256–7,

260–1, 263–4, 266–70, 273–4, 278–80, 282–3, 285–94, 298–303, 306–16, 323–31, 339–40, 343–55

Villarceaux (France), 105

Wachau (Lower Austria), 329

Wagner, Cosima, 12, 101, 131; Letters to Mahler, 267–70

Wagner, Karl, 257

Wagner, Richard, 26–27, 44, 51–52, 58, 60, 79, 81, 92–93, 113, 122, 125, 130, 135, 238–9, 269, 272, 275, 287, 290, 296–7, 305, 324–5, 345–6, 349–50, 352; *Eine Faust Ouvertüre*, 309; *Der fliegende Holländer*, 168; *Götterdämmerung*, 34, 63, 154, 282; *Lohengrin*, 44, 53, 106, 114–15, 122, 310; *Die Meistersinger*, xli, 14, 154, 207, 211, 293, 309, 315, 323; *Parsifal*, 125, 160, 268; *Das Rheingold*, 77, 154; *Siegfried*, 45, 131, 133, 154, 315; *Siegfried Idyll*, 309; *Tannhäuser*, 79, 168; *Tristan und Isolde*, 31, 34, 54–55, 58, 62, 91, 96, 104, 113, 128–32, 145–6, 151, 154, 163, 205, 263–4, 268–9, 310, 316–17, 338; *Die Walküre*, 44, 60–61, 83, 106, 113, 131, 133, 154; Letters to M. Wesendonck, 237–40; prose works, 92

Wagner, Siegfried, 268–70; *Der Bärenhäuter*, 268–9; *Bruder Lustig*, 268, 270; *Herzog Wildfang*, 269; *Der Kobold*, 268–9

Waldheim und Eberle, 176

Walker, Frank: *Hugo Wolf*, 63

Walter, Bruno, xli, plate opp. 99, 104, 113, 198, 228, 244–5, 250, 260, 289, 354; *Gustav Mahler*, 354; *Theme and Variations*, 112

Walter (violinist), 296

Wanamaker's (New York), 86

Warsaw, 295

Weber, C. M. von, 110; *Die Drei Pintos*, 110–11; *Euryanthe*, 53–54, 71; *Oberon*, 291, 344; grandson and wife, 110–11

Wedekind, Frank, 126, 285, 354; *Franziska*, 15; *Frühlings Erwachen*, 283–4

Weidemann, Friedrich, 82, 311, 354

Weidt, Lucy, 311

Weimar, 90, 94, 110

Weingartner, Felix, 90, 124–5, 292, 302, 310–15, 318, 355; Letter to Mahler, 302; *Orestes*, 327

Weiss, Joseph, 164–6, 355; compositions for piano, 165; arrs. of Bach and Brahms, 164

Weissenkirchen (Wachau, Lower Austria), 329

Wesendonck, Mathilde: Letters to Wagner, 237–40

West Roosevelt, *see* Roosevelt

Wiener Wald (Lower Austria), 225, 293

Wiesbaden (Germany), 137–8, 222–3, 258, 293–4

Wilde, Oscar, 239, 278; *Salome*, 88

Wilhelm II, Kaiser, 167

Winternitz, Arnold, 315, 355

Wolf, Hugo, xxv, 62–65, 177; *Der Corregidor*, 62, 64–65; *Lieder*, 177; *Rübezahl*, xxv, 64, 143

Wolff, Hermann, 281, 283, 285, 345, 355

Wolff, Louise, 267, 282–3, 286, 355

Wolfgangsee (Upper Austria), 141

Wolfrum, Philipp, 230, 355

Wolfskehl, Karl, 90

Wondra, Herr, 262, 292, 314

Wörthersee (Carinthia), 43–46, 79, 98, 121, 140, 238–9, 328

Wydenbruck, Misa, 257, 355

Yeats, W. B.: 'Byzantium' poems, 354

Zaandam (Holland), 248

Zandvoort (Holland), 252

Zemánek, Vilem, 306, 355

Zemlinsky, Alexander von, 4–5, 16, 69, 77–78, 80, 84, 125–6, 182, 279, 289, 355; *Das goldene Herz*, 4

Zend-Avesta (Zoroastrian scriptures), 226

Zichy, Géza, 10, 355

Zilcher, Hermann: *Fitzebutze*, 271

Zögernitz (Vienna), 126, 221–2

Zola, Émile, 87, 149; *J'accuse*, 87

Zuckerkandl, Bertha, 3–5, 14–15, 18, 50, 62, 84, 355; Diary-extract, 303

Zuckerkandl, Emil, 3–5, 14, 18, 50 84 355

Zwerenz, C. L., 108

Zwerenz, Mizzi, 108

THE MEMOIRS OF HECTOR BERLIOZ

Ed David Cairns

Writing with unreserved candour and emotion, sparing no one's feelings – least of all his own – Hector Berlioz began, when he was forty four (in 1848) to set down a memoir of this musical and personal life. Twenty one years later, the work was completed. It is regarded to this day, as one of the greatest of all biographies.

David Cairns, renowned Berlioz scholar and author of the definitive biography, has further updated and revised his original translation of 1969.

'By some alchemy, the unmistakable voice of Berlioz himself, passionate, witty, enraged, high-spirited, sardonic, tormented and infinitely proud, speaks from these pages. An overwhelming sense of identity unites life, book and translation . . . Of the composers of the nineteenth century only Berlioz was a genius in the use of words. His *Memoirs* are more than a great musician's vivid account of his life. They are a crucial document of their age, for they illuminate as little else the early romantic temperament and its relations with the outside world'
Observer

0 7474 0582 4
BIOGRAPHY

CARDINAL

T. S. ELIOT
Peter Ackroyd

'Perceptive and assured . . . the fullest and most plausible portrait
achieved'
Frank Kermode, *Guardian*

'A major biography . . . the result does justice to the complexity of E
genius, and builds up a commanding case for the unity of life and we
We are unlikely to have a better biography of Eliot for many year
John Carey, *Sunday Times*

0 7474 0182 9   NON-FICTION

THE LIFE AND DEATH OF MOZAR
Michael Levey

'Essential reading for all Mozartians' *The Times*

Mozart's reputation as a composer continues in the ascendant, yet
curiously, our understanding of the man has been clouded: his
personality has been seen as irreconcilable with the musical
genius. This picture is unsatisfactory and unsatisfying. Michael
Levey sees behind that darkened varnish the clear image of
a man of immense liveliness and great humanity not at all at
odds with the genius we acknowledge in the music. Simply,
Michael Levey reveals the real Mozart.

0 7474 0150 0   NON-FICTION

CARDINAL

YOUNG BETJEMAN
Bevis Hillier

'If he was England's best-selling poet since Lord Byron, he was also, like Byron, as good value in the flesh as in verse, if not better . . . A delicious volume which takes the late Laureate from birth to marriage'
Sunday Telegraph

'Of my contemporaries who have made a name in the world, I have no hesitation in saying Betjeman was the most unusual, in background, talents, various erudition and way of life . . . Bevis Hillier has tackled a lot of intricate material remarkably well'
Anthony Powell, *The Times*

'A model of biography, and fascinatingly documented. The chapters on the mass of literary influences that combined to produce Betjeman's unique poetic voice are little masterpieces in themselves. All the personal material is wonderfully rich and unsimplified. It will be hard to wait patiently for volume two'
John Carey, Sunday Times

0 7474 0467 4   BIOGRAPHY

CARDINAL

HEMINGWAY

Kenneth S. Lynn

'This brilliant biography . . . Hemingway studies will never be the
same again'
Daily Telegraph

'Kenneth S. Lynn's magnificent biography . . . Accomplished,
revealing and, all in all, profoundly sympathetic'
Times Literary Supplement

Kenneth S. Lynn reveals a man dogged with the fear that he could n
support his own myth. Two contemporaries, both female, already
sensed this: Zelda Fitzgerald put it tersely – 'No man could be as ma
as all that' and Gertrude Stein said 'What a book would be the real sto
of Hemingway, not those he writes, but the confessions of the real
Ernest Hemingway'. This is that book; a detective story which track
down Hemingway's real debts and obsessions. This brilliant biograph
may appear to be the case against Hemingway, but Hemingway final
emerges as a genuine hero. As Norman Mailer put it: 'he carried a
weight of anxiety with him which would have suffocated any man
smaller than himself.'

0 7474 0320 1   NON-FICTION

CARDINAL

FOUR DUBLINERS
Richard Ellmann

'...mann's four Dubliners are Wilde, Yeats, Joyce and Beckett, and his ...im, rich book comes up with new material on each . . . His gift for ...iting critical insight with biography is as freshening, as undogmatic and as humane as ever' John Carey, *Sunday Times*

'In Ellmann's best manner' Frank Kermode, *Guardian*

'A skilful and distinguished book' P N Furbank, *Sunday Telegraph*

'This brief, witty book . . . is a model of literary perception' William Trevor, *Observer*

0 7474 0276 0   NON-FICTION

All Cardinal books in this series are available from good bookshops, or can be ordered from the following address:

Sphere Books
Cash Sales Department
P.O. Box 11
Falmouth
Cornwall, TR10 9EN

Please send cheque or postal order (no currency), and allow 60p for postage and packing for the first book plus 25p for the second book and 15p for each additional book ordered up to a maximum charge of £1.90 in U.K.

B.F.P.O. customers please allow 60p for the first book, 25p for the second book plus 15p per copy for the next 7 books, thereafter 9p per book.

Overseas customers, including Eire, please allow £1.25 for postage and packing for the first book, 75p for the second book and 28p for each subsequent title ordered.